Models and Strategies
for
Training Design

Edited by
Karen L. Medsker
and
Kristina M. Holdsworth

A Publication of the
International Society for
Performance Improvement

Models and Strategies for Training Design

Printed in the United States of America

Published by
International Society for Performance Improvement
1400 Spring Street
Suite 260
Silver Spring, MD 20910
301.587.8570
Fax: 301.587.8573

Visit our website at www.ispi.org

Edited by Karen L. Medsker and Kristina M. Holdsworth

About ISPI

Founded in 1962, the International Society for Performance Improvement (ISPI) is the leading international association dedicated to improving productivity and performance in the workplace. ISPI represents more than 10,000 international and chapter members throughout the United States, Canada, and 40 other countries. ISPI's mission is to develop and recognize the proficiency of our members and advocate the use of Human Performance Technology. Assembling an Annual Conference & Exposition and other educational events—including the award-winning HPT Institute, publishing several periodicals, and producing a full line of publications and resources are some of the ways ISPI works toward achieving this mission. For more information, please write ISPI, 1400 Spring Street, Suite 260, Silver Spring, MD 20910; website: www.ispi.org; email: info@ispi.org.

*In memory of
our fathers*

Herschel Bailey
1904–1949

*He would have been surprised and pleased to see me
become a professor and writer of books.*

Ken Holdsworth
1942–2000

*The compass rose represents the moral and life
guidance my father gave me as well as the sense of
adventure and exploration we shared.*

Acknowledgments

Chapter Authors

Marian V. Barnwell	Paul T. Haley
Naomi Berkove	Kristina M. Holdsworth
Dede Bonner	Craig Locatis
Brandy Christin	Ramona L. Lush
Bill Combs	Karen L. Medsker
Letitia A. Combs	Bobbie Moore
Cynthia J. Demnitz	Peter J. Pallesen
Linda J. Elengold	Fran Peters
Theresa Falance	Kristin Radcliffe
John P. Fry	Cynthia Vorder Bruegge
Maureen Giannotti	Dina E. Widlake
Amy A. Greene	

Contributors

The following individuals assisted the chapter authors by providing information, explanation, references, case studies or examples, or reviewing content. The editors and the authors are grateful for their contributions.

Dr. John Burgoyne	Dr. Elwood F. Holton III
Dr. Alan Collins	Dr. David H. Jonassen
Ms. Marirose Coulson	Dr. M. David Merrill
Ms. Susan Crawford	Dr. Joseph M. Scandura
Dr. Robert Gagné	Dr. Jane Kathryn Vella

Cover Art and Graphics

Sterling Spangler

Graphics and cover art provided by Sterling Spangler, freelance graphic artist and multimedia specialist. Sterling's career has ranged from a public relations officer for a large hospital system to a multi-media specialist in the field of earth science. His graphics have appeared in Victoria Bruce's *No Apparent Danger*, published by HarperCollins. He specializes in print and electronic media and is currently a resident of the greater Washington/Baltimore metropolitan area.

Preface

Training, of course, is not the answer to every performance problem. Performance gaps and their causes must be analyzed to determine the right mix of performance improvement interventions. When training is the answer, however, the designer must base the design on something. That something should be one or more instructional models or strategies that have been verified by formal research or in the broader laboratory of teaching/learning experience. This book explains, in what we hope is a format readily accessible to practitioners and students alike, some of the major models and strategies that guide the experts who design instruction for adult learners. We have selected the models and strategies from a broad range of theoretical perspectives, including behavioral, cognitive, humanistic, and social, and we have tried to show when and how each model or strategy may be used most effectively.

With the recent explosion of technology-based instruction, especially web-based training, we are often asked, "How is instructional design different for technology-based delivery systems, compared with design for classroom training?" On that topic, a chapter has been included that describes many of the special considerations required for electronically delivered multimedia instruction. However, it should be noted that the human brain has not evolved as rapidly as have the technologies available for instructional delivery. Fundamentally, people still learn pretty much in the same old ways, about which we are ever trying to learn more. Thus, most of the proven models and strategies, based on sound learning theories, are as applicable as always and can be adapted to the newer delivery systems.

Writing this book has been a three-year effort involving many people. First, we thank our friends, the chapter authors, for their hard work, creativity, and patience with our many requests for changes. We are also indebted to the researchers and model-builders who originated the models and strategies we describe. Many of these people helped us by providing insights by telephone or email and by reviewing chapter drafts. Our graphic artist, Sterling Spangler, graciously provided the figures within and covers on the book. At ISPI, Matthew Davis is to be congratulated for believing in our book, and April Davis deserves great thanks for following through with the publication process.

KLM
KMH

Table of Contents

Introduction

Karen L. Medsker

Training is only one performance improvement intervention within the larger context of individual, group, and organizational performance improvement. Yet training continues to be an important and complex part of what performance technologists do. This book attempts to help instructional designers design better training (and thus enhance client performance) by choosing and using a variety of proven models and strategies.

The last decade has seen substantial growth in awareness and application of human performance technology (HPT). During the 1990s, the professional societies devoted to training changed their emphasis to HPT (or performance improvement, usually considered to be synonymous with HPT). The National Society for Performance and Instruction, which had long been an advocate of HPT, became the International Society for Performance Improvement. The American Society for Training and Development also became an advocate for performance improvement, rather than for training alone, though not changing its name. Thousands of organizations rushed to convert their training departments to performance consulting or performance improvement departments. Articles, books, and seminars on how to make the transition proliferated. Organizations even began announcing position vacancies for performance technologists and performance consultants. What is HPT, why is it gaining ground, and what is still needed for its greater success?

What Is HPT?

HPT has a definite philosophy. A basic tenet of HPT philosophy is that a systemic approach to improving human performance is most effective. One should consider the entire system in which human performance occurs: aspects of the tasks, the performers, and the environment in which the tasks are performed. HPT also assumes that the performance of individuals, groups/teams, and organizations can best be improved through systematic methods, following the steps outlined below:

1. Identify and measure performance gaps (desired versus actual outcomes).
2. Assess causes for the performance gaps.
3. Prescribe performance "interventions" (i.e., solutions, strategies, initiatives) that directly address the causes.
4. Design and implement interventions.
5. Evaluate the impact of interventions on performance.

HPT is an interdisciplinary field, drawing from theory and research in psychology—especially learning psychology, industrial/organizational psychology, ergonomics and human factors, operations research, education, management and organizational behavior, and organization development. Experimental and quasi-experimental studies are conducted in HPT to determine what interventions are effective and under what conditions.

A classic model for analyzing causes of human performance gaps, or planning new human performance systems, is that of Gilbert (1978, 1982). Gilbert's Behavior Engineering Model serves to illustrate the scope of factors that influence human performance. An adaptation of the model is shown in Table 0.1. Three sets of factors on the left relate to the person, and the three factors on the right are about the environment in which the person performs.

The Person	The Environment
Skills and Knowledge	Data or Information
Capacity	Tools and Settings
Motives	Incentives

Table 0.1
Behavior Engineering Model

Models and Strategies for Training Design

Gilbert's model emphasizes the distinction between skills and knowledge (stored in the performer's head) and data and information (stored in external sources, such as job aids, reference manuals, and online help systems). This is a useful distinction, because training often can be avoided or reduced through the use of well-constructed job aids or reference material, which may be relatively quick and inexpensive to develop and deliver. The goal of training is to store skill and knowledge in the learner's head, but training is expensive and time consuming to develop and deliver. Often, a job aid is preferable to training, because the task is infrequently performed, easily forgotten, has many steps, involves burdensome recall of information, or involves decisionmaking that requires support during performance.

Gilbert's other four categories usually do not call for training solutions. If performers lack physical, mental, or emotional capacity to perform, solutions such as job redesign, performance support, selection of different performers, career counseling, or medical interventions may be appropriate. If the tools or physical environment are not adequate, ergonomic solutions are recommended. Motivational solutions include selecting and placing people in jobs they are already motivated to perform, designing jobs that are intrinsically motivating, and ensuring career development opportunities. Related to motivation are incentives, which can be tangible or intangible. Incentive systems can be formally structured, with rewards contingent on specific performance, or they can be informal and administered at the discretion of individual supervisors.

Based on ideas from Gilbert's model and others (e.g., Harless, 1989; Rummler & Brache, 1995), Table 0.2 illustrates how HPT can be used to analyze a hypothetical performance gap and identify possible interventions. The Cause Categories column lists a variety of factors that can support or hinder desired performance. Possible Causes gives sample deficiencies related to the hypothetical performance gap in the medical laboratory, and Possible Interventions lists ways to bridge the performance gap by addressing the causes.

- Current Performance: 10% of the test results coming from a medical laboratory are inaccurate.
- Desired Performance: The goal must be a 0% error rate, because of the impact on human life.

Cause Categories	Possible Causes	Possible Interventions
Vision/Mission	• Vision and mission for the laboratory are clear, but lab employees are not informed.	• Improve orientation program to emphasize vision and mission. • Post vision or mission on laboratory wall.
Goals/Objectives/Expectations	• Lab employees do not know that 0% error rate is the goal.	• Inform employees of the performance expectations.
Values/Norms	• Cultural values are not performance oriented. Employees are just "putting in their time."	• When new employees are hired, screen for needed values. • Managers model and reward desired behaviors.
Motivation/Incentives	• Employees are paid hourly, with no incentive for accuracy. • Employees do not see any potential career path—they feel "stuck." • The lab techs perceive little meaning in their tasks.	• Track individual or group performance on accuracy and give bonuses. • Counsel employees about advancement opportunities within and beyond the lab. • Provide means for lab techs to see the results of their work—e.g., patient contact.
Capacity	• Employees lack required physical stamina, visual acuity, mental health, or other personal attributes. • Employees are sleep deprived or on drugs.	• Select different people for these jobs. • Provide health and fitness facilities. • Provide personal counseling.
Organization and Job Structures	• Centralized laboratory does not promote accountability to client departments. • Work is divided so that each job is repetitious, with little variety.	• Decentralize medical laboratory functions, distributing lab techs to client departments. • Redesign jobs to include more variety of tasks, with greater opportunities for learning.

Table 0.2
Sample Performance Gap

Cause Categories	Possible Causes	Possible Interventions
Documentation and Standards	• Lab tests are computerized, but systems lack help screens.	• Add user-friendly help screens for complex decisionmaking steps in testing procedures.
Job Aids, Signage, and Labels	• Lab techs forget the steps for infrequently used equipment. • Lab equipment and supplies are stored in haphazard ways.	• Post job aids on or near the equipment. • Organize storage areas with clear labels, so that correct choices are easy to make.
Physical Facilities/Space	• Work space is crowded, lighting is inadequate, or space is poorly ventilated.	• Redesign work space, improve task and ambient lighting, and enhance ventilation.
Skills and Knowledge	• Employees lack basic education for the job tasks. • Employees do not know how to follow specific procedures.	• Hire people who are better qualified, or encourage employees to continue their education. • Provide job-relevant training and on-the-job coaching.
Resources	• Essential laboratory materials are not sufficient or are of poor quality.	• Make high-quality products available as needed.
Tools	• Laboratory equipment is out of date, in poor repair, or out of adjustment. • Not enough equipment is present, causing lab techs to rush each test.	• Invest in better equipment and maintenance contracts. • Ensure enough equipment is available.
Processes/Procedures/Practices	• Lab procedures are inefficient and involve unnecessary paperwork.	• Re-engineer lab procedures to streamline paperwork and reduce redundancy.

Table 0.2

Sample Performance Gap (cont.)

The Advance of HPT

Many reasons account for the recent surge in HPT. Some organizations have grown weary of business fads and "flavors of the month" that promise quick success for minimal investments. Even some substantially good ideas that have come and gone could have been more enduring if they were part of a systemic approach, rather than isolated interventions. HPT is not a fad, but a comprehensive, research-based approach that leads to measurable results. Although HPT can produce some results quickly, much of its analysis, application, and evaluation requires hard work and long-term investment to achieve organizationwide, sustainable payoffs. Fortunately, organizations seem more willing to make this commitment than they have in the past. To advance the field of HPT and make it even more useful, more research is needed, and closer ties need to be formed between research and practice (Stolovitch, 2000). Academic programs that prepare HPT researchers and practitioners must also be increased in number and strength (Medsker, et al., 1995).

The Role of Training in HPT

The expansion and acceptance of HPT has increased awareness that training and education (instructional interventions) are appropriate only to address skill and knowledge deficiencies, that training often must be combined with other interventions to bridge performance gaps, and that many performance gaps should not be addressed by training at all. Nevertheless, many critical factors in the performance environment of organizations today seem to increase, rather than decrease, the need for instructional interventions. The so-called knowledge explosion ensures that, overall, there is more to learn. Rapidly changing technology and environmental conditions affecting organizations create needs for almost constant learning and relearning. Globalization requires many to learn more about multinational business and other cultures. And the fact that people change jobs and careers more frequently than ever implies that they must always be learning new skills. The training and education market is huge and growing, evidenced by the trend toward setting up corporate universities.

HPT professionals, then, face several challenges related to training and education. Besides convincing clients that training is not the answer to every problem, we must also build more effective training faster. We must do quicker and more accurate needs assessments, improve training design and development, select from an intimidating array of available delivery systems, and prove the value of training. This book addresses the challenge of greater training effectiveness: designing instructional interventions that match the needs of the learners, the content, and the performance context.

When training is needed, HPT practitioners typically employ a systems approach to training development, also known as instructional systems design (ISD). ISD consists of five phases: analysis, design, development, implementation, and evaluation; frequently referred to as the ADDIE model. An innovative approach in the 1970s, ISD has now become a standard for training development, at least for large organizations that require training effectiveness and efficiency (Gagné & Medsker, 1996).

However, ISD has also come under attack for being rigid, clumsy, slow, unscientific, and costly and for producing training products that are boring, static, and don't meet business needs (Gordon & Zemke, 2000). Especially for multimedia and web-based training, the traditional "waterfall" approach to ISD (where each step is completed and in turn serves as input to the next step) has been supplanted by approaches in which four of the five ADDIE phases get done almost simultaneously. Tennyson (1999) describes the Fourth Generation ISD (ISD[4]) model, in which six functions or domains are done interactively, through dynamic interaction: situational evaluation, foundation, design, production, implementation, and maintenance. Typically, a "rapid prototype" is put together for the client to evaluate. Based on the client's reaction, the creators refine the prototype, or junk it and start over. In this process, the ADDIE phases or the ISD[4] domains all occur together, rather than as separate steps. This makes sense, especially when a client would have difficulty imagining the "look and feel" of a technology-based product without seeing the prototype.

The Role of Design in Training

Whether using the old waterfall or the newer ISD[4] approach, the design function must occur. Design includes selection of specific content, goals and objectives; sequencing of content; selection of learning and teaching activities; and detailed specification of how these activities will occur. The developers, with or without client input, must decide what the actual learning experiences will be like. People representing behavioral, cognitive, humanistic, and social philosophies of learning advocate different ways of approaching design tasks.

The thesis of this book is that carefully chosen design models and strategies can contribute both to the effectiveness and to the appeal of the learning experience.

Theoretical Perspectives and This Book's Organization

The term "instructional design" is often narrowly defined to mean a set of models and practices that are systems oriented, consistent with ISD, and based on behavioral or cognitive approaches to learning. This book takes a broader view and includes some models and strategies that are not systems oriented, are inconsistent with ISD, or are based on humanistic and social approaches to learning. Thus, instructional design here includes any deliberate arrangement of conditions and experiences in which learning can take place. This more inclusive set of models and strategies reflects, to some extent, the diversity of approaches that is actually used in the real world of adult learning and workplace training. It also presents to the instructional designer an illustrative, though not exhaustive, array of tools from which to choose. Some of the models and strategies are for general purposes and have broad application, while others are for special purposes.

Instructional design, whether narrowly or broadly defined, is not an exact technology based on an exact science, but is (as yet, at any rate) a combination of science, technology, craft, art, and intuitive leaps. The wise practitioner, then, avoids locking into a single theoretical framework, but rather maintains an eclectic stance, drawing from each theoretical perspective the principles and techniques that work, and putting them together in proven, logically defensible, and creative ways to meet specific instructional needs. The goal of this book is to assist designers in this complex and challenging process.

Part I of the book includes three models in the behavioral tradition. Behaviorists emphasize the importance of specifying the behavior to be learned, breaking the final behavior down into smaller components, providing repeated practice of the behavior, shaping the desired behavior through successive approximations, and reinforcing the behavior when it is exhibited. Behaviorists focus on observable events, avoiding discussion of learning events or processes that occur inside the learner. Behaviorism was the prominent school of thought during most of the 20th century; behaviorists generated impressive scientific evidence for their approaches in clinical and classroom settings as well as in the laboratory.

Part II has eight chapters on cognitive models and strategies. Some of these cognitive approaches to learning and instruction grew out of the behaviorist tradition. Rather than rejecting behaviorism, many cognitive psychologists during the 1970s and later sought to build on the successes of behaviorism by attempting to study the inner workings of the human organism. Still observing behavior as the outward manifestation of learning, cognitive psychologists build and test models for what is happening in the brain or mind. For example, the information-processing model compares human learning to computer information input, processing, storage, retrieval, and output. Other cognitive learning models, labeled "discovery" or "inquiry," were not inspired by behaviorism but by the practical successes of master teachers who were able to capitalize on learners' innate curiosity and motivation to seek and create their own knowledge. These inquiry-oriented models aim more to help learners develop thinking, learning, and problemsolving processes than to help them acquire specific content knowledge and skills. Inquiry-oriented models have been advocated and used, in one form or another, at least as far back as Socrates.

Part III provides samples of humanistic, social, and affective models and strategies. Both the popular education and the adult learning models embody the humanistic perspective that learners, not designers or instructors, know best what should be learned and how it should be learned. The role of a humanistic instructor, in fact, is more that of a facilitator than a presenter of information or director of learning activities. Learners take on most of the decisionmaking in the learning process and are responsible for their own learning. Cooperative learning stresses the importance of learning in groups and of learners teaching each other. This approach is both humanistic and social, and it can be used to learn social and team skills, as well as other content. Keller's motivational design model can be used in conjunction with any general-purpose model to add motivational (affective) elements to enhance learning. The Lancaster model is an "umbrella" model that emphasizes both active learning (discovery) and cognitive reflection. Lancaster is not specifically behavioral or cognitive, and it is included in this section because it spans across all theoretical perspectives.

Brethower (2000) expresses an interesting point of view regarding the distinctions and frequent disputes among various theoretical orientations to learning and performance improvement. He suggests that cognitivists and behaviorists are really saying much the same thing—just using different language to describe their theories—and that their instructional design prescriptions actually are quite similar. Constructivists in recent years have created considerable turmoil by labeling both behaviorists and cognitivists as "hopeless objectivists" who don't understand that knowledge is "constructed" within each learner, rather than transmitted to the learner. Brethower says that the constructivist view of knowledge acquisition is not only correct and important, but well supported by behavioral and cognitive research! He urges practitioners to look at what works and to worry less about surface differences in language. This book, while pointing out differences among theories and models, recommends that instructional designers use what works, matching models and strategies from various theoretical origins to their best uses.

Chapter 11, for example, advocates the integration of constructivist and objectivist strategies.

Part IV of this book contains a job aid for selecting models and strategies, given specific situational learning needs. The final chapter provides guidance on applying the models and strategies to develop multimedia (technology-based) learning experiences, as well as general design guidance for technology-based delivery systems.

Genesis of This Book

Marymount University's School of Business offers a Master of Arts program in Human Performance Systems (HPS). This program, formerly Human Resource Development, was renamed to reflect its evolution from a training emphasis to a performance emphasis (Medsker & Fry, 1992). The program includes core courses in performance analysis (diagnosing performance needs), performance improvement strategies (survey of nontraining interventions), and research and evaluation (assessing the impact of HPT interventions). Because Marymount also offers Master's programs in Human Resource Management (HRM) and Organization Development (OD), elective courses for HPS students include a wide array of HRM topics that relate to performance improvement, such as compensation and benefits, labor relations, personnel selection and appraisal, and HRM planning, as well as OD topics such as diagnosis, intervention, and change management. Students may also take courses from other departments, such as financial management or information management, to prepare themselves to be strategic business partners within, or consultants to, government, business, and nonprofit organizations.

Graduate students may also earn an Instructional Design Certificate, as part of a HPS, HRM, or OD degree, or as a stand-alone certificate. This certificate includes a basic instructional design course, in which students learn ISD, using the Dick and Carey (1996) and Gagné and Medsker (1996) texts. The certificate also includes an "advanced" instructional design course, in which students learn to apply a variety of models and strategies from different theoretical perspectives—behavioral, cognitive, humanistic, social. Going beyond a narrow definition of instructional design, the course includes models and strategies whose originators call themselves educators rather than instructional designers and who do not consider themselves as following a systems approach. The purpose of the course is to provide the student practitioners with a variety of tools that will make their instructional products more effective and exciting. Thus, the course discusses best uses of each model and strategy.

This book was first conceived as a textbook for the "advanced" instructional design course described above. However, a second purpose was to provide a handbook or reference book that would be useful to training practitioners. It includes some models and strategies from the "green book" (Reigeluth, 1983), some from Joyce and Weil (1999), and a few other favorites and "must haves" from other sources. (For example, the Lancaster model was unearthed during a class trip to the United Kingdom.) The goal in selecting the models and strategies for inclusion was not to be exhaustive, but to provide samples from diverse theoretical perspectives, comprising a selection that would help designers be more flexible and creative in their course designs. Other criteria for inclusion of models and strategies in this book were these: usefulness with adult audiences in practical settings; research support and/or a history of successful practice; and intuitive appeal.

Using This Book

Professors and students of instructional design may use this book in different ways. One way is to make the book a supplement in a basic instructional design course. A core text that covers the basic skills of instructional design (e.g., how to write objectives and test items; how to select media; how to conduct formative evaluation) could be used for skill building, and this book could provide material for discussion of alternative views of design. Alternatively, this book can be used as a core text, with the goal of having students actually learn to use the models this book presents. In the latter approach, individuals or teams can choose models to present to the class. To maximize involvement, each student or student team can conduct (in class) a demonstration lesson that illustrates key attributes of the assigned model. These demonstration lessons provide a concrete basis for discussing features, strengths, and limitations of each model. They also enhance retention of content by providing a memorable, involving experience led by classmates.

Instructional design practitioners can use this book as a reference in the early stages of a project. A good place to start may be the job aid in Chapter 17, which suggests possible models and strategies to use under certain instructional circumstances. Chapter 18 includes design guidelines and model applications for use with technology-based training delivery. If users are unfamiliar with any of the models, they might read selected chapters, and quickly review chapters on familiar models, to spark design ideas. The implementation guide in each chapter lists the critical steps for designing with each model or strategy and can be used as a job aid. If a model or strategy has particular applicability in the designer's practice, consulting the references may be helpful.

References

Brethower, D.M. (2000). Integrating theory, research, and practice in human performance technology: Examples from behavioral, cognitive, and constructivist theories. *Performance Improvement, 38*(4), 33–43.

Dick, W., & Carey, L. (1996). *The systematic design of instruction* (4th ed.). Glenview, IL: HarperCollins.

Gagné, R.M., & Medsker, K.L. (1996). *The conditions of learning: Training applications*. Ft. Worth, TX: Harcourt Brace.

Gilbert, T.F. (1978). *Human competence: Engineering worthy performance*. New York: McGraw-Hill.

Gilbert, T.F. (1982). A question of performance. Part 1: The probe model. *Training and Development Journal, 36*(4), 21–29.

Gordon, J., & Zemke, R. (2000). The attack on ISD. *Training, 37*(4), 42–53.

Harless, J. (1989). *Front-end analysis workshop*. Newnan, GA: Harless Performance Guild.

Joyce, B.R., & Weil, M. (1999). *Models of teaching* (6th ed.). Boston: Allyn & Bacon.

Medsker, K.L., & Fry, J.P. (1992). Toward a performance technology curriculum. *Performance and Instruction, 31*(2), 53–56.

Medsker, K., Hunter, P., Stepich, D., Rowland, G., & Basnet, K. (1995). HPT in academic curricula: Survey results. *Performance Improvement Quarterly, 8*(4), 6–21.

Reigeluth, C.M. (1983). *Instructional design theories and models: An overview of their current status*. Hillsdale, NJ: Lawrence Erlbaum Associates.

Rummler, G.A., & Brache, A.P. (1995). *Improving performance: How to manage the white space on the organization chart* (2nd ed.). San Francisco: Jossey-Bass.

Stolovitch, H.D. (2000). Human performance technology: Research and theory to practice. *Performance Improvement, 38*(4), 7–16.

Tennyson, R.D. (1999). Instructional development and ISD[4] methodology. *Performance Improvement, 38*(6), 19–27.

About the Author

Karen L. Medsker is professor and chair of the Human Resources Department at Marymount University, where she teaches graduate courses in Instructional Design and Performance Improvement. She also consults and writes on training and performance issues and is a long-time member of the International Society for Performance Improvement. Her PhD is from Florida State University, in Instructional Systems. Previously, she worked at AT&T/Bell Laboratories and Indiana University-Purdue University at Indianapolis.

Behavioral Models and Strategies

During the first 70 years of the 20th century, behaviorism was the predominant psychological approach to research in learning and performance. Behaviorism's scientific accomplishments are substantial, its applications are demonstrably successful, and its contributions are lasting. Clinical psychology, industrial psychology, and education have been greatly advanced by the behavioral movement. Specific ideas that behaviorism contributed to the theory and practice of instructional design and training are as applicable today as ever:

- Focus on observable behavior as the outcomes of learning.
- Specify behavioral objectives to guide the focus of instructional design.
- Analyze desired behavior into small units, to be learned individually.
- Increase the likelihood and frequency of desired behavior through positive reinforcement.
- Decrease unwanted behavior by ignoring it or through negative reinforcement or (less frequently) punishment.
- Provide opportunities for frequent responding (practice) by the learner.
- Ensure that all learners achieve the objectives by providing enough time and support.

Early researchers, such as Thorndike, Watson, Ebbinghaus, and Pavlov, discovered the principles of associations (stimulus-response connections), discrimination and generalization, interference (competition among associations), classical conditioning, and the law of effect (later called the principle of reinforcement). It was B.F. Skinner, however, who built upon previous research to formulate reinforcement theory (or operant conditioning) and who led behaviorism to the forefront of theory, research, and practice. Practical applications were made in mental health clinics and in both regular and special education classrooms. Since the 1960s, research has demonstrated the effectiveness of behavioral techniques to overcome learning problems, reduce phobias, eliminate poor habits, and establish desirable habits. Skinner (1968) applied his theories especially to formal instruction, and behavioral technologies were widely used in schools to manage classroom behavior and enhance academic achievement. Through his books *Walden Two* and *Beyond Freedom and Dignity*, Skinner excited and frightened his readers about the potential of behavior management to change society. What are these principles that have so much power?

Behaviorism focuses on observable events (behaviors), not internal states or processes within the learner. It avoids terms such as "thinking" and "mind," so that what happens inside the learner is considered a "black box." Learning is defined as a relatively permanent change in behavior not due to growth or maturation. All learning is thought to occur as a result of contingencies in the environment, either planned or accidental. Operant conditioning changes behavior by deliberately manipulating the consequences of behavior (contingency management). Behaviors that are reinforced (rewarded) tend to be strengthened, and behaviors that are ignored or punished tend to be weakened or extinguished. Shaping occurs when the desired behavior is gradually brought about through reinforcement of successive approximations to the desired behavior.

Models Based on Behaviorism

The following are some prominent instructional models from the behaviorist tradition, three of which are represented by chapters in this book.

Behavior Modification

One direct application of behaviorism is behavior modification (MacMillan, 1973). In this paradigm, specific target behaviors are identified and precisely described. The target behaviors are measured to establish a baseline. Then an intervention program is begun, in which the desired behaviors are reinforced and unwanted behaviors are ignored or punished (in other words, the contingencies are managed according to some pre-determined scheme). The target behaviors continue to be measured until they reach the desired levels. Once the target behaviors are well established or extinguished, additional contingency management may be required to maintain the behaviors at their desired levels. Behavior modification has been successfully used in classrooms and in mental health settings to bring about positive behavior change and learning. "Token economies" give small, frequent, symbolic rewards for each behavior, which can later be exchanged for more significant rewards.

Behavior modification (Chapter 1) offers strong research support, applicability in the workplace for building a variety of work-related and personal habits, and principles that can be integrated with other models for training development.

Programmed Instruction

Programmed instruction is a specific method of teaching and learning based on behaviorist principles. Quite popular during the 1960s, programmed instruction was developed for use in military and other government-sponsored training, corporate training, and school learning. It was so important that it inspired the founding of a new professional society, the National Society for Programmed Instruction. The Society still thrives today, though its name is now the International Society for Performance Improvement and its mission is considerably broader.

Programmed instruction was usually workbook based but sometimes was implemented via mechanical teaching machines. Content was presented one small idea or skill at a time in sections called "frames." Learners responded to questions or other practice opportunities and received immediate feedback, with opportunities to try again or get remedial help if they were at first unsuccessful. The programs were self-paced, but a human tutor was often available to help with trouble spots, especially when the instruction was presented in a learning center or classroom. Success was almost guaranteed, because the steps were so small that virtually all learners could respond correctly to the practice exercises, and by virtue of remediation and self-pacing. Branching was frequently used to route learners to specific sections of the instruction, based on their individual learning needs or their performance on prior activities.

Programmed instruction lost its great popularity by the early 1970s, although it is still occasionally used today. Because the stimulus and response patterns varied little, learners often found the training repetitive and boring, which made them lose interest. Critics said that higher-order behaviors were difficult to teach and learn in this restricted format. In any case, the principles of programmed instruction have survived and are often the basis for today's interactive technology-based instruction. Computer screens and web pages reflect the old frames of programmed instruction, although greater variety is incorporated to enhance interest. Computer-based and multimedia instruction use self-pacing, frequent responding, immediate feedback, and branching extensively.

Gropper's Behavioral Approach

George Gropper's work in instructional design theory (Gropper, 1983) integrated most of what was known from behavioral learning research, extended that knowledge in some areas, and resulted in a detailed, prescriptive model of instructional design. For this reason, Gropper's model was chosen as the subject of Chapter 2.

Gropper's approach is to analyze specific, detailed requirements of the subject matter (objective) to be learned. For example, what does the objective require the learner to do (e.g., recall facts, solve problems)? What are the component skills of the objective (e.g., chaining, stimulus discrimination)? What are the stimulus properties of the component skills (e.g., response similarity, number of stimulus properties)? Answers to these questions lead to treatment prescriptions: routine, shaping, or specialized. Generally, routine treatments are used when learning tasks are not too difficult and when stimulus and response properties are less confusing. Routine treatments consist of examples, cues, practice, and feedback. When skills are more difficult because of obstacles such as confusing stimulus or response properties, or because of challenging performance conditions, shaping treatments are prescribed. These treatments gradually increase the difficulty of practice opportunities by varying the size of the unit of behavior, the nature of the stimulus situation, the cue strength (help), the mode of responding, or other variables. Specialized treatments (e.g., backward chaining, practice of errors) are used in unusual circumstances that require them.

In addition to his prescriptions for analyzing and teaching individual objectives, Gropper also gives advice for sequencing multiple objectives. Objectives may be related to each other vertically (one is prerequisite to the other), horizontally (one is performed temporally prior to the other but need not be learned first), or not at all. Two objectives may also share the same subordinate objective. He points out the importance of determining learning contingencies versus performance contingencies in identifying the best learning sequence. More recent prescriptions for conducting instructional analysis and sequencing (e.g., Dick & Carey, 1996; Gagné, Briggs, & Wager, 1992) follow Gropper's principles.

Mastery Learning

Mastery learning is another model based on behaviorist principles. The ideas are to break down the learning content into small units; have learners study these units in a recommended sequence at their own speed; supply feedback, praise, and encouragement; provide plenty of remedial practice; and allow progression to the next unit only when the previous unit is mastered. Carroll (1971) and Bloom (1971) brought this model to the forefront, building on work by Morrison in the1930s (Saettler, 1990). The core principle of this model is to hold achievement constant at a high level by allowing time to vary—given enough time and assistance, virtually all learners can master the objectives.

Many instructional programs were developed using this model, especially during the 1970s. Individually prescribed instruction was a mastery learning system developed for use by elementary and secondary school students by the Learning Research and Development Center of the University of Pittsburgh. Other examples include systems for teaching foreign languages in language laboratories. Meta-analyses of the research on mastery learning systems support modest but consistent learning advantages, compared with learners in non-mastery control groups (Kulik, Kulik, & Bengert-Drowns, 1990). Principles of mastery learning have been and are easily incorporated with other instructional design models, when individual learner pacing is possible.

Behavior Modeling

Social learning theory (Bandura, 1977), adds an interesting twist to behaviorism by acknowledging the demonstrated strong effects of an admired human model in getting people to behave in desired ways: People imitate the behavior of those they admire, such as celebrities, family members, peers, or leaders. Behavior modeling uses this principle as a key feature of its training method, as well as the powerful behaviorist principle of positive social reinforcement. As described by Robinson (1982), behavior modeling is a highly prescriptive model for teaching interpersonal or "people" skills, such as those needed by managers, customer service personnel, and virtually everyone in today's collaborative work environment. With slight modifications, it can also be used for other types of training, including technical skills, or any skill that can be demonstrated. First the learner sees the videotaped model being successful (getting reinforced) when he or she uses the recommended behaviors (critical steps). This reinforcement is all the more effective because the person getting reinforced is an admired human model. Next, during skill practice exercises, learners get opportunities to try out the recommended behaviors in simulated situations. Every behavior they perform correctly is socially reinforced as the class members and instructor deliver specific, tailored feedback. Errors and omissions are corrected by suggestions of "alternative positive behaviors." Behavior modeling was selected for inclusion in this section (Chapter 3) because of its solid research base and its widespread acceptance as an effective model.

References

Bandura, A. (1977). *Social learning theory*. Englewood Cliffs, NJ: Prentice-Hall.

Bloom, B.S. (1971). Mastery learning. In J.H. Block (Ed.), *Mastery learning: Theory and practice*. New York: Holt, Rinehart & Winston.

Carroll, J.B. (1971). Problems of measurement related to the concept of learning for mastery. In J.H. Block (Ed.), *Mastery learning: Theory and practice*. New York: Holt, Rinehart & Winston.

Dick, W., & Carey, L. (1996). *The systematic design of instruction* (4th ed.). Glenview, IL: HarperCollins.

Gagné, R.M., Briggs, L.J., & Wager, W.W. (1992). *Principles of instructional design* (4th ed.). Fort Worth, TX: Harcourt Brace Jovanovich.

Gropper, G.L. (1983). A behavioral approach to instructional prescription. In C.M. Reigeluth (Ed.), *Instructional design theories and models: An overview of their current status* (101–161). Hillsdale, NJ: Lawrence Erlbaum Associates.

Kulik, C.C., Kulik, J.A., & Bengert-Drowns, R.L. (1990). Effectiveness of mastery learning programs: A meta-analysis. *Review of Educational Research, 60,* 265–299.

MacMillan, D.L. (1973). *Behavior modification in education*. New York: Macmillan.

Robinson, J.C. (1982). *Developing managers through behavior modeling*. Austin, TX: Learning Concepts.

Saettler, P. (1990). *The evolution of American educational technology*. Englewood, CO: Libraries Unlimited, Inc.

Skinner, B.F. (1968). *The technology of teaching*. New York: Appleton.

CHAPTER 1

Behavior Modification

Linda J. Elengold

Behavioral models of performance management are based on the theory that environment shapes behavior and that desired behaviors can be taught by manipulating their consequences. Behavior modification as a training method uses the well-substantiated principle that behaviors that are rewarded tend to be repeated, while behaviors that are ignored or punished either diminish or become extinct. In this model, the goal of learning is to modify particular behaviors. The learning environment is structured so that positive reinforcers (rewards) are identified and applied to increase the frequency of desirable behavior, whereas undesirable behaviors are ignored, or even punished, to reduce their frequency. Also known as contingency management, a behavior modification program presents reinforcement only when the desired behavior appears. (The reinforcement is contingent on the desired behavior.)

Behavior modification's effectiveness is well supported by laboratory and field research. The approach has been used successfully in mental health settings (e.g., to establish socially acceptable behaviors and self-care practices), in educational settings (e.g., to control disruptive classroom behavior and to increase on-task study behaviors), and in workplace settings (e.g., to establish habits consistent with recommended safety procedures). In addition, desirable health-related behaviors, such as exercise, smoking cessation, alcohol abstinence, weight management, and stress reduction, have all been successfully adopted using behavior modification as a framework for learning.

Origins

Behavior modification practices have been used for centuries to alter maladaptive behavior. Forness and MacMillan (1970) trace procedures consistent with behavior modification principles back as far as Plato and Erasmus. Around 1800, Jean Itard used positive and negative reinforcement to control and teach disruptive students, and Johan Christian Reil used "non-injurious torture" to treat insanity. Both achieved good results (MacMillan, 1973). Moviegoers in 1999 may remember the effective contingency management practiced on King George III to restore his mental health in *The Madness of King George*. And many readers will themselves have had their behavior manipulated by Grandma's Law: You can have dessert only if you eat your vegetables.

However, it was toward the end of the 19th century and during the early 20th century that the experiments of Ebbinghaus, Pavlov, and Thorndike created the scientific basis for behavior modification. J.B. Watson's famous experiment with 11-month-old Albert, in which Albert learned to fear a harmless white rat (conditioned stimulus) through pairing of the rat with a disagreeable sound (unconditioned stimulus) demonstrated how maladaptive behaviors can be learned through classical conditioning (Watson & Rayner, 1920). Jones (1924) used desensitization to eliminate children's fears. Burnham (1924) made significant strides in applying previous behavioral research to education, advocating principles that later developed into programmed instruction.

The 1930s and 1940s saw much refinement and expanded applications of the principles of behavior modification, but it was the decade of the 1950s and the theoretical work of B.F. Skinner that brought about a surge of large-scale, high-quality research and application with a variety of experimental subjects in a wide range of settings. For example, stuttering, stammering, tantrums, anxiety, phobias, juvenile delinquency, and writer's cramp were treated effectively, and cooperative behavior among young children was effected using operant conditioning. Social reinforcers were found to be effective.

Skinner identified two types of conditioning: respondent (classical) and operant. In respondent conditioning, as with Pavlov's dogs, an unconditioned stimulus (UCS) such as an audible tone is paired with a conditioned stimulus (CS) such as food until the USC produces the same response as the CS—in this case salivation. The focus in respondent conditioning is on the antecedents to the desired behavior. In operant conditioning, the focus is on reinforcement following the desired behavior, rather than on the antecedents. Operant conditioning is most often used to modify human behavior. Skinner identified primary reinforcers, which satisfy primary needs, and secondary reinforcers, which provide other less direct forms of satisfaction.

In the 1960s and 1970s, clinical and educational settings used behavior modification principles widely, both in regular and special education classrooms. Concurrently, programmed instruction, another application of behavioral principles, was in common use. Programmed instruction, a system of self-study adopted by the U.S. Armed Forces and some industrial groups, was very popular during these years. Based on Skinner's work, programmed instruction taught the subject matter in small steps, or frames, in a workbook or on a machine. Students were prompted for frequent responses and provided immediate feedback to reinforce correct answers. Success was almost guaranteed. Programmed instruction allowed students to progress at their own pace as they learned individually, either inside or outside the classroom.

In the 1970s, cognitive approaches to learning became popular, and behavioral approaches lost much support in the education and training communities. Behaviorism was criticized for its apparent inability to develop complex behaviors, such as higher-level thinking skills and creativity. Humanists have always viewed behavior modification unfavorably, as they see behavior modification as manipulative, which is unacceptable in their frame of reference. Nevertheless, behavior modification principles are still used today and often incorporated into training programs based on other paradigms.

Description

Behavior modification assumes that all behavior, good and bad, is learned through events in a person's environment. From this assumption follows the assumption that learning principles can be used to establish new behaviors and to change existing behaviors to more desirable ones. Causes of behavior such as internal states of motivation and personality characteristics are rejected—only observable events and behaviors are considered.

Basic Concepts

To implement a behavior modification program, one must first understand the basic concepts underlying the model. Certain definitions are necessary for that understanding.

Biographical Sketch

Burrhaus Frederick Skinner was born on March 20, 1904, in Susquehanna, Pennsylvania. Growing up with a typical turn-of-the-century, small-town childhood and education, he was interested in his own inventions and physics and chemistry experiments. He became interested in animal behavior while keeping a variety of turtles, snakes, toads, lizards, and even chipmunks. After graduation from Hamilton College in 1926 with a bachelor's degree in English Literature, Skinner devoted two years to becoming an author and pursuing his hobbies of painting, sculpture, and music.

Deciding that he wasn't destined to be a writer, he enrolled at Harvard from 1928 to 1931, earning a doctorate in Psychology. In 1936, he married Yvonne Blue, a graduate of the University of Chicago, who encouraged his interest in literature. They moved to the University of Minnesota, where Skinner taught until 1945, when he became chair of the Department of Psychology at Indiana University. Skinner was experimenting with learning and reinforcement in pigeons and formulated the beginnings of his theory that all behavior is a product of the environment. His "Skinner box" was a small, soundproof chamber that isolated animals so he could experiment on specific conditions. He used it to train rats and pigeons to press a lever to obtain food. He returned to Harvard in 1948.

Skinner's 1940 novel *Walden Two* about utopian society is based on his theories of behavior modification and reinforcement. From 1941 to 1957, he raised two children. His second child, Deborah, was the famous "baby in the box." In the late 1950s, he began to study contingency management and programmed instruction in schools.

In 1964, Skinner received a Career Award from the National Institute of Mental Health, which supported his research for 10 years, including an analysis of cultural practices from the point of view of an experimental analysis of behavior. Skinner's major publications include *Science and Human Behavior* and *Beyond Freedom and Dignity*. In these works, Skinner suggests that many individual and social problems could be better solved by a behavioral modification approach rather than punishment. Punishment is ineffective, he postulated, because the results are of short duration.

Skinner died in 1990.

Eliciting Stimulus. The antecedent condition(s) under which behavior occurs. The stimulus, or stimuli, could be a social situation, a set of verbal cues, a sound, a visual image, a command, or a physical environment.

Response. The behavior that occurs when certain stimuli are present. Operant responses are those that are under the control of the person (not involuntary or reflexive) and that "operate" on (do something to) the environment.

Positive Reinforcer. An environmental stimulus that, when presented after a behavior, increases the probability of that behavior occurring again. It is important to note that not everyone finds a particular stimulus reinforcing. Thus, reinforcers must be individually determined. In addition, a person may find a stimulus (e.g., food) reinforcing at one time (after long food deprivation) but not at another time (e.g., after a full meal). So reinforcement must also be determined situationally.

Negative Reinforcer. Termination of an aversive stimulus. An aversive stimulus is one that the person will avoid if given a choice (e.g., solitary confinement).

Figure 1.1 displays the basic components of behavior modification.

Figure 1.1
The Behavior Modification Model

Punishment. Presentation of an aversive stimulus, or the withdrawal of a positively reinforcing stimulus. An example of the former would be public ridicule; the latter, a reduction in pay.

Target Behavior. The desired response or behavior that is to be established by a behavior modification program. The target behavior must be carefully selected and exactly defined in observable and measurable terms (e.g., remain seated for five-minute intervals).

Contingency. A relationship in which an environmental event (e.g., reinforcer) occurs only after a specified behavior (target behavior). The contingent event does not necessarily have to follow the behavior, but it does not occur unless the behavior occurs.

Desensitization. Unlearning a previously learned negative response, through repeated pairing of the stimulus with pleasant stimuli. For example, a student who fears math could be given ice cream when working on math problems.

Counterconditioning. Learning a positive response (desirable behavior) that replaces an undesirable behavior. For example, learning to chew gum instead of smoking.

Modeling. Imitation of the behavior of others (e.g., parent, supervisor, peer, or celebrity). This phenomenon is not adequately explained by either the respondent or operant conditioning paradigms, but it is often used successfully in behavior modification programs, especially in developing a target behavior that the learner does not already possess. Human models are more effective with human learners than are nonhuman models.

How Behavior Modification Works

Behavior modification is the use of rewards in a systematic way to establish or alter behavior. The ultimate goal of any behavior modification/contingency management training is to establish the desirable behavior in the learner's everyday life and to allow the new behavior to be transferred to similar new situations. The new behavior must be "durable;" that is, the new behavior will become intrinsic and under the learner's self-control and self-monitoring.

Reinforcing consequences, or rewards, is the key to establishing or maintaining a behavior. Reinforcers can be internal to the learner or social, material, or preferred activities. Although there are what might be called "universal reinforcers" (e.g., money), reinforcers are person and time dependent. Often in learning environments, knowledge of results (e.g., a test score of 100%, achieving the correct solution to a problem, or the ability to parallel park a car) can be self-reinforcing. That is, the learner is rewarded simply by knowing that he or she has been successful. Praise or recognition from instructors, peers, coworkers, or family members may be very effective reinforcers. Cash bonuses or other material rewards may also work well. And often people will learn or perform a less-preferred activity if a preferred activity is the reward. (For example, as soon as I finish the assignment, I will go to a movie.)

Reinforcers are most effective when given immediately after the desired behavior occurs, and they may lose some of their power when delayed. However, this depends somewhat on the person, as some people seem to be more willing to work for delayed gratification. Reinforcers may be given continuously (every time the desired behavior is emitted) or intermittently (reliably but not every time). Much research has been done to test the effectiveness of different "schedules of reinforcement." Continuous reinforcement is usually used when establishing a new behavior or at the beginning of a behavior management program. An intermittent schedule can be a ratio (e.g., given every third time) or variable (e.g., random). Intermittent schedules are usually used to maintain a desired behavior once it has been established. If reinforcement is given too often, the learner may reach saturation—a point at which the reinforcer is no longer reinforcing.

Phases of a Behavior Modification Program

Five phases are used to design, implement, and evaluate a behavior modification (contingency management) program:

- Phase 1: Specify a Target Behavior
- Phase 2: Establish a Baseline
- Phase 3: Design the Contingencies
- Phase 4: Institute the Program (Intervention)
- Phase 5: Evaluate the Program

Phase 1: Specify a Target Behavior. The objective of Phase 1 is to specify the desired behavior and to determine how this behavior will be measured. One of Skinner's major contributions was to define learning outcomes in terms of observable behaviors (objectives). The first step is always to answer the question "What do you want the learner to be able to do as a result of the instruction?" To maximize success, only one or a small number of related behaviors should be targeted at one time. Other target behaviors can be added later in the program.

To complete this phase, you must make sure that the desired behavior is observable, positively stated, and measurable. For example, "The participant will walk for at least 10 consecutive minutes," or "You will keep an accurate daily journal of all foods eaten and their calories, which should total between 1000 and 1200 calories per day." Define what will be considered successful. The more precisely and explicitly the behavior can be described, the better. The goal should almost be guaranteed to be achievable so that the learner is not set up to fail. The success criteria will often increase over time; for example, "The participant will walk at least four days during the first week and five days the second week."

Phase 2: Establish a Baseline. In Phase 2, the current frequency of the desired behavior (if any) is recorded. This supports the assessment of a performance gap and creates a baseline for comparison. Charting is particularly helpful in this phase, and during Phase 4 as well. During Phase 2, additional information is collected about the antecedent conditions under which the undesirable behavior (or lack of desired behavior) occurs, as well as any reinforcers that may be sustaining an undesirable behavior. For example, uncontrolled eating may occur during certain times of the day, when specific food cues are present, or under high-stress conditions. Failure to exercise may occur when social pressure reinforces other activities incompatible with exercise.

The baseline also helps to determine the success criteria (interim and final) for the target behavior. If the performance gap is large, it may be best to set goals that are small and achievable at first, to improve the chances of success and positive reinforcement. Figure 1.2 shows the baseline data and data from later phases of the program.

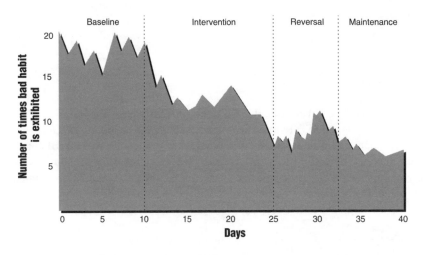

Figure 1.2
Sample Behavior Modification Program: Extinguishing a Bad Habit

Phase 3: Design the Contingencies. During this phase, you structure the situation or environment for success, select the reinforcers and reinforcement schedule for shaping behavior, finalize the behavior modification plans, and determine the duration of the program. For a weight-loss program, for example, you might prepare menus and shopping lists in advance; select the reward for each day that actual eating follows the plan; decide that after the first month, rewards will taper down to a weekly schedule; and determine that the program will last for three months.

In designing the contingencies (interventions), many decisions are required. If an undesirable behavior needs to be weakened, several methods are possible. Extinction may be brought about by ignoring the behavior or through a counterconditioning process. Punishment may be used in the form of removal of a positive reinforcer (e.g., no television until I lose 10 pounds). Satiation may be considered (i.e., making the person "sick" with an "overdose" of the undesirable behavior, such as smoking). If a fear is involved, densensitization may be needed. Removing harmful antecedent or reinforcing conditions surrounding the behavior may also be helpful. For example, removing all junk food from the house and staying away from certain social situations may be useful.

To strengthen a behavior that already exists, positive reinforcement (tokens, tangible social reinforcement, or activities) may be used, designed to fit the person. Negative reinforcement may be used in addition. Again, antecedent and reinforcing stimuli must be controlled. For example, to strengthen healthful eating habits, the kitchen should be stocked with "safe" foods, and activities around "safe" people should be planned.

To develop a new behavior (one that is not currently in the person's repertoire), shaping, prompting and fading, or modeling may be required. Shaping involves the gradual development of the behavior through successive approximations. For example, a weight-lifting program requires new skills. Therefore, easier routines should precede more difficult ones. Prompting and fading could be accomplished by personalized coaching (e.g., using a personal trainer to establish a weight-lifting routine), then having the learner gradually perform without the aid of the coach. Human modeling is also effective in teaching people new behaviors. Again, a personal trainer should demonstrate the moves to be learned. Modeling is also used frequently in weight-loss programs, by using instructors (and videos of successful clients) who have succeeded in losing weight and maintaining their weight loss.

Phase 4: Institute the Program (Intervention). In Phase 4, the program is implemented as designed. The learner, if not previously involved in the program development, is informed of the conditions of the program. The environment is arranged to support the success of the program. For example, all junk food is removed from the house. Finally, occurrences of the desired behavior are recorded and the reinforcers are given as scheduled. Charting is important in this phase.

Phase 5: Evaluate the Program. In Phase 5, at the end of the planned time for the program, success is evaluated by comparing the baseline measurements of the behavior with the ending level of occurrences of the target behavior. Reinforcers may be discontinued ("reversal of contingencies") and the frequency of the desired behavior measured again to determine the level of internalization of the desired behavior. A longer or redesigned intervention phase may be necessary if the behavior pattern reverts to an undesirable level. Maintenance of the desired behavior is necessary with continued monitoring.

Strengths and Weaknesses of Behavior Modification

Behavioral approaches deal only with observable behaviors, antecedents, and consequences. The model does not account for unobservable events, thoughts, and/or feelings. Learning is defined as a relatively permanent change in behavior, rather than as an internal cognitive process. Therefore, the model has been criticized as limiting and as applicable only to simple behaviors. This model does, however, serve as a basis for the cognitive-behavioral approaches that include internal events such as thoughts and emotions when considering the factors that precipitate and maintain behaviors. In cognitive-behavioral approaches, learning techniques such as repeated practice, modeling, and reinforcement are used to modify not only behavior, but thoughts and emotions as well.

One strength of this model is that, by defining the desired behavior, the learner knows exactly what is expected. In a well-designed contingency program, improved performance can be achieved and habits can develop that result in future performance, even after the reinforcement is discontinued. Using behavior modification, the participant can accomplish small tasks, building incrementally into larger tasks or behaviors. If the contingency management program is designed and implemented by others, especially without the consent of the learner/performer, then the approach may be viewed as manipulative or even coercive and unethical. If used by the learner/performer to regulate his or her own behavior, however, or with help from a professional or trusted coach, behavior modification can be a valuable tool for self-directed learning.

Using this model for group instruction may have practical drawbacks. It can be difficult to find a reinforcer that is rewarding to everyone in the group; yet rewarding individuals differently may be perceived as unfair. If the time period for group training is limited, some members may lag behind in reaching the goals. Continuing the behavior modification program alone, individuals may fail.

Research Support

Operant conditioning, the theory that underlies behavior modification, is well established in the behavioral psychology literature. Principles of behavior change through contingency management have been well established by the work of B.F. Skinner and others. Even today, research continues into methods of modifying behaviors and maintaining behavioral change.

James O. Prochaska, a psychologist and director of the Cancer Prevention Research center at the University of Rhode Island, has studied how thousands of people overcome behavioral problems and how we can apply behavior modification to life-style issues that impact health (Prochaska et al., 1994). At the University of Washington, G. Alan Marlatt, professor of psychology and director of the Addictive Behaviors Research Center, has spent nearly a decade researching the application of behavior modification in the prevention and treatment of addictive behaviors, such as alcoholism. In 1992, he began teaching a course, "Self-Directed Change—Skills for Life-style Goals," to test his theory that when students learn the principles of behavior modification, they can apply these principles to specific behaviors in their lives. The students set their own behavior modification goals and chart their progress over the semester (Monaghan, 1992).

The National Institutes of Health, (NIH) cites six leading causes of death that are behaviorally based: AIDS, violence, smoking, accidents, substance abuse, and diet. Since HIV is most commonly transmitted by specific behaviors, NIH is targeting HIV/AIDS for researching the factors influencing change in risk behaviors and the success rate of preventive interventions for specific populations. The Prevention Science Working Group in NIH's Office of AIDS Research is studying the success of behavior modification strategies for high-risk behaviors and needle exchange programs (American Psychological Association, 1998).

Other behavior modification studies currently center on drinking and driving, particularly in teenagers. In a presentation to the American Psychological Association 1997 annual convention, John R. Mattox of the University of Memphis concluded that the most effective programs for teenage drivers

Research Support, cont.

included not just instruction, but also enforced consequences for inappropriate behaviors. Consequences included police enforcement of curfews, speeding and DWI laws, and graduated licensing, where experience and competency were rewarded with longer driving hours (American Psychological Association, 1997).

In 1999, the National Institutes of Mental Health (NIMH) formed a new Division of Neuroscience and Basic Behavioral Science to perform basic behavioral research. Other work on behaviorism is ongoing in its Division of Mental Disorders, Behavioral Research and AIDS, which focuses on relating behavioral research to public health issues and mental disorders. Its research includes patients' adherence to medical treatments and health-related behavior changes and health services, including studies on whether people seek medical treatment and what determines whether they subsequently behave according to medical advice (Azar, 1999). NIMH and the National Institute on Drug Abuse are also funding research into relapse to high-risk behaviors after behavior change (American Psychological Association, 2000).

Best Uses

Behavior modification is often used in children's classrooms to teach socially desirable behavior, such as staying in one's seat, raising one's hand, and cooperation skills.

For adults, behavior modification is used to deal with such workplace problems as tardiness and poor work habits. Behavior modification techniques can be used to increase the use of a new method or procedure, to increase the timeliness of report filing, and/or to improve job performance outcomes, such as number of sales calls made or speed of problem resolution.

Often, behavior modification is used by groups and individuals to modify their own behaviors in such areas as staying on a budget, decreasing television viewing, or managing time. Health-related areas use behavior modification extensively for changing behaviors in adults: exercise, smoking cessation, alcohol/drug abstinence, weight-loss programs, and stress reduction. Groups such as Weight Watchers, Diet

Workshop, and Alcoholics Anonymous stress behavior modification as a technique for successfully changing existing habits. The program may be customized to the individual by a physician, counselor, or other expert, or within a group context. Often the individuals are responsible for monitoring their own behavior and administering some of the predefined reinforcements. Social reinforcement is also used in group settings.

For academic content, other behavioral models and strategies, such as mastery learning, programmed instruction, or behavior modeling, are more appropriate.

Model in Action

Employee wellness and fitness have become important factors in the 21st-century workplace. Many companies recognize these areas as critical to employee productivity and performance improvement. Smoking cessation programs, treatment of eating disorders, alcohol and drug abuse treatment programs, and stress management programs offer classic examples of behavior modification ("Health Behavior Modification," 1995), and these are often offered in the workplace. Many commercial weight-reduction programs offer participants a variety of behavior modification techniques to facilitate weight loss and even bring their programs to the workplace.

Weight-loss programs recommend a variety of behavior modification techniques. The "desired behaviors" may include eating on a smaller plate to make portions appear larger, eating smaller but more frequent meals to sustain a feeling of fullness, keeping a daily journal of all food eaten to ensure conscious choices, weighing and measuring all food before eating, and documenting physical activity. The programs all include an educational component, where participants are taught the desired behaviors and are told exactly what is expected of them (e.g., a completely filled-out food diary for the following week). The programs provide social reinforcers, such as public acknowledgment and applause, and tangible awards including ribbons, pins, and prizes. Reinforcement is given often, as participants are encouraged to accomplish small tasks, such as exercising three times next week, with the desired result being a long-term cumulative effect. Positive behavior is modeled by "leaders" and instructors who can document their own individual successes, which they achieved by implementing the desired behaviors. Participants are encouraged to provide their own rewards to continue behavioral modifications learned once they finish the program.

Implementation Guide

Model Phase	Activities
1. Specify the Target Behavior	• Identify the desired behavior. • Precisely and explicitly describe the behavior. • Determine how it can best be observed and measured.
2. Establish a Baseline	• Systematically observe the current behavior. • Measure current behavior or competing behaviors. • Assess antecedent conditions and reinforcing stimuli.
3. Design the Contingencies	• Identify reinforcers (positive or negative) that are appropriate to the target population. • Determine how often reinforcement will be provided. • Select other appropriate aspects of the intervention, such as environmental conditions, punishments, counterconditioning, desensitization, or modeling.
4. Institute the Program (Intervention)	• Inform the learner of the conditions. • Structure the environment for success where possible. • Reinforce the desired behavior. • Continue to measure and chart behavior.
5. Evaluate the Program	• Compare intervention phase data to baseline data. • Use reversal to check for internalization of new behavior. • Withdraw reinforcement, but continue to monitor during maintenance phase.

References

American Psychological Association. (1997). *Combination of interventions are found to be most effective in improving drinking behavior among teenagers* [On-line]. Available: http://www.apa.org/releases/traffic.html

American Psychological Association. (1998). *Why behavioral research on HIV/ AIDS?* [On-line]. Available: http://www.apa.org/ppo/faids.html

American Psychological Association. (2000). *Prevention of relapse to high-risk behaviors* [On-line]. Available: http://www.apa.org/science/ nimh_high_risk.html

Azar, B. (1999, February). *NIMH reshuffles behavioral research. APA Monitor On-line* [On-line]. Available: http://www.apa.org/monitor/feb99/nimh.html

Burnham, W. (1924). *The normal mind*. New York: Appleton.

Forness, S.R., & MacMillan, D.L. (1970). The origins of behavior modification with exceptional children. *Exceptional Children, 37*, 93–100.

Health behavior modification—A commitment to change. (1995, October). *Journal of Physical Education, Recreation, & Dance, 12*.

Jones, M.C. (1924). The elimination of children's fears. *Journal of Experimental Psychology, 7,* 382–390.

MacMillan, D.L. (1973). *Behavior modification in education*. New York: Macmillan.

Monaghan, P. (1992). Psychology course links theory and practice of behavior modification. *The Chronicle of Higher Education*, A31–A33.

Prochaska, J.O., Norcross, J.C., & Diclemente, C.C. (1994). *Changing for good*. New York: William Morrow and Company, Inc.

Watson, J.B., & Rayner, R. (1920). Conditioned emotional reactions. *Journal of Experimental Psychology, 3,* 1–14.

Bibliography

B.F. Skinner Foundation. (1999). *A brief survey of operant behavior* [On-line]. Available: http://www.bfskinner.org/Operant.asp

Epstein, R., & Skinner, B.F. (Eds.). (1982). *Skinner for the classroom*. Champaign, IL: Research Press.

Joyce, B., & Weil, M. (1992). *Models of teaching*. Boston: Allyn and Bacon.

Public Broadcasting System. (1998). *A science odyssey: People and discoveries: B. F. Skinner* [On-line]. Available: http://www.pbs.org/wgbh/aso/databank/entries/bhskin.html

Skinner, B.F. (1953). *Science and human behavior*. New York: The Free Press.

Skinner, B.F. (1958, October 24). Teaching machines. *Science*, 969–977.

Skinner, B.F. (1964, May 20). New methods and new aims in teaching. *New Scientist*, 122.

Skinner, B.F. (1965, October 16). Why teachers fail. *Saturday Review*, 80–81, 98–102.

Skinner, B.F. (1968, February 16). Teaching science in high school—What is wrong? *Science*, 704–710.

Skinner, B.F. (1973). Some implications of making education more efficient. In *Seventy-Second Yearbook of the National Society for the Study of Education*. Chicago: University of Chicago Press.

Skinner, B.F. (1974). *About behaviorism*. New York: Alfred A. Knopf.

Skinner, B.F. (1986, October). Programmed instruction revisited. *Phi Delta Kappan*, 103–110.

About the Author

Linda J. Elengold has more than 10 years of experience in managing, designing, developing, and evaluating human performance and training projects. She provides consulting expertise to government agencies and commercial clients to identify performance problems, determine appropriate solutions to support business goals, and lead design and development efforts. Linda designs performance-centered systems interfaces, electronic performance support systems, interactive multimedia, computer- and web-based training, online help systems, and other performance improvement solutions. She also evaluates training and performance support interventions for usability, effectiveness, and return on investment. A project manager for WPI, Inc., a division of SI International, Linda has developed and taught workshops in both ISD and return on investment for performance support, and presents at industry conferences. She earned a master's degree in Human Performance Systems at Marymount University and serves on the board of directors of the Maryland Chapter of the American Society for Training and Development.

CHAPTER 2

Behavioral Approach

Maureen Giannotti and Kristin Radcliffe

George L. Gropper developed a behavioral approach to instructional design and published it in several related works in the 1970s and 1980s. The model was built on the behavioral learning theory that had been extremely popular during the previous two decades. Gropper's model prescribes systematic treatments, or instructional strategies, based on the type of objective, the underlying component skills, and their stimulus and response (S-R) characteristics that will produce the desired change in overt behavior.

This model offers a methodical and structured approach to the design of practice for five types of behavioral objectives, addressing each with three types of prescriptions. Five key steps are used to develop instruction:

1. Define the objective(s).
2. Break the objective(s) down into component skills.
3. Analyze the conditions that affect the ease or difficulty of learning the skills (stimulus and response characteristics).
4. Analyze the performance criterion.
5. Prescribe instructional treatments.

Gropper's model emphasizes analysis of the performance conditions and criteria for each objective. The selection of an instructional treatment depends on the mix of skills that compose the learning objective, a determination of how easy or difficult those skills are to master, and an assessment of whether the learner will have to recall or transfer what is learned.

Consistent with the behavioral tradition, active practice and reinforcement are central to Gropper's approach, and learners must practice the behaviors in the appropriate context. The instructional goal is to have particular stimuli elicit the desired behavioral response. This is accomplished by repeated practice of the behavior in the presence of the controlling stimuli, followed by reinforcement. In fact, all three types of treatments (routine, shaping, and specialized) are variations on what is practiced and the method and sequence in which it is practiced.

Origins

Gropper's model is deeply rooted in behavioral learning theory, which dominated the instructional landscape especially from the early 1950s through the mid 1970s. This approach to instructional design gained strength when psychologists responsible for training troops during World War II defined training outcomes in performance terms, which were directly related to the soldiers' job tasks (Gropper, 1983). Task analysis and performance objectives became two basic tenets of the behavioral approach to instructional design.

B.F. Skinner was the most significant contributor to the development of behavioral learning theory, and his research was, of course, most influential to Gropper's work in instructional design. Skinner's theory of operant conditioning emphasizes the effective control of behavior through a series of S-R relationships. He applied this theory to learning and instruction, including the development of programmed instruction, which made central use of active practice and reinforcement. During the 1960s, behavioral analysis methods developed further (Mechner, 1967), and comprehensive behavioral models of instructional design began to emerge (e.g., Gagné, 1970). These developments were influential in Gropper's work.

Gropper (1973, 1974) integrated most of what was known about behavioral approaches to instruction, and he extended this knowledge to form a detailed and comprehensive prescriptive model.

Biographical Sketch

George L. Gropper received an AB in Social Relations from Harvard College in 1948, an MA in Psychology from the University of California at Berkeley in 1953, and a PhD in Psychology from the University of Pittsburgh in 1956. He retired in 1991 from Digital Equipment Corporation, where he served as an advisor and consultant to technical writers who prepared technical manuals and to course developers who prepared courses on computer usage. In his role as a consultant, he has provided advice and training on all major instructional design tasks. He has also made significant contributions to programs concerned with broader educational issues and quality assurance.

Previously, Dr. Gropper served for two years in a faculty development role at the University of Pennsylvania and for one year as a visiting professor in the Department of Educational Research at Florida State University. Prior to that, he spent 15 years in research and development at the American Institutes for Research. Through those years, he did research on the role of visuals in instruction, applied programming techniques to educational television, and developed an instructional design model.

His research and development led to several major publications: *Managing Problem Behavior in the Classroom* (Appleton Century Crofts, 1970); and (from Educational Technology Publications) the following four volumes— *Criteria for the Selection and Use of Visuals in Instruction* (1971); *Instructional Strategies* (1974); *Diagnosis and Revision in the Development of Instructional Materials* (1975); and *Text Displays: Analysis and Systematic Design* (1991).

Description

Gropper's behavioral approach to instructional design establishes a set of prescriptive treatments for specific behavioral learning goals. His intent was to provide the instructional designer with more detailed and useful guidance than the principles of operant conditioning or behavioral learning theory previously offered. The result is a complex model based on years of research and practical experience. Gropper breaks down the design process into five steps (see Figure 2.1):

1. Define Objectives
2. Analyze Component Skills
3. Assess the Difficulty of Acquiring Skills
4. Analyze the Performance Criterion
5. Prescribe Treatments

Define Objectives

Gropper identifies five specific types of objectives:

1. Recalling Facts
2. Defining and Illustrating Concepts
3. Giving and Applying Explanations
4. Following Rules
5. Solving Problems

Gropper leaves the task of defining these learning outcome categories to others, and he does not create a unique taxonomy.

Analyze Component Skills

Gropper identifies four types of component skills that may comprise behavioral objectives: discriminations, generalizations, associations, and chaining. The designer must dissect the learning objective into its component skills, because each of these skill types has certain stimulus and response properties that will affect how they are learned.

Discrimination. These skills require that learners distinguish among stimuli. For example, when learning to drive a car, students must learn to distinguish visually between safe and unsafe stopping distances at different speeds. When playing soft-ball, the batter must discriminate between a pitch that is a strike and a pitch that is a ball. Each stimulus requires a different response.

Generalization. Generalization occurs when learners can recognize similarities among a class of stimuli. Here, each member of the class requires the same response. In baking, for example, recipes may require mixing the liquid ingredients together. The baker must recognize milk, water, and vegetable oil as belonging to a

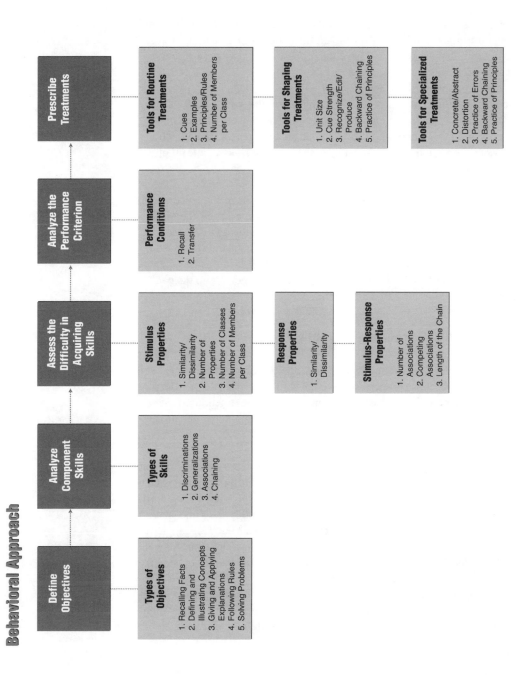

Figure 2.1
Behavioral Approach

class called liquids. Given another recipe, the baker must generalize the term liquid ingredients to fruit juice and honey. In softball, the batter must generalize across different types of pitches that may all have the properties of a strike (e.g., curve ball, fast ball, slider) and must swing at all of them.

Association. Association is the process of linking a stimulus with a desired response. Often, multiple associations must be learned. Examples include links between names and faces, states and capitols, road sign shapes and driver actions (e.g., slow, yield, stop). In the softball example, the batter must associate all pitches within strike range with the response of swinging the bat.

Chaining. Chaining is assembling a series of S-R associations in sequence to complete a task. An example is opening a bottle of wine with a corkscrew. The foil is the stimulus to cut off the foil. The exposed cork is the stimulus to insert the corkscrew. When the screw has reached the proper depth, this is the stimulus to withdraw the cork. Each of the steps in the chain involves discriminations, generalizations, and/or associations. In softball, a chain consists of picking up the bat, swinging at a pitch, hitting the ball, and running the bases.

Assess the Difficulty of Acquiring the Skills

During this step, the designer examines the S-R properties of each component skill and determines whether those properties make the skill easy or difficult to learn. Findings here will have a direct impact on the instructional treatment used. Several factors affect the level of difficulty in learning a discrimination, generalization, association or chain, as described below.

Discriminations. Learning can be more difficult if the stimuli are similar or if there are many kinds (classes) of stimuli. Consider the task of identifying apples if no signs are present. Although there are many types of apples, some have very similar stimulus properties. All apples have a similar shape, are roughly the same size, have stems, are shiny, and are green, yellow, or red. MacIntosh and Gala apples are quite similar in color and size, while Granny Smith and Yellow Delicious may also be confused. To identify a particular type of apple reliably, the learner must make relatively fine distinctions in color, size, shape, and shininess. Birdwatchers have an even more difficult time learning to identify species of birds. Non-native speakers of English may be confused by words such as red and read or wait and weight, because the sound stimuli are the same but the written stimuli are different, and the meanings are different as well.

Generalizations. Learning generalizations can be difficult if a large number of stimuli belong to one class and the stimuli are not similar. For example, consider a teenager trying to learn to classify cars by sight into brand categories (e.g., Chevrolet, Toyota, Honda, Chrysler). Each brand has a variety of models, styles, years, colors, and sizes. These diverse properties of examples within each class make generalization difficult.

Dissimilarity among members of a class can also make it difficult to form a generalization, especially when the learner is confronted with a new member of the class (Gropper, 1983). Art history students must frequently classify paintings as belonging to a particular artistic period (e.g., Gothic, Baroque, Italian Renaissance). This is a particularly difficult skill for a novice because, on the surface, two Baroque paintings will not be identical or even nearly so. They share certain properties that make them a member of the class of Baroque paintings, but their differences may obscure these common properties for the learner.

Associations. Learning can be easier or more difficult depending on the strength of the existing S-R associations. For instance, consider a child learning to ride a two-wheel bicycle. The learning experience will be easier for the child who learned first how to pedal on a tricycle and then a two-wheeler bike with training wheels. Although balancing the bike does require new learning, the response of pedaling the bike to make it go is very strong and supportive of the new behavior.

Chains. Learning difficulty can depend on the length of the chain (number of steps). The chain's learning difficulty also depends on the difficulty of individual links in the chain. For example, if an auto mechanic is working on a different type of car than practiced previously, the repair job may require generalization at certain critical steps in the chain.

Analyze the Performance Criterion

The final phase of analysis, prior to selecting the appropriate instructional treatment, requires that the designer determine how the skill will be used once it has been learned. Gropper identifies two types of performance requirements: *recall* and *transfer*.

Recall tasks require the learner to perform only what has been previously encountered and practiced during training. When all members of a class of stimuli have been encountered during instruction, then the performance depends only on recall. For example, an instructional design student might be asked to recall what activities occur within each phase of the ISD model, after all these activities have been presented and discussed during class. When the skills learned during training must be applied to a situation that has not been previously encountered, then successful performance depends on transfer. The transfer requirement is more common and is more difficult than recall. For example, instructional design students are taught to use the five-step ISD process (analyze, design, develop, implement, and evaluate). Effective performance requires that they apply the ISD process to new situations they have not encountered during class. They need to transfer the skills they learned in the classroom and apply them to the workplace.

Prescribe Treatments

The final step in Gropper's model is to prescribe an instructional treatment. Gropper strives to give the designer specific techniques, rather than generic steps, that will bring about the desired behavior change. Treatments must address the needs identified in the analysis of the component skills, the ease or difficulty of learning the skills, and the performance criterion.

The most basic element of any instructional treatment is practice, followed by reinforcement. To design effective practice, however, the designer must answer these questions:

- What should be practiced (content)?
- How much should be practiced (size of unit)?
- How should it be practiced (mode)?
- In what order should it be practiced (sequencing)?
- How much help should the learner have with the practice (cueing and fading)?

These are precisely the questions that Gropper's prescriptions address. There are three types of treatments: *routine treatments*, *shaping progressions*, and *specialized treatments*. Each of these instructional strategies refines and elaborates the design of practice tasks.

Routine Treatments. The simplest and most direct approach is to have the learner practice, right away, the entire criterion behavior. A routine treatment provides—

- Instructions (what to do and how to do it)
- Varied examples of correct performance (demonstration)
- The rules or principles governing the performance
- Practice of the entire behavior, in final form

Frequent or repeated practice ensures recall of the skill, while varied practice (using a number of different examples) ensures transfer.

A routine treatment for teaching how to use the "cut" and "paste" features in a word processing software package (a transfer task consisting of a chain) would require the instructor to follow the steps below:

1. Give the learners verbal or written instructions on how to cut and paste.
2. Demonstrate how to cut and paste.
3. Explain when it is appropriate to cut and paste and how to avoid any pitfalls.
4. Provide a variety of practice examples.

Shaping Progressions. For behavioral objectives that are more complex or difficult to master (based on their S-R properties), the practice of a complete criterion behavior from the start may be unrealistic. In this instance, Gropper suggests practice on a series of approximations that will eventually lead the learner to perform the behavior at a criterion level. This is called a shaping progression. The designer has several treatment tools to use to shape the behavior. These tools provide learners with additional aid as they work toward achievement of the criterion behavior. These include the following:

- **Fade the cues.** Cues are stimuli that already elicit the response that the learner must practice. Cues are a form of added help for the learner. Oral or written instructions, pictures, symbols, sounds, or job aids of any sort may all serve as cues. During instruction, control is transferred from the cues to the actual stimuli that must control the response (criterion stimuli). For example, an instructor teaching a basic computer class tells students to hit the escape key each time they see a particular error message on the screen. The verbal instructions are the cue for the response of hitting the escape key. After the behavior has been learned, the error message itself will elicit the desired response. In a shaping progression, the designer may fade the cues. Fading involves the gradual weakening and eventual elimination of the cues until the learner can perform the criterion behavior with no cues present. A common fading technique is to diminish the need for the use of a given job aid. As learners rely less and less on the job aid, the criterion stimulus begins to control the response.

- **Vary the unit of practice.** For objectives that involve a long chain of S-R units, like a procedure or complex rule, the designer may choose to have the learner practice the component parts individually, thereby varying the unit of practice. When teaching someone to swim, the instructor will usually have the learner practice floating, kicking, and breathing separately until each individual skill is mastered. Only then will students be asked to practice swimming in its entirety. In a more complex procedure such as equipment repair, the learner may benefit from practicing parts of the chain (e.g., diagnosing the problem, taking the equipment apart, replacing the deficient component, etc.).

Designers can also vary the unit of practice by adjusting the standards or integrity of the behavior to simplify the task for the learner. For example, when someone learns to scuba dive, he or she often starts in a swimming pool, then progresses to a lake and finally to a real dive site in the ocean.

- **Change the mode of practice (recognize/edit/produce).** Another treatment tool available to the designer is changing the mode of the practice. Most behavioral learning objectives require that students exhibit some form of behavior. In a progression leading up to that behavior, the student is first asked to practice identifying the correct response. Later, the student is asked to edit responses that are incorrect. Finally, the student is asked to produce a correct response on his or her own. This graduated practice is known as the "recognize-edit-produce" progression. An instructor can profitably use this progression to teach beginning instructional designers how to write performance objectives. Learners are given a list of performance objectives and asked to identify the condition, behavior, and criterion or any missing components in each (recognize). Then they are asked to rewrite performance objectives that are written incorrectly (edit). Finally, students write performance objectives of their own (produce).

- **Gradually increase example difficulty.** Varying the level of difficulty in the practice examples is another shaping technique. This tool is especially important in learning a generalization or when criterion performance requires that the skills be transferred. Instructors often use role-play activities when teaching sales representatives how to make an effective sales call. They may start with an easy role-play and progressively get more difficult, for example, requiring the sales rep to deal with a customer who has very limited time or who is argumentative.

- **Gradually increase performance standards.** Instrumental music teachers are familiar with this tool. When learning a new piece, the student is allowed to play slowly and is permitted to make a few mistakes. Later, the tempo must increase, and fewer errors are allowed. Finally, the piece must be played at the standard tempo and with no errors. As another example, telephone sales or customer service workers are often measured by the number of calls they complete per hour or their success rate. Time and success standards can be gradually raised during the training period and during the first days or weeks on the job.

All these treatment tools can be used alone or in combination with one another to achieve an effective shaping progression.

Specialized Treatments. These treatments are reserved for the most difficult behaviors to learn and are used less frequently than are routine or shaping treatments. A number of specialized treatments are available, as described below.

- **Concrete/abstract progressions.** For concepts or principles in which the criterion mode is abstract or highly technical, changing the mode of practice to something concrete through the use of visual or verbal examples is an instance of a concrete/abstract progression. Computer instructors, when teaching first-time computer users the concept of storing files on the hard drive, often use a visual example of a file cabinet, with manila file folders, and documents inside the file folders. Students practice describing the relationship of the documents to the folders and the folders to the file cabinet in the visual example and then practice describing the same relationship on the computer using the technical terms. This is the same principle used to teach the concept of fractions by using pieces of pie as a concrete expression.

- **Distortions of stimulus or response.** Distortions involve exaggerating the practice examples. In playing tennis, students practice serving the ball by slowing down the motion, reaching back to scratch their back with the racquet, moving the racquet to a 12:00 noon position, and then following through on the opposite side of their body in an exaggerated manner. This is an example of a distortion of response. When training medical students, instructors may use the distortion of stimulus, initially exaggerating symptoms to aid the diagnosis of an illness or condition. Gradually, students are given examples with more subtle symptoms.

- **Practice of errors.** When practicing behaviors that are prone to errors or even slight variations, it is often helpful to practice the wrong behavior as well as the right behavior so that the learner can "feel" the difference when the response is practiced correctly. For instance, violin students might practice holding the instrument incorrectly and then correctly, so that they can feel and get to know the difference. Foreign language learning may also benefit from comparing incorrect and correct pronunciation of sounds. This is known as practice of errors.

- **Backward chaining.** Another specialized treatment tool is backward chaining. This involves reversing the sequence in which the component skills of a criterion behavior is practiced. The advantage of starting with the last step of a procedure and working backward is that the learner has the opportunity to see the end result and model that behavior. For example, novice instructional designers are often given the task of revising course materials (the last step of the ISD process). As a result, they see the outcome of the design process, which they can model when they develop materials, design instruction, or analyze tasks.

- **Practice of principles.** Finally, for some behaviors it is necessary to understand a whole set of principles prior to practicing the behavior. For example, new pilots need to learn and practice the principles of aerodynamics before they can practice flying a plane.

  Note: For designers with a cognitive orientation, this idea is central, not just a "specialized treatment."

Matching Treatments to Objectives. Since each of the five types of objectives may contain a mix of the four component skills, it follows that they could possibly have common treatments. The three treatments discussed above—*routine*, *shaping*, and *specialized*—are common to all objectives. The question that obviously presents itself is, "How do you know when to use which treatment?"

Prescribing the treatment is difficult, because it requires judgment on the part of the designer. The treatments differ in the manner in which they address the potential learning difficulties of each component skill and the criterion for performance (recall or transfer). The most direct route to achieving an instructional goal is to have the learner practice the intact criterion behavior. Therefore, Gropper recommends that routine treatments be considered first for all five types of objectives. If the analysis of the S-R properties in the component skills make those skills more difficult to learn, then shaping progressions should be considered to gradually bring the learner up to criterion behavior. Shaping progressions, however, take longer to implement, because learners must practice noncriterion behaviors prior to the practice of criterion behaviors. Last, for the most difficult behaviors, based on the length of the chain, strength of existing associations, or "fine-grained" similarities that make discriminations a challenge, the use of a specialized treatment is warranted. This type of instructional strategy is the most time consuming and most difficult to develop.

Sequencing Multiple Objectives

Gropper's views on sequencing multiple objectives are based on the conduct of task description, which reveals either vertical, horizontal, or no relationship between each two objectives (Gropper, 1983). A vertical relationship exists when one objective must be learned before another, an idea that is the same as Gagné's idea of a learning prerequisite. For example, a person cannot learn to construct a meaningful flowchart until he or she first learns the associations between the flowchart symbols (rectangle, diamond, etc.) and their meanings (task, decision, etc.). Gropper calls the process of identifying these vertical relationships *task description*. Horizontal relationships exist between objectives of coordinate status. That is, the learning of one is not contingent on the learning of the other. In this relationship, however, one task may be performed first in time. For example, in baking bread, kneading the dough is performed before shaping the loaf. However, the baker can learn to shape the loaf before learning to knead the dough. In other cases, neither horizontal nor vertical relationships may exist between two objectives.

Research Support

Gropper's model is supported by a strong research base. The types of component skills in his model (discriminations, generalizations, associations, and chaining) have all been subjects of extensive programs of behavioral research. Instructional treatments that Gropper advocates have also been studied extensively. For example, Alden (1978) reports on the effectiveness of backward chaining, citing earlier work by Gilbert (1962a, 1962b) and Harless (1969, 1970). Balkenius (1996) summarizes studies on generalization. Strategies that promote transfer (as distinct from those that promote recall) have been widely researched over many decades. The findings, even those from more recent work, are consistent with Gropper's prescriptions regarding the criticality of frequency and variety of practice, graduated difficulty, and understanding of underlying principles (Patrick, 1992).

Best Uses

This model provides designers with a structured approach to instructional design, including a number of tools for analyzing content and a variety of methods for structuring learning experiences, especially practice. Although the approach is structured, it does not yield cookie-cutter designs. A variety of treatments are offered, and the choice of prescriptions is left to the designer's judgment, based on an assessment of the ease or difficulty of the learning task. The model's complexity and requirement for designer judgment, however, may prove to be a hindrance to the novice designer.

We often associate behavioral learning with motor skills, but Gropper's model addresses a wide variety of objectives, from recalling facts to solving problems. The model may be successfully applied to verbal information, motor skill, and intellectual skill learning tasks. While the model specifically includes problemsolving as a type of learning, the analytical and treatment tools lend themselves better to problemsolving within well-defined domains. Those learning objectives that target open-ended problemsolving, creativity, and complex cognitive strategies are probably best addressed by other models. Gropper does not specifically address attitude learning. Specific tools, such as exaggeration, recognize-edit-produce, and backward chaining, can be used separately to complement designs using other models. For example, where behavior modeling is being used to teach interpersonal skills, a shaping progression can be incorporated to increase the complexity of the role-play situations gradually.

One limitation of the model is that it does not directly address individual differences among learners, including their acquisition of prerequisite skills. These learner variables can also affect the ease or difficulty in attaining mastery of a particular skill.

Model in Action

As a result of an outbreak of poison ivy rashes among visitors to a nature preserve, the education center has decided to offer a seminar that will help visitors identify and avoid poison ivy on the nature trail.

In this case, the objective is to define and illustrate poison ivy. This objective requires that learners do the following:

- Discriminate instances of poison ivy from non-instances.
- Generalize among plants that look slightly different but that belong to the same class as poison ivy.
- Associate a definition of poison ivy with the respective plants.
- Associate poison ivy with the act of avoidance.
- Transfer the skills learned during the seminar to instances not previously encountered.

Several considerations went into the prescription of an instructional treatment. First, many classes of plants exist on the nature trail, several of which have characteristics similar to poison ivy. In addition, there are several varieties of poison ivy, and although they have certain features that distinguish them as members of the poison ivy family, they are different enough to cause a potential learning difficulty. Finally, learning must be transferred from the classroom in the visitor's center to actual experience on the nature trail.

The treatment prescribed in this case to accommodate the potential learning difficulties was a shaping progression. The lesson plan is described below.

Identifying the Poison Ivy Plant

- The instructor introduces the topic by asking the class how may of them have ever experienced a poison ivy rash. Students share their experiences with the class. The instructor validates their experiences by discussing the uncomfortable symptoms that result from contact with the poison ivy plant and explains that by simply knowing what plants to avoid, they could forgo this uncomfortable experience. Note: This step is included because it's good practice (gains attention), but it is not derived from Gropper.

- Next, the instructor shows an actual poison ivy plant and discusses its distinguishing characteristics with the class. Then the instructor shows five slides with pictures of different poison ivy plants (beginning with one that is commonly recognized as poison ivy and progressing to those that are more difficult to recognize as poison ivy). Students practice identifying the distinguishing characteristics that make each plant a member of the poison ivy family. The instructor provides feedback (*varied examples*).

- The instructor provides students with a quick reference guide that has pictures and descriptions of poison ivy plants most commonly found in the nature preserve (*cues*).

- Next, the instructor shows a series of slides, some of which are poison ivy plants and some of which are not. Students practice identifying the poison ivy plants with the use of the quick reference guide. Discussion follows and the instructor provides feedback.

- Students view a new set of slides containing some poison ivy plants and some distracters and practice identifying the poison ivy; however, this time they cover up the pictures on their quick reference guide and use only the descriptions of the plants (*fading*). The instructor provides feedback.

- Next, the slides are scrambled and students practice the activity several more times without the aid of the quick reference guide (*fading*). The instructor provides feedback.

- The instructor now introduces five different plants; examples are the real thing this time. Students are asked to identify the one that is the poison ivy plant using the quick reference guide and what they learned looking at the slides. Students must identify what characteristics distinguish the poison ivy plant from the others.

- Finally, the instructor takes the students on the nature trail, points to a plant, and asks students to identify whether it is a poison ivy plant. Ten to fifteen examples are used. Students may use their quick reference guides.

- At the end of the lesson, the instructor tests the students' performance by asking them to identify poison ivy plants along the trail. The learners have to correctly identify instances of poison ivy.

Implementation Guide

Figure on page 29 serves as a more detailed implementation guide for using Gropper's model. However, a brief summary of the design steps is included here.

Step	Design Task	Options
1	Define and classify objectives.	1. Recall facts. 2. Define and illustrate concepts. 3. Give and apply explanations. 4. Follow rules. 5. Solve problems.
2	Analyze component skills for each objective.	1. Discriminations 2. Generalizations 3. Associations 4. Chaining
3	Assess the degree of difficulty in skill acquisition.	1. Stimulus properties 2. Response properties 3. S-R properties
4	Analyze the performance criterion.	1. Recall 2. Transfer
5	Prescribe treatments.	1. Routine 2. Shaping 3. Specialized

References

Alden, J. (1978). Backward chaining: Teaching task performance. *The instructional design library: No. 6*. Englewood Cliffs, NJ: Educational Technology Publications.

Balkenius, C. (1996). Generalization in instrumental learning. In P. Maes, M. Matarie, J.A. Meyer, J. Pollack, & S. Wilson (Eds.), *Proceedings of the Fourth International Conference on Simulation of Adaptive Behavior*. Cambridge, MA: The MIT Press/Bradford Books.

Gagné, R.M. (1970). *The conditions of learning* (2nd ed.). New York: Holt, Rinehart & Winston.

Gilbert, T.F. (1962a, January). Mathetics: The technology of education. *The Journal of Mathetics*, 7–73.

Gilbert, T.F. (1962b, April). Mathetics II: The design of teaching exercises. *The Journal of Mathetics*, 7–56.

Gropper, G.L. (1973). *A technology for developing instructional materials*. Pittsburgh: American Institutes for Research.

Gropper, G.L. (1974). *Instructional strategies*. Englewood Cliffs, NJ: Educational Technology Publications.

Gropper, G.L. (1983). A behavioral approach to instructional prescription. In C.M. Reigeluth (Ed.), *Instructional design theories and models: An overview of their current status* (101–161). Hillsdale, NJ: Lawrence Erlbaum Associates.

Harless, J.H. (1969). *Construction of teaching exercises*. McLean, VA: Harless Performance Guild, Inc.

Harless, J.H. (1970). *Describing behavior in successive approximations*. McLean, VA: Harless Performance Guild, Inc.

Mechner, F. (1967). Behavioral analysis and instructional sequencing. In P.C. Lange (Ed.), *Programmed instruction*. Chicago: NSSE.

Patrick, J. (1992). *Training: Research and practice*. London: Academic Press.

Bibliography

Deighton, L.C. (1971). *The encyclopedia of education: Vol. 6*. Crowell-Collier Educational Corp. (MacMillan Company & The Free Press).

Gropper, G.L. (1991). *Text displays: Analysis and systematic design*. Englewood Cliffs, NJ: Educational Technology Publications.

About the Authors

Maureen Giannotti

Maureen Giannotti has more than seven years of experience in training, instructional design, and management. She has designed, developed, and delivered training for a wide range of target audiences on six different proprietary database products as well as on a variety of nontechnical topics. Currently employed by American Management Systems in Fairfax, Virginia, Maureen serves as an instructional designer in the Training Services Business Unit. Ms. Giannotti received her BA from Dickinson College in 1990. In addition, she has a Graduate Certificate in Instructional Design from Marymount University.

Kristin Radcliffe

Kristin Radcliffe received a BS in Business Administration from York College of Pennsylvania in 1993 and a MA in Human Resource Development with a Certificate in Instructional Design from Marymount University in 1997. She is currently employed by American Management Systems in Fairfax, Virginia, as an instructional designer involved in the training and design aspect of a financial-based computer system implementation. Previously, she was employed as a designer at Cable & Wireless, designing sales/product training and other performance improvement solutions.

CHAPTER 3

Behavior Modeling

John P. Fry and Dede Bonner

Since its first controlled application in the early 1970s, behavior modeling has become a major factor in modern training methods.

—Donald Tosti, 1980

Behavior modeling presents trainees with a model that demonstrates key behaviors and provides structured skill practice exercises for trainees to practice the key behaviors. Based on social learning theory, behavior modeling has become the most effective, robust method currently known for training people in interpersonal or "soft" skills. Interpersonal skills are often hard to grasp, since situations in which they are used are similar, but different. The effectiveness of behavior modeling is derived from its solid grounding in and application of research-based learning principles, as well as its high face validity for learners who just want to improve their skills. Behavior modeling is also unique in that it attempts to change behaviors directly, as compared to lecture-oriented training, which seeks to impart knowledge with only the distant hope that the new knowledge will ultimately change behavior.

Design of a typical behavior modeling-based program begins with identification of best practices or desired behaviors for handling a given problem/interpersonal situation, by interviewing subject matter experts (SMEs) and role models. The instructional designer then boils down the experts' actions and strategies into a short sequence of critical steps. Critical steps are the synthesis of role models' actual, effective behaviors in real-life situations. The designer then checks academic references to verify and clarify the SME descriptions. Finally, the designer uses these critical steps to drive the creation of a video modeling display, an introductory lecturette, and realistic skill practice exercises.

In the classroom, the critical steps or desired behaviors are introduced and then demonstrated via a video modeling display. After the behaviors that the model uses are analyzed, trainees practice using the critical steps in realistic skill practice exercises and receive feedback from their peers, facilitated by the instructor, with an emphasis on specific feedback and positive reinforcement. Although trainees learn the critical steps through imitation, rehearsal, practice, analysis, and positive feedback, the primary emphasis of behavior modeling training should be on practice and feedback, and more practice and feedback, until trainees can perform the critical steps unconsciously. To be called a skill, interpersonal behaviors need to be able to be used effectively whenever the need arises.

Behavior modeling methodology has been used primarily for management and supervisory interpersonal skill acquisition. Examples of the wide variety of topics with which behavior modeling works well include routine management situations, such as delegation, dealing with difficult employees, and leading meetings; interpersonal situations, such as customer service, assertiveness, first aid training, and hand-to-hand combat techniques (Russ-Eft, 1997); and computer skills (Simon & Werner, 1996). For class projects in a graduate-level behavior modeling course, students have even designed training for topics such as criticizing your spouse without being critical, conducting a power lunch, getting the second date, and initiating safe sex. In general, the more sensitive and more potentially embarrassing situations are, the more people avoid them and welcome a controlled environment, such as behavior modeling-based training as a solution.

Origins

Behavior modeling has been around longer than humans have; higher-order animals use it to demonstrate behaviors that they want their offspring to imitate or mimic. The apprentice system of passing on trade skills is a crude form of today's behavior modeling. The Chinese philosopher Confucius also knew that learning by doing had merit when he said—

> I hear and I forget
> I see and I remember
> I do and I understand.

Social Learning Theory

Behavior modeling is rooted in the extensive research on social learning theory by Bandura and his associates (1977, 1986). Bandura's research demonstrated that humans learn new behaviors by imitating other humans and through the social reinforcement of these imitative behaviors. For example, children adopt a new behavior (and are socialized) by imitating family members and then being rewarded for using appropriate behaviors. Adults often observe and then imitate admired human models at work, in sports, and on television, especially if positive consequences clearly follow the demonstrated behavior.   Thus, learning new behaviors comes either directly from experiencing the consequences of using these behaviors or from observing others in the act of using behaviors and noting the consequences (a process known as vicarious reinforcement).

It is worthwhile to note that behavior modeling is based on social learning theory rather than on Skinner's reinforcement theory. For example, behavior modeling can be considered "no-trial learning"—an individual can learn new behavior just from observing and without direct experience and reinforcement. Nonetheless, training programs make extensive use of social reinforcement to motivate learners and provide knowledge of results from peers.

Biographical Sketch

Arnold P. Goldstein and **Melvin Sorcher** were the first researchers and practitioners to use social learning theory in corporate settings and thereby to pioneer the use of what is now called behavior modeling training methodology. Dr. Goldstein earned his PhD from Pennsylvania State University and was a professor of Psychology at Syracuse University. He has authored several books on behavior modification and has written more than 40 articles on staff training, management training, and behavior change.

Dr. Sorcher (PhD, Syracuse University) has written numerous articles dealing with motivation and behavior modification approaches to training in industrial and educational settings. He was manager of field personnel research for General Electric Company when he and Goldstein wrote *Changing Supervisor Behavior.* They influenced James Robinson, while he was working at Agway, and then continued work on behavior modeling with Development Dimensions International.

Before behavior modeling, managers were trained and educated primarily by lecture methods. Research results showed little evidence that such traditional, theory- and knowledge-based methods were effective in changing on-the-job "soft-skill" behavior (Campbell, 1971; Goldstein & Sorcher, 1974). Typically, 80% of these managers experienced no transfer to their jobs. Furthermore, of the 20% who did experience change, less than 20% of what they were supposed to learn transferred to the job.

Even when training methods began to emphasize active participation, the results were no better. First, unstructured role playing or abstract exercises were used to elicit participants' normal behavior and then, through discussion of the consequences of their behavior, participants were expected to gain insight that would cause them to change their on-the-job behavior. Second, where "how-to" behavior was stressed, the focus was on general behavior in general situations, rather than on specific behavior in specific situations. Rarely were appropriate behaviors modeled or demonstrated for use in specific situations.

As a result, when managers returned to work, they were unable to respond appropriately to interpersonal situations for two reasons. First, they couldn't remember or didn't know what specific behaviors were appropriate. Second, the managers typically received little feedback and no reinforcement for using appropriate behaviors on the job. The burden of translating theory into practice, or transferring new behavior to the job, was placed on the trainee. Only highly motivated and determined individuals actually managed to make the change; the effort was just too daunting for the average manager.

Early Applications

In the earliest work with behavior modeling in organizations, Goldstein and Sorcher (1974) worked with hard-core unemployed personnel in an attempt to reduce the high turnover rate of unskilled labor at General Electric (GE). Goldstein and Sorcher reasoned that these employees lacked good role models and friends who had histories of steady jobs and that their supervisors also lacked role models on how to deal effectively with this type of employee. Parallel but separate behavior modeling skill-based programs were created for both groups, which resulted in long-term cost savings for GE through reduced turnover.

In contrast to previous methods, behavior modeling training has proven to be markedly effective in changing behavior on the job. In 1975, at the annual conference of the American Psychological Association, the first reports of corporate-based research (AT&T, GE, IBM) clearly demonstrated that behavior modeling was a breakthrough training methodology; it actually changed supervisor behavior on the job (Robinson, 1982). Later research results showed that when all the components of the method are fully implemented, 80% of the graduates of behavior modeling-training use, on the job, roughly 80% of what they are supposed to learn and apply (Fry & Cliborn, 1975).

Research Support

Throughout the 1970s and 1980s, numerous companies reported widespread success with behavior modeling techniques in such venues as improving sales performance (Smith, 1976) and managerial training (Sims & Manz, 1982). In one of the best designed research studies of a training program (Latham & Saari, 1979), a group of supervisors who attended behavior modeling sessions demonstrated greater improvements in all of Kirkpatrick's four evaluation levels—reaction, learning, behavior change, and results— both immediately after training and several months later. Further, when the control group was later included in the behavior modeling training, it too demonstrated the same levels of improvement. More recent research has corroborated these findings. Burke and Day (1986), using a meta-analysis of several different approaches to managerial training, reported that behavior modeling is one of the more effective methods. Summaries of a series of studies of behavior modeling training programs undertaken in corporate settings, which lend research support for this model, may be found in the works of Russ-Eft and Zenger (1995), Pescuric and Byham (1996), Russ-Eft (1997), and Medsker and Fry (1997).

Today behavior modeling is still proving itself, as it has adapted well to the rapid changes in organizations' and learners' changing expectations for more nonclass-room formats. As preferences for learning methodologies gravitate to convenience and the ease of computer-based training, behavior modeling is being used in various combinations of classroom delivery, self-paced study, and other nontraditional learning systems (Byham & Pescuric, 1996; Pescuric & Byham, 1996). For example, online learners benefit from mastering the key skills at their own pace and with more time to analyze them as needed, thus providing a time and cost-saving alternative for geographically dispersed employees.

Description

There are six major components of the behavior modeling methodology:

1. Prescribed Critical Steps/Behaviors—The course designer identifies critical steps/behaviors that competent practitioners use when they successfully carry out specific job tasks.

2. Credible Model—The trainees are shown a video model of the critical steps/behaviors being used effectively in a typical and realistic problem situation.

3. Skill Practice Exercises—Trainees repeatedly rehearse and practice the critical steps/behaviors in realistic problem situations.

4. Specific Feedback and Social Reinforcement—As trainees are successful in using the critical steps/behaviors, the instructor facilitates feedback from their peers that is specific and positively reinforcing.

5. Transfer Strategies—Transfer to the workplace is greatly enhanced by progressively increasing the difficulty and reality of the skill practice exercises.

6. On-the-job Reinforcement—The supervisors of the trainees are also trained in how to use the same skills, how to coach trainees, and how to reinforce their subordinates' attempts to use the critical steps/behaviors.

These components are described in detail for a typical training scenario. Note: It is assumed that the instructional designer will also be the instructor in the scenario.

Scenario

The training and development department is asked to solve a workforce performance discrepancy or problem that appears to be interpersonal in nature. The problem (or task) involves the inability of supervisors to give effective feedback about poor performance. The instructional designer completes a front-end analysis, which includes asking the target population this key question, "Could you perform this task, as desired, if your life depended on it?" (Mager, 1988). As a result of negative responses—thus verifying that the discrepancy is the lack of interpersonal skills—the instructional designer is satisfied that behavior modeling training is an appropriate intervention.

Prescribed Critical Steps/Behaviors. The instructional designer needs to identify accurately the behaviors or critical steps that make a significant difference between effective and ineffective handling of the interpersonal discrepancy in question. First, the designer identifies individuals or SMEs who have firsthand, real-life experiences with the interpersonal discrepancy. These SMEs are the performers themselves (e.g., supervisors who use either effective or ineffective behaviors when interacting with employees), recipients of these interactions (e.g., employees or customers in other scenarios), or those who observe these interactions (e.g., managers of the supervisors). One caution: Individuals who have been performing the task for a long time, and now perform the task unconsciously, are often unable to specify what it is that they do that makes them effective. Direct observation may be the only way to identify what it is that they do that makes them effective or ineffective on the job.

The Critical Incident Technique (Flanagan, 1954; Zemke & Kramlinger, 1982) is an extremely useful means for stimulating detailed recall of specific behaviors in challenging situations. Ask the SMEs to think back over the recent past and recall specific incidents where they had performed or observed the task being performed either very well or very poorly. As the SMEs describe the critical incident, the designer elicits answers about the circumstances that surrounded the incident, what the individual did or observed that was effective or ineffective, and how the incident affected the task that the individual was performing. Typically, SMEs will be able to recall incidents where performance was highly effective or highly ineffective—incidents that made a difference.

The number of interviews needed depends on the scope of the discrepancy. Once the interviewer begins to hear redundant answers, there is little reason to conduct more interviews.

The instructional designer should search the literature only after effective and ineffective behaviors have been elicited by using the Critical Incident Technique. Training manuals, articles, and books by experts often describe behaviors that may not be available from interviews or observation. However, they may be out of date. In behavior modeling, the emphasis is on what really works in the workplace, not on academic theory or on research that has been conducted without field experience that attests to its reliability and validity. However, a combination of observations, interviews, and literature reviews will reveal a variety of situations under which the behaviors are used. These situations are useful for two reasons: First, to serve as a test of the behaviors in practice; second, for use when the designer is creating realistic skill practice exercises.

Once a list of effective and ineffective behaviors (and behaviors common to both effective and ineffective performers) has been identified, the instructional designer examines the effective and common ones. They are arranged into an effective-behavior sequence (or a logical order of action based on the SMEs' stories and common sense) that appears appropriate to the interpersonal discrepancy situation. Most trainees like a step-by-step approach. In some cases, rather than being in a linear sequence, the critical steps may best be stated as circular, such as "active" listening that requires ongoing verbal and nonverbal eliciting and reinforcing behaviors.

Usually there are too many behaviors in the sequence. To condense the list to a manageable one (usually between five and seven critical steps), the instructional designer needs to eliminate behaviors that are not critical to one's effectiveness in handling the target situations. The designer should keep behaviors that moved the interaction along in a positive manner. Behaviors that were obtained from interviews with recipients (e.g., customers) are usually the most reliable; good performers often find it difficult to distinguish which of their behaviors make a significant difference in their effectiveness.

The specificity of the steps is another concern. If the task analyzed involves a clearly defined series of specific behaviors that must be accomplished in a specific order and the learner must repeat them, precisely, over and over again to develop a skill (e.g., how to serve a tennis ball), then the critical steps or behaviors need to be very specific. However, such specific behaviors (often called "hard skills") usually do not transfer to other similar situations (e.g., squash or racketball). In contrast, interpersonal skills need to be written as general behaviors for several reasons:

1. There is more than one way to complete the task.
2. When the behaviors are used, no two situations/scenarios are ever exactly the same.
3. Trainees need to be prepared to use the critical steps in a variety of situations.

Therefore, behavior modeling-based critical steps (often called "soft skills") typically subsume specific behaviors. Instructional designers can try writing descriptive statements that combine similar behaviors or that subsume specific behaviors that occur simultaneously (e.g., "active" listening).

For example, below are the Critical Steps for improving employee performance (Robinson, 1982). Note that each critical step begins with an action verb, is succinct and easy to remember, understand, and visualize doing:

1. Describe the problem in a friendly manner.
2. Ask for the employee's help in solving the problem.
3. Discuss causes of the problem.
4. Identify and write down possible solutions.
5. Decide on the specific action to be taken by each of you.
6. Agree on a specific followup date.

Ideally, the critical steps should be concise and descriptive enough that the learner can memorize them for use in challenging real-life situations. For example, consider a confrontation between a supervisor and an employee over a performance appraisal. If the critical steps for dealing with confrontations were short and memorable, it improves the odds that the supervisor will still be able to recall them, even in such a tense moment.

Credible Model. The next component of behavior modeling is a credible modeling display that clearly demonstrates the use of the critical steps. A modeling display is the entire vignette that shows the model using the steps and receiving positive consequences for their use. The model (e.g., a supervisor) demonstrates the behaviors that the learner is to emulate. If the critical steps displayed by the model in the modeling display are specific and produce positive results, learners will know precisely what behaviors they are to learn and what the consequences should be if they use them themselves on the job.

Videotape is the current predominant medium used for presenting modeling displays. Where individualized instruction occurs, CD-ROM is the preferred delivery method. The length of the typical videotape modeling display is short, typically about seven minutes, in order to not overtax observers' memories.

When developing credible modeling displays, the designer must answer three questions that reflect the thinking of the target population (Robinson, 1982):

1. *Could the situation displayed have happened in real life?* The problem situations used in the modeling displays should be realistic and represent typical scenarios and problems that actually occur on the job. To be credible, the model must be shown handling a difficult and challenging situation, one the observers can imagine themselves being in or remember having actually been in, that they would like to be able to handle more effectively. Finally, the trainees need to see real, positive consequences for using the critical steps. Otherwise, they'll ask, "So what?"

   To further enhance credibility (and realism), the model must also appear as someone who the observer can identify with. Goldstein and Sorcher (1974) assert that behavior changes significantly more when the model is viewed as highly competent, knowledgeable, friendly, helpful, having high status, or controlling desired resources.

2. *Does the model handle the situation effectively?* The modeling display should show only effective, positive behaviors. Since in the corporate world employees are already keenly aware of inappropriate or dysfunctional behavior, there is little value in showing ineffective behavior. There are exceptions, however. A very short contrast model might be used as an attention grabber at the beginning

of the training session, to vividly demonstrate the purpose of the training. Also, if situations arise for which employees are not aware of the negative consequences of their normal behavior, they will need a contrast model to help discriminate between what is and is not appropriate. For example, consider an American making a sales call in Saudi Arabia, where cultural differences are apparent; knowing the appropriate behavior is critical.

3. *Am I capable of doing that well?* Learners must perceive that they can do as well as the model. Therefore, modeling displays should depict satisfactory, not necessarily exemplary, skill levels. Whereas satisfactory behavior appears achievable, exemplary behavior could appear to be beyond the learner's ability level and will cause them to give up.

Skill Practice Exercise: Design. Although often confused with role playing, behavior modeling skill practices do not require trainees to play a role or assume a character. Rather, trainees rehearse the critical steps demonstrated in the modeling display and then practice them in problem situations that simulate incidents that they typically and frequently confront on the job. Since the simulated problem situations are taken from the trainees' workplace and/or the trainees are asked to describe incidents (problem situations) that have occurred to them, the skill practice exercises are not so much role plays as practice in handling the real thing.

Practice makes perfect. Therefore, 80% of trainees' time in behavior modeling sessions should involve skill practice. Through repeated practice and specific feedback, skill practice exercises develop not only the desired skill, but also the confidence that is necessary for trainees to use these skills on the job. Georges (1996) points out that most soft-skill training is a myth; it really is soft-skill education. What he means is that without repeated skill practice, until overlearning occurs, trainees will know what to do, but they will not know how to do it or do it effectively.

To develop confidence, skill practice exercises must be designed to appear realistic and eventually present challenges just as difficult as those faced in real life. The exercises need to also be sufficiently challenging to prevent boredom and enable trainees to "test" the critical steps adequately. If trainees are asked to "experiment" with the critical steps and the steps actually enable them to solve realistic problem situations, trainees will "sell" themselves that the critical steps really work. If skill practice exercises are too easy, unchallenged trainees will lose interest. Also, easy exercises often give trainees false confidence; they may think that because they have been successful in the classroom, they will be able to handle any real situation. Obviously, if they fail, they are not likely to use the critical steps again.

Initial skill practice exercises should be designed to be similar in difficulty to those displayed by the video model. Then, as trainees take part in repeated practice and their competence increases, they should be given exercises that have been designed to present increasingly more difficult problem situations. This design strategy will increase both competence and confidence, the key to transfer of training.

Initial skill practice exercises should also be designed with content that presents general content situations or includes content that is sufficiently different from topics that they are familiar with on the job. If the content is too similar to the trainees' real job, they will be distracted by it (they'll want to discuss the content) and will not pay attention to the process skills (critical steps) that they are supposed to be learning.

The ideal source of data for the design of skill practice exercises is from critical incident technique interviews, where typical problems and issues frequently being encountered by the workforce surface. The more precise the details collected are, the more realistic the exercises will be. Likewise, the background data in the exercises need to contain sufficient detail for the situation to be handled satisfactorily by use of the critical steps. In other words, designers need to create problem situations where win-win solutions are possible.

Management often causes workplace problems; they hire the wrong employees, fail to train them properly, give ambiguous directions and standards, or give little or no accurate feedback and reinforcement. Therefore, when designing skill practice exercises in which supervisors interact with employees about a work-related problem situation, designers must avoid having an employee be completely at fault. Not only will adding "fault" to the supervisor's role make the exercise more challenging, it will also make it more realistic. Even more realistic skill practice exercises can be designed from data obtained from the trainees themselves. Since they will be concerned about how to use the critical steps at work, they are typically willing to share pertinent data to construct a replica of a problem situation that they want to use the critical steps on when they return to work. This also enhances the transfer of training.

As a general rule in the design of skill practice exercises, the greater the variety of real and commonly occurring problem situations that the trainees are exposed to, the more they will be able to generalize their skills to handle new or novel situations that are similar in scope.

Skill Practice Exercises: Rehearsal, Coaching, and Practice. At this point, the instructional designer needs to focus on the instructor's role; understanding what takes place in the classroom can only help to maximize the design and impact of behavior modeling training.

For example, after gaining the trainees' attention, the instructor provides a short overview of the module by describing the need for learning the critical steps (hopefully based on a needs assessment), the benefits to the trainees and the company, and the critical steps.

Next, the instructor prepares the trainees to view the video modeling display. First, to establish a context, he or she describes the scenario and the context. Then, the trainees are cued about what will be shown in the video model, especially to alert them to pay particular attention to responses by the model to others' behavior in the video. Finally, the trainees observe and record (on a sheet of paper that lists the critical steps) specific and significant ways in which the model uses each of the critical steps.

After they have viewed the video model, the trainees describe how the model effectively used each critical step. During the analysis, the instructor reinforces trainees who accurately report specific and significant behaviors. In addition to facilitating the trainee's learning, the instructor's objective at this point is to train the trainees to observe, record, and report accurately.

Next the trainees are provided with a rationale for participating in skill practice exercises. After the scenario is described, the instructor requests volunteers for the skill practice. When they have finished reading their role information, the instructor asks a series of questions, such as those below, which serve as a rehearsal of what they will do in the actual exercise:

- Who are you? What is your objective for this interaction?
- What specific problem are you going to discuss?
- How are you, as a supervisor, going to use each of the critical steps?
- What behaviors do you, as the employee, plan to exhibit?

If their answers are not on target, the instructor coaches them by providing cues until the instructor feels comfortable with the answers and the volunteers feel confident that they can successfully use the critical steps in the skill practice exercise. Sometimes asking the volunteers to visualize how they will use the critical steps helps to overcome anxiety.

It's important for the instructional designer to write enough coaching questions, especially those that are specific to the scenario, to support the instructor's coaching role adequately. Coaching questions help the volunteers to visualize and mentally rehearse their scripts and roles. The instructor's level of preparation and ability to coach the volunteers often makes the difference between a competent and a poorly executed skill practice.

The extent of coaching delivered by the instructor depends on the skill level and confidence level of the volunteers. In general, the instructor will need to provide more coaching during the first few skill practice exercises and less later on, as trainees build both competence and confidence. As the instructor gradually withdraws coaching and prompting help, trainees will gradually become independent and ready to use (transfer) the prescribed skills on the job.

While the rehearsal and coaching is going on, the remaining trainees should be paying attention. Their "listening in" will not only serve to prepare them for their observer roles, but also will help them to learn the critical steps.

To further increase involvement (and learning), trainees can be asked to help rehearse and coach the volunteers. Two beneficial outcomes result: First, all trainees will be involved in thinking about how to use the critical steps for the given problem situation. Second, because they identify with the person they coach, they will "root" for them to be successful. As a result, they themselves will learn the critical steps more readily and give more accurate feedback.

When the volunteers are ready to begin, the instructor asks the remaining trainees to be observers. "Observer notes," which list the critical steps, are distributed with instructions to record specific and significant behavior that describes how effectively each of the critical steps are used. Instructions to also record dialogue (exact quotes) help facilitate accurate feedback later.

With competent coaching, skill practice exercises almost always are successful. However, if the volunteers deviate from the information in their roles to the point where the critical steps aren't being used effectively, the instructor must stop the exercise, ask the volunteers to keep to their roles, and restart the action.

In the worst case, the volunteer using the critical steps "freezes up." To protect that person's self-esteem, the instructor needs to stop the action and ask the volunteer to think through what has happened and to consider alternative ways of behaving. The instructor should not offer solutions; it's best just to describe what has happened and let the volunteer come up with his or her own solution and try again (and again, if necessary), until he or she is successful. The instructor's emphasis at this point is to guarantee success in using the critical steps, to whatever extent possible. Trainees need to know that if they are applied correctly, the critical steps will work. Such knowledge will inspire them to transfer their newly learned skills to their workplace.

Specific Feedback Through Social Reinforcement. Social reinforcement, as described below, plays an important role in trainees' initial acceptance of new behaviors. In addition, since feedback is more readily accepted if it comes from peers, the instructor should facilitate the feedback so that trainees (observers) give all the feedback.

Unless it's by accident, humans cannot improve their performance unless they receive accurate and specific feedback. In addition, humans usually continue to do things that they have found to be effective and/or which are reinforced by others. Likewise, they also usually avoid doing things that they have found to be ineffective and/or that go unrecognized. In addition, they will more readily adopt new ways of doing things if they receive feedback in a form that is acceptable to them.

Therefore, the instructor needs to manage the feedback in a structured and positive manner. For effective performance, he or she should elicit specific, positive reinforcement from the observers; specific feedback enables volunteers to know precisely what it was they did that made their skill practice successful. For ineffective performance, observers offer specific, alternative positive behaviors. "Negative" feedback in the form of "alternative positive behaviors" makes it easier to accept than other forms of "constructive" feedback. It not only maintains the self-esteem of the volunteers, but it tells them precisely what they should do next time to be successful.

When a skill practice exercise ends, volunteers should give feedback first. Self-assessment is the most readily accepted feedback; it can include self-generated alternative positive behaviors even before the observers give their feedback.

The volunteer who received the critical steps is asked for feedback first to assess whether the objective of the interaction was accomplished, so the person who used the steps will get an overall sense of whether he or she was successful. Then the volunteer who used the steps tells whether he or she would do anything differently if an opportunity to repeat the skill practice exercise occurred. Next the observers are instructed to follow these rules:

1. Speak directly to whom you are giving feedback.
2. Be brief, but focus on significant observations.
3. Be specific, but include your rationale.
4. Be honest, but maintain self-esteem.

5. If you think of "a better way," then offer an alternative positive behavior and your rationale.

The observers then describe briefly how each critical step was used effectively. The instructor reinforces the observers for being specific and focusing on significant behaviors. This reinforcement continues to "train" them to give accurate feedback.

If an observer gives an alternative positive behavior, the instructor should ask the recipient of the feedback if he or she agrees. If there is disagreement, the instructor then facilitates a discussion with the intent of deriving even better alternatives.

Transfer Strategies. As with other training methodologies, the designer wants to ensure that the learners are able to apply what they learned in the classroom to real-life situations. A variety of strategies can be used to facilitate transfer of training:

1. The problem situations selected represent real problems with real solutions.
2. No more than six to eight trainees take part in a training session.
3. The sequencing of training moves from simple to complex.
4. Training schedules are designed for distributed rather than massed practice. If training is spaced over four to six weeks (distributed) with a week interval between sessions, trainees will be able to apply the critical steps on the job, receive feedback, and share it with their classmates. If they have been unsuccessful, they can practice in the classroom before trying the steps again.
5. Participants are asked to write their own problem situations, ones that they will confront when they return to work. Practice in the classroom becomes rehearsal for real situations.

On-the-Job Reinforcement. All the components described above are necessary, but without reinforcement in the actual work environment, skill transfer is unlikely. To ensure that there is skill transfer, the supervisors, managers, and peers of the trainees need to reinforce the trainees' use of their newly acquired skills back on the job. If they don't, the trainees will view them as barriers to skill transfer.

Development Dimensions International (Robinson, 1982) offers a 2 ¾-day training program for those who supervise trainees (the target population). It is called a management-reinforcement workshop. Mid-level managers learn how to do the following:

1. Reinforce their first-line supervisors' use of their newly acquired skills.
2. Help these supervisors diagnose critical situations in the workplace.
3. Use the skills themselves so they can be a model for their supervisors.

Best Uses

Covey (1989) defines a habit as being made up of three parts: *knowledge* (the what, where, when, and why), *attitudes* (the want to) and *skills* (the how to). Knowledge is often learned by textbooks, computer-based training, CD-ROM, and lectures. Experiential learning is often used to develop awareness and improve attitudes. However, at the end of awareness training, trainees often ask for "how to" behavioral skills; they now want to take action. In comparison, behavior modeling focuses on neither knowledge nor attitudes, but directly on behavior change. It is noteworthy that a byproduct of behavior modeling training is awareness and attitude change. Obviously skills alone won't result in effective work habits. But without skills, all the knowledge in the world (often the primary focus of education) will not be adequate.

Behavior modeling training is best used for solving soft-skill or interpersonal skill discrepancies. In contrast with technical skills, where there is usually one best way to perform a task, interpersonal skills typically take place in situations that are similar but always different. Behavior modeling training enables trainees to learn to transfer and adjust their skills to the similar but different situations. The same principles of behavior modeling can be used for technical training.

From the perspective of the instructional designer, behavior modeling works extremely well when the following conditions are present: an experienced instructor, a clear set of behavior skills to learn, repeated practice and feedback (social reinforcement) from other trainees, and on-the-job reinforcement by the trainees' managers. Behavior modeling scores higher than other forms of training design on transfer of learning and meaningfulness because of its focus on realistic applications. The costs for the development and administration of a behavior modeling program are typically in the middle range.

Model in Action

Giving Effective Feedback

During the 1999 spring semester 1999 at Marymount University, three graduate students in HPS 501 Training Adults: Behavior Modeling formed a team to design a behavior modeling module, a requirement for the course. One of the students on the team, Stephen O'Connor, a sales manager for Mobil Oil Corporation, identified an interpersonal discrepancy that became the team's project for the semester.

Mobil's marine sales department had set up a system where veteran sales managers would accompany new (rookie) salespersons while they made sales calls on prospective clients. After each sales call, the sales manager, who was generally silent during the sales call, was required to give feedback to the new salespeople to improve their sales skills. Following complaints by the workers, an investigation revealed that sales managers were deficient in how they gave their feedback.

The team followed all the requirements of the course: They designed an introduction, a seven-minute video model (of a sales manager giving effective feedback to a new salesperson), two realistic skill practice exercises, and all the necessary handout material. The success of their presentation of their prototype module in HPS 501 motivated Stephen to risk using it at Mobil Oil.

The module, including the team's video and skill practice exercises, has now been incorporated into Mobil Marine's Coaching for Sales Seminar, which is conducted for sales managers globally. After two seminars, one in Asia Pacific and one in Latin America, comments such as the following were received from managers who participated:

> I adopted the coaching skills in training and had candid communication with my subordinate. By asking specific questions, listening patiently, and expressing my understanding, we have a good chance with a major marine target account during the tender process.

> I have a new employee (two months) who had difficulties. I showed understanding and let him know he was doing a good job for two months in the field. We then freely discussed ideas and business issues and established a business plan for the region.

> I found it very useful for me personally and it reduces gaps in managing people— for supporting and improving performance, to give or receive feedback properly, effectively, basically on a sales call. I would like to thank this excellent group for inviting me to participate and congratulate them for the excellent organization, alignment, focus, and professionalism in executing this session.

U.S. Army Noncommissioned Officers

The first author of this chapter used behavior modeling to train U.S. Army officers and senior noncommissioned officers at Fort Bliss, Texas, during the early 1970s and discovered some useful techniques for overcoming resistance to learning participative management skills.

Authoritarian supervisors, such as senior U.S. Army noncommissioned officers (NCOs), often resist learning new interpersonal, soft-skill behaviors, especially if the new skills focus on participative skills that are directly at odds with their ingrained ways of leading and managing. The officers say, "I didn't get where I am by being soft!" Instead of arguing with them, appealing to them with research data, or trying to sell them on the new behaviors, the best approach is just to have them take part in the training and learn at their own pace. It is best to permit only one authoritarian person in a training group of six to eight participants. In this case, the other participants were officers who all had been exposed to the theory of participative leadership/management in college and were receptive to learning skills that would enable them to actually be a participative leader/manager.

On occasion, the senior NCOs' resistance took the form of asking to use their existing skills to handle the problem situation during a skill practice. This request was honored, but with two conditions: First, they had to listen to accurate feedback (most likely for the first time in their careers), and second, if the feedback showed their performance to be inadequate, the officers had to promise to redo the skill practice using the skills that they were supposed to be learning. Typically, the participants were able to use the new skills successfully. However, that experience and others, at first, did not change their attitudes; the officers still verbally condemned the new skills. Cognitive dissonance was at work.

Fortunately, the officers were involved in a series of training modules and their attitudes eventually came around in line with their new behavior. When asked about what they were thinking, the participants said that they only knew one way of dealing with subordinates—the authoritarian way. When the officers were shown alternative ways to achieve the same goals (keeping discipline through performance counseling) and were allowed to discover for themselves that the new skills were effective, the officers sold themselves that the skills work. Exhortation and logic would never have sold these participants.

Implementation Guide

Step	Instructional Delivery
1	Identify critical steps that address the identified skill discrepancy.
2	Introduce content of the module and relate its purpose, value, and application to the needs of the participants and the organization.
3	Introduce and describe the critical steps.
4	Clarify the setting and cue the use of the critical steps in the video model.
5	Instruct the trainees to record specific and significant uses of the critical steps.
6	Show a model of the critical steps being used effectively by a credible person in a credible problem situation.
7	Facilitate a discussion of the trainees' observations of critical step use and reinforce feedback that is specific, significant, and accurate.
8	Ask for volunteers to practice using the critical steps in a prepared skill practice exercise.
9	Rehearse the volunteers regarding the objective of the meeting and how each critical step will be used.
10	Instruct the observers to record specific and significant uses of the critical steps.
11	Facilitate a discussion of the observers' social reinforcement feedback to the skill practice participants on how effectively they used the critical steps.
12	Ask trainees to write skill practice exercises based on their work settings.
13	Ask for volunteers to practice critical steps on trainee-written situations.
14	Ask trainees to use critical steps on the job and report their success at the next session.
15	Train managers to reinforce trainees' attempts to apply the critical steps on the job.

References

Bandura, A. (1977). *Social learning theory*. Englewood Cliffs, NJ: Prentice-Hall.

Bandura, A. (1986). *Social foundations of thought and action*. Englewood Cliffs, NJ: Prentice-Hall.

Burke, M.J., & Day, R.R. (1986). A cumulative study of the effectiveness of managerial training. *Journal of Applied Psychology, 71*, 232–245.

Byham, W.C., & Pescuric. A. (1996, December). Behavior modeling at the teachable moment. *Training* 51–56.

Campbell, J. (1971). Personnel training and development. In P.H. Mussen & M.R. Rosenzweig (Eds.), *Annual review of psychology*. Palo Alto, CA: Annual Reviews.

Covey, S.R. (1989). *The 7 habits of highly effective people*. New York: Simon & Schuster.

Flanagan, J.C. (1954). The critical incident technique. *Psychological Bulletin, 51*, 327–358.

Fry, J.P., & Cliborn, R.E. (1975). *Development, implementation, and evaluation of leadership/management training within army battalions*. Alexandria, VA: Human Research Resource Organization.

Georges, J.C. (1996, January). The myth of soft skills training. *Training*, 48–51.

Goldstein, A.P., & Sorcher, M. (1974). *Changing supervisory behavior*. New York: Pergamon Press.

Latham, G.P., & Saari, L.M. (1979). Application of social-learning theory to training supervisors through behavioral modeling. *Journal of Applied Psychology, 64*, 239–246.

Mager, R.F. (1988). *Making instruction work*. Belmont, CA: Lake Publishing.

Medsker, K.L., & Fry, J.P. (1997). Acquisition of interpersonal communication skills: A research-based approach. *Telematics and Informatics, 14*(III), 209–218.

Pescuric, A., & Byham, W.C. (1996, July). The new look of behavior modeling. *Training and Development*, 24–33.

Robinson, J.C. (1982). *Developing managers through behavior modeling*. Austin, TX: Learning Concepts.

Russ-Eft, D. (1997). Behavior modeling. In L.J. Bassi, & D. Russ-Eft (Eds.), *What works* (105–149). Alexandria, VA: American Society for Training and Development.

Russ-Eft, D.F., & Zenger, J.H. (1995). Behavior modeling training in North America: A research summary. In M. Mulder, W.J. Nijhof, & R.O Brinkerhoff (Eds.), *Corporate training for effective performance* (89–109). Boston: Kluwer Academic.

Simon, S.J. & Werner, J.M. (1996). Computer training through behavior modeling, self-paced and instructional approaches: A field experiment. *Journal of Applied Psychology, 81*, 648–59.

Sims, H.P., & Manz, C.C. (1982). Modeling influences on employee behavior. *Personnel Journal, 61*(I), 58-65.

Smith, P.E. (1976). Management modeling training to improve morale and customer satisfaction. *Personnel Psychology, 29*, 351–359.

Tosti, D.T. (1980, August). Behavior modeling: A process. *Training and Development Journal,* 70–74.

Zemke, R., & Kramlinger, T. (1982). *Figuring things out: A trainer's guide to needs and task analysis.* Reading, MA: Addison-Wesley Publishing.

Bibliography

Decker, P., & Nathan, B. (1985). *Behavior modeling training.* New York: Praeger Scientific.

Goldstein, I.L. (1980). Training in work organizations. *Annual Review of Psychology, 31*, 229–272.

Noe, R.A. (1999). *Employee training and development.* Boston: McGraw-Hill.

About the Authors

John P. Fry, PhD

John Fry is associate dean and director of Corporate Outreach, Marymount University, in Arlington, Virginia. Dr. Fry initiates and manages corporate-university partnerships, directs an MS in Organizational Leadership and Innovation program, and has taught HPS 501 *Training Adults: Behavior Modeling* every semester for the past 17 years.

After receiving his doctorate in Industrial/Organizational Psychology from Michigan State University in 1970, he served as a senior scientist for Human Resources Research Organization (HumRRO), where he conducted research and designed behavior modeling-based training for U.S. Army officers.

Dede Bonner, EdD

Dede Bonner is president of New Century Management, Inc., a consulting firm established in 1988 in Leesburg, Virginia. Dr. Bonner helps Fortune 500 companies, high-technology firms, academic groups, and government agencies develop knowledge management and learning strategies for competitive business growth. Dr. Bonner teaches behavior modeling and other human resources courses at Marymount University and the University of Virginia. She is the editor of the book *In Action: Leading Knowledge Management and Learning*, published by the American Society of Training and Development, and served as the chair for the editorial review for *Training and Development* magazine, which has a circulation of more than 70,000 worldwide. She received her doctoral degree from George Washington University's Executive Leadership Program. Dr. Bonner has actively practiced the principles of behavior modeling while teaching more than 19,000 people.

Cognitive Models
and Strategies

The cognitive school of instructional design encompasses a large and rather diverse group of models and strategies. In contrast to behaviorism, cognitive models deal directly with events and processes that occur—or are hypothesized to occur—within the learner's mind. Cognitive models can be roughly divided into two camps: One camp, which may be called expository, builds on the behaviorist tradition, adopting principles of behaviorism but adding theoretical constructs and research findings from the newer cognitive approaches to learning and instruction that became prominent during the1970s. Models in the other camp, inquiry or discovery, are derived more from philosophical ideas about how people learn and from observation of the practices of master teachers and their students.

Expository Models and Strategies

Expository models generally approach teaching and learning as a problem of how to store skills and knowledge in the learner's head in efficient ways, making use of what is known about human information processing. Expository models rely at least partly on "telling" as an instructional technique.

Advance Organizer Model

An early expository model is that of David Ausubel (discussed in Chapter 9). Ausubel (1968) did not use behavioral principles such as active responding and reinforcement, yet his prescriptions opposed the discovery methods and experiential learning practices popular with his contemporaries. Ausubel's primary focus was to help students learn organized bodies of subject matter from expository teaching methods (i.e., lecture, reading, and other forms of direct presentation). His theory of meaningful verbal learning addresses how content is organized, how the mind works to process and store new information, and how courses and lessons can be organized to make verbal learning more efficient and more lasting. According to

Ausubel, instruction should help the learner create and strengthen a cognitive structure that accommodates, organizes, and integrates old and new knowledge. A key tool for doing this is the advance organizer—an overarching idea that can be represented verbally or graphically—that creates or reinforces a cognitive structure, tying together existing knowledge and new knowledge within a coherent, organized scaffolding. The advance organizer concept itself, among all of Ausubel's ideas about teaching and learning, has been supported by a substantial body of research and has enjoyed widespread acceptance.

Structural Learning Theory

Scandura's structural learning theory (SLT) is a model that bridges behaviorism and cognitivism. As Chapter 8 explains, SLT's approach (as it applies to instructional design) is to analyze learning tasks as procedures represented by algorithms, and to continue analyzing steps into the smallest possible units or steps of behavior (Scandura, 1983). Paths of varying complexity, and a hierarchy of paths from simplest to most complex, are then identified. Learning begins with the simplest unmastered path and continues through paths of increasing complexity. Though these ideas derive from behavioral analysis principles, Scandura also concerns himself with cognitive issues such as how learners process information, use higher-order rules to generate new rules, and achieve automatization. Since SLT focuses most on how to analyze and sequence learning tasks, and little on how to teach the tasks, in this book SLT is considered not to be a stand-alone model. That is, another model would be needed to design an actual lesson based on the content chosen and sequenced according to SLT. Nevertheless, SLT's applicability is strong, especially for individualized and computer-based instruction. Another similar model not covered in this book is Landa's algo-heuristic theory of instruction (Landa, 1983).

Conditions of Learning and Component Display

Chapters 4 and 5 present conditions of learning model (Gagné, et al., 1992) and component display theory (Merrill, 1983), which are examples of stand-alone, general-purpose models that combine both behavioral and cognitive theory- and research-based principles. Each of these models presents its own taxonomy of learning outcomes, and each gives detailed prescriptions for how to design lessons for particular types of learning outcomes. Both are based on the assumption that different conditions are required for optimal learning of different categories of outcomes. While these models strongly advocate active learner practice, they also emphasize telling or exposition as a strategy for most learning objectives. Component display theory (CDT) evolved from Merrill's attempts to clarify Gagné's theory for his students (Merrill, 1983). CDT's taxonomy is a two-dimensional matrix of learning outcomes (content and performance), whereas the Gagné-Briggs taxonomy has one dimension. Gagné and Briggs use rather general principles to describe their prescriptions (e.g., ensure mastery of prerequisites). Merrill and his associates, in trying to make instructional prescriptions both easier to apply and more automatic (for computer-aided design), developed a more detailed structure in which a limited number of set prescriptions (e.g., show multiple, new examples) could be selected according to set rules. Both of these models have become standards in the instructional design community.

Mnemonics

Mnemonics, as described by Joyce and Weil (1996), is a special-purpose, cognitively based instructional technique for helping people memorize (retain and retrieve at will) information effectively, including associations (such as names and labels), ordered steps in procedures, lists of items, rules of thumb, and facts. Memorization should not be viewed as a trivial activity, since life requires everyone to remember many bits of important and useful information. In addition, memorized data can provide the basis for other performances, including rule use and problemsolving. Further, by learning mnemonic methods, individuals can increase their ability to memorize. Various mnemonic systems have been developed, and some of these are covered in Chapter 6. While not a stand-alone instructional design model, mnemonics can be incorporated with many other models. The tools are applicable in either designer-controlled or learner-controlled environments, because specific mnemonics can be developed by instructional designers and by the learners themselves.

Inquiry or Discovery Models and Strategies

Cognitive models in the inquiry or discovery camp have origins that predate behaviorism. Generally, these models stress the importance of the learning process itself, with the goal of increasing thinking and creative problemsolving skills, or "learning how to learn," often giving these goals priority over the learning of particular subject matter. Some of these models attempt to teach the scientific method: problem finding, hypothesizing, data gathering and analysis, and forming conclusions. Of these, some recommend starting by analyzing learner misconceptions, then providing inquiry experiences by which learners correct these misconceptions. Others attempt to enhance nonrational creative abilities. Some methods prescribe teacher direction and control of the learning process, while others insist on self-direction by learners. Most advocate beginning a unit or lesson with a puzzling event or question, to provide intrinsic motivation for the inquiry process. Some models are more appropriate for individualized instruction, while others are intended for use with class groups. Most of these theories and models are derived inductively, from observation or transcripts of master teachers at work. Although a chapter is not devoted to Jerome Bruner (1961, 1968), he deserves special mention as a leader in the cognitive inquiry movement.

Most inquiry or discovery models were developed with school learning in mind. However, a great deal of management and team training is conducted using discovery approaches. Structured experiences (from self-assessment inventories, to "desert survival" exercises, to outdoor adventure experiences) provide participants with opportunities to discover insights about themselves, how they perform in a group or team, principles of group dynamics, power relationships, or human behavior in general. For example, training in team skills may provide a group exercise during which the team learns in a vivid way the advantages of cooperation versus competition among members.

Cognitive Inquiry Theory

Cognitive inquiry theory, as presented in Chapter 10, represents a more designer- or instructor-controlled approach (Collins & Stevens, 1983). The designer sets specific goals or objectives, and learners achieve the objectives through a teacher-controlled structure that employs specific techniques. The techniques, however, ensure that learners are cognitively very active and are discovering content rather than being "told." Cognitive inquiry methods are motivational for learners and can be very effective for teaching principles and causal relationships, as well as the more general inquiry skills themselves. Inquiry training methods can be combined effectively with cooperative learning (see Chapter 14). They are, however, less effective for teaching facts, and in general are more time consuming than expository methods.

Synectics

Synectics (Chapter 7) is a special-purpose instructional model that uses analogies to enhance creative thinking. Originated by Gordon (1961) as a method for creative problemsolving in business and industry, it was later adapted for use in instruction. Synectics is based on the idea that creativity involves putting together ideas that do not usually occur together. Employing a specific sequence of analogic thinking, a facilitated group either "makes the familiar strange" in order to break their mental set and find creative solutions to a situation or problem; or the group "makes the strange familiar" by comparing a new concept or technology to something well known. Becoming adept at the methods, people can apply them to a variety of situations, thus enhancing their own creative thinking and problemsolving capacity.

Constructivism

During the 1990s, discovery approaches experienced a resurgence in the form of constructivism (Duffy & Jonassen, 1993; Jonaassen et al., 1998). Constructivism goes further, however, than discovery or inquiry models, in that it puts even greater control in the learner's hands. The designer's job is to create a resource-rich environment in which the learners are free to set their own learning goals, determine their own learning methods and sequence, explore at will, consult different experts with multiple perspectives, and evaluate their own learning against their own emerging criteria. In this regard, constructivism shares some views with humanism (see Part III of this book), but it is classified here as a cognitive model, because it lacks the humanistic emphasis on feelings and values. Constructivism, described in Chapter 11, is based on the premise that all knowledge is constructed subjectively in the mind of the individual learner. In fact, there is no such thing as objective knowledge outside the individual learner, so to suppose that knowledge can be transmitted from instructor to learner is wrong. Both behavioral and cognitive approaches to learning are labeled as "objectivist," and are generally rejected by constructivists. Radical constructivists believe that all learning should happen in rich but unrestricted learning environments (electronic or otherwise) that simulate or actuate real-world problems and tasks (a sort of sink-or-swim approach). Less radical adherents suggest that objectivist approaches may be appropriate for novices in a discipline or performance area, and that once basic skills are learned, the learner should then enter realistic constructivist environments and be confronted with authentic tasks. While constructivists have targeted their efforts to school learning at all levels, some business organizations have tried to apply constructivist principles to their training operations, for example, by replacing traditional training with self-directed learning. All in all, constructivism has challenged the instructional design community to think about, defend, and even modify or expand its practices.

Contributions of Cognitive Approaches

Cognitive approaches have made many contributions to instructional design. For example, cognitive task analysis goes beyond behavioral task analysis in identifying knowledge and skill components that cannot be directly observed. When these are identified and taught, learning is more complete, and higher-order learning goals are more readily achieved. Some cognitive models have contributed taxonomies of learning outcomes, facilitating the designer's ability to match instructional strategies to types of learning outcomes, based on theoretical and research-based principles. Methods such as think-aloud protocols (in which subjects describe their thinking during a learning or problemsolving task) have enabled researchers to find out more about the mental processes that occur during a learning experience. This knowledge helps designers arrange external events that support those internal processes. Meanwhile, advocates of discovery-oriented models raise awareness of the importance of learner control in the learning process.

References

Ausubel, D.P. (1968). *Educational psychology: A cognitive view*. New York: Holt, Rinehart & Winston.

Bruner, J.S. (1961). *The process of education*. Cambridge, MA: Harvard University Press.

Bruner, J.S. (1968). *Toward a theory of instruction*. New York: Norton.

Collins, A., & Stevens, A.L. (1983). A cognitive theory of inquiry teaching. In C.M. Reigeluth (Ed.), *Instructional design theories and models: An overview of their current status* (247–278). Hillsdale, NJ: Lawrence Erlbaum Associates.

Duffy, T.M., & Jonassen, D.H. (Eds.). (1993). *Constructivism and the technology of instruction: A conversation*. Hillsdale, NJ: Lawrence Erlbaum Associates.

Gagné, R.M., Briggs, L.J., & Wager, W.W. (1992). *Principles of instructional design* (4th ed.). Fort Worth, TX: Harcourt Brace Jovanovich.

Gordon, W.J.J. (1961). *Synectics*. New York: Harper & Row.

Jonassen, D.H., Peck, K.L., Wilson, B.G., & Pfeiffer, W.S. (1998). *Learning with technology*. Englewood Cliffs, NJ: Prentice Hall.

Joyce, B.R., & Weil, M. (1996). *Models of teaching*. Boston: Allyn & Bacon.

Landa, L.N. (1983). The algo-heuristic theory of instruction. In C.M. Reigeluth (Ed.), *Instructional design theories and models: An overview of their current status* (163–211). Hillsdale, NJ: Lawrence Erlbaum Associates.

Merrill, M.D. (1983). Component display theory. In C.M. Reigeluth (Ed.), *Instructional design theories and models: An overview of their current status* (279–333). Hillsdale, NJ: Lawrence Erlbaum Associates.

Scandura, J.M. (1983). Instructional strategies based on the structural learning theory. In C.M. Reigeluth (Ed.), *Instructional design theories and models: An overview of their current status* (213–246). Hillsdale, NJ: Lawrence Erlbaum Associates.

CHAPTER 4

Conditions of Learning

Bobbie Moore

Beginning in the 1960s, R. M. Gagné and L. J. Briggs each published articles and books about their research in the psychology of learning. Together, they developed a theory of instruction that relies on a systematic analysis of the tasks to be learned. Their model prescribes instructional treatments that match desired learning outcomes, based on cognitive information-processing theory and research.

Two premises distinguish the Gagné-Briggs instructional theory. The first is that all subject matter tasks should be analyzed to identify their learned components, some of which may require learning in a specific order because of hierarchical (dependent) relationships. Knowledge of the subject matter's learning structure is essential in planning the necessary sequence of instruction. The second premise distinguishes five categories (domains) of learning and identifies different instructional conditions that will support learning in each domain. Domains of learning outcomes used by Gagné-Briggs consist of the following categories:

- intellectual skills
- cognitive strategies
- verbal information
- attitudes
- motor skills

The Gagné-Briggs model posits that, based on how information is processed, instruction must generally include nine events to ensure learning:

- gain attention
- state objectives
- recall prior learning
- present content
- provide learning guidance
- elicit performance
- provide feedback
- assess performance
- enhance retention and transfer

A central tenet of the Gagné-Briggs model is that the events of instruction combined with the conditions of learning provide for instruction that is complete, efficient, and effective.

Origins

Gagné and Briggs dedicated their careers to understanding the psychology of human learning. Gagné contributed a now-classic work to the field of human learning research: *The Conditions of Learning and Theory of Instruction* (1985). Gagné acknowledged the influences of behavioral learning theorists, including Pavlov and Watson (conditioned response) and Skinner (reinforcement theory).

However, Gagné departed from behavioral theory by emphasizing the learner's internal processing in addition to externally observable behaviors. For the development of the information-processing theory, Gagné acknowledged the work of contemporaries such as Tulving and Donaldson (1972) and Greeno and Bjork (1973). Other learning theorists who influenced Gagné and Briggs include Ebbinghaus (1913), Köhler (insight theory) (1927), Harlow (learning sets) (1949), and Ausubel and coauthors (cognitive structure) (1978).

Gagné's study of information-processing incorporated knowledge then being developed about the mechanisms of short-term (working) memory, long-term memory, and encoding information for storage and enhanced retrieval. The methodical study of the mechanics of learning led directly to the formulation of the nine events of instruction as well as a reliance on learning analysis to develop instructional objectives.

Gagné and Briggs treated the systematic analysis of the learning environment and the learning task as a critical aspect of instructional design. This approach coincided chronologically with the development of a general instructional systems design (ISD) model (in which effort Gagné was a leader) and is therefore not only consistent with ISD procedures but could be said to provide the scientific basis for the design phase of ISD.

The Gagné-Briggs systems approach and emphasis on behavioral objectives reflect a preoccupation with technical and scientific supremacy during and after World War II. The "space race" created a demand for mathematics and science education, as well as a generalized desire for accountability in education and in workplace training. Both Gagné and Briggs contributed to military and business training research and applications. Their work also coincided with the rise of computer science, which drove a desire to understand how computerized information-processing could be made to imitate human information-processing (Gagné & Medsker, 1996).

Description

This section first describes the information-processing learning model that is the foundation of the Gagné-Briggs instructional theory. Next it describes the five categories or domains of learning outcomes into which subject matter is divided. Recommendations for using standard verbs for writing learning objectives are given next. Then the internal and external conditions that facilitate each of the five learning domains are discussed. There is a discussion of learning analysis—the breakdown of a learning task into its prerequisite learning components. Finally, the nine events of instruction that Gagné and Briggs prescribe for lessons of all types are described.

Information-Processing Model of Learning

Figure 4.1 depicts an information-processing model of learning that is the foundation of the Gagné-Briggs theory of instruction. It compares hypothetical mental functions in the brain with analogous functions in a computer system.

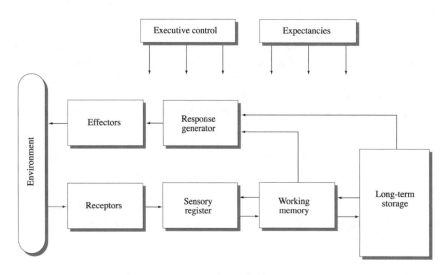

Figure 4.1
Information-Processing Model[1]

One element of the information-processing model that is important to learning is the sensory register, where incoming information resides very briefly, perhaps for a few hundredths of a second (Gagné & Medsker, 1996, p. 46). Sensory register processing includes pattern recognition and selective perception, in which some of the data received is recognized and some screened out or ignored. Therefore, attracting the learners' focus is a compelling need. As we shall see, the first instructional event—gaining attention—relates to providing a change in stimulus to get the learner focused on the upcoming instruction.

Another key element, important for instructional design purposes, is working memory, where conscious information-processing ("thinking") occurs. Since the capacity of working memory is limited, instructional designers should plan to present new information in manageable quantities.

Research into cognitive processes has shown that information must be semantically or meaningfully encoded so that it is placed into storage in an organized manner.

[1.] Adapted from *The Conditions of Learning—Training Applications,* 5th ed., by Gagné & Medsker, © 1996. Reprinted with permission of Wadsworth, a division of Thomson Learning. Fax 800-730-2215.

Encoding, which occurs in working memory, may employ visual images, spatially related items in a table, hierarchical structures, and so forth; it is essential to actually learning (retaining) new information for subsequent retrieval.

Information not properly encoded is not actually learned and therefore cannot be accessed or retrieved for purposes of association with new information. Encoding determines the structure of knowledge in long-term memory. The way new content is presented can enhance encoding.

The "response generator" impels muscles to move, allowing the learner to emit a response: for example, answer a question or perform a task. Thus, practice and feedback are required to complete the learning process and assess learning.

Five Domains of Learning Outcomes

To capture the breadth of learned capabilities possible in humans, Gagné and Briggs propose five major categories, elaborated in several of their works (Gagné, 1985; Gagné, Briggs, & Wager, 1992; Gagné & Medsker, 1996).

Intellectual Skills. These are the "know-how" skills, also called "procedural knowledge," that enable us to use symbols to classify, use rules, and solve problems. The Gagné-Briggs model assumes four hierarchically related categories of intellectual skills:

1. *Discrimination*: This is the capability to discern differences, such as between shapes, colors, tastes, and sounds; being able to tell the difference between an octagonal sign and a triangular sign is an example. Other examples:
    •Distinguish differences between two types of skin rashes' appearance.
    •Distinguish between font sizes used for screen displays of text.
2. *Concepts*: Previously learned discriminations combine to form concepts—the skills that allow us to classify phenomena using critical attributes. For instance, a "full stop" when driving a car means the driver stops the car for a count of three seconds. Other examples:
    •Classify by name several types of skin rashes.
    •Classify examples and non-examples of programming languages.
3. *Rules*: These specify relationships among two or more concepts and are often stated as propositions. For instance, "Heavy vehicles need greater stopping distance than lighter ones," and "Left turns are more dangerous than right turns" are examples of driving rules. Other examples:
    •Determine from examination of a patient's rash one diagnosis that can be eliminated.

•Establish whether a given software tool has the capability to meet a client's need.

4. *Higher-order rules*: These require combining multiple rules in order to perform a task. For example, knowing how to drive a car in icy conditions requires knowing additional rules beyond those needed for dry-pavement driving. Additional examples:
    •Interpret one's own symptoms to determine whether to see a doctor.
    •Design software to meet a new customer need.

Cognitive Strategies. Strategic knowledge and metacognition are additional terms used to describe cognitive strategies. They help learners manage their own thinking and learning, regardless of the domain of learning outcome. For instance, people often invent mnemonic devices to memorize names of new people they meet, or visualize themselves performing motor skills to improve performance. Cognitive strategies may be simple or complex. The following behaviors require cognitive strategies, in addition to other types of learned capabilities:

    •Create a new scheduling procedure that permits a doctor to adhere to a posted schedule.
    •Invent a new surgical procedure.

Verbal Information. Names, dates, descriptions, and other declarative knowledge are examples of verbal information. The general guideline is that if the learner must state, tell, or describe something, and will be called on only to recall it, the domain is verbal information (Gagné & Medsker, 1996). For instance, a driving student may be asked to state the local speed limit. Other examples:

    •State the name of the heart's main pumping chamber.
    •Without notes, explain the features of a new software package.

Attitudes. Attitudes have three components: cognitive (beliefs), affective (emotions), and behavioral (actions). Since attitudes are internal, only their external expression can be observed. The Gagné-Briggs model focuses attention on action choices people make as the observable expression of their attitudes. For instance, choosing to drive within the speed limit would require an attitude change for many motorists. While attitudes may be challenging to teach, attitudes are often a critical component of desired behavior in an educational or work setting. Paying attention to the attitudinal component of instructional challenges can greatly enhance instructional effectiveness. Additional examples of attitudes:

    •Choose to advise patients that the doctor is behind schedule.
    •Choose to employ structured design methods in a software development project.

Motor Skills. Motor skills require physical movements to be executed with proper smoothness and timing. For instance, balance is required for climbing telephone poles or scaffolding. Strength and timing may be required for handling packages. Motor skills must typically be combined to perform tasks such as swimming, playing ball sports, or driving a car. Other tasks involving motor skills:

·Draw blood or inject medications.
·Use a computer keyboard efficiently.

Biographical Sketches

Robert Mills Gagné (1916–) obtained his undergraduate degree at Yale University and his PhD in Experimental Psychology at Brown University. From the 1940s through the 1960s, he taught at several universities, researched and developed training at various Air Force bases, and supervised research programs on instructional methods at the American Institutes for Research. From 1969 until his retirement in 1994 he was instrumental in establishing Florida State University's graduate program in instructional systems; he is currently Professor Emeritus of Educational Research at Florida State University. His many publications include professional journal articles on human learning and books such as *The Conditions of Learning and Theory of Instruction* (1985), and *Principles of Instructional Design* (1992).

Leslie John Briggs (1919–1988) earned his BS in Education at Kansas State College and his PhD in Psychology at Ohio State University. During the 1950s, he taught Psychology at the University of Hawaii, conducted personnel training research for the Air Force, and directed the instructional methods program at the American Institutes for Research. Since 1968 he has been Professor of Instructional Design and Development at Florida State University. His publications include articles on sequencing instruction and several books, among them *Instructional Design* (1977) and, with R.M. Gagné, *Principles of Instructional Design* (1988).

Learning Objectives

Gagné, Briggs, and Wager (1992) provide standard verbs for stating learning objectives. Table 4.1 indicates the standard verbs suggested for objectives falling in each learning domain. The intent of the list is to help the designer communicate without ambiguity what performance is expected by using these capability verbs in

---

constructing instructional objectives. More information about how to write training objectives is readily available (e.g., Dick & Carey, 1996; Mager, 1975).

Desired Learning Outcome	Descriptive Verb
Intellectual skills	
Higher-order rule	Generate
Rules	Demonstrate
Concepts	Identify or classify
Discriminations	Discriminate
Cognitive strategies	Adopt
Verbal information	State
Attitude	Choose
Motor skill	Execute

Table 4.1
Standard Verbs for Writing Objectives

Conditions of Learning

Both internal and external conditions can enhance learning in each domain. Internal conditions describe what must be available within the learner to support encoding and storage of new information. External conditions are those provided by the instructional environment. This section describes both types of conditions.

Intellectual Skills.

- *Internal*: For learning intellectual skills, mastery of prerequisite skills is vital, as intellectual skills are hierarchically related. Higher-order rules have rules as prerequisites, rules require concepts, and concepts have discriminations as prerequisites. Learning about safe stopping distance in icy conditions (higher-order rule) requires knowing that stopping distance increases with speed (rule), how to estimate stopping distance (rule), that following distance can be adjusted using either the brake or the accelerator (concepts), and feeling/seeing whether a road is icy (discrimination).

- *External*: To assist the internal conditions of learning intellectual skills, prerequisite skills must be learned in order from simple to complex and reminders or practice used to recall previously learned skills. Further, since generalization is an essential feature of intellectual skills learning, a variety of examples is required. In the safe stopping distance example, use of repeated visual examples that demonstrate both safe and unsafe stopping distances would be helpful.

Cognitive Strategies.

- *Internal*: Learning cognitive strategies depends on an existing storehouse of information and skills. Consider a package-delivery employee: Planning a route that will meet certain performance criteria for timeliness and efficiency requires knowing speed limits in the area, alternate routes in the event of construction or traffic delays, and what intersections are dangerous. In this case, there is a significant attitude component as well. That is, the employee should want to meet the performance criteria.

- *External*: Providing repeated and varied opportunities to discover and try out cognitive strategies appears to be an effective method of stimulating cognitive strategy learning. Discovery of one's own cognitive strategies may be more effective than learning those of others. A verbal description and example of the strategy may be helpful. For example, an experienced delivery person could explain and demonstrate her own route-planning strategies. Then the new employees may use this information as the basis for developing their own strategy for route plans and further develop the strategy by trial and error.

Verbal Information.

- *Internal*: For learning both labels and facts, it is very helpful for the learner to have a pre-existing set of organized knowledge (a meaningful context). The existing knowledge must be capable of retrieval, and the new verbal information is learned by being incorporated into the existing knowledge. Also, the learner will master new facts or labels better if the learner has various cues to encode information. For example, planets of our solar system will be more easily learned if some basic knowledge of astronomy is recalled and if the first letters of the planets spell something recognizable (a cue).

- *External*: Verbal information acquisition is enhanced by providing a meaningful context, such as sentences, images, or linked information that may be used for retrieval. For example, learning new words (labels) is accomplished by using the words in sentences. Fact learning has been shown to be enhanced by simple devices such as topic sentences (Gagné, 1985). Simply stating the objective of the learning is helpful with verbal information (e.g., Will learners need to state the information verbatim or rephrase it in their own words?). More sophisticated devices such as Ausubel's advance organizers and mnemonic devices help place more complex, new information in context.

Repetition alone has not proven reliable in learning verbal information, but spaced practice retrieving the verbal information has been related to fact and label learning.

Attitudes.

- *Internal*: Although attitudes are internal, they are demonstrated as behaviors. Several internal conditions have been identified as desirable for attitude learning. One is that the learner must possess prerequisite intellectual or motor skills; enjoying piano or ballet lessons, for example, will be more achievable if the learner has necessary intellectual skills such as reading music, or motor coordination for dance steps. A second condition is necessary if what is being learned is imitation of another's behavior—the learner must admire the person modeling the behavior, as when a professional athlete urges adolescents not to use drugs.

  Another condition enabling attitude learning is cognitive dissonance, or a situation in which the learner is holding two incompatible beliefs, such as "I am a good driver" and "I regularly exceed the speed limit." Confronting the dissonance may help the learner acquire an attitude more compatible with learning safe driving habits.

- *External*: External conditions that support attitude learning are ensuring the prerequisite learning (of any domain), and supplying an admired human model who exhibits the desired behavior, whether someone known to the learners or actors in a video. Supplying information or experiences that could induce cognitive dissonance may be helpful. Also important is providing direct reinforcement for demonstrating the desired behavior, either by praise, recognition, or avoidance of an unpleasant consequence. Vicarious reinforcement (observing another person being reinforced for the behavior) may also be effective.

Motor Skills.

- *Internal*: Learning motor skills requires an executive subroutine that consists of a procedural sequence. For example, to parallel park a car, a common sequence of events involves using the front door of the car in front of the space as a guideline, then backing until your head is even with the other car's rear bumper, then turning the steering wheel toward the curb until you are behind the other car, and so forth. Being able to remember the subroutine is an important condition for learning the new skill. In addition, learning all the component skills, such as backing the car in a straight line, is important.

- *External*: Repeated practice with knowledge of results is the primary external condition for learning motor skills. Typically, feedback includes kinesthetic (internally sensed) feedback, self-assessment using indicators such as reducing the number of attempts before achieving success, and coached feedback.

Table 4.2 recaps the five domains of learning outcomes, along with examples and conditions of learning.

Learning Analysis

The Gagné-Briggs model pays close attention to the sequence of instruction, primarily determined by an analysis of the task to be learned. That analysis results in identification of learning objectives and determines what objectives require prerequisites to be learned. For example, intellectual skills are hierarchically related, as described earlier. Higher-order rules require less-complex rules, rules have concepts as prerequisites, and concepts require the learner to be able to discriminate (e.g., between red and green to recognize a traffic signal). In these cases, the prerequisites are essential to the new learning. Other prerequisites, outside of the intellectual skills domain, may be important but supportive rather than essential. Attitudes, for example, often play a supportive role in learning skills in other domains, such as intellectual and motor skills.

In the design sequence, a task analysis will often look like a procedure, but when tasks are analyzed to identify prerequisites, a learning hierarchy or instructional curriculum map (ICM) is called for. See Figure 4.2 on page 93 for an example of an ICM. Instructions for creating ICMs and multiple examples are provided by *The Conditions of Learning* (Gagné & Medsker, 1996) and *The Effective Design of Instruction* (Dick & Carey, 1996). The Gagné-Briggs model holds that learning analysis will create efficient instruction, because only the essential content will be included, and it will be effective because prerequisites are learned before the higher-level skills (sequencing is correct).

Domain of Learning	Sample Learned Outcome	Conditions of Learning
Intellectual Skills	• Classify diseases by sight and sound. • Use advanced features of office software.	*Internal*: Master prerequisite skills. *External*: Teach from simple to complex; use practice to recall previously learned skills; use a variety of examples.
Cognitive Strategies	• Develop mnemonic devices to learn procedural steps. • Create novel approaches for reducing poverty.	*Internal*: Use existing knowledge base of information and skills. *External*: State or model strategy; provide varied opportunities to discover and practice.
Verbal Information	• Match names and faces of project team members. • Explain the gist of the organization's mission statement.	*Internal*: Use pre-existing organized knowledge and incorporate cues for retrieval. *External*: Provide meaningful context—sentences and images; provide spaced practice retrieving the information.
Attitudes	• Choose to use public transit to save energy. • Give up habits known to be unhealthful.	*Internal*: Prerequisite learning often must be present; have admiration for a human model. *External*: Demonstrate desired behavior using an admired human model; reinforce desired behavior directly or vicariously.
Motor Skills	• Keyboard rapidly and accurately. • Hang wallpaper.	*Internal*: Learn executive subroutine. *External*: Provide repeated practice with feedback on results.

Table 4.2
Conditions of Learning by Domain

The Events of Instruction

The model proposes a "deliberately arranged set of external events designed to support internal learning processes" (Gagné et al., 1992, p. 11). Table 4.3 shows the relationship between internal information-processing events and external events of instruction in a numbered list, as presented by Gagné et al. (1992), and provides advice for designers. Designers should remember that all these events may not be needed for every lesson. Gagné and Briggs point out that sometimes learners themselves—especially experienced, self-directed learners—supply some of the instructional events.

Because of the differences in conditions of learning among domains, events for verbal information acquisition are designed differently from those designed for intellectual skills, and so forth.

Learner's Internal Processes	External Events of Instruction	Instructional Design Prescriptions
Reception	1. Gain attention	Provide stimulus change.
Expectancy	2. State the learning objective	Tell learners what they will be able to do after learning.
Retrieval from long-term memory	3. Stimulate recall of prior learning	Elicit previously learned knowledge or skills.
Selective perception	4. Present content	Show/explain/demonstrate the content with distinctive features.
Encoding	5. Provide learning guidance	Suggest a meaningful organization or cues.
Responding	6. Elicit performance	Ask learner to perform.
Reinforcement	7. Provide feedback	Give specific feedback.
Responding and reinforcement	8. Assess performance	Ask learner to perform again and give specific feedback.
Retrieval and generalization	9. Enhance retention and transfer	Provide varied practice opportunities and spaced reviews.

Table 4.3
Events of Instruction in the Learning Process

Event 1: Gain Attention. This event is not greatly differentiated among the domains of learning outcomes. It is typically accomplished by providing a change in stimulus (activity or media), such as a pertinent short video, skit, surprising event, cartoon, or visual image. A message whose content is related to that of the lesson objective is usually more effective.

Event 2: State the Learning Objective. Gagné and Briggs prescribe more than a simple verbal statement of the learning objective. For intellectual and motor skills, they recommend demonstrating the skill (showing an example), so that the learner has an accurate picture of what the desired performance looks like, as well as the end result. This demonstration sets up an expectancy and provides direction for the learner. (It may also provide motivation.) For verbal information, this event should describe exactly what the learner will be expected to learn and in what form it should be recalled. For example, must labels be recalled in scrambled order, or only in a prescribed sequence? Must information be learned verbatim, or can the learner paraphrase? For cognitive strategies, a demonstration may help, but usually a verbal statement of the strategy—or a statement of what the strategy (to be discovered) must accomplish—is considered sufficient. For attitudes, the objective often is not stated early in the lesson, but may be linked most productively with Event 5, learning guidance. (It may be counterproductive to tell a learner, "Our objective is to change your attitude.")

Event 3: Stimulate Recall of Prior Learning. Since intellectual skills are hierarchically related, most intellectual skill objectives have simpler intellectual skill prerequisites, without which the terminal objective cannot be learned. These prerequisites, and any other supportive enabling skills, should be ensured (ideally through demonstration by the learner) before learners undertake new learning. For other types of learning, recall of prerequisites is also required, but the prerequisites vary in nature. Cognitive strategies may depend on previous learning of all types. Verbal information depends primarily on well-organized bodies of information and concepts (for meaningful context). Motor skills may rely on the prior learning of an executive subroutine (procedure) and any part skills that make up the total skill, and learners should demonstrate these prerequisites. For example, swimming is made up of kicking, breathing, and stroking skills. Attitudes, by contrast, depend on recall of the situation and action involved in the desired personal choice (e.g., you are faced with an angry customer) and, ideally, the acceptance of an admired human model.

Event 4: Present Content. For intellectual skills, this event consists of detailed presentation, with explanations, demonstrations, and a variety of examples of the skill to be learned. For example, if teaching students how to fill out income tax forms, several different clients with different financial circumstances should be illustrated. For cognitive strategies, the choice is whether to present the strategy, through a verbal statement only or through a demonstration of the strategy, or whether to present only the need for a strategy, allowing the learners to discover their own strategies in future events. Presenting the content is straightforward for verbal information. The content should be presented in a logical, memorable format, structured, if possible, in a way that is easy to remember (e.g., visual, table, mnemonic device). In attitude learning, the message should be presented, to the extent possible, by an admired human model and by using media that involve the senses (e.g., film or video). This event for motor skills may include a detailed demonstration accompanied by verbal cues.

Event 5: Provide Learning Guidance. This event, which is often combined with Event 4, consists of cues, tips, and other forms of guidance to assist the learner with the encoding process. This event can also be combined with Events 6 and 7 (practice and feedback), since additional guidance may be needed at that point in the learning sequence. For intellectual skills and cognitive strategies, a variety of examples is important, as well as verbal cues and guidance from an expert performer. Job aids with verbal and visual cues may be used, then faded as the learning progresses. Verbal information learning may be enhanced by elaboration on the content, relating it to known bodies of knowledge, as well as the use of images and mnemonics. For attitudes, admired human models may be observed making the desired action choice and being reinforced for their choices. For example, the manager in the video uses the preferred conflict resolution skills and wins the negotiation. For motor skills, the key form of learning guidance is specific, informative feedback. For example, if a novice golfer slices his drives, the instructor must give individually tailored tips on the stance and swing.

Event 6: Elicit Performance. This event is relatively undifferentiated by learning domain. In each case, the learner must practice the behavior specified in the learning objective. Depending on complexity or difficulty, practice may be designed to elicit, at first, only a part of the final performance, or the entire performance at a reduced level of difficulty or to a reduced standard of quality. Assistance and coaching may also be used during the early stages of practice. Gradually, the scope, difficulty, learner autonomy, and quality of the performance may be increased.

Event 7: Provide Feedback. Feedback is relatively undifferentiated by learning domain. More important, perhaps, is the complexity of the performance being learned. Simple verbal information, intellectual skills, and motor skills can be taught with "right" or "wrong," "great" or "try again" responses to practice attempts. Complex behaviors in every domain may require more elaborate forms of feedback, explaining exactly what was wrong, perhaps why, and advice for the next practice attempt. Where possible, the learner should observe the natural consequences of performance so he or she may then be able to self-reinforce or take corrective action.

Event 8: Assess Performance. This event is an opportunity (formal or informal) for the learner (and instructor) to determine how well learning has occurred. As in Event 6, the performance required (in this case, the "test") should match the objective. At the assessment phase, however, the learner should perform without assistance or coaching, and should perform to the full standards stated in the objective. The most difficult domain to assess may be attitudes, where artificial opportunities (such as role plays or simulations) may be constructed to provide conditions for personal action choices, or learners may have to wait until real occasions occur and be observed in those conditions.

Event 9: Enhance Retention and Transfer. Retention is a critical issue for verbal information, because this domain is especially subject to forgetting. Verbal information decays more rapidly than other types of learning. Retention can be enhanced, however, through repeated, spaced practice (which, in the extreme, results in "overlearning"), through the provision of job aids and reference materials, and through refresher training. Transfer is not a major issue for verbal information, because typically the learned information need not be applied in a variety of situations. The opposite, however, is true for intellectual skills and cognitive strategies, where transfer is everything. Transfer to new situations can be enhanced by additional practice on varied problems, in variable circumstances, and through immediate and frequent application on the job. Learners may retain and transfer attitudes through additional opportunities to make action choices and through social reinforcement of desired choices. Motor skills are maintained primarily through spaced practice over time, and transfer is not usually a major issue.

Best Uses

The Gagné-Briggs model is a general-purpose model intended to apply to all subject matter and all domains. Over time, the model has become a standard for use in structured environments such as military training design and some corporate settings. This association is partially attributed to the model's emphasis on rigorous analysis of the content structure, which some instructional designers (e.g., Gayeski, 1998) regard as time consuming. However, the model is actually in wide use across all five domains of learning outcomes in a variety of settings. Some (e.g., Zemke, 1999) regard Gagné's book (*The Conditions of Learning*) as a basis for a "science of instruction."

The rigor that characterizes the Gagné-Briggs model doesn't limit its usefulness; instead, the model may be relied on to deliver instruction that is efficient (doesn't include extraneous information) and effective (includes all necessary learning). Therefore, the model is especially helpful in any situation where instructional design must be successful, either because of the critical nature of the performance (e.g., training fighter pilots) or because resources are extremely scarce (as in non-profit organizations or those that are publicly accountable).

Research Support

Substantial research supports the information-processing view of learning on which the Gagné-Briggs instructional theory is based. Use of the model has reportedly strengthened computer-based training design by reinforcing knowledge of how learning takes place (Clark, 1992). Gagné and Briggs themselves (Gagné, 1985; Gagné et al., 1992) conducted research to test their theories on the importance of task analysis, performance objectives, the events of instruction, and the conditions of learning. The individual conditions of learning for each domain are well supported by theory and empirical studies (Gagné & Medsker, 1996).

Learning hierarchies associated with intellectual skills were validated by research (White & Gagné, 1978) verifying that prerequisites can be identified and are important to learning concepts, rules, and higher-order rules. In addition, that research showed verbal information (facts and labels) was not a prerequisite for intellectual skills.

Most research testing the model's premises appears to have been done at the same time as the model's development. For example, Branson (1977) and Boutwell (1977) reported on studies conducted in the military and medical professions, respectively, that supported systematic instructional design using task analysis and performance objectives. There appears to be little current research into the nine events of instruction, although that aspect of the model is widely used.

Model in Action

Consider a situation in which learners have had their driving licenses suspended for driving under the influence of alcohol. They have been mandated to take a formal course on finding alternatives to driving while under the influence of alcohol. The learners must pass this course, which has several sessions, before they will be able to regain their licenses. None of the learners has yet had a serious incident behind the wheel, and none has previously taken a class of this kind.

The school's instructional designer drafts an instructional curriculum map (ICM), of which Figure 4.2 is an excerpt. The top box (goal or terminal objective) represents an attitude, and a variety of other attitudes, intellectual skills, and verbal information are judged to be prerequisite to the goal. The triangles denote a change in learning domain.

Once the ICM is completed, the instructional designer groups the boxes into lessons, based on required sequencing of prerequisites, logic, and time constraints for individual lessons. The sample lesson shown in Table 4.4 uses the nine events to teach the highlighted boxes (1 and 2) in the ICM (Figure 4.2). Note that this is an intellectual skills lesson, and thus includes the condition of a variety of examples.

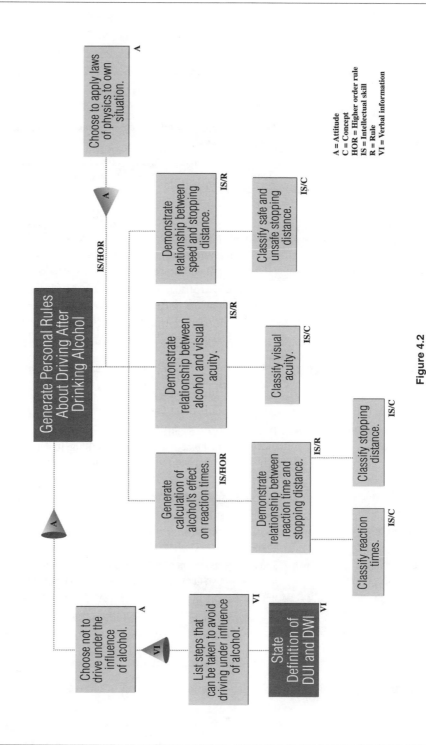

Figure 4.2
Partial Instructional Curriculum Map

Event	Lesson Plan
1. Gain Attention	Show the learners a videotape that dramatically depicts the result of driving while impaired—an accident at high speed that causes a fatality.
2. State the Learning Objective	Present the objectives on a transparency. At the conclusion of this module, learners will be able to demonstrate the relationship between alcohol consumption and visual acuity. Demonstrate one example.
3. Stimulate Recall of Prior Learning	Lead discussion of visual acuity concept learned in previous lesson, using a variety of examples showing excellent to poor visual acuity, accented by images that represent differences in visual acuity.
4. Present Content	Lead discussion of alterations of visual acuity that take place because of alcohol consumption. For example, under the influence of a certain amount of alcohol, acuity is reduced by a corresponding percentage. Demonstrate with several examples.
5. Provide Learning Guidance	Use tools such as specially designed glasses that distort vision in a manner consistent with DWI/DUI, and ask participants to describe what they can and cannot see using the glasses.
6. Elicit Performance	Have the learners recall and use the concepts and rules in multiple, varied practice items such as filling in the blanks, matching, and stating definitions or descriptions aloud.
7. Provide Feedback	Provide feedback to each learner about errors and correct answers.
8. Assess Performance	Have each learner solve several problems that demonstrate the effects of alcohol on visual acuity.
9. Enhance Retention and Transfer	Tell a story about a personal incident with DUI/DWI, then assign two questions for the next session: What is the worst problem you've had with DUI/DWI? What do you want to avoid? State that these questions will be used to open the next session.

Table 4.4
Sample Lesson Plan

Implementation Guide

Step	Design Instructions
1	Categorize the overall or terminal learning task as to domain or type of learning outcome.
2	Analyze the task for prerequisites.
3	Create a learning hierarchy or instructional curriculum map.
4	Create an objective for each map component.
5	Divide hierarchy or map into lessons.
6	Structure each lesson using the nine events and conditions of learning.

References

Ausubel, D.P., Novak, J.D., & Hanesian, H. (1978). *Educational psychology: A cognitive view* (2nd ed.). New York: Holt, Rinehart & Winston.

Boutwell, R.C. (1977). Medical education and instructional design. In L.J. Briggs (Ed.), *Instructional design: Principles and applications* (423–459). Englewood Cliffs, NJ: Educational Technology.

Branson, R.K. (1977). Military and industrial training. In L.J. Briggs (Ed.), *Instructional design: Principles and applications* (353–390). Englewood Cliffs, NJ: Educational Technology.

Briggs, L.J. (Ed.). (1977). *Instructional design: Principles and applications*. Englewood Cliffs, NJ: Educational Technology.

Clark, R.C. (1992). Computer-mediated instruction. In H.D. Stolovitch & E.J. Keeps (Eds.), *Handbook of human performance technology* (449–472). San Francisco: Jossey-Bass.

Dick, W., & Carey, L. (1996). *The systematic design of instruction* (4th ed.). New York: HarperCollins.

Ebbinghaus, H. (1913). *Memory: A contribution to experimental psychology*. (H.A. Ruger, Trans.). New York: Teachers College.

Gagné, R.M. (1985). *The conditions of learning and theory of instruction* (4th ed.). Fort Worth, TX: Holt, Rinehart & Winston.

Gagné, R.M., Briggs, L.J., & Wager, W.W. (1992). *Principles of instructional design* (4th ed.). Fort Worth, TX: Harcourt Brace Jovanovich.

Gagné, R.M., & Medsker, K.L. (1996). *The conditions of learning: Training applications*. Fort Worth, TX: Harcourt Brace.

Gayeski, D.M. (1998, April). Out-of-the-box instructional design. *Training & Development, 52*, 36–40.

Greeno, J.G., & Bjork, R.A. (1973). Mathematical learning theory and the new 'mental forestry.' *Annual Review of Psychology, 24*, 81–116.

Harlow, H.F. (1949). The development of learning sets. *Psychological Review, 56*, 51–65.

Köhler, W. (1927). *The mentality of apes*. New York: Harcourt.

Mager, R.F. (1975). *Preparing instructional objectives* (2nd ed.). Belmont, CA: Fearon-Pitman.

Tulving, E., & Donaldson, W. (Eds.). (1972). *Organization of memory*. New York: Academic Press.

White, R.T., & Gagné, R.M. (1978). Formative evaluation applied to a learning hierarchy. *Contemporary Educational Psychology, 3*, 87–94.

Zemke, R. (1999, July). Toward a science of training. *Training, 36*, 32–36.

Bibliography

Dick, W., & Carey, L. (1990). *The systematic design of instruction* (3rd ed.). Glenview, IL: HarperCollins.

About the Author

Bobbie Moore earned a master's degree in Human Performance Systems and a certificate in Instructional Design at Marymount University in Arlington, Virginia. She finds daily opportunities to apply rigorous performance improvement principles in her work as a Development and Learning Associate with Schiff Consulting Group. In this capacity she provides support to Fortune 500 finance executives, with emphasis on helping corporate finance personnel to become value-added business partners.

Bobbie holds a bachelor's degree in Spanish Language and Literature from Middlebury College, is a Certified Management Accountant, and is presently working on a doctorate in Adult Education through Nova Southeastern University.

CHAPTER 5

Component Display Theory

Naomi Berkove and Bobbie Moore

M. David Merrill first began developing the underlying principles of component display theory (CDT) in the early 1970s. Motivated by an interest in designing effective instruction, Merrill created this structured method for categorizing learning outcomes and prescribing learning strategies.

Merrill's theory resembles the Gagné-Briggs model in that both prescribe different instructional approaches based on desired learning outcomes. In contrast to the Gagné-Briggs model, however, Merrill's prescriptions treat only the cognitive domain and do not address all of the Gagné-Briggs model's Nine Events of Instruction. Merrill's approach considers three instructional phases: presentation, practice, and testing performance. For a given cognitive learning outcome, CDT prescribes instructional methods in more detail than the Gagné-Briggs model does.

A distinguishing feature of CDT is its highly structured approach. CDT dissects learning into small pieces or *components* and assigns individual strategies to each. The resulting product is rich in detail, providing specific guidance on techniques for each phase: presenting content, eliciting practice, and testing performance. What CDT offers in depth, however, it lacks in breadth. As stated above, CDT treats only cognitive learning, not instruction in motor skills or attitude.

Furthermore, CDT narrowly focuses on "microstrategies." These are instructional strategies for teaching a single concept or a single process. CDT does not address broader "macro" issues, such as how content should be selected, how instruction should be sequenced or delivered (i.e., by classroom training, computer-based training, etc.), or even what methods to use. In fact, Merrill (1983) has argued that—

> a given micro strategy, as specified by CDT, can be used with a wide variety of subject matters and content organizational schemes, with virtually any delivery system, and with a wide variety of different techniques for managing the instruction (p. 284).

An important element of CDT's structure (and another contrast with Gagné's taxonomy) is that its instructional prescriptions use two dimensions to classify learning objectives: the level of learner performance desired and the content type. CDT's two-dimensional scheme for classifying objectives is known as the performance-content matrix, generally accepted as a notable contribution to instructional design theory. Although CDT's terminology is challenging[1], it is widely acknowledged that Merrill has developed a precise vocabulary for describing instructional presentation variables. These presentations are the *display* in CDT.

In practical terms, CDT's users generally select from its prescriptions and adapt its principles for their specific applications, rather than applying the theory as a whole. Applications of CDT often appear in the context of technology-based instruction because of the theory's detailed approach. Merrill himself developed several electronic instructional design products using concepts evolved from CDT. CDT's principles have also been applied in nontechnical environments, and Merrill's work with several corporations encouraged them to use CDT as a tool for developing their own in-house instructional design processes.

Origins

According to Merrill et al. (1996)—

> If an instructional experience or environment does not include the instructional strategies required for the acquisition of the desired knowledge or skill, then effective, efficient, and appealing learning of the desired outcome will not occur (p. 5).

---

[1] CDT's terminology reflects Merrill's deliberate attempt to choose words that convey a precise meaning. It is Merrill's belief that precise language leads to more effective instructional design, and his later instructional theories and new terminologies continue to reflect this philosophy (personal communication, M.D. Merrill, 1998).

Merrill's search for what makes good instruction is as relevant now as it was when he first developed CDT. Although his current theoretical and practical work

---

Biographical Sketch

M. David Merrill (1937-) is Professor of Instructional Technology at Utah State University. Merrill earned a BA at Brigham Young University and both an MA and PhD at the University of Illinois. He has taught at the University of Southern California (USC), among other institutions.

Merrill has written numerous books, papers, and articles, and has codeveloped products that rely on CDT and are used to improve instructional design processes, especially for computer-based instruction. (The Electronic Trainer and the Instructional Simulator are two more recent examples of products introduced in collaboration with other members of ID2, a Utah state research group.) His work on CDT includes authoring chapters in Charles Reigeluth's *Instructional Design Theories and Models* (1983) and *Theories of Instructional Design in Action* (1987). Merrill also wrote a chapter on applying CDT in the 1988 publication *Instructional Designs for Microcomputer Courseware* (D.H. Jonassen, Ed.). A collection of some of his other articles and publications on CDT can be found in his 1994 book, *Instructional Design Theory.*

---

focuses on course structures instead of lessons, and "instructional transactions" rather than presentations, it is based on the same philosophies that shaped CDT.

CDT may be categorized along with the Gagné-Briggs model as a cognitive theory of instructional design. Merrill's theory also draws on the work of Bruner, Evans-Glaser-Homme, Rothkkopf, Skinner, Gropper, and others.

The first edition of Gagné's *Conditions of Learning* (1965) impressed Merrill, who liked Gagné's catalogue of conditions for acquiring specific learning outcomes. Merrill perceived a need, however, for further detail about what constituted effective instructional presentation. His concern with the details of presentation yielded what were for him the core components of good instruction—generalities and examples in presentation and practice—and the two dimensions of instructional objectives—performance and content. Merrill's first paper based on CDT principles appeared in 1973 (Merrill & Boutwell). By 1983, Merrill had more fully developed CDT, and a complete description of the theory appeared in Reigeluth's *Instructional Design Theories and Models* (Merrill, 1983).

During the 1970s and 1980s, CDT generated widespread discussion in academic circles, and it also received testing and use in a range of working environments. Because of its highly structured approach and terminology, CDT enjoyed some popularity in environments where a formalized work style and technical language were already accepted, including military and instructional technology communities. One of the first military training applications of CDT, the Instructional Quality Inventory (Ellis & Wulfeck, 1978), was used by the U.S. Navy to evaluate existing instructional materials. Merrill's work with IBM and Arthur Andersen relied on CDT to help these companies create their own instructional development processes. Developers of technical training and computer based instruction in particular report continued use of CDT concepts as a tool for designing technical training.

Description

Merrill's CDT assumes that there is a best way to design instruction. Merrill (1983) maintained that "for each type of objective, there is a unique combination of…presentation forms that will most effectively promote acquisition of that type of objective" (p. 283). CDT is the expansion of this philosophy into a complete instructional theory. It represents Merrill's efforts to define different types of cognitive learning and then prescribe the instructional strategy most appropriate for each type.

CDT at a Glance

Component display theory has two basic parts: The first part analyzes and classifies the components of cognitive learning. The second part identifies the most appropriate instructional strategy for each component. It should be noted that the second part is substantially more difficult than the first. This is not because of lack of clarity in the theory, since the theory is precise in prescribing what strategies fit each component of learning. On the contrary, it is exactly this precision that makes it challenging to keep track of the prescriptions assigned to each component once all the components are assembled.

Classifying the Components. Merrill categorized cognitive learning along two dimensions: content and performance. CDT describes each component of learning by these two aspects. In addition, Merrill created a structure to describe how instruction is presented. He classified instruction by using four different presentation forms that also identify whether material is presented in a general manner or as a specific example. These classification schemes comprise the basis of CDT.

Assigning Strategies. Once each instructional component is defined, the next step involves assigning an instructional strategy to each component. In CDT, strategies are assigned for three phases: presenting the content, providing practice, and testing or evaluating learner performance. Using the previously mentioned classification schemes, CDT prescribes instructional strategies that should be used to ensure the most effective learning. Specific directions explain how each phase of instruction should be presented, depending on the content of the material and the desired performance.

After defining the basic presentation strategy, CDT also provides additional tips to enhance learning. Consistent with the rest of the theory, each tip is linked to the type of content, performance, and presentation of the individual components. Finally, CDT offers overall strategies to use across the various phases of instruction. These strategies provide meaningful links among the presentation, practice, and testing phases of instruction.

The Components of CDT

Content. The basis of CDT is the classification of different types of learning. CDT classifies each cognitive learning objective along two dimensions: content and performance. The four categories of content in CDT are fact, concept, procedure, and principle:

- *Fact* refers to a piece of information, such as a date, a name, or an event.
- *Concept* refers to a group of objects or symbols that share one or more common characteristics, such as "user interface" or "balanced scorecard."
- *Procedure* refers to a set of steps to accomplish an activity or produce a product, such as repairing a copier or operating a switchboard.
- *Principle* refers to an explanation or prediction of why things work the way they do, such as market fluctuation models or the mechanics of compound interest.

Except for *fact*, each of these content categories can be represented as either a specific example or as an abstract generality. For instance, it is possible to describe in abstract the concept of a computer network, or the concept can be explained by referring to a particular computer network. Similarly, the law of gravity can be represented by a formula or by dropping an object. According to CDT, facts cannot be described in abstraction. Facts are always represented as specific examples.

Performance. In addition to defining the content, CDT classifies components of instruction according to what the learner is to do with the content. The three categories of performance are remember, use, and find.[2]

- *Remember* refers to recalling information either verbatim or paraphrased, such as reciting a poem or citing a law.
- *Use* refers to applying information, such as operating a bulldozer or classifying management styles.
- *Find* refers to the process of creating or deriving something new, such as identifying the reason for low classroom attendance or inventing a new security system.

With the exception of *fact*, any of the content categories can be combined with any of the performance categories (*fact* can only be combined with *remember*). For example, the content category *procedure* would be combined with the performance category *remember* if the learner were to retrieve from memory the steps for performing a fire safety inspection. If the learner were required to perform the inspection, the correct classification would be *use-procedure*. If the learner were given the task of creating a new inspection process, the learning would be classified as *find-procedure*. According to Merrill (1983), it is not possible to *use* or *find* facts, since they cannot be represented in an abstract form. In CDT, *remember-fact* is the only possible *fact* combination. Additional examples are shown in Table 5.1.

	REMEMBER	USE	FIND
FACT	Name the four emergency exits on the airplane.		
CONCEPT	Explain the term "learning curve."	Determine whether the patient's weight is above average.	Create a logo that reflects the company's philosophy.

Table 5.1
Performance-Content Matrix With Examples

---

2. Merrill's performance categories of remember, use, and find may be compared to Gagné's categories of verbal information, intellectual skill, and cognitive strategies.

	REMEMBER	USE	FIND
PROCEDURE	State the steps for applying for a promotion.	File a tax return.	Determine the best method for testing this new software.
PRINCIPLE	State the second law of physics.	Explain why a broken seal could lead to contamination of the contents.	Determine the effect of replacing sugar with corn syrup in candy production.

Table 5.1
Performance-Content Matrix With Examples (cont.)

Putting Together the Components

Primary Presentation Forms. CDT's next step is assigning an instructional strategy to each defined type of learning. CDT identifies three distinct phases of instruction: presentation, practice, and testing performance. For each phase, CDT outlines the most appropriate strategy for the type of learning. Specifically, CDT does this by prescribing when it is most appropriate to use each of four presentation forms:

1. generality
2. specific example[3]
3. expository method (tell)
4. inquisitory method (ask)

The expository method is always used during the presentation phase, since content is explained or provided to the learner during this phase. The inquisitory method is always used during the practice and testing performance phases, since the learner is asked to provide an answer or do an action both to practice the material and to perform (i.e., be tested on) the instruction.

Using these four presentation forms (generality, specific example, expository method, inquisitory method), CDT defines an instructional strategy based on the action the learner is to do. This means that there are distinct strategies depending on whether the learner is to *remember*, *use*, or *find* the content.[4] Table 5.2 depicts how

---

[3.] Merrill refers to this as an *instance*. We have used *example* for the sake of clarity.

[4.] Merrill maintained that separate instructional strategies should be used for remembering a generality versus remembering a specific example, so he added another category to the performance matrix.

these strategies are combined.[5] Where appropriate, Merrill indicated when new or multiple examples (or generalities) should be offered to enhance learning. He also indicated when it would be appropriate to paraphrase a response.

Understanding the instructional strategy for each of the categories requires some interpretation. For example, the instructional strategy for *use*, such as duplicating pages on a new photocopy machine, would be to present the content both in a general form as well as through a number of specific examples, each of which would be a new representation of the content to be learned. The learner would then practice the skill, using multiple examples not previously encountered. A proper testing strategy would use a number of new examples to determine learner performance.

The words *generality* and *specific example* have distinct meanings according to CDT. CDT defines these terms differently, depending on whether the content is classified as fact, concept, procedure, or principle. The definitions also change depending on whether the information is delivered in the presentation phase or in the practice/testing performance phases of instruction. Table 5.3 displays these definitions.

With this additional layer, the instructional strategy becomes decidedly more intricate. To return to our earlier example, duplicating pages on a new copier would be categorized as *use-procedure*. Table 5.2 indicates that the instructional strategy for the presentation phase of *use* is a generality plus multiple new examples. Table 5.3 shows what is meant by a generality of a procedure. In this case, it translates into describing the process. A proper description would include the name of the functions that can be done with the copier (i.e., sorting, stapling, etc.), the goal of these functions, the basic steps involved, the order of those steps, a distinction between the basic process and the points where judgment might be required, and some of the alternatives in the process.

---

5. While we have attempted to preserve as much of Merrill's terminology as possible, we thought that his shorthand for the instructional strategies might be confusing. We have therefore chosen to use fewer abbreviations in our charts and tables. We have also removed references to *expository method* and *inquisitory method*, as these do not vary within each phase of instruction. The reader is asked to remember that the *expository method* is always used during the presentation phase, and the *inquisitory method* is always used during the practice and testing performance phases.

Category of Performance	Presentation		Practice		Testing Performance	
Find			Gen. (New)	Ex. (Mult., New)		
Use	Gen.	Ex. (Mult., New)		Ex. (Mult., New)		Ex. (Mult., New)
Remember Generality	Gen.	Ex. (New)	Gen. (Para.)		Gen. (Para.)	
Remember Instance		Ex.		Ex.		Ex.

Gen. – Generality
Ex. – Specific Example
Mult. (Multiple) – More than one
New (New) – Content not previously presented
Para. (Paraphrased) – Not verbatim; restated in learner's own words

Table 5.2
Primary Presentation Forms

The multiple new examples required by the prescription are also meticulously defined. According to Table 5.3, an example of a procedure is a demonstration of the procedure by simulation if necessary. Each demonstration would include the name of the procedure to be demonstrated (i.e., making double-sided copies), a description of the desired outcome, and the equipment necessary to accomplish the procedure.

Referring to Table 5.2, the practice and testing performance strategies for *use* require that the learner be exposed to multiple new examples of the procedure. According to Table 5.3, this means that the learner would need to demonstrate various procedures using the new copier (i.e., copying from single-sided to double-sided, making darker copies, etc.) These procedures should be new—not previously presented to the learner. The instructional strategies appropriate for the other learning classifications can be similarly identified using Table 5.2 and Table 5.3.

Secondary Presentation Forms. Stopping here in the design process would provide a solid basis for instruction, but it would not represent a complete strategy according to CDT. Merrill (1983) held that it is important to use certain helping techniques when delivering different parts of the instruction. He postulated that such techniques "facilitate the students' processing of the information or ... provide items of interest" (p. 308). For example, he suggested accompanying generalities with some type of elaboration, such as a mnemonic or a diagram, to help learn the information. He also stated that feedback "should always accompany practice at every performance level" (p. 322).

He identified the following techniques, which he called secondary presentation forms, as enhancing learning efficiency:

- Use attention-focusing help such as arrows, colors, bold lettering, etc. (help)
- Use alternative representations of the content, such as charts, formulas, symbols, etc. (representation)
- Provide contextual information, such as the historical background of an event, an anecdote relating to an example, a discussion of the importance of a principle, etc. (context)
- Provide prerequisite information, such as definitions of more basic concepts. (prerequisite)
- Use mnemonics to assist in memory retention. (mnemonic)
- Provide feedback for both correct and incorrect responses, including supplying attention-focusing help or corrective guidance. (feedback)

As with the earlier parts of CDT, these techniques are linked with the individual phases and types of instruction. Table 5.4 shows how these techniques are applied with the previously described instructional strategies.

Interdisplay Relationships. Until this point in the design process, the focus has been on analyzing the individual components of instruction in a highly detailed manner. The last step of CDT switches to a wider lens and looks at the instructional strategy as a whole. Merrill (1987) made the case that it is important to pay attention not only to the individual parts of instruction, but also to how those parts relate to each other. The instructional strategies for presenting content, providing practice, and testing performance should be coordinated to fit together with each other, since "the relationship between [them] also affects the learning that will occur" (p. 209).

Type of Content	PRESENTATION		PRACTICE / TESTING PERFORMANCE	
	Generality	**Example**	**Generality**	**Example**
Fact	N/A	Match • Symbol to symbol • Object to symbol • Event to symbol	N/A	Match • Symbol to ? • Object to ? • Event to ?
Concept	Definition including— • Name • Superordinate concept • Distinguishing features • Relationship between features	Classification of example • Using name • Can be an object, event, or symbol • Must be a representation that has all the critical attributes	State definition, either verbatim or paraphrased.	Classify a new symbol, object, or event by supplying name or definition (verbatim or paraphrased) as appropriate. Example should exhibit all critical attributes.
Procedure	Describe procedure including— • Name of procedure • Goal • Identification of steps, conditions, and loops • Order of steps • Distinction between process and decision • Alternatives	Demonstrate procedure indicating— • Name of procedure • Desired outcome • Required materials • Representation of procedure if no actual demonstration	State steps in a procedure, either paraphrased or verbatim or in a flow chart representing the procedure. Learner should be given the name and goal of the procedure.	Demonstrate procedure, symbolically if necessary. Learner should be given the name, goal, materials and/or symbols necessary to execute the procedure.
Principles	Describe principle including:— • Name • Identification of component concepts and events involved • Statement of causal relationship	Explain principle including— • Name • Specific situation where the principle applies • Execution of the process to which the principle applies	State the relationship between the principle and proposition, either verbatim or paraphrased.	Explain principle given a new problem situation, using representation if necessary. Learner may be asked to predict the outcome.

Table 5.3

Primary Presentation Form-Content Matrix[a]

[a]. In Merrill's later work, he elaborates on the practice/testing performance categories by making a further distinction for the find level (Merrill & Twitchell, 1994).

Category of Performance	Presentation		Practice		Testing Performance	
Find			Gen. (New)	Ex. (Mult., New)		
			• Feedback (Use)			
Use	Gen.	Ex. (Mult., New)		Ex. (Mult., New)		Ex. (Mult., New)
	• Help • Prereq. • Alternate represent.	• Help • Prereq.		• Alternate represent. • Corrective feedback		
Remember Generality	Gen.	Ex. (New)	Gen. (Para.)		Gen. (Para.)	
	• Mnemonic	• Alternate represent.	• Corrective feedback • With help			
Remember Instance		Ex.		Ex.		Ex.
				• Corrective feedback		

Note: Learner Control and Isolation should be used across all levels.

Help – Use attention-focusing help such as arrows, colors, bold lettering, etc.

Prereq. – Provide prerequisite information, such as definitions of more basic concepts.

Alternate represent. – Use alternate representations of the content, such as diagrams, formulas, etc.

Mnemonic – Use mnemonics to assist in memory retention.

Corrective feedback – Provide feedback indicating the correct response.

With help – Provide feedback which includes attention-focusing help such as arrows or colors.

Feedback (Use) – Provide feedback by having the learner use the concept, procedure, or principle created to see if it "works."

Table 5.4
Primary and Secondary Presentation Forms

Specifically, Merrill identified what he called interdisplay relationships, so named because they are instructional strategies that are applied across the different segments of instruction. The most significant of these interdisplay relationships is the idea that learners should have a degree of control over the instruction they receive. To a certain extent, learners should be able to determine the sequence of instruction, the number of examples and practice items, and the amount of elaboration they receive. Rather than a one-size-fits-all approach, Merrill contended that instruction is most effective when it adapts to learner needs.

Merrill argued that—

> it is unlikely that a single student will need all of the material provided, but it is equally probable that in a group of students, each of the components included will be used by at least some of the students. If every student is required to use every prescribed component, the mateials [sic] will be considerably less efficient than is necessary (1983, p. 327).

The focus on learner control may be one reason that CDT has found acceptance among computer based instruction (CBI) developers. According to CDT, the learner control concept should be applied to all levels of instruction for all content and performance types. CDT does not address how to ensure the learners make appropriate choices.

Merrill also identified other interdisplay relationships, many of which he associated with types of performance. Specifically, he named the following:

- Present a set of facts in a different order each time they are encountered (random order).
- Limit the maximum number of new items a learner must remember to seven (chunking).
- Match good examples with non-examples (examples that do not have the critical characteristics) to help learners distinguish between the two (matching).
- Gradually reduce the amount of help provided (fading).
- Use valid examples with noncritical characteristics that are as different from each other as possible (divergent).
- Require learners to recall new facts immediately (no delay).
- Use examples with a range of difficulty (range).
- Isolate each of the primary presentation forms from the surrounding text so that the learner can easily identify the main ideas and key points (isolation).

Table 5.5 shows how these interdisplay relationships fit with the primary and secondary presentation forms.

Research Support

Many of the individual instructional prescriptions of CDT have been well established in laboratory research. For example, fading is a technique whose effectiveness is supported by extensive behavioral learning research, and cognitive researchers have shown mnemonics to be effective. Research on concept learning supports the use of examples and non-examples. A lengthy list of additional research on individual elements of CDT is cited in Merrill's 1994 book. These include primary presentation forms (generality, example, presentation and practice), attention-focusing help, presenting a range of instances, and learner control of primary presentation form sequence. The search for independent research that tests the efficacy of the theory as a whole, however, produced fewer results. It yielded an array of research conducted by Merrill's university and business colleagues, but the search for independent studies was less successful.

Best Uses

In Merrill's own view, CDT's main contribution to ISD has been its focus on a precise terminology for instructional design (personal communication, M.D. Merrill, 1998). While this same structured terminology and highly formalized approach may make CDT unappealing to classroom instructors, developers of programmed instruction in general and CBI in particular appear to have benefited from its precision (Wilson, 1987). The complex structure of CDT lends itself well to automating the instructional design process, where computer logic would generate the prescriptions. Merrill himself created an instructional authoring system called TICCIT while he was developing CDT.

Conditions favoring CDT's use in CBI have continued to the present. Merrill's concern with instructionally sound interactive courseware has led to evolution of a more integrative theory, called instructional transaction theory (ITT). Products advertised on the Internet that rely on ITT are primarily multimedia tools (i.e., authoring system "plug-ins"), but ITT appears to have appeal beyond the instructional technology community.

Category of Performance	Presentation		Practice		Testing Performance	
Find			**Gen.** (New)	**Ex.** (Mult., New)		
			• Feedback (Use)			
			Divergent/Range			
Use	**Gen.**	**Ex.** (Mult., New)		**Ex.** (Mult., New)	**Ex.** (Mult., New)	
	• Help • Prereq. • Alternate represent.	• Help • Prereq.		• Alternate represent. • Corrective feedback		
	Divergent/Range Matching Fading		Divergent/Range No matching Fading feedback		Divergent/Range No matching No help	
Remember Generality	**Gen.**	**Ex.** (New)	**Gen.** (Para.)		**Gen.** (Para.)	
	• Mnemonic	• Alternate represent.	• Corrective feed-back • With help			
Remember Instance		**Ex.**		**Ex.**	**Ex.**	
				• Corrective feedback		
	Random Order Chunking		Random Order No Delay 100% Accuracy		Random Order No Delay 100% Accuracy	

Note: Learner Control and Isolation should be used across all levels.

Divergent – Use examples where the critical characteristics are different from each other.

Range – Use examples with a range of difficulty.

Matching – Match good examples with non-examples to help learners distinguish between the two.

Fading – Gradually reduce the amount of help provided.

Random Order – Present a set of facts in a different order each time they are encountered.

Chunking – Limit the maximum number of new items a learner must remember to seven.

No Delay – Require learners to recall new facts immediately.

100% Accuracy – Require that all answers be correct.

Learner Control – Give learners some control over the instructional content and strategy.

Isolation – Isolate each of the primary presentation forms from the surrounding text so that learners can easily locate, skip, or repeat a given item.

Table 5.5
Primary and Secondary Presentation Forms and Interdisplay Relationships

Although the principles of CDT can be applied to a variety of learning situations, the model's structured approach makes it a good match for technical training where the content is well defined, rather than "soft" or interpersonal skills training. Ruth C. Clark, author of *Developing Technical Training* (1989), uses an adaptation of Merrill's content-performance matrix as the basis of her book, and states "[h]aving used his content-performance matrix to teach hundreds of technical experts how to design training, I find it provides a succinct and powerful model" (p. viii). Its detailed attention to effective instructional prescriptions for all three phases of presentation, practice, and performance also make CDT an attractive model when high levels of learner achievement are desired.

It is important to recall that CDT's applications include only cognitive instruction, not motor skills or attitudes.

Model in Action

Employing a narrow focus—one performance-content combination—and addressing the presentation prescriptions for that type of objective helps to demonstrate CDT. This section focuses on *use-concept* as the performance-content type. In keeping with CDT's limited scope, the result does not describe the delivery or sequencing decisions that the instructional designer would need to make.

This section shows how to develop presentation attributes for the following objective:

> During a customer product complaint phone call, classify the customer's product using the product ID number: Is it a refrigerator under warranty from our company or not?

From Table 5.2, we see that the instruction must present the generality and use multiple new examples in presentation, practice, and testing performance. From Table 5.3, we learn that presentation of the generality must include the name, distinguishing features, relationship between those features, and the superordinate concept definition—the general concept into which this concept fits. Using Table 5.5, the learner must receive during the presentation phase:

- Reference to any prerequisites (prereq.)
- An alternate representation of the concept with attention-focusing help (alternate represent., help)
- Examples that are matched to appropriate non-examples (matching)

- Examples as well as non-examples with a divergence in critical characteristics encompassing a range of difficulty (divergent/range)
- A reduced amount of help as the learner progresses (fading)

Putting all these prescriptions together yields the presentation prescriptions shown in the following example. All the bulleted items should be included in the instruction, although CDT does not prescribe any particular order for presenting them.

Presentation

For the following items, italics designate CDT prescriptions.

- Define the concept:

   "A product sold by our company is under warranty if its product ID date is within a stated period of today's date, regardless of the manufacture location. The warranty period for refrigerators is seven years."

   Name, superordinate concept (warranty), and prerequisite concept (refrigerator warranty)

- Include all concept attributes:

   "Product ID numbers contain the information necessary to decide whether the product is a refrigerator under warranty at the time of the customer's call. A refrigerator under our warranty must have a product ID number that—

   • begins with MA
   • has a model number (1 to 25 for refrigerators)
   • has a country code: U, B, or C for United States, Brazil, or Canada
   • ends with a four-digit number indicating a month and year of production

   Prerequisite concept (product ID), distinguishing features, and relationship between features

- Present an alternate representation:

   Present the product ID number in a manner different from a simple verbal description (e.g., a photo of a refrigerator product ID number). Use colors, arrows, or circled areas to help focus attention on important information.

   Alternate representation with help

- Present examples:

  "Examples of in-warranty product IDs as of May 1, 2015; all are our refrigerators:

    •MA4C0810 (Made in Canada, August 2010)
    •MA25U0309 (Made in the United States, March 2009)
    •MA5B0608 (Made in Brazil, June 2008)"

  Examples have all critical attributes, are divergent, and include a range of difficulty

- Present non-examples:

  "These product IDs are not under our refrigerator warranty as of May 1, 2015:

    •RA4C0810 (not our company's product ID)
    •MA27A0309 (production location does not match)
    •MA5B0208 (product manufactured over 7 years prior)"

  Non-examples match examples, include a range of difficulty, and are divergent

According to Table 5.2, the practice and testing performance phases use an inquisitory method involving multiple new examples. Table 5.3 tells us that the learner must classify previously unencountered examples exhibiting all critical attributes. From Table 5.5 we see that—

- An alternate representation should be used during practice, and the learner should receive corrective feedback.

- Examples should be divergent in critical characteristics and include a range of difficulty.

- The learner should receive fading help during practice and no help during performance testing.

Practice/Testing Performance

For the following items, italics designate CDT prescriptions.

- Classify previously unencountered examples:

  Determine whether these products are under our refrigerator warranty as of May 1, 2015.

    •MA4U2103
    •MA25D0410
    •MA16B102
    •CE12U0808

Examples have all critical attributes, are divergent, and include a range of difficulty.

•Classify examples using an alternate representation.

Ask learners to determine whether a refrigerator is under warranty using a manner different from a simple verbal description. Provide attention-focusing help and corrective feedback during practice but not during the testing performance phase.

Alternate representation with fading help and corrective feedback during practice.

CDT does not tell the instructional designer how to fulfill these prescriptions. A game or flash cards might be appropriate for helping the learner classify new examples. The generality might be presented after the examples. What matters is not the delivery or the sequencing but the prescriptions.

The same principles hold true whether designing instruction for classroom presentation or CBI. CDT postulates that instruction will achieve its objectives, given adherence to these principles.

Implementation Guide

Step	Instructions
1	Classify the type of learning according to content and performance (refer to Table 5.1 for guidance).
2	Based on the type of performance, use Table 5.2 to determine the basic instructional strategy.
3	Based on the type of content, use Table 5.3 to interpret the instructional strategy from Step 2.
4	Use Table 5.5 to identify the appropriate supplemental techniques to use.

References

Clark, R.C. (1989). *Developing technical training: A structured approach for the development of classroom and computer-based instructional materials.* Reading, MA: Addison-Wesley Publishing Company, Inc.

Ellis, J.A., & Wulfeck, W.H. (1978). *Interim training manual for the instructional quality inventory.* NPTROCTN 78-5. San Diego: Navy Personnel Research and Development Center.

Gagné, R.M. (1965). *The conditions of learning.* New York: Holt, Rinehart & Winston.

Merrill, M.D. (1983). Component display theory. In C.M. Reigeluth (Ed.), *Instructional design theories and models: An overview of their current status* (279–333). Hillsdale, NJ: Lawrence Erlbaum Associates.

Merrill, M.D. (1987). A lesson based on the component display theory. In C.M. Reigeluth (Ed.), *Instructional design theories in action* (201–234). Hillsdale, NJ: Lawrence Erlbaum Associates.

Merrill, M.D. (1988). Applying component display theory to the design of courseware. In D.H. Jonassen (Ed.), *Instructional designs for microcomputer courseware.* Hillsdale, NJ: Lawrence Erlbaum Associates.

Merrill, M.D., & Boutwell, R.C. (1973). Instructional development: Methodology and research. In F.N. Kerlinger (Ed.), *Review of research in education* (Vol. 1). Itasca, NY: Peacock.

Merrill, M.D., Drake, L.D., Lacy, M., Pratt, J., & the ID2 Research Group. (1996). Reclaiming instructional design. *Educational Technology, 36*(5), 5–7.

Merrill, M.D. with Twitchell, D.G. (Eds.). (1994). *Instructional design theory.* Englewood Cliffs, NJ: Educational Technology Publications.

Wilson, B.G. (1987, February 26-March 1). *Computers and instructional design: Component display theory in transition.* Paper presented at the Annual Convention of the Association for Educational Communications and Technology, Atlanta, GA.

Bibliography

Clark, R.C. (1999). *Developing technical training: A structured approach for developing classroom and computer-based instructional materials.* Silver Spring, MD: International Society for Performance Improvement.

Gagné, R.M., & Medsker, K.L. (1996). *The conditions of learning: Training applications.* Fort Worth, TX: Harcourt Brace.

Merrill, M.D. (1997). *Instructional transaction theory (ITT): Instructional design based on knowledge objects.* Posting to the ITFORUM Listserv, September 19. ITFORUM@UGA.CC.UGA.EDU and http://www.coe.usu.edu/it/id2/ddc0997.htm

Twitchell, D. (Ed.). (1990). Robert M. Gagné and M. David Merrill in conversation: Number 3 in series. *Educational Technology*, *30*(9), 36–41.

Twitchell, D. (Ed.). (1990). Robert M. Gagné and M. David Merrill in conversation: Number 4 in series. *Educational Technology*, *30*(10), 37–45.

Twitchell, D. (Ed.). (1990). Robert M. Gagné and M. David Merrill in conversation: Number 5 in series. *Educational Technology*, *30*(11), 35–39.

Twitchell, D.G., Anderton, G., & Parry, K. (1990). A simplified approach to the application of component display theory. *Educational Technology, 30* (4), 11–18.

About the Authors

Naomi Berkove

Naomi Berkove is an instructional designer with ACS Technology Solutions in Chicago, IL. She has consulted to both the government and private industry, designing technical and soft-skills training materials for various federal agencies and Fortune 500 companies. She completed her graduate work in instructional design at Marymount University in Arlington, Virginia.

Bobbie Moore

Bobbie Moore earned a master's degree in Human Performance Systems and a certificate in Instructional Design at Marymount University in Arlington, Virginia. She finds daily opportunities to apply rigorous performance improvement principles in her work as a development and learning associate with Schiff Consulting Group. In this capacity she provides support to Fortune 500 finance executives, with emphasis on helping corporate finance personnel to become value-added business partners.

Bobbie holds a bachelor's degree in Spanish Language and Literature from Middlebury College, is a Certified Management Accountant, and is presently working on a doctorate in Adult Education through Nova Southeastern University.

CHAPTER 6

Mnemonics

Paul T. Haley

Whether verbal, visual, musical, or poetic, mnemonics are techniques that help us remember things like names, dates, lists, and telephone numbers. Such labels and facts, for which mnemonics are designed, underlie most kinds of training, even when the focus is on problemsolving and conceptual skills.

Orators in ancient Rome used mnemonic aids. Rhymes have helped generations of bad spellers to handle "beliefs" and "receipts"[1], even on months with only 30 days[2]. Systematic research in memory developed along with cognitive and information processing models of psychology. Study of keywords as mediating links for acquiring foreign language spurred research in the 1970s and 1980s, with significant contributions from Michael Pressley and colleagues.

Mnemonics can help us organize our thoughts, remember steps in a procedure, recall the components of a formula or list, or relate two different sets of data. Mnemonic methods include loci, pegwords, and first-letter acronyms and acrostics. They can help us learn strange words via keywords and images. An investment in mastering a digit-consonant system can yield improved memory for all those numbers in our lives: phones, PINs, credit cards, HMOs.

---

[1]. "i before e except after c"

[2]. "30 days hath September, April, June, and November..."

Integrating mnemonics into the flow of training is crucial, for whatever model of learning a designer uses, mnemonics can help establish the underlying verbal knowledge needed. While not a stand-alone instructional design model, mnemonics can easily be incorporated, with big payoff, into lesson plans based on most models.

Origins

Roman orators could not write down their main points on handy 3 x 5 cards, so they used what they saw in front of them. The method of *loci* (Latin for "places") was born when an orator first decided on a series of places he would look (perhaps within the senate building) and then mentally associated each major point of his speech with a specific place. Thus he might envision grain piled against a particular column. That mental image could serve as his cue to remember to discuss grain prices.

Even when orating to legions camped along the Rubicon, a speaker could use the mental picture of those familiar places to keep on track. Today, people may base their method of loci on furniture arranged in their living rooms or stores along a shopping street.

The *peg* system was developed in 17th century England as an outgrowth of loci. Instead of places as markers, this system substituted common objects that resembled numbers. Thus 1 = candle, 8 = spectacles. The objects made it easier for people to create memorable images; to remember to talk about, say, bulldogs as the eighth item in a list, one could visualize a dog wearing spectacles. This peg system was expanded two centuries later by items chosen not for their shape, but for their rhyme: 1 = bun, 2 = shoe, 8 = gate. Here, the bulldog could be jumping over a gate.

The 17th century also saw the first *digit-letter* system to represent numbers as sequences of letters. Word forming became easier later when only consonants represented digits, with vowels just filling in (Higbee, 1993).

Though the *keyword* method had been used for some time, especially for acquiring foreign language, Atkinson and Raugh focused research on it in the mid-70s (Atkinson, 1975; Atkinson & Raugh, 1975). Their work on "acoustic" and "imagery" links was further developed by Michael Pressley, Joel Levin, and colleagues (Pressley, Levin, & Delaney, 1982).

Biographical Sketches

Michael Pressley is the Notre Dame Professor of Catholic Education and Professor of Psychology at the University of Notre Dame. He serves there as the director of the Masters in Education program.

Professor Pressley is the author of more than 200 books, articles, and chapters, making substantial contributions to the fields of children's memory, the development of reading skills, and teaching.

He currently serves as the editor of the *Journal of Educational Psychology* and is a member of a dozen other editorial boards. Mr. Pressley has been a member of the faculty of California State University, Fullerton; University of Western Ontario; University of Maryland at College Park; and University at Albany, State University of New York. In 1981 Michael married Donna Lynn Forrest. He and Donna are the proud parents of Timothy, who is now 11 years old.

Joel R. Levin is currently at the University of Wisconsin. Among his most recent publications is a book chapter, "Mnemonic Strategies for Adult Learners" (Carney & Levin, 1998).

Description

Mnemonic techniques use existing knowledge and associations to organize or encode new verbal knowledge (Bellezza, 1996). We organize things we already know to make sure we include everything and get it all in the right order. Thus, the mnemonic HOMES helps us should we ever need to name all five Great Lakes, the names of which we pretty much know. Organizing is no help for completely new labels or facts; we have to encode them.

Encoding starts by searching for anything familiar that reminds you of the new word. Imagine that you had never heard of Lake Ontario—had never even heard the word before. The first sound, "on," is a familiar preposition. Then there is "air" or a "tear," and the end is a bit like the cereal Cheerios. Now instead of one new word to remember, you have three old ones. That would be no great improvement except for our ability to create and remember images. The three words can be captured in a memorable (and unlikely) image of a person sitting on a giant inflated innertube and desperately trying to fix a tear in it before it sinks. Yes, the innertube looks like a Cheerio that is floating in one of the Great Lakes.

Organizing Mnemonics

Loci. The method of loci goes back Roman orators, but we use it every day in its simplest form. For its full potential, the method first requires memorizing a set of locations, real or imaginary, to which one can attach associations: points to make, things to do. The locations can be real; they do not have to be memorized. Create an image of your front door looking like a giant book, and chances are you will remember to take that overdue library book with you when you leave the house. Anniversary? Imagine the steering wheel of your car made of twisted rose stems, complete with thorns. Tomorrow you will buy roses.

Trainers can take advantage of places the trainees will see and touch on the job and use those loci as cues for associated memories. Keep it simple and involve as many senses as possible.

Pegword. Pegwords are just an extension of loci. The Roman senator might have held an image of wheat piled against one pillar of the senate building to remind him to talk about farm subsidies. A particularly ugly statue might cue the next point, and so on around the room. Pegwords are objects that are common enough and distinct enough to form vivid images. To place these mental objects in order, the most common technique has them rhyme with numbers (1 is a bun, 2 is a shoe, 3 is a tree, 4 is a door, etc.). Thus, a modern-day senator could remember to talk subsidies as his second point by remembering a giant shoe with wheat growing up through the laces.

The loci and pegword methods have the advantage of being multi-use and extrinsic. If one takes the time and effort to learn a system once, then those organizing cues will be available for years to come. Both systems are preferable to simple linking of cues through a link story. In that approach, the learner creates images that tie each item to the next. That pile of wheat might have a stream of water flowing through it to remind our orator of his next point: aqueduct construction. Next might come an image of soldiers floating down the water, cueing some remarks on defense. Linked intrinsic images like this share the weakness of cheap Christmas tree lights: lose one and abandon all hope. With loci or pegwords, a missed step can be skipped. Cues can also be brought up in reverse or any order.

Interference is a potential problem with any multi-use memory system. Those same sticks for point number six may be associated with so many different things that the user loses track. Studies have found that contextual cues usually help keep pegs straight, and there are techniques for varying the number or the setting of the pegs or loci (Higbee, 1993). Difficulty and effort attend this and any mnemonic system. Verhaeghen's study of mnemonic systems with older adults used the method of loci and found increasing non-compliance with age (Verhaeghen & Marcoen, 1996).

First Letters. First-letter mnemonics are inescapable in our world. An *acronym* is a group of initials that can be pronounced as a word: NASA, RAM, MADD, NAFTA, KISS. These are more memorable than abbreviations, which are pronounced letter by letter: NAACP, URL, NBA, FCC. Creating really good acronyms is a challenge that becomes a bit easier when order is not important. HOMES includes all the Great Lakes, but in no geographic order. That mnemonic is no help to remembering the positions of the lakes from west to east (SMHEO).

When the order of items is important, learners can try forming a sentence in which the first letter of each word is the same as the first letter of each item to be remembered. This is an *acrostic* sentence. The trick is to make the sentence vividly memorable, and ideally somehow associated with the subject. Examples of acrostics include the order of arithmetic operations: "Bless My Dear Aunt Sally" for brackets, multiplication, division, addition, and subtraction. Seattle residents remember the order of downtown streets, two per letter, from Jefferson and James to Pike and Pine with the mnemonic "Jesus Christ Made Seattle Under Pressure."

In this example from a career development workshop, the word "MOVIES" served as both a mnemonic device and an overall theme. As an acronym, the word helped participants to remember the six critical elements (that have related competencies) for managing their careers:

M	Marketplace
O	Opportunities
V	Values
I	Interpersonal networks
E	Education and Experience
S	Synchronicity

The workshop's designers carried out the "Movies" theme by highlighting parallels between personal career development and the scripting, casting, and production of a film. They even put up movie posters on the training room walls to reinforce the theme.

Rhymes and Alliteration. These are the ones that can live on for generations:

- Thirty days hath September. . . .
- Red Right Returning (for the color of buoys marking boating channels)
- Columbus sailed the ocean blue . . . .

Encoding Mnemonics

Keyword. Atkinson described the keyword method for learning foreign words as consisting of an "acoustic link" and an "imagery link" (1975). Pressley elaborates this into a rule composed of five parts (Pressley & El-Dinary, 1992). Notice in Table 6.1 how one could build a keyword mnemonic for a foreign word. The first step is to find an English word that sounds like the foreign word. Then an imagery link makes that sounds-like keyword stand out in memory.

Step		Description	Example
acoustic link	(a)	Identify a portion of the foreign word that physically resembles an English word.	Farsi/Persian word for "my friend" is *doostam*. The English word *dust* sounds a little like the first part.
image 1	(b)	Retrieve an image of the keyword referent.	Dust is the keyword. Imagine dust.
image 2	(c)	Retrieve an image of the referent of the foreign word translation.	Imagine a friend or friends; see an image.
	(d)	Identify a semantically meaningful context that includes both the keyword and translation referents.	How could a friend and dust act together? Friends can run to each other. Running feet kick up dust.
imagery link	(e)	Use the images of the keyword and translation referents to construct an image consistent with the semantically meaningful context.	Create an image of two friends, separated for years, happily running toward each other, not minding the dust they kick up.

Table 6.1
Keyword Method

Digit-Consonant (Phonetic). Compared to a series of numbers, words are much easier to remember. That accounts for part of the popularity of vanity license plates. Since every telephone keypad has a built-in conversion table (three letters associated with each number), businesses can advertise mnemonic phone numbers: a florist at 800-FLWRTIME, a caterer at 800-EAT-GOOD, plus GE-CARES, TRUGREEN, or 560-ROOF. There is even a website (PhoNETic.com) that will search for word conversions in any phone number.

The digit-consonant mnemonic system is a more generalized system for turning numbers into words. It uses a conversion table loosely based on graphic similarities between numbers and letters. There may be variations on the number-letter links, but Higbee describes a fairly standard conversion table. He prefers to call it the phonetic system, since it is based on the sounds consonants make in a word. Thus, both "boring" and "barring" have a single "R" sound in the middle. See Table 6.2 for some sample conversions (Higbee, 1993, p. 176).

Digit	Sound	Connection	Examples
1	t, th, d	*t* has single stroke like 1	tot (11), thin (12)
2	n	two strokes in *n*	noon (22), inner (24)
3	m	three strokes in *m*	mummy (33), minor (324)
4	r	*R* like backward 4	rat (41), ornate (421), armorer (4344)
5	l	*L* = Roman numeral 50	lily (55), little (515), lantern (52142)

Table 6.2
Digit-Consonant Method

As with the keyword method, conversion must be followed by an imagery link. Thus if the phone number of your school is 515-3241, you might create an image of a tiny rodent in a space suit ("little moon rat") walking through the school's front door.

Digit-consonant mnemonics can be applied to locker combinations, credit cards, PINs, decimal values of pi, etc. The practice can also be used to create hundreds of pegwords for organizing mnemonics. The system's power and usefulness are enormous, but so is its difficulty. To some people, however, it can become addictive; every number becomes a word puzzle.

Research Support

Several studies over the past three decades have demonstrated that mnemonic techniques enhance retention of verbal information. Now there is particular interest in individual differences, especially on aging adults (Verhaeghen & Marcoen, 1996) and learning disabled children (Mastropieri, et al., 1987). A statement by Francis Bellezza sums up current research needs:

> . . . [N]ot all mnemonic devices are successful for all types of learners, although some mnemonic procedures will be helpful for all. It follows from this conclusion that a basic problem with mnemonic instruction books written by experts is that they may be of relatively little use to a large number of interested novices, for they do not provide instruction and exercises for a variety of levels of ability and skill. Neither do they provide realistic estimates of how much practice is necessary for the average learner to move from one level of performance to the next. (Bellezza, 1996, p. 371)

Carney & Levin (1998) review much of the research on mnemonics. Among their findings are the following points:

- The keyword method has been validated in studies covering a wide range of subject matter: second language vocabulary, science concepts, states and their capitals, presidents of the United States, city attractions, etc. The method has proven generally successful for people of varying ages and abilities.

- The digit-consonant (phonetic) system for numbers and dates has met with mixed success. In one study, use of this system actually impaired recall of two-digit dates compared to the control group. In other studies it has been successful, especially when it has been kept simple.

- The method of loci has proven more successful in studies with college students than with the elderly. A followup study of the elderly found that many just stopped using the system after they learned it, even though it had brought them good results.

- The pegword method of organizational mnemonics has also been validated as more successful with college students. Older subjects achieve mixed results.

Research Support, cont.

• Delayed recall after five or more days has been worse in some studies of the pegword and keyword systems. Despite immediate recall advantages, mnemonic groups seemed to experience a more rapid rate of forgetting over time compared to control groups. Overlearning through additional rehearsal may alleviate this effect.

In their studies of the long-term durability of mnemonic effects, Hwang et al. emphasize the importance of the instructional purpose for which information is to be used (Hwang et al., 1999). If individual dates are critical (e.g., In what year was the Battle of Gettysburg? When was the Erie Canal completed?), then methods such as digit-consonant work well. If the point of the instruction is the relation of historical dates, they must be learned differently, for instance, with a timeline.

Best Uses

Mnemonics are best used for learning verbal information—things that must be recalled, such as names, labels, lists (in order or not), steps in procedures, etc. This kind of knowledge decays easily, and we want it to remain accessible in long-term memory A synopsis of sample uses for mnemonic devices is shown graphically in Figure 6.1, and is further described in Table 6.3.

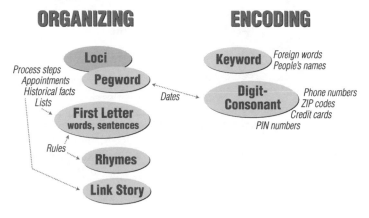

Figure 6.1
Organizing and Encoding

Use	Method	Examples
Process steps (order important)	Loci or Pegword, first-letter sentence or word	Loci (in a house) for photo darkroom steps: 1. Enter through door ...developer 2. Next visit bathroom ...wash 3. Then the kitchen ...fixer The ABC steps of CPR rescue: • A: Airway • B: Breathing • C: Circulation
Lists (order not important)	Loci, Pegword, first-letter word or sentence	"RICE" treatment for sports injury: Rest, Ice, Compression, Elevate
Rules	First letter or rhyme	"A pint's a pound the world around."
Dates	Digit-Consonant Pegword	1512—"tell town"
Names	Keyword	Renfrew sounds like *run throw.* Imagine Ms. Renfrew in a javelin competition.
ZIP code, PIN number	Digit-Consonant	22141 = "none to read"
Foreign words	Keyword	"endaxi" means OK in Greek. Sounds like *in taxi.* Imagine a happy traveler in a taxi.

Table 6.3
Uses for Mnemonic Methods

Model in Action

Using public transportation is part of the orientation of new employees in this example set in the Virginia suburbs of Washington, DC. Many employees will use the Metrorail system for travel between downtown sites and suburban offices. Memorizing the names and order of stations along one line will help trainees feel more comfortable in their new surroundings.

José, the trainer, limits the task to the stations on Metrorail's orange line west of the Potomac. There are nine stops. He knows it is unlikely the initial letters will form a word, especially since they must be kept in order. The letters could, however, be used to form a rather long acrostic sentence (like "Bless my dear Aunt Sally"). Complicating matters, several names are longer than one word. Ideally, José would like to choose words that suggest these compound names. Table 6.4 shows his first ideas:

Station Name	Initial	First Try	Second Try
Vienna	V	Very	Vinny
Dunn Loring	Dl	Delicious	Delivers
West Falls Church	Wfc	Westfall	Waffles (at)
East Falls Church	Efc	Eastfill	Easter (then)
Ballston	B	Ball, bell	Borrows
Virginia Square	Vs	Virgins	Viagra (for)
Clarendon	Cl	Clans	Clams
Courthouse	Co	Count	Courting
Rosslyn	R	Roses	Roses

Table 6.4
First-Letter Acrostic for Stations

The resulting acrostic sentence is long and awkward: "Vinny delivers waffles at Easter, then borrows Viagra for clams courting roses." Its only virtue is that it contains some memorable images, such as carrying giant waffles into a church (Falls Church) decked out for Easter.

José goes back to the drawing board. Perhaps he was trying to have the mnemonic do too much. He decides to concentrate on the order of the stations. The uneven number nine means there is one station in the middle, Ballston, with four on either side. This brings to mind an image of a plank balancing over a ball. This is a simple, memorable image that serves two purposes. The keyword "ball" cues the name "Ballston," and the balancing image chunks the remaining stations into two manageable groups of four.

Encouraged, José takes another look at first letters: V D W E B V C C R. This time he notices a word embedded there: WEB. With a major stretch, he considers "ViDeo WEB ViCCaR." Every consonant represents a station so long as everyone remembers to misspell "vicar."

At this point José talks with his trainees about the difficulties he has had. They like the image of balancing on Ballston but think José is trying too hard to get every-thing else to fit. One student says her main problem is remembering the station between Vienna and the two Falls Church stops. Someone suggests the keyword "dawn" for Dunn Loring. Immediately José puts together an image and statement of backward cosmography: "Vienna dawns from west to east." The first trainee really likes this. From now on, every time she thinks of the Vienna station, she will imagine that town's musical namesake in the pink light of dawn. That will remind her of Dunn Loring, with West and East Falls Church right after that.

Encouraged by their success with that chunk of four stations, José and the trainees turn their attention to the "VCCR" on the other side of Ballston. One of the trainees says that remembering Rosslyn is no problem; it is a major station and a junction of two Metro routes. The hard part, he says, is remembering the order of Courthouse and Clarendon. Which comes first? Someone else in the class says she always for-gets about Virginia Square completely. José suggests that they use the strong image of the ball for Ballston and imagine that ball rolling into a square. It could be a child's playground game of four-square.

Someone then suggests a way to handle the Clarendon-Courthouse confusion. She says that Rosslyn reminds her of roses (keyword), and she can see an image of roses growing just outside a house. That establishes the Courthouse station next to Rosslyn. Next, a trainee in the back speaks up to offer a rhyming link for Claren-don. It half rhymes, he says, with its neighbor, Virginia Square/Clar-endon. Several trainees groan, but they are not likely to forget.

José tells the trainees that he hopes the experience of coming up with keywords, images, rhymes, and acrostics will help them throughout all their learning. He admits that looking for mnemonic devices can become addictive. In this little exer-cise about station names they learned the importance of not trying to do too much with a mnemonic device. Just concentrate on clearing up the areas of confusion, and remember: K.I.S.S.

Implementation Guide

Step	Design Instructions
1. Identify Opportunities	Survey the entire instructional process and body of content to identify opportunities for using mnemonic techniques. These opportunities might include major themes (like the "MOVIES" example), critical dates or people, unfamiliar terms or foreign words, process steps (as in the ABCs of CPR), and things that are easily confused (buoy should be on the left or right?).
2. Select Technique	Select an appropriate mnemonic technique (see Table 6.3). Consider whether you need an organizing or an encoding device and whether the order of items is important.
3. Create Mnemonic	Create the mnemonic and/or decide to involve trainees in creation. This may require brainstorming or even synectics. If time allows, encourage trainees to generate their own mnemonic associations as much as possible. Be sensitive to a reluctance to create mental imagery, found more often among older adults. Provide "starter" keywords, images, etc., as needed to avoid frustration. Children younger than sixth grade tend to do better with provided images (Higbee, 1993).
4. Insert in Lesson Design	Insert in overall lesson design. Use it several times if possible. Integrate and expand it throughout the lesson. Present the new technique in a context of need-to-know information. Provide lots of opportunities to practice and for trainees to monitor their own progress.
5. Encourage Rehearsal	Encourage participants to rehearse often and "overlearn" the material. Do not be surprised if you have to resuggest using mnemonic techniques that trainees previously learned and applied.

References

Atkinson, R.C. (1975). Mnemontechnics in second-language learning. *American Psychologist, 30*, 821–828.

Atkinson, R.C., & Raugh, M.R. (1975). An application of the mnemonic keyword method to the acquisition of a Russian vocabulary. *Journal of Experimental Psychology: Human Learning and Memory, 1*, 126–133.

Bellezza, F.S. (1996). Mnemonic methods to enhance storage and retrieval. In E.L. Bjork & R.A. Bjork (Eds.), *Memory: Handbook of perception and cognition* (2nd ed.) (345–380). San Diego: Academic Press.

Carney, R.N., & Levin, J.R. (1998). Mnemonic strategies for adult learners. In M.C. Smith (Ed.), *Adult learning and development: Perspectives from educational psychology* (159–175). Mahwah, NJ: Lawrence Erlbaum Associates.

Higbee, K.L. (1993). *Your memory: How it works and how to improve it* (2nd ed.). New York: Paragon House.

Hwang, Y., Renandya, W.A., Levin, J.R., Levin, M.E., Glasman, L.D., & Carney, R.N. (1999). A pictorial numeric system for improving students' factual memory. *Journal of Mental Imagery, 23*(1–2), 45–69.

Mastropieri, M.A., Scruggs, T.E., & Levin, J.R. (1987). Learning-disabled students' memory for expository prose: Mnemonic versus nonmnemonic pictures. *American Educational Research Journal, 24*, 505–519.

Pressley, M., & El-Dinary, P. (1992). Memory strategy instruction that promotes good information processing. In D. Hermann et al., (Eds.), *Memory improvement: Implications for memory theory*. New York: Springer-Verlag.

Pressley, M., Levin, J., & Delaney, H. (1982). The mnemonic keyword method. *Review of Educational Research, 52*, 61–91.

Verhaeghen, P., & Marcoen, A. (1996). On the mechanisms of plasticity in young and older adults after instruction in the method of loci: Evidence for an amplification model. *Psychology & Aging, 11*(1), 164–178.

Bibliography

Gruneberg, M. (1992). The practical application of memory aids: Knowing how, knowing when, and knowing when not. In M. Gruneberg, & P. Morris (Eds.), *Aspects of memory* (2nd ed.) Vol. 1: The practical aspects. New York and London: Routledge.

Healy, A.F., & Sinclair, G. (1996). The long-term retention of training and instruction. In E.L. Bjork & R.A. Bjork (Eds.), *Memory: Handbook of perception and cognition* (2nd ed.), (525–564). San Diego: Academic Press.

McCormick, C., & Pressley, M. (1997). *Educational psychology: Learning, instruction, assessment.* New York: Longman.

Rupp, R. (1998). *Committed to memory.* New York: Crown.

About the Author

Paul T. Haley is a performance technologist with Human Performance Systems, Inc. in Washington, DC, where he specializes in instructional design and instructional delivery systems. Recent clients include Goodwill Industries, ITT Systems, Allegis Group, Caliber Learning, and The World Bank. Paul earned a BA in English from Stanford University, an MA in Communications from the University of Pennsylvania, and an Instructional Design Certificate from Marymount University. He taught English as a Peace Corps volunteer in Iran and served as a media designer and audiovisual producer for the American Red Cross. Later, he taught computer skills and served as a distance learning production specialist at Central Piedmont Community College, Charlotte, North Carolina. More recently, he taught seminars on using the World Wide Web for the Arlington County (VA) schools and George Mason University.

CHAPTER 7

Synectics

Letitia A. Combs and Ramona L. Lush

Synectics is an instructional method for enhancing creative thought. It is based on structural processes of invention and creative problemsolving that have been used successfully in business for designing and modifying products (Gordon, 1961). The word synectics has its base in the Greek word *syn*, meaning "together" and *ectics*, chosen arbitrarily (Prince, 1982) and meaning joining together of different and apparently irrelevant elements (Gordon, 1961; Prince, 1970).

William J. J. Gordon coined the term synectics for his particular approach to creative problemsolving. This approach consists of two primary methods. The first method is making the strange familiar, using what is already known to understand that which is not known. The second method is making the familiar strange, developing a new understanding by viewing something that is known in a new, creative way (Sanders & Sanders, 1984).

The synectics model is based on Gordon's original creative problemsolving method—using metaphor and analogy. Through metaphor and analogy the learner can view a problem in a new way, establish a relationship of likeness between two items, and connect the familiar with the unfamiliar. The strange can be made familiar by comparing the new concept with a known concept. Conversely, the learner can also use metaphor and analogy to gain a new outlook through making the familiar strange.

For learning to progress, learners often need to view familiar things in a new way. Synectics can be used to facilitate that process. Through the use of metaphor and analogy, learners examine designated items from a fresh perspective. Thereby, they can gain a new understanding of those items or situations, can empathize with previously unfamiliar objects, create new solutions, or redesign familiar things.

A second important situation is for learners to understand and assimilate new material. In this case, synectics can be used to analyze the new information. Using analogies, learners can compare the new with the familiar to identify similarities and differences between the new and the known, gradually gaining understanding of the new.

Origins

Evolution of the Synectics Process

Gordon first started research on creative thinking in his Harvard laboratory in the 1940s. How creativity can (or should) be defined has been in dispute throughout the history of academic study of the concept. Traditional views held that you either had it or you didn't, and that it was inspired and artistic in nature. Gordon's research was directed toward dispelling the elitist view of the creative process and changing that process to an egalitarian activity. He sought to identify the quality of creativity and to develop an approach to teach individuals to become creative.

In 1944, Gordon and his associates began a series of observations of the process of *invention*. They observed that four inter-related psychological states were present when invention occurred:

1. *Detachment and Involvement*—The feeling that an inventor described as being removed from the outside world while experiencing closeness with the subject of his work. This could also be characterized as initially taking an omnipotent view, and then moving to a first-person view.

2. *Deferment*—The sense that it was difficult, though necessary, to guard against premature attempts at solution.

3. *Speculation*—The ability to let the mind run free.

4. *Autonomy of Object*—The feeling described at the end of the invention process that the invention is a thing on its own, separate from the inventor.

During the next few years, further research conducted with both artists and scientists led to the identification of "increasingly clear, recurrent patterns of mental activity which accompanied the creative process" (Gordon, 1961).

As early as 1956, Gordon was using an approach that he called *operational creativity*—a precursor of his synectics process. Although Gordon originally targeted his work for use in industrial settings, he speculated that his methodologies also had educational functions and potential for applications in other environments (Gordon, 1956).

He believed that the only way to truly understand the nature of creativity was through observation of the creative process and by changing that process while in action. From his research with industrial groups and his observation of the creative problemsolving process, Gordon developed the following assumptions that challenged conventional views of creativity:

1. Creativity is important in everyday activities.
2. The creative process in human beings can be concretely described, and that description can be used in teaching methodology to increase the creative output of both individuals and groups.
3. The cultural phenomena of invention in the arts and in science are analogous and are characterized by the same fundamental psychological processes.
4. Individual process in the creative enterprise is directly analogous with group process (Gordon, 1961).

Synectics Assumptions

Gordon (1961) formalized his assumptions into a working theory of creative problemsolving. His synectics theory was based on these assumptions:

1. Creative efficiency can be markedly increased if people understand the psychological process by which they operate.
2. In the creative process, the emotional component is more important than the intellectual; the irrational is more important than the rational.
3. It is the emotional, irrational elements that must be understood to increase the probability of success in a problemsolving situation.

Application

Armed with the theory, Gordon's company conducted synectics sessions with hundreds of different businesses and institutions (Gordon, 1972) that yielded a variety of innovative products. For example, a synectics session produced the concept and design of Pringles potato chips. The stated problem was how to pack chips compactly, without breaking them, and the inspiration for the solution came from wet leaves stacked together. Other examples of successful inventions conceived through the use of the synectics process are a trash compactor, the electric knife, an early NASA space suit closure device, disposable diapers, a Ford truck frame suspension system, an accelerated wound-healing system, and operating table covers (Davis, 1999).

Biographical Sketch

William J. J. Gordon's background includes quite a spectrum of experiences. He has been a schoolteacher, horse handler, salvage diver, ambulance driver, ski instructor, sailing schooner master, college lecturer, and pig breeder. Gordon holds numerous patents and his creative writing collaborations with colleagues have been published in *The New Yorker* and *The Atlantic Monthly*. His publications have garnered an O. Henry Short Story Award and a Science Fiction Award (Davis, 1999).

Gordon first developed the concept of *operational creativity* while conducting industrial research with the Invention Design Group of Arthur D. Little, Inc. In 1966, he and coworker George Prince left to form their own company, Synectics, Inc. (Gordon, 1961; Prince, 1970). In the early 1970s, the name of their company changed to Synectics Educational Systems (SES), the structure under which Gordon and Prince published a number of synectics creative problemsolving workbooks.

Description

In synectics, the creative process is defined as the mental activity that results in artistic or technical creations. Synectics is not concerned with the motivations for creative activity, nor is it intended to be used to judge the ultimate product of an aesthetic or technical invention (Gordon, 1961). It is concerned with how creativity occurs and with how groups and individuals can use the creative process.

Synectics makes creativity a conscious process. Gordon (1961) described his work as "an attempt to describe those conscious, preconscious and subconscious psychological states which are present in any creative act." Creative activity depends on, and emerges from, participants' knowledge and experiences, helping to connect ideas from familiar content to those from new content or to view familiar content from a new perspective. Use of the synectics strategies puts into practice the various principles of synectics theory (Gordon, 1961). The model is shown graphically in Figure 7.1

Synectics focuses on metaphor and analogy to prompt creative connections in the learner's mind. The use of metaphor and analogy encourages development of a novel viewpoint and lessens the tendency to overanalyze a situation by focusing attention on emotional elements.

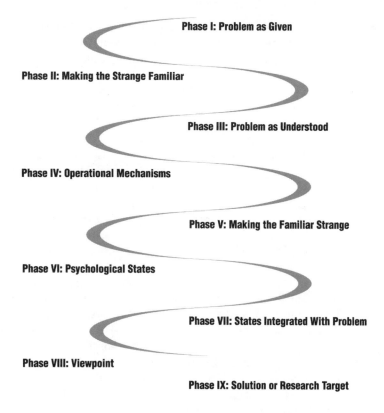

Phase I: Problem as Given

Phase II: Making the Strange Familiar

Phase III: Problem as Understood

Phase IV: Operational Mechanisms

Phase V: Making the Familiar Strange

Phase VI: Psychological States

Phase VII: States Integrated With Problem

Phase VIII: Viewpoint

Phase IX: Solution or Research Target

Figure 7.1
Synectics Model

Making the Familiar Strange and Making the Strange Familiar

Gordon's research observations convinced him that the two most effective strategies for a group to collectively reach the required psychological states (*detachment and involvement, deferment, speculation*, and *autonomy of object*) for creative problemsolving were making the familiar strange and making the strange familiar (Gordon, 1961; 1976). Both strategies use the same metaphorical mechanisms to facilitate the creative process. Making the familiar strange (to create something new) requires the learners to create a series of analogies, without logical constraints, to free the imagination and increase conceptual distance. In making the strange familiar, the learners seek to understand new or difficult concepts, using familiar metaphors to help analyze the unfamiliar material (Joyce & Weil, 1996).

The Metaphorical Way of Learning and Knowing

Metaphor is an expressed or implied comparison that produces simultaneously meaningful intellectual illumination and emotional excitement (Gordon, 1961). Lakoff and Johnson (1980) see metaphor as a mechanism by which we live—"metaphors partially structure our everyday concepts, and that this structure is reflected in our literal language." This structure includes both orientational (up-down, front-back, on-off, center-periphery, and near-far) metaphors and ontological (entity and substance, container, and personification) metaphors.

Recently, the concept of metaphor has been revitalized as a result of the convergence of interest from a variety of disciplines, including neurobiology, linguistics, and cognitive sciences. Metaphor is viewed as being rooted in two senses: first, metaphor is used to organize bodily sensation cognitively, especially affects; second, metaphor is rooted in the body as it rests on the border between mind and brain. Metaphor is therefore considered as a developmentally early, mental function and also as an emergent property of mind (Modell, 1997).

From this perspective of metaphor as a way of learning and knowing, synectics takes advantage of a naturally occurring phenomenon: "Metaphor is principally a way of conceiving one thing in terms of another, and its primary function is understanding" (Lakoff & Johnson, 1980). The most familiar types of metaphor are analogy and simile. Analogy focuses on a similarity of relations or function. Simile emphasizes the excitement generated when two relatively unlike things have qualities attributed to each other (Gordon, 1961). Gordon incorporates elements of both analogy and simile in the four metaphorical mechanisms that he instituted with his synectics approach to creative problemsolving.

Metaphorical Mechanisms

Gordon believed that these four mechanisms (personal analogy, direct analogy, fantasy analogy, and symbolic analogy) constituted the basis for creative learning and innovation. He saw these mechanisms as indispensable, specific, and reproducible mental processes for the implementation of synectics—tools to initiate the motion of creative process that are necessary to sustain and renew that motion. He further stated that through practice, they become habitual ways of seeing and acting. Even individuals who by habit unconsciously use one or more synectics techniques have been observed to intensify their own creative effectiveness through use of the formalized synectics process (Gordon, 1961).

Personal Analogy. Personal identification with the elements of a situation releases the individual from viewing the problem in terms of its previously analyzed elements and therefore can result in new insights. Learners must identify with the ideas or objects to be compared. They must empathize with and become the object. For example, by identifying himself with a snake swallowing its tail, Kekule developed an insight into the benzene molecule in terms of a ring rather than a chain of carbon atoms. There is also Keat's own description of his writing of Endymion: "I leaped headlong into the sea, and thereby have become better acquainted with the sounds, the quicksand, and the rocks, than if I had stayed upon the green shore and piped a silly pipe, and took tea and comfortable advice" (Gordon, 1961).

The application of personal analogy requires loss of self. As the loss of self becomes more extensive, the likelihood that an innovative result will occur becomes greater.   Gordon identifies four levels of personal analogy:

- *First-person description of facts*—Known facts are stated, but no new insights are presented. For example, students in a Civil War history class could be asked, "You live in Gettysburg and you are watching the battle take place around you. Describe what you see."

- *First-person identification with emotion*—Known emotions are stated, but no new insights are presented. The same students could be asked to describe the emotions they feel as residents of Gettysburg or as soldiers fighting in the battle.

- *Empathetic identification with a living thing*—Emotional and kinesthetic identity is established with the subject of the analogy. After watching the movie *Gettysburg*, the students can feel the emotions of the residents and soldiers at Gettysburg, not just describe those emotions.

- *Empathetic identification with a nonliving thing*—Identity is established with an inorganic object and a situation is explored from the perspective of that object. For example, a student may describe the current state of the Gettysburg battlefield: "I feel tired, so many people walk on me every day. My grass is worn down. But I also feel proud that visitors come here to learn about my history" (Joyce & Weil, 1996).

Direct Analogy. Direct analogy is the comparison of unlike items. The purpose is to gain understanding about the new item by comparing it with a familiar item. Learners create a simple comparison of two objects or concepts. For example, insight into emotions is often gained by comparison with colors (e.g., red = anger). The use of mechanical tools can often be better understood by comparing them to similar natural items, such as a comparison between a helicopter rotor and a maple seed twirling its way to the earth. During World War II, Gordon participated in an emergency response group charged with removing a sunken ship blocking Tripoli harbor. An Army colonel's visualization of his mother, separating clumps of dirt from her garden and raking it smooth, suggested the eventual solution—blasting the ship into pieces and "raking" it level (Davis, 1999).

Fantasy Analogy. The fantasy analogy requires the learner to imagine the wildest, far-out, wonderful, ideal solutions, which through the process of working backward from ideal goals stimulates practical ideas. Gordon (1961) used the expression "conscious self-deceit" to indicate that "the problem solver must be aware of the laws which conflict with his ideal solution—yet he must be willing to pretend the laws don't exist." For example, to escape a traffic jam, the person might imagine the car sprouting wings and flying over the traffic. He viewed this approach as a kind of Freudian wish-fulfillment strategy. A similar approach, described by Prince, is the "get fired technique" in which the original idea must be so outrageous that if you presented it in the initial form to the company president, he would immediately fire you (Davis, 1999).

Symbolic Analogy. Symbolic analogy, also known as compressed conflict, uses apparent oxymorons to describe items in a creative manner. Prince (1975) also refers to this mechanism as essential paradox. Learners develop a two-word description of an object or concept in which the words seems to be contradictory, or in opposition. For example, the process of sublimation of dry ice can be described as "cold steam." Or chocolate can taste "bittersweet." Similarly, conflicting images and concepts can be placed in juxtaposition with one another. Learners can be asked if a volcano has a right to erupt, or what the city of Washington, DC would be like if it were suddenly transported to Morocco.

Best Uses

Synectics is best used in situations requiring creative thought or action. It works well for enabling learners to view situations from a fresh perspective. Some of the best opportunities for the use of synectics techniques in educational environments occur when the learners are examining an abstract concept, exploring a social issue, or solving a problem (including conflict resolution). Synectics techniques can also be used during creative writing to gain fresh perspectives and break writer's blocks (Joyce & Weil, 1996).

Strengths

As a model of instruction, synectics has several strengths. It is appropriate for use in both business and educational environments (Gordon, 1961). It can also be used successfully with a wide range of ages. Additionally, the model works well with learners who withdraw from more academic learning activities because they are not willing to risk being wrong (Joyce & Weil, 1996).

Synectics can be used as a stand-alone approach or combined easily with other models of instruction. As a stand-alone model, synectics can be used to teach creative problemsolving. In combination with other models, it can stretch concepts being learned from an information-processing perspective; or it can open dimensions of social issues being explored through role playing and group investigation (Joyce & Weil, 1996). Synectics can also be used to complement other instructional models such as inquiry training, by encouraging divergent thinking while examining issues and generating hypotheses. In today's business environment, synectics could be used very effectively with business process re-engineering teams or other teams charged with creating innovative strategies or products. A synectics session could also do double duty as a team-building exercise.

Limitations

Creative problemsolving is time intensive. The synectics process as a creative problemsolving methodology becomes more effective over time. Learners need some time to get comfortable with the techniques and assimilate their use as "second nature." It is better suited to a group that works together on a continuous basis rather than a group that's just forming or is together for a very short period (Gordon, 1961). Additionally, high achieving learners who are only comfortable giving an answer that they can document as "right" are often reluctant to participate (Joyce & Weil, 1996).

Model in Action

Divergent thinking is critical to crafting innovative business and management strategies. The example in Table 7.1 illustrates how the imaginative, and often emotional, aspects of synectics can be used in such cases. In this illustration, the participants have been asked to craft a new vision statement for their own small consulting business. The facilitator's role is to guide the participants in employing the metaphorical mechanism and selecting analogies to take forward through the process.

Sample Synectics Exercise

Phase	Description
Current Situation	Facilitator has participants describe and profile their consulting business. Participants list and discuss what they see as the three key characteristics of their specific consulting business and use them to create a draft corporate vision statement.
Direct Analogy	Participants are given a small white box full of small, assorted objects and asked to describe it. A sample collection of items might contain multicolored jelly beans, buttons, push pins, toy figurines, a door hinge, coins, nails, safety pins, twist ties, a feather, a rock, and a small mirror. Time allowed: 5–10 minutes.
	Participants are asked to compare the collection of items in the box to the consulting business. Responses are recorded. One analogy—"A consulting business is like a kaleidoscope"—is selected and the participants describe why this is so in further detail.
Personal Analogy	Participants are asked to "become" a kaleidoscope. Personal analogies are created to describe what it is like to be a kaleidoscope. The facilitator guides the participants through first-person description of facts, first-person identification with emotion, and empathetic identification with a nonliving object. Responses include "I feel as though all light and color pass through me. I have the power to separate that light and color into many different patterns from simple forms to complex."

Table 7.1
Sample Synectics Exercise

Phase	Description
Compressed Conflict	Participants review their analogies from phases two and three, suggest several compressed conflicts, and choose one. Systematic randomness is selected for further study.
Direct Analogy	Students generate and select another direct analogy, based on the compressed conflict of systematic randomness. The selected direct analogy is, "The consulting business is like systematic randomness." A good consultant needs to know how to spot trends and find the pattern of the customer's needs. Participants use the selected direct analogy to rewrite their vision statements. Time allowed: 10–20 minutes. The group compares the resulting "visions" to the original works.

Table 7.1
Sample Synectics Exercise (cont.)

Implementation Guide

Instructional strategies using synectics are designed to provide a structure through which students can free themselves to apply imagination and insight into everyday activities (Joyce & Weil, 1996).

Synectics can be used alone to create something new, or it can also be used in conjunction with other models to allow students to view a familiar subject in a new way. The role of the facilitator is to guide the learner through all the steps of invention and specifically guard against closure.

Joyce and Weil (1996) developed instructional models for implementing both synectics strategies. The following implementation guides summarize and illustrate these models.

Making the Familiar Strange

Scenario: Participants in a seminar are learning to develop creative websites. Their current challenge is to come up with an engaging theme for a new website, which will be designed as a class project. The seminar facilitator has chosen to use a synectics strategy to get participants to be more creative in developing theme ideas.

Phase	Description	Example
Current Situation or Problem	Learners describe and examine a current situation or problem, isolating key aspects to enhance their own understanding of the situation or problem.	Facilitator engages participants in a discussion of what makes an engaging theme for a website, the importance of matching the theme to the intended audience, and reasons to avoid certain themes (e.g., cultural sensitivity).
Direct Analogy	Learners select an analogy that provides the strangest comparison with the problem situation. They explore (describe) the analogy's characteristics, then compare them with the original problem situation.	Facilitator asks participants to brainstorm possible analogies and posts all their ideas. Participants select a rhinoceros as being the strangest comparison on the list. They brainstorm characteristics of a rhinoceros, then say how these characteristics apply to a website.
Personal Analogy	Learners "become" the analogy selected in the direct analogy phase and identify the feelings of the analogy.	Learners describe how it feels to be a rhinoceros. The facilitator focuses them on feelings, not characteristics, and posts their ideas.
Compressed Conflict	Learners select pairs of words (from lists already posted) that argue or conflict with each other, then select one pair that expresses the truest conflict.	Learners generate a list of possible conflict pairs. Through discussion, they finally select "humble-powerful" as the word pair that expresses the truest conflict.
Direct Analogy	Learners select another direct analogy, based on the chosen compressed conflict—the one that seems the most exciting.	Several possible images that represent "humble-powerful" are generated. Through discussion, the participants finally select a mountain-climbing guide as the most exciting analogy.
Original Situation or Problem	Learners use entire experience to solve the original problem or reflect on the situation in new ways.	Participants explore the possibility of using mountain climbing as a theme for their website. Other possible themes emerge through reflection on the whole exercise.

Making the Strange Familiar

Scenario: Engineering professors are participating in an instructional design seminar. The goal is for them to improve the instructional design of the courses they teach. In this segment, they are being introduced to the concept of "behavioral objective." Previously, none of the participants have used behavioral objectives, and past experience indicates that participants will find it difficult to write their own behavioral objectives.

Phase	Description	Example
Information on New Topic	Instructor provides information on a new or difficult topic to be learned.	Instructor provides an overview of what behavior objectives are, why they are important for improving instruction, and the three key components of a behavioral objective.
Direct Analogy	Instructor suggests a direct analogy and asks learners to describe the analogy.	Instructor suggests that behavioral objectives may be compared with engineering requirements or specifications. Participants are asked to describe and give examples of engineering requirements and specifications.
Personal Analogy	Learners "become" the analogy and identify the feelings of the analogy.	Instructor asks participants to put themselves in the place of engineering requirements and specifications and describe how they feel. (This activity should help to raise awareness of the central purpose and critical importance of requirements and specifications.)
Compare Analogies	Learners explore points of similarity between the direct analogy and the new topic.	Instructor asks participants to compare engineering requirements and specifications with behavioral objectives for instruction. Participants list points of similarity (e.g., guide design activities, support measurable results).
Contrast Analogies	Learners explore points of difference between the direct analogy and the new topic.	Instructor asks participants to contrast engineering requirements and specifications with behavioral objectives for instruction. Participants list points of dissimilarity (e.g., human vs. nonhuman).
Original Situation or Problem	Learners explore the original topic.	Participants discuss the purpose, value, and key components of behavioral objectives.
New Direct Analogies	Learners provide their own direct analogy and explore similarities and differences.	In this case, further analogies may not be required, but another possible analogy would be professional certification criteria.

References

Davis, G.A. (1999). *Creativity is forever.* Dubuque, IA: Kendall/Hunt Publishing Company.

Gordon, W.J.J. (1956). Operational approach to creativity. *Harvard Business Review, 34*(6), 41–51.

Gordon, W.J.J. (1961). *Synectics: The development of creative capacity.* New York: Harper & Row.

Gordon, W.J.J. (1972). On being explicit about the creative process. *Journal of Creative Behavior, 6*(4), 295–300.

Gordon, W.J.J. (1976). Metaphor and invention. In A. Rothenberg & C.R. Hausman (Eds.), *The creativity question* (251–255). Durham, NC: Duke University Press.

Joyce, B., & Weil, M. (1996). *Models of teaching* (5th ed.). Boston: Allyn and Bacon.

Lakoff, G., & Johnson, M. (1980). *Metaphors we live by.* Chicago and London: The University of Chicago Press.

Modell, A.H. (1997). The synergy of memory, affects, and metaphor. *The Journal of Analytical Psychology: An International Quarterly of Jungian Practice and Theory, 42*(1), 105–117.

Prince, G.M. (1970). *The practice of creativity: A manual for dynamic problem solving.* New York: Harper & Row.

Prince, G.M. (1975). Creativity, self, and power. In I.A. Taylor & J.W. Getzels (Eds.), *Perspectives in creativity* (249–277). Chicago: Aldine Publishing Co.

Prince, G.M. (1982). Synectics. In S.A. Olsen (Ed.), *Group planning and problem solving methods in engineering* (62–68). New York: Wiley.

Sanders, D.A., & Sanders, J.A. (1984). *Teaching creativity through metaphor.* New York: Longman, Inc.

Bibliography

Alexander, T. (1978). Inventing by the madness method. In G.A. Davis & J.A. Scott (Eds.), *Training creative thinking.* Melbourne, FL: Krieger.

Couch, R. (1993). *Synectics and imagery: Developing creative thinking through images*. (Clearinghouse No. IR16449). Dublin, OH: OCLC Online Computer Library Center, Inc. (ERIC Document Reproduction Service No. ED36330).

Gordon, W.J.J. (1965). The metaphorical way of knowing. In G. Kepes (Ed.), *Education of vision*. New York: George Braziller.

Gordon, W.J.J. (1966). *The metaphorical way of learning and knowing*. Cambridge, MA: Porpoise Books.

Gordon, W.J.J. (1974a). *Making it strange*. Books 1–4. New York: Harper & Row.

Gordon, W.J.J. (1974b). Some source material in discovery by analogy. *Journal of Creative Behavior, 8*, 239–257.

Gordon, W.J.J. (1980). Discovery by analogy. *Chemtech, 10*(3), 166–171.

Gordon, W.J.J. (1987). *The new art of the possible: The basic course in synectics*. Cambridge, MA: SES Associates.

Gordon, W.J.J., & Poze, T. (1971a). *The basic course in synectics*. Cambridge, MA: Porpoise Books.

Gordon, W.J.J., & Poze, T. (1971b). *The metaphorical way of knowing and learning*. Cambridge, MA: SES Associates.

Gordon, W.J.J., & Poze, T. (1972a). *Teaching is listening*. Cambridge, MA: SES Associates.

Gordon, W.J.J., & Poze, T. (1972b). *Strange and familiar*. Cambridge, MA: SES Associates.

Gordon, W.J.J., & Poze, T. (1980a). *Non-literal analogy practice in the basic course in synectics*. Cambridge, MA: Porpoise Books.

Gordon, W.J.J., & Poze, T. (1980b). SES synectics and gifted education today. *Gifted Child Quarterly, 24*, 147–151.

Gordon, W.J.J., & Poze, T. (1980c). *The new art of the possible*. Cambridge, MA: Porpoise Books.

Gordon, W.J.J., & Poze, T. (1981). Conscious/subconscious interaction in a creative act. *Journal of Creative Behavior, 6*(4), 295–300.

Indurkhya, B. (1992). Metaphor and cognition: An interactionist approach. *Studies in Cognitive Systems, 13*, 411–413.

Isaksen, S.G., & Parnes, S.J. (1992). Curriculum planning for creative thinking and problem solving. In S.J. Parnes (Ed.), *Source book for creative problem solving: A fifty year digest of proven innovation processes* (422–440). Buffalo, NY: Creative Education Foundation Press.

Khatena, J. (1975). Creative imagery and analogy. *The Gifted Child Quarterly, 19*(2),149–160.

Malaga, R.A. (1998). *The effect of stimuli modes in individual creativity enhancing decision support systems.* Unpublished doctoral dissertation, George Mason University, Fairfax, VA.

Maltzman, I. (1960). On the training of originality. *Psychological Review, 67*(4), 229–242.

Osborne, A.F. (1963). *Applied imagination: Principles and procedures of creative problem-solving.* New York: Charles Scribner's Sons.

Prince, G.M. (1992a). The operational mechanism of synectics. In S.J. Parnes (Ed.), *Source book for creative problem solving: A fifty year digest of proven innovation processes* (168–177). Buffalo, NY: Creative Education Foundation Press.

Prince, G.M. (1992b). The mindspring theory: A new development from synectics research. In S.J. Parnes (Ed.), *Source book for creative problem solving: A fifty year digest of proven innovation processes* (177–193). Buffalo, NY: Creative Education Foundation Press.

Shekerjian, D. (1990). *Uncommon genius: How great ideas are born.* New York: Penguin Books.

Stein, M.I. (1992). Creativity programs in sociohistorical context. In S.J. Parnes (Ed.), *Source book for creative problem solving: A fifty year digest of proven innovation processes* (85–88). Buffalo, NY: Creative Education Foundation Press.

Von Oech, R. (1986). *A kick in the seat of the pants.* New York: Harper & Row.

About the Authors

Letitia Combs

Dr. Letitia Combs joined the faculty of Virginia Polytechnic Institute and State University (Virginia Tech) in 1995 and served as Assistant Director of the Virginia Tech Northern Virginia Center from 1996 to 1997. She teaches graduate courses in instructional design, instructional facilitation, distance learning, knowledge management, and educational research and evaluation. Dr. Combs received her MS and EdD in Vocational Technical Education from Virginia Tech. She has been national President of Omicron Tau Theta, the professional honorary society in vocational and technical education, and she is the founder and an editorial board member of the *Journal of Vocational and Technical Education.*

She is additionally employed at Vertex Solutions, a distance learning and educational technology firm. She has developed prototype programs that prepare Welfare to Work recipients and displaced workers to meet information technology (IT) job needs. Dr. Combs has directed four national workforce certification testing programs that were administered to more than15,000 workers. She has conducted occupational analyses and developed education programs for fields including computer science and electrical engineering. She has designed occupational aptitude tests and accompanying student programs to meet IT industry needs. She has also developed leadership, life skills, employability and technical education programs for residents of low-income housing developments and has directed a $5 million national training program of 200+ annual programs.

Ramona L. Lush

Ramona L. Lush is a senior acquisition analyst for the Department of Defense (DoD). Her primary role is lead analyst for development and implementation of defense acquisition policy. Ms. Lush has been actively involved in a variety of business re-engineering initiatives for DoD acquisition and currently has a lead role in an initiative to establish a knowledge management system for the defense acquisition workforce. She is a two-time recipient of the Vice President's National Performance Review Heroes of Reinvention Award. In addition to her re-engineering work, Ms. Lush also serves as a consultant to the Defense Acquisition University on developing and updating courses for the university and as a guest lecturer for the advanced program management classes. Ms. Lush is currently a doctoral student at Virginia Tech. She received her MS in Adult Learning and Human Resource Development at the same university.

CHAPTER 8

Structural Learning

Marian V. Barnwell

Scandura's structural learning theory (SLT) includes research methodologies and an array of content and population-specific theories not presented in this chapter (Scandura, 1983). For the purposes of this book, SLT focuses on Scandura's prescriptions for selecting and sequencing content to provide the most efficient instruction possible to the individual learner. While the approach can be adapted to group instruction, its best application is for the individual learner, especially using technology-based delivery systems that can adapt to individual needs.

The designer using a structural learning approach first identifies instructional goals and the cognitive processes (rules) by which the learner should perform the desired tasks. Then, using structural analysis, the designer breaks the rules down into small (atomic) steps (operations and decisions) and develops flow diagrams to analyze and document these steps. The resulting procedures are analyzed to identify the simplest path through the procedure, and paths of increasing complexity.

When delivering instruction, the instructor or instructional system tests the learner to see what he or she already knows. Instruction then begins with the simplest path that the learner cannot yet perform, and continues with paths of increasing complexity until the entire rule has been learned. Structural learning does not emphasize teaching/learning strategies themselves, but emphasizes the importance of the content and sequence of what is taught.

Origins

SLT emerged about 1960 with Scandura's work on problemsolving instruction and rule-governed behavior. Strongly believing that good instructional theory must be precise, operational, and comprehensive, Scandura (1996) finds it useful to represent the rule as the basic learning component. His earlier works include substantial research on rule learning (Scandura, 1972) and *Structural Learning I* and *Structural Learning II* outline the extensive work of Scandura and others on complex human learning and the emergence of SLT (Scandura, 1973; Scandura, 1976). These two volumes discuss the problematic inter-relationship among competence, behavior, and learning and stress the need for continued work in this area. In the mid-1970s, SLT appeared with "important refinements, extensions, and applications to education" (Scandura, 1983, p. 225). Of important note is Scandura's emphasis that SLT is not a single, specific theory but a "unified theoretical framework" surrounding a broad range of complex human behavior phenomena (Scandura & Brainerd, 1978). In essence, SLT combines theories of learning and instructional and developmental procedures by prescribing rigorous analysis of the content, testing for learner competence, and sequencing instruction incrementally.

Description

SLT calls for a highly analytical approach to designing instruction. Its major emphasis is on content selection and sequencing strategies. Scandura believes that what people do and can learn "depends directly and inextricably" on what they already know (Scandura, 1983, p. 237). Consequently, SLT endeavors to address what Scandura views as the critical interrelationships among content, cognition, and individual differences in achievement.

SLT applies to the design of instruction primarily for the cognitive domain, and Scandura offers some key prescriptions. Most important is the prescription that all content is to be analyzed and taught as rules. For SLT, learning and knowledge are both hierarchical in nature and can be represented as sets of hierarchically organized rules. Of equal importance is the prescription for a simple-to-complex instructional sequence. The principle is to teach the simplest path through a rule first, and then to teach paths that are progressively more complex until the learner has mastered the entire rule. This calls for a prior assessment of learner competence, which is the basis for deciding which paths the learner already knows and which rules are to be taught. As SLT requires mastery of each "equivalence" class

> ## Biographical Sketch
>
> **Joseph M. Scandura**, PhD, chair of Scandura-Flexsoft International, has authored more than 175 publications including eight books in educational research, psychology, artificial intelligence, mathematics, and software engineering. He also chairs the Board of Scientific Advisors at Merge Research Institute. His original work in structural learning was published in two volumes (1973 and 1976) and was selected as a Citation Classic in the Institute for Scientific Information's Current Contents (July 1987). He authored chapters in Charles Reigeluth's *Instructional Design Theories and Models* (1983) and *Theories of Instructional Design in Action* (1987). He is the founder of Intelligent Micro Systems and Editor-in-Chief of the *Journal of Structural Learning and Intelligent Systems.*
>
> Dr. Scandura earned a bachelor's and a master's degree from the University of Michigan and a doctorate from Syracuse University and received an honorary master's degree from the University of Pennsylvania. An Emeritus and Adjunct Professor at the University of Pennsylvania, Dr. Scandura has also taught at the State University of New York-Buffalo and Florida State University.
>
> > The long history of structural learning research shows the more precisely one identifies what must be learned the better one can teach [the corresponding content] (J.M. Scandura, personal communication, August 2, 1998).

(or homogeneous problem) of each rule, instruction begins at the lowest or simplest level in which such mastery is not yet achieved.

SLT has no focus on taxonomy of learning outcomes since all content must be analyzed in the same way. Scandura's structural analysis is more precise than traditional task analysis. According to Scandura, task analysis identifies the ingredients or prerequisites for performance at successive levels of abstraction, yet it fails to specify cognitive processes sufficient for actually solving problems in the domain. On the other hand, structural analysis is a type of cognitive task analysis that expressly provides for higher- and lower-order knowledge (Scandura, 1996). Performing a structural analysis allows you to determine the optimal presentation sequence for teaching those rules selected for instruction.

An essential characteristic of SLT is that both data and process (i.e., content and rules) are represented at the same level of abstraction. The fundamental components of a structural analysis are specification of the problem domain and identification of the rules needed to solve the problems (Scandura, 1983). Scandura details how this is done through a series of steps (Scandura & Brainerd, 1978). The first step requires the analyst to decide a suitable way to represent the given facts in a problem and solutions associated with the domain. Next, the analyst selects a finite sample of instances from the problem domain and then devises methods for solving the sampled problems that are consistent with how target learners might be expected to solve them.

Scandura's structural analysis is the bridge between content selection and sequencing. It identifies the specific rules to be learned; in particular, it provides a systematic method to select content in the right sequence for the instruction. Besides sequencing, SLT prescribes no specific guidance for instructional strategies.

The Language of SLT

"People use rules to solve problems and if an individual has learned a rule for solving a given problem or task, then he will use it" (Durnin & Scandura, 1973, p. 264). One of the first and most prominent concepts introduced in SLT is that of rules. In Scandura's terms, these are theoretical constructs used to represent all kinds of human knowledge. SLT assumes that the competence underlying any given problem domain can be represented by rules (Scandura, 1983). There must be a finite set of rules to cover a given topic, each broken into smaller or alternate rules.

Scandura's rules have several components:

- *Domain*—Problem situations requiring successful performance by the learner
- *Range*—Expected output or result generated by the rule
- *Operation*—Series of actions applied to the domain elements, connecting the domain and the range

Atomic rules are the smallest steps in a procedure; these cannot be decomposed into simpler actions. Higher-order rules are the cognitive processes that enable the learner to combine several atomic rules into more complex rules.

When a rule is used to solve a problem or achieve an instructional objective, it is considered the solution rule. Each sequence of atomic rules that results in solving the problem is a path and each path defines an equivalence class of the domain. The complexity level of a path determines if it is subordinate or superordinate to another. Automaticity (expert, efficient performance) results from complete learning, enabling performance with less conscious thought.

To illustrate Scandura's unique terms, let us relate them to an instructional situation for workers in an interior decorating firm that specializes in making custom draperies. We start with an objective that specifies what the worker must be able to do after the instruction. Custom drapes can be designed with different styles of headers. Our objective is for the worker to make three variations of a drape header. While this objective requires previously acquired motor skills, the new learning is cognitive. Figure 8.1 illustrates all the decisions and actions required for this objective. Our worker must be able to make three different headers, each with an increased level of difficulty. What the workers already know and are able to do will directly affect the drape makers' ability for successful performance. Scandura emphasizes that the key instructional implication of SLT is the designer's judgment about what individual learners know and what they are able to do. This requires a very close look at what we believe learner characteristics to be. The analysis is only as accurate as our assumptions are accurate. In this case, our analysis assumes that target workers already know sewing basics. If this assumption is incorrect, then the analysis must be modified accordingly, or the worker will be unable to perform successfully.

Domain. The domain is the set of encoded inputs to which the rule applies. To achieve performance, the worker must have a situation, materials, tools, or other resources to start with. (These are similar to the "conditions" or the "given" in an instructional objective.) For successful construction of the drape header, the worker must have fabric, sewing equipment, tools, and notions. Thus, we can define the domain as: (given) any single panel of fabric cut to correct dimensions, sewing machine, thread, pins, etc. and the requirement to make drape headers—these describe the situation and important conditions under which the performance is to occur.

Range. The range is a set of outputs that the rule is expected to generate. It is the outcome—finished product or the results—the performer is to produce. In this case, we want our worker to be able to make three variations of a drape header: one with a rod pocket, one with a rod pocket and ruffle, and one with pleats. The range consists of products with all three variations.

Operation. The operation (or procedure) represents the actions and decisions the learner applies to elements of the domain. This is how the learner gets from the domain to the range (e.g., measure the fabric, use the sewing machine). Figure 8.1 shows the operation or all the steps and decisions required of our worker to make the drape header—from the first measure (step #1) through all the steps up to and including the last stitch (step #18).

Atomic Rule. An atomic rule represents a single unit of behavior (Stevens & Scandura, 1987). SLT assumes that before training, an individual in the target population can perform these simplest, most basic steps either perfectly or not at all. The solution rule for our drape header objective (Figure 8.1) shows a number of cognitive actions that are considered atomic.

Higher-Order Rules. In SLT, higher-order rules include behavioral phenomena such as rule derivation, motivation, rule selection, problem definition, storage, and retrieval (Scandura, 1983). Since higher-order rules make learning and performance more efficient, they should be taught whenever possible. A rule is higher order relative to another if it operates on the other rule. In this sense, higher order rules do not correspond to the higher order rules as used more commonly to indicate rules associated with higher levels in a learning hierarchy (Scandura, 1983). Rather than being a combination of lower order rules, Scandura's higher-order rules describe the processes by which lower-order rules are combined to form rules that are more complex and solve problems. Scandura's higher-order rules may be compared to what others have called cognitive strategies or metacognition. They allow learners to focus on the covert, thought-based steps required for an action. Higher order rules facilitate the analysis and specification of complex tasks.

Scandura posits clear advantages to interposing higher-order rules whenever possible (1983). First, they enable the instruction and delivery of relatively complex domains in an efficient manner. Second, higher-order rules optimally represent individual knowledge—they make it easy to identify the exact point of confusion if a learner does not master a rule. And finally, higher-order rules facilitate the required structural analysis of content. Some higher-order rules (generation) produce new knowledge and some (automatization) make existing rules more efficient (Scandura, 1996).

In the drape header flowchart (Figure 8.1), higher-order rules are not explicitly identified. They would be whatever cognitive processes the learner uses to combine atomic rules (e.g., steps 11–16) into more complex rules (e.g., calculate the size of each pleat and space).

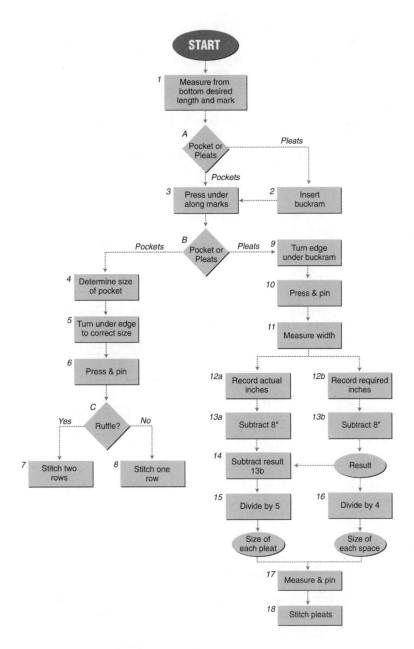

Figure 8.1
Atomic Solution Rule for Drape Header Objective

Solution Rule. "A rule that is used to solve a problem is a solution rule for that problem" (Stevens & Scandura, 1987, p. 163). It is the series of actions and decisions necessary to achieve the instructional objective. Figure 8.1 shows all the atomic rules that comprise the solution rule in our drape header problem.

Path. A path generally refers to rule sequencing. For Stevens & Scandura (1987), a path is the sequence of a rule's atomic components in such a way that their performance will satisfy an objective to a particular degree of difficulty. Our solution rule requires three paths (Table 8.1), one for each type of drape header (final outcome). The level of complexity is implied by the conditions of the objective or the domain elements provided in the instructional situation.

Equivalence Class. Each path defines a type of problem or Scandura's equivalence class. Paths 1, 2, and 3 (Table 8.1) represent the equivalence classes of the three drape headers: pocket without ruffles, pocket with ruffles, and pleats.

Path 1 (pocket, no ruffle)	Path 2 (pocket with ruffle)	Path 3 (pleats)	Teaching Sequence of Paths
1	1	1	
A	A	A	
3	3	2	Path 3
B	B	3	
4	4	B	
5	5	9	
6	6	10	
C	C	11	Path 2
8	7	12 a,b	
		13 a,b	
		14	
		15	Path 1
		16	
		17	
		18	

Table 8.1
Solution Rule Paths (Equivalence Classes)

Subordinate or Superordinate. A path is subordinate when it is less complex than other paths through the same solution rule. The converse is true of superordinate paths. To proceed with instruction at the superordinate path, it is assumed that the learner has mastered the performance required on the subordinate path. As illustrated in Table 8.1, Path 3 is superordinate to Paths 1 and 2, and Path 1 is subordinate to Paths 2 and 3.

Automaticity. When learning is well established, information processing occurs without conscious control. In taking the required measurements for the drape header, our worker uses little cognitive capacity in performing the requisite psychomotor activities (e.g., handling the measuring instrument, using the machine, etc.). Automaticity describes the ability to execute a task quickly, effortlessly, and accurately with little conscious attention. The steps in Figure 8.2 demonstrate this, conceivably, as the expected performance of a more experienced worker. Normally, automaticity is unintentional, involuntary, and autonomous. For instance, once we learn how to subtract, we do not have to think about what steps to follow to solve subtraction problems.

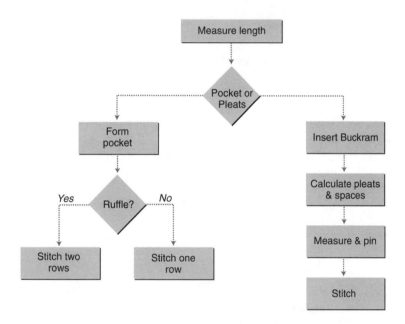

Figure 8.2
Automated Solution Rule for Drape Header Objective

Path Selection Strategy

SLT demands a systematic approach for deciding which path to teach. It requires the development of an adaptive test for each path. Such a test is derived directly from the equivalence classes: The test items should require the learner to perform all steps in the path corresponding to that equivalence class (Stevens & Scandura,

1987). In making decisions regarding instructional sequence, each learner is tested on one randomly selected test item from each equivalence class. (This seems to be the first instance where the learner is actively involved in the lesson design.) Scandura considers this testing critical to identifying precisely and unambiguously what learners know and what they do not know. Begin by testing the learner on the superordinate path. Success with the test items implies potential success on all other items from the same equivalence class. If the learner fails, then test at a lower path and keep testing until you find the learner's first level of competence.

The content sequencing strategy follows directly from this—identify what the learner has not mastered and teach that. In other words, begin teaching one path above the highest path already mastered and continue until all paths are mastered. In teaching each higher path, present and explain the new rules or unmastered material to be learned.

While testing may be easily done with target learners for individualized instruction and computer-based training, it can be quite challenging for groups. This is especially so of adult learners, who may not feel comfortable with letting others know before the instruction what they do not know. In addition, it is not especially motivating for any learner to begin a lesson with a difficult test that may lead to a failure. For some content, it may facilitate instruction delivery to give adult learners an opportunity to self-assess their knowledge. Even so, this can be equally discomforting, as such learners may not wish to share this information. SLT does not address how to handle this situation.

Best Uses

Structural analysis is particularly useful for analyzing complex cognitive content. SLT's precision for content selection and sequencing that match learner needs facilitates the design of instruction for procedural knowledge as well as complex subject matter having a high volume of detail to be learned. Examples include mathematical and scientific curricula and technical procedures such as equipment diagnosis and repair. SLT can be used with learners who have little or no previous knowledge of the subject matter because the content taught results from the initial tests used to determine what the learner knows (Stevens & Scandura, 1987). Although delivering SLT-designed instruction can be an arduous challenge for groups, as Scandura observed, it has a rigorous base that makes it useful in designing individualized instruction (Scandura, 1983). Designers of web-based and computer-managed instruction will find SLT's exacting and systematic approach uniquely appealing. Empirical evidence shows that the SLT provides one of the "most comprehensive and reliable foundations on which to build a [computer-aided instruction] system" (Scandura, 1977, p. 555).

Over the past decade, Scandura's work with structural learning has focused on software engineering. He has been applying SLT principles in developing automated software tools and packages (Scandura, 1997). The resultant enabling technologies gave rise to applications and tools that allow commercial enterprises to optimally develop, test, and integrate e-business models.

Research Support

Substantial research results can be found that support individual SLT principles and prescriptions rather than SLT as a whole and its application as an instructional design tool. Dating as far back as the early 1960s, Scandura and his colleagues have conducted a large number of studies on rule learning, rule-governed behavior, problemsolving, sequencing, processing capacity, and structural analysis (Scandura, 1976). Other research involves the impact of higher-order rules on individual performance (Scandura, 1980). Results show that curricula that are characterized in terms of rules and higher-order rules provide explicit basis for instruction and make specific provisions for remote transfer. Additionally, empirical results have demonstrated the practicality of structural analysis and its application to emerging technologies (Scandura, 1997).

Model in Action

In today's workplaces, electronic messages (email) are perhaps even more common for communicating with others than the telephone: They are now considered the standard. This section illustrates the application of SLT principles in the design and delivery of new-hire training for using a specific email system.

A group of program coordinators needs to disseminate current information on available training courses and programs to personnel throughout the country. After instruction, each coordinator will be able to send emails, including attached files, to one or more recipients by replying to or composing a new email message. For successful performance on this objective, each coordinator must have basic computer skills, a fully functioning computer with an email system installed, a personal email account, email addresses of employees, and current information on training courses and programs.

SLT requires an analysis of all content. The first step is to identify the exact nature of the job tasks required and to select a sample of each type of email the coordinators will send. Our analysis reveals four different email tasks to be learned:

1. Reply to a message.
2. Reply to a message and attach a file.
3. Compose a new message and attach a file to one recipient.
4. Repeat Task 3, and send to multiple recipients (instead of one) on a newly self-created list.

The email application uses a toolbar (Figure 8.3) for recurring functions, and the training is designed using it as a basis.

Figure 8.3
Standard Toolbar

Next, we identify the procedures to be learned for sending each type of email. In this case, the analysis assumes that all coordinators have basic computer and email skills, including operating a computer (using a keyboard and mouse) and opening and reading email messages. (Basic skill levels of the coordinators were obtained from a pre-employment test and the test results are the basis for this assumption.)

The correct learner performance is easily determined. When a procedure is performed incorrectly, the system displays an error message requesting missing information. For instance, each message must contain information in the Subject field before the Send command will work. If the learner tries to use the Send command while the field is left blank, an error message will appear requesting that the Subject field be filled in. In another instance, the system will display an error message when the coordinator clicks the Attach File button and does not select a file to attach.

Table 8.2 illustrates the atomic solution rule for the four different email tasks. These are the series of actions and decisions necessary to achieve the instructional objective of sending emails with attached files to one or more recipients. The instructional materials give the coordinators added information relating to each action and decision by displaying explanatory text with graphics. For example, the materials will show various icons with text explanations as used by the email system. There are four paths to the atomic solution rule with increasing levels of difficulty corresponding to the sample type of emails to be sent. These paths are displayed in Table 8.3.

Step	Action
1.	Click *Reply* on toolbar (opens message reply window).
2.	Click in *Message* window.
3.	Type message.
4.	Attach a file?
	If Yes, go to #18.
	If No, go to #21.
5.	Click *New Message* on toolbar (opens new message window).
6.	Click in *To* field.
7.	Click *Address Book* on toolbar (dialog box pops up).
8.	Create a group list?
	If yes, click *New Group* (opens *Group Properties* box).
	If no, go to #12.
9.	Click in *Name* field.
10.	Type in a name for the group.
11.	Click *Add/Remove Members* button.
12.	Double click recipient's name from the list.
13.	Add another name?
	If yes, go to #12.
	If no, click *OK* (returns to *Select Name* box)
14.	Double click the group name just created in #10.
15.	Click *OK* again (returns to *To* field on new message).
16.	Click in the *Subject* field.
17.	Type subject of the new message.
18.	Click *Attach File* on toolbar (dialog box pops up).
19.	Select the file to attach.
20.	Click *OK* button (returns to message box).
21.	Click *Send* on toolbar.

Table 8.2
Atomic Solution Rule

Path 1 Reply	Path 2 Attach	Path 3 New	Path 4 List
1	1	5	5
2	2	6	6
3	3	7	7
4	4	8	8
21	18	12	9
	19	13	10
	20	15	11
	21	16	12
		17	13
		2	14
		3	15
		4	16
		18	17
		19	2
		20	3
		21	18
			19
			20
			21

Table 8.3
Atomic Solution Rule Paths

As learning takes place and the coordinators gain experience, they will be able to perform the steps more quickly and accurately with little effort. Actions such as selecting the appropriate icon or button to click will become automatic and involuntary. Information processing becomes easier and several steps are combined into steps that are more complex. Thus, the 21 steps in the atomic solution rule are combined into 8 steps as the *automated solution rule* for sending emails in Table 8.4. The four paths to the *automated solution rule* are shown in Table 8.5..

Step	Action
S1	Open Message Reply window.
S2	Type message.
S3	Attach file.
S4	Send message.
S5	Open New Message window.
S6	Fill in email address of recipient(s).
S7	Create a group distribution list for several addresses.
S8	Fill in subject of message.

Table 8.4
Automated Solution Rule

Path 1 Reply	Path 2 Reply & Attach	Path 3 New w/ Attach	Path 4 New w/ List & Attach
S1	S1	S5	S5
S2	S2	S6	S7
S4	S3	S8	S6
	S4	S2	S8
		S3	S2
		S4	S3
			S4

Table 8.5
Automated Solution Rule Paths

In selecting the sequence for instruction, the subordinate path comes first. Thus, in both paths (atomic and automated), Path 1 is taught first and, once the procedures for Path 1 are mastered, SLT prescribes the unique procedures for Path 2—attaching a file. Explaining the uniqueness of each new path is repeated until the coordinator masters the procedures for all four paths. Built-in error checks serve as the test of the coordinator's level of competence. Any instance of unsuccessful performance causes a prompt for further instruction and practice until the procedure is mastered.

Implementation Guide

Phase	Step	Instruction
D E S I G N	1	For each objective, specify the domain, range, and operation.
	2	Analyze the operation to identify all decisions and actions (rules).
	3	Identify different paths through the solution rule.
	4	Identify which paths are subordinate to the others and construct a hierarchy of paths.
	5	Develop a test for each path (equivalence class).
D E L I V E R Y	1	Test learner on the superordinate class. If learner fails, test at the next-lower path. Keep testing at successively lower paths to determine which paths the learner has already mastered.
	2	Teach one path above the path already mastered.
	3	Repeat until all paths are mastered while explaining the uniqueness of each new path.
	4	Use further practice to teach the combination of several atomic rules as a single cognitive step, that is, higher-order rule to achieve automation.

References

Durnin, J.H., & Scandura, J.M. (1973). An algorithmic approach to assessing behavior potential: Comparison with item forms and hierarchical technologies. *Journal of Educational Psychology, 65*(3), 262–272.

Reigeluth, C. (1998, September 1). *Elaboration theory* [On-line]. Available: http://www.gwu.edu/~tip/reigelut.html

Scandura, J.M. (1972). What is a rule? *Journal of Educational Psychology, 63*(3), 179–185.

Scandura, J.M. (1973). *Structural learning I: Theory and research.* New York: Gordon and Breach Science Publishers.

Scandura, J.M. (Ed.). (1976). *Structural learning II: Issues and Approaches.* New York: Gordon and Breach Science Publishers.

Scandura, J.M. (1977). *Problem solving: A structural/process approach with instructional implications.* New York: Academic Press.

Scandura, J.M. (1980). Theoretical foundations of instruction: A systems alternative to cognitive psychology. *Journal of Structural Learning, 12*, 313–328.

Scandura, J.M. (1983). Instructional strategies based on the structural learning theory. In C.M. Reigeluth (Ed.), *Instructional design theories and models: An overview of their current status* (213–246). Hillsdale, NJ: Lawrence Erlbaum Associates.

Scandura, J.M. (1996). Role of instructional theory in authoring effective and efficient learning technologies. *Computers in Human Behavior, 12*(2), 313–328.

Scandura, J.M. (1997). A cognitive approach to reengineering. *Crosstalk, The Journal of Defense Software Engineering, 10*(6), 26–31. Available: http://www.stsc.hill.af.mil/Crosstalk/1997/jun/cognitive.html

Scandura, J.M., & Brainerd, C.J. (Eds.). (1978). *Structural/process models of complex human behavior.* Alphen ann den Ryn, the Netherlands: Sijthoff & Noordhoff International Publishers.

Stevens, G.H., & Scandura, J.M. (1987). A lesson design based on instructional prescriptions from the structural learning theory. In C.M. Reigeluth (Ed.), *Instructional theories in action.* Hillsdale, NJ: Lawrence Erlbaum Associates.

Bibliography

Gagné, R.M., & Medsker, K.L. (1996). *The conditions of learning: Training applications*. Fort Worth, TX: Harcourt Brace.

Jeeves, M.A., & Greer, G.B. (1983). *Analysis of structural learning*. New York: Academic Press.

Scandura, J.M. (1985). Structural learning: the science of cognition, instructional and intelligent systems engineering. *Journal of Structural Learning, 8*, i–ii.

Scandura, J.M. (1995). Theoretical foundations of instruction: Past, present and future. *Journal of Structural Learning, 12*, 231–243.

Scandura, J.M. (1999). *Structural learning theory in the year 2000* [On-line]. Available: http://www.scandura.com/Articles/SLT%20Y2K.pdf

Scandura, J.M., & Scandura, A.B. (1980). *Structural learning and concrete operations: An approach to piagetian conservation*. New York: Praeger Scientific Publishers.

About the Author

Marian V. Barnwell is director of internal audits for a major Department of Defense agency in the metropolitan Washington, DC area. She has more than 20 years of progressive experience in work group processes. During the past seven years, she has developed and implemented process improvement initiatives to meet the unique needs of professional employees in the inspector general community. These initiatives include facilitating and developing staff skills in customer satisfaction, teambuilding, problemsolving, project management, work group productivity, and intra- and intergroup relations.

Ms. Barnwell earned a Certificate in Instructional Design and an MA in Human Performance Systems from Marymount University. She is a Certified Public Accountant in the Commonwealth of Virginia.

CHAPTER 9

Advance Organizer

Cynthia Vorder Bruegge and Dina E. Widlake

> *... meaningful learning takes place if the learning task can be related in nonarbitrary, substantive (non-verbatim) fashion to what the learner already knows, and if the learner adopts a corresponding learning set to do so.*
>
> *—David P. Ausubel, 1968*

Based on his cognitive instructional theory developed in the 1960s, David P. Ausubel's advance organizer strategy focuses on enhancing meaningful verbal learning. Drawing on what the learner might already know, a lesson based on the three-step model presents the advance organizer tool, presents the learning content, and strengthens the cognitive structure. In so doing, the model helps learners build a cognitive structure, link new knowledge to any existing knowledge, and create a basis for meaningful learning. The advance organizer model focuses on learning through presentation or lecture, and its strategy stresses logical, organized instruction. Thus, the model is ideal for verbal learning in any field, including computer software material, product knowledge, manufacturing procedures, employee benefit plans, and corporate policies and procedures. The advance organizer model can also be used in conjunction with other models, such as mnemonics, ARCS motivational model, and structural learning.

Origins

Ausubel began writing about his model in an article called "The Use of Advance Organizers in the Learning and Retention of Meaningful Verbal Learning" (1960). He later published a comprehensive book on his learning theory (1968). The central concept of Ausubel's model—meaningful verbal learning—did not originate with him. Ausubel acknowledged researchers D.O. Lyon, M.G. Jones, H.B. English, and others who worked earlier in the 1900s to link meaning and learning.

Ausubel was a cognitive theorist during the time when behavioral theories were prominent. During much of Ausubel's career, educational systems accepted and widely adopted the principles of behavioral psychology. One of the most influential books in the field of educational psychology, *Theories of Learning* by Ernest R. Hilgard, was first published in 1948 and was updated three times. Many of the theories in Hilgard's book were based on the principles of behavioral psychology, which dominated the entire discipline of psychology throughout much of the 20th century. Even in the 1975 edition of his book, Hilgard included a discussion of Gagné's work *Conditions of Learning* (1965), but failed to address Ausubel's theory.

Despite the lack of enthusiasm initially shown for his work by his colleagues, the American Psychological Association honored Ausubel with the E. L. Thorndike Award in 1976.

Biographical Sketch

David P. Ausubel received his doctorate from the City University of New York and his medical training from the Mental Health Department of the Lutheran Medical Center in Brooklyn, New York. In 1952, he published his first book, entitled *Ego Development and the Personality Disorders: A Developmental Approach to Psychopathology*. He worked in the field of developmental psychology studying such areas as adolescent development and drug addiction. He also published *Theory and Problems of Adolescent Development* (1977) and *What Every Well-Informed Person Should Know About Drug Addiction* (1980).

Description

Summary

Ausubel believed people retain information better and longer if they can make sense of new concepts by integrating them into an organized cognitive structure. He made a clear distinction between meaningful learning and rote learning. What differentiates meaningful learning is its connection and relationship to what the learner already knows.

The vocabulary Ausubel chose to articulate his advance organizer theory is complex and detailed. He introduced concepts such as subsumers, cognitive structure, concept assimilation, advance organizers, reception learning, progressive differentiation, integrative reconciliation, obliterative assimilation, obliterative subsumption, and derivative and correlative subsumption (Ausubel, 1968). This vocabulary has perhaps contributed to the difficulty people experience in understanding Ausubel's theory. Once you understand these concepts, the theory becomes clear and intuitively appealing.

Components of the Model

Cognitive Structure. Ausubel used cognitive structure to describe ". . . the substantive content of an individual's structure of knowledge and its major organizational properties . . ." (Ausubel, 1968). In other words, Ausubel believed individuals carry information around in their heads in an organized, hierarchically structured way—just as documents are stored in a filing cabinet or a computer hard drive. If information is stored in an organized way, a person can more easily retrieve it when necessary. Ausubel identified this mental organization as a cognitive structure.

Subsumers. According to Ausubel, subsumers are thoughts, concepts, and categories that make up the cognitive structure. These branch-like configurations result from learning. When learning occurs, the brain cells change and create different paths. As greater amounts of information are learned about a particular topic, the subsumer becomes more complex, with a greater number of small branches extending from the main branch. A cognitive structure can have many subsumers, depending on the number of varied disciplines a person knows or the varied kinds of experience a person has had. Continuing the analogy with computer files: As new information is introduced into the existing structure, new folders are created, and new files are created within existing folders.

For example, a woman who took an ethics course in college has a subsumer called "ethics" and several subordinate concepts attached to "ethics" as branches, such as names of ethical philosophers. In her first job, she reads the company manual containing the company's "business ethics." This is a new idea to her, but related to "ethics." "Business ethics" becomes a new branch attached to the larger subsumer "ethics" and, in fact, a new subsumer in itself, within which she can subsume the ethical principles of her employer.

Progressive Differentiation. Ausubel advocated that instructional presentations adhere to the principles of progressive differentiation. The instructor should articulate information by presenting ". . . the most general and inclusive ideas" first and follow with the more specific and detailed parts of these ideas (Ausubel, 1968). This sequencing parallels how the learner's cognitive structure is organized. The material in a cognitive structure is organized hierarchically so that the most general components of the material reside at the top. As you move down the hierarchy, the related information becomes more specific and detailed. This movement from the very general to the very specific is called progressive differentiation.

For example, an instructor teaching a class about how to make ethical decisions in the workplace demonstrates the use of progressive differentiation by beginning his lecture describing the various theories of moral philosophy. Then the instructor narrows his presentation by introducing an ethical decisionmaking model, describing the various levels at which ethical decisionmaking occurs—societal to corporate to individual. From the individual level, the instructor becomes even more specific by identifying the kinds of questions an individual must ask when determining what decision is the most ethically sound in a given case.

Integrative Reconciliation. The complement to progressive differentiation is integrative reconciliation. If progressive differentiation is the process of presenting material from the very general to the very specific, then integrative reconciliation is the reverse process. Ausubel argued it is not enough simply to organize a presentation in accordance with the principles of progressive differentiation. Learners often experience cognitive dissonance with such a presentation. Learners may be introduced to a concept that already exists in their cognitive structure, but the new way in which the concept is presented may be different or may even conflict with how the learners understood that concept. To help work through the cognitive dissonance, an instructor should organize a presentation to move back up the hierarchy, from the very specific to the very general. This helps the learner reorganize the subsumers involved, if necessary.

As an example, an instructor teaching a class about how to make ethical decisions in the workplace begins his lecture identifying the varying theories of moral philosophy. The instructor then differentiates through the decisionmaking models (societal, corporate, individual) and identifies the specific kinds of questions an individual must ask to reach the most ethically sound decision in a given case. (So far, the instructor is using progressive differentiation.) The instructor then demonstrates integrative reconciliation by starting with a specific ethical decision and moving back up the hierarchy, concluding with identifying the theories of moral philosophy used in that decision.

Advance Organizer. Ausubel's learning theory gets its name from its best known tool or strategy—the advance organizer. Advance organizers are very general ideas: concepts, relationships, or structures that combine and associate the material about to be learned. An instructor uses the advance organizer to arrange material in a lesson so the most general concepts are presented first. Much discussion and even confusion exists among researchers, instructional designers and instructors about what an advance organizer really is. While Ausubel was general, and perhaps even vague, in his description of the advance organizer, it is understood that the advance organizer—

- must connect to the learner's existing cognitive structure (to help bridge the gap between what the learner already knows and the new material being learned).
- must be at a higher level of abstraction than the new content itself.
- may be represented visually or verbally by a picture, diagram, story, chart, or oral description.

Figure 9.1 shows an advance organizer that provides an overview of sports games, showing the sports graphics, players, and fields. An instructor would use this organizer to introduce a lesson about the players and positions as well as the rules of various games. Another example of an advance organizer is the systems design model shown in Figure 9.2. An instructor would use this organizer to introduce a lesson about any phase of a systems design model.

Choosing the Advance Organizer

Choosing or designing an advance organizer itself is challenging, because an effective organizer must fit both the content and the learners. Ausubel describes two types of advance organizers to be used in different circumstances.

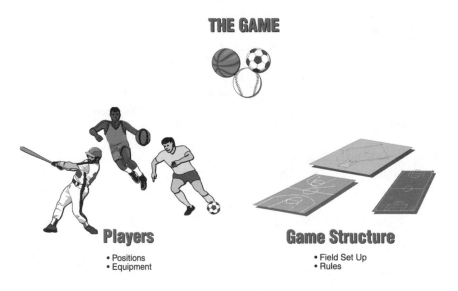

Figure 9.1
Sports Advance Organizer

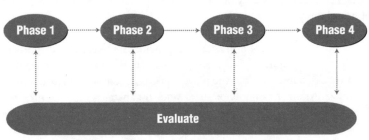

Figure 9.2
Systems Design Advance Organizer

Comparative Advance Organizer. A comparative advance organizer compares and contrasts two concepts, theories, or processes to prevent confusion brought on by their similarities. When a company replaces one word-processing application with another, a comparative organizer might very well help employees learn how to use the new application. All word processing applications accomplish the same tasks; they just do them differently. A comparative organizer shows the similarities and differences between the original word processing application and the new one.

For example, both applications provide a tool to insert graphics into a page, but the tool names and where they can be found are different. Building on functional similarities and how the new application accomplishes a similar function in a different way, the instructor helps the employees understand how to use the new tool. Learners may eventually use the tool independently, relating what is known about the old system to discover how to do the same thing in the new application. The semantic and ergonomic differences between the two applications no longer are a barrier to the use of the new application, and similarities are used to facilitate learning.

Expository Advance Organizer. An expository advance organizer provides anchors for learning unfamiliar materials. For example, an expository advance organizer can be used when teaching learners who have no prior knowledge or experience with computers to use the Internet in a networked environment. In this case, the advance organizer can be an image of a spider web with each site in this worldwide network being represented as a main anchor on the web and the links between these places being represented by the lines of the spider's web, connecting users from site to site.

When teaching a concept using the advance organizer tool, consider the following questions:

1. With regard to the subject you want to teach, what related ideas, at a very general level, already exist for the learners? If the subject matter being taught is about keyboarding, find out what level of typing background the learners have.
2. How can you draw links between what the learners know and what is to be taught? For instance, if the learners do have some previous experience or training on a typewriter, build a comparative organizer to link the rules of using a typewriter to that of using a computer keyboard.

Ausubel argues that the new material must be organized; maintaining and presenting organized material is key to establishing meaningful learning. When using this model to design instructional material, it's important to remember that the advance organizer tool does provide a familiar setting or structure to anchor new, potentially strange, material. The tool does not ask learners to recall what they did last week, tell learners what they will do tomorrow, ask learners to recall a personal experience and indicate that the lesson resembles that situation, or present the objective of the course.

Approach

Table 9.1 summarizes the lesson design steps, using an advance organizer.

Step	Action	Results
1.	Conduct a needs assessment to determine any existing knowledge of learners that is relevant to the new knowledge.	• Clarifies learner's level of knowledge on the subject • Determines the level of difficulty for the instruction • Determines start point for the instruction
2.	Based on the results of needs assessment, select the type of advance organizer. • Comparative advance organizer will be used if new material resembles existing knowledge • Expository advance organizer will be used if material is unfamiliar to the learners	• Determines start point for the instruction • Determines the nature of the organizer to be used
3.	Select and develop the concept for the advance organizer by constructing a high-level "picture" of the overall concept that will be taught.	• Provides a structure for the lesson content • Builds a cognitive bridge when existing knowledge is relevant
4.	Plan to use the advance organizer to— • Present the organizer • Present the learning content (using progressive differentiation) • Strengthen cognitive structure (using integrative reconciliation	• Completes a lesson plan for meaningful verbal learning

Table 9.1

Lesson Design Using the Advance Organizer

Subway Example

The example of travelers learning to use a subway system in an unfamiliar city or foreign country can illustrate the value of the advance organizer model. Anyone who has experienced this challenge understands the confusion that may result, made worse if a language barrier is also involved. Which stop is closest to my destination? Which train or trains must I take to reach that station most efficiently? How do I purchase a ticket or pay the fare? How much is the fare? How long will the trip take? Travelers who have used other subway systems may have some advantages, but negative transfer may occur because the traveler may incorrectly assume that a feature of the familiar system is also a feature of the new system.

Imagine how much easier a new subway system would be to learn if travelers could be presented with an Ausubel-style lecture before descending into the subway station. An advance organizer, perhaps in the form of a diagram or chart, could be used to illustrate that all subway systems have common high-level features: for example, maps (routes, lines, and stops), schedules, evidence of payment (tickets, tokens, or farecards), fare structures, and norms of conduct (e.g., no eating). Travelers could be encouraged to use their experience with previous subway systems to construct a comparative organizer. (Features of the new system could then be compared and contrasted with the known system.) Using progressive differentiation, the particular features of the unfamiliar system would then be explained, moving from the general features to the specific rules and procedures. Moving back up the hierarchy, from specific to general (integrative reconciliation), the presentation would help participants strengthen their cognitive structures regarding subway systems in general and how this particular one fits into a general scheme. Travelers would be better prepared for future encounters with yet unfamiliar subway systems.

As travelers learn to use more and more subway systems, their cognitive structures regarding subway systems become very rich and detailed, helping them to remember the details of previously learned systems and also allowing them to adapt more easily to new systems.

Research Support

More than 200 studies have been conducted to determine the effectiveness of the advance organizer on learning and retention. The outcomes of these studies have been mixed, and the conclusions are often conflicting (Story, 1998). Some of the early studies may have suffered from methodological problems, as well as from lack of agreement on exactly what an advance organizer is (e.g., What, exactly, did Ausubel mean when he said the organizer should be at a higher level of abstraction than the content?). However, Novak (1977) provided educators a comprehensive (and comprehensible!) learning theory based on Ausubel's work, which seemed to clarify the meaning and application of the advance organizer. Joyce and Weil (1996) summarize the history of advance organizer research and report that reviews of later investigations (1970s and 1980s) yielded generally positive results, often with large effect sizes. Long-term studies show better results than short-term studies, and illustrations appear to add to the effectiveness of advance organizers. Organizers seem to have the greatest effect on recall of facts and formulas, but they have been shown to improve learning of many types.

Organizers are helpful for the learning of multiple, interrelated concepts. For example, Moore and Readence (1984) demonstrated that both individual concepts and their inter-relationships were better learned using a graphic organizer. Hirumi and Bowers (1991) used graphic organizers to improve the learning of psychological concepts and their inter-relationships.

Application of Ausubel's model, though not explicit, is also seen in the work of Tony Buzan. Buzan developed a tool called the mind map that is meant, in one way, to parallel how information is stored in the mind (1989).

Ausubel's model has had a significant impact on learning, is widely known and accepted, and is used extensively by instructional designers and trainers today. Ausubel's focus on meaningful learning and cognitive structure has inspired much work in the field of learning.

Best Uses

Ausubel's advance organizer model was designed for teaching what Gagné calls verbal information and concepts, but it is also useful for other types of learning. Meaningful learning can occur through presentation, if the presentation is well organized hierarchically. Because this model is so focused on learning through presentation, instructors will find it ideal for training both groups and individuals, whether by live lecture, text, video, or computer.

Because of its emphasis on organization as an aid to assimilation and retention, the model is especially useful when introducing very new information or very large amounts of information. Its strength lies in its parallel between the structure of content and the cognitive structure of learners. Through the use of this model, learners benefit not only from meaningful learning, but also from a strengthening of their cognitive structures. This model's greatest strength is the way it manages to show the "big picture" first, which is greatly appreciated by many intuitive learners.

In school learning, most subjects, such as history, biology and chemistry, are well-suited candidates for Ausubel's model. Advance organizers are useful in both technical training and "soft skills" training, providing a meaningful structure of context for the details that are to follow. Comparative organizers are particularly helpful for transition training to a new system, policy, or procedure.

The advance organizer is a versatile model. Other training models are more suited for instructors to use when teaching motor and intellectual skills, but Ausubel's model can be used to introduce such material prior to a skill demonstration and practice. Instructors may also use the advance organizer model to summarize steps required of a specific skill. Ausubel's model is limited by its dependency on the creativity of the designer and the organizational strength of the presenter. To be most effective, the organizer must be carefully selected, well designed, and skillfully used.

Model in Action

Two European-born soccer players, Helmut and Marietz, came to the United States to work and settle with their families. After several years of coaching youth soccer for fun, they decided to start a business. They saw an interest developing among the parents of the children they taught and thought a soccer school for the parents could succeed. The timing was perfect. The United States had just hosted a World Cup tournament and Major League Soccer (MLS) was growing as a professional sport.

Helmut and Marietz knew the game of soccer inside and out but were not sure how to begin training adults. They hired consultants to develop a program that would effectively introduce these older newcomers to the sport. The consultants recommended that the first part of the program consist of a series of presentations on the sport: its history, rules, equipment, and guidelines. Helmut and Marietz believed that people could not really learn from lectures and presentations. The consultants agreed that for teaching the mechanics (motor skills) of the game—how to kick, trap or throw the ball—this approach would not work. However, because they wanted the beginning of the program to be about the concepts related to the game, the approach would work beautifully.

Each lesson would be designed based on an analysis of what their students already knew, thereby ensuring learning would take place. They saw questions in the eyes of both Helmut and Marietz. "In other words," the first consultant continued, "we will identify what your clients already know about soccer, other similar sports, or sports in general, and design the lectures using that knowledge as a place to connect what they will learn with what they already know." This is the basic premise of Ausubel's model.

The aim of one lesson would be to enable an individual who currently has little or no experience with soccer to watch, with understanding, a professional soccer match. The organizer for this lesson would be a graphic of a soccer ball, player, and field that presented the general concepts of the game.

The lesson would include the advance organizer model's three steps. Within the first step—present Advance Organizer—they would conduct activities to clarify the aims of the lesson and to prompt the participants' awareness about the sport or similar sports (comparative organizer). The activities would include a question-and-answer session, a presentation of the objectives to be met by the end of the session, and a show of some soccer highlights. Then they would present or introduce the advance organizer tool (Figure 9.3).

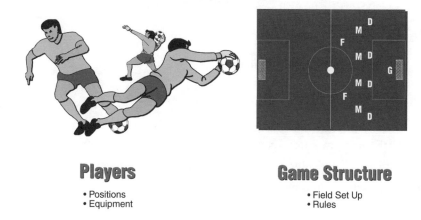

THE GAME OF SOCCER

Players

• Positions
• Equipment

Game Structure

• Field Set Up
• Rules

Figure 9.3
Soccer Advance Organizer

For the second step—present learning content—they would actually present the material, continuing to use the advance organizer graphic. The presentation would be hierarchically structured so that the most general ideas would be presented first. Through progressive differentiation, more general ideas (i.e., what the field looks like, where the players are located on the field) would be followed by more detailed ideas (i.e., number of players, parts of the field). Progressive differentiation would conclude with the most specific material being presented (i.e., explanation of positions, rules of the game). References to the organizer would be made regularly.

For the final step—strengthen cognitive organization—activities would allow for integrative reconciliation and active reception learning on the part of the participants. The new concepts, through the use of the advance organizer, would be reviewed from the detailed level to the general (integrative reconciliation) so that the participants would have a chance to reconcile any conflicts between these new concepts and any existing concepts, and avoid cognitive dissonance. The activities would also be designed to encourage the participants to make the new concepts meaningful in their own way.

Implementation Guide

Once you design a lesson using an advance organizer, implementing the lesson consists of three steps:

1. Present advance organizer
2. Present learning content
3. Strengthen cognitive organization

This three-step approach helps in the following ways:

- It taps into the learner's existing cognitive structure.
- It helps link new information with existing information.
- It transforms unfamiliar material into more familiar material.
- It makes the abstract more concrete.

The following Implementation Guide summarizes the recommended method for presenting a lesson based on an advance organizer.

Step	Components	Considerations
1. Present Advance Organizer	• Identify defining attributes. • Give examples. • Provide context. • Repeat.	• Explore the essential features of the advance organizer and the lesson content. • Prompt awareness of learner's relevant knowledge and experience.
2. Present Learning Content	• Present material. • Use progressive differentiation. • Maintain attention. • Make organization explicit. • Make logical order of learning material explicit.	• Do what Ausubel describes as "providing ideational scaffolding for the incorporation and retention of the more detailed and differentiated material that follows." That is, group and link things together so they make sense for your learners. • Break down concepts from top to bottom. • Engage learners where appropriate. • Show how the material relates to the advance organizer. • Show learners how material fits into their cognitive structure.
3. Strengthen Cognitive Organization	• Anchor the new learning material in the learner's existing cognitive structure. • Use integrative reconciliation. • Promote active reception learning. • Elicit critical approach to subject matter. • Clarify.	• Link new ideas to the bigger picture. • Remind students of the ideas (the "big picture"). Ask for a summary of the major attributes of the new learning material. Repeat precise definitions. Ask for differences between aspects of the material. Ask students to describe how the learning material supports the concept or proposition that is being used as the organizer. • Ask learners to describe how the new material relates to the organizer. Ask for additional examples of the concept or propositions in the learning material. Ask learners to verbalize the essence of the material, using their own terminology and frame of reference. Ask learners to examine the material from alternative points of view. • Ask students to recognize assumptions or inferences that may have been made in the learning material, to judge and challenge the assumptions and inferences, and to reconcile contradictions among them. • Ensure that links have been established in learners' cognitive structure.

References

Ausubel, D.P. (1960). The use of advance organizers in the learning and retention of meaningful verbal learning. *Journal of Educational Psychology, 51,* 267–272.

Ausubel, D.P. (1968). *Educational psychology: A cognitive view.* New York: Holt, Rinehart & Winston.

Ausubel, D.P. (1980). Schemata, cognitive structure, and advance organizers: A reply to Anderson, Spiro, and Anderson. *American Educational Research Journal, 17,* 400–404.

Buzan, T. (1989). *Using both sides of your brain.* New York: Penguin Books USA Inc.

Concept mapping. (1998, July 1). [On-line]. Available: http://www.spjc.cc.fl.us/0/SPNS/Lancraft/mapping/usescmapping.html

Gagné, R.M. (1965). *The conditions of learning.* New York: Holt, Reinhart & Winston.

Hirumi, A., & Bowers, D.R. (1991). Enhancing motivation and acquisition of coordinate concepts by using concept trees. *Journal of Educational Research, 84*(5), 273–279.

Joyce, B., & Weil, M. (1996). *Models of teaching.* Boston: Allyn & Bacon.

Moore, D.W., & Readence, J.E. (1984). A quantitative and qualitative review of graphic organizer research. *Journal of Educational Research, 78*(1), 11–16.

Novak, J.D. (1977). *A theory of education.* Ithaca, NY: Cornell University Press.

Story, C.M. (1998). What instructional designers need to know about advance organizers. *International Journal of Instructional Media, 25*(3), 253–261.

Bibliography

GSU Master Teacher Program. (10/27/97). *On learning styles.* [On-line]. Available: http://www.gsu.edu/~dschjb/wwwmbti.html

Instructional Design I - MM1200. (6/1/00). [On-line]. Available: http://cville.northatlantic.nf.ca/~mcoady/IDlinks.htm

Kiewra, K.A., et al. Effects of advance organizers and repeated presentations on students' learning. *Journal of Experimental Education, 6*(2), 147–159.

Learning theory: Ausubel. (10/31/97). [On-line]. Available: http://www.seas.gwu.edu/student/sbraxton/ISD/ausubel.html

R511 Instructional Technology Foundation. (9/26/97). *Historical timelines project* [On-line]. Available: http://copper.ucs.indiana.edu/~yichen/page1.html

Teaching models in art teacher education. (10/25/97). [On-line]. Available: http://ag.arizona.edu/~lgalbrai/teachmod.htm

The concept mapping home page. (10/27/97). [On-line]. Available: http://www.to.utwente.nl/user/ism/lanzing/cm_home.htm

Williams, T.R., & Butterfield, E.C. (1992). Advance organizers: A review of the research—Part I. *Journal of Technical Writing & Communication, 22*(3), 259–272.

About the Authors

Cynthia Vorder Bruegge

Cynthia Vorder Bruegge earned her MBA and Graduate Certificate in Instructional Design from Marymount University, and her BS in Industrial/Organizational Psychology from George Mason University. A training and instructional design professional, her career spans the technical and health care industries and includes involvement in all phases of the ISD model. Her most recent accomplishment was assessing, designing, developing, implementing, and evaluating a training course for data warehousing software.

Dina E. Widlake

Dina E. Widlake earned an MA in Human Resource Development and a Certificate in Instructional Design from Marymount University. She has worked as both a Training Specialist and Training Manager for EDS. She is currently a test development manager for Brainbench, where she oversees the development of tests delivered over the web.

CHAPTER 10

Cognitive Inquiry

Peter J. Pallesen

Cognitive inquiry theory turns learning into problemsolving. For learners to become involved in either creating new theories or recreating old theories that were developed over centuries is exceptionally motivating. Probably the best payoff to the cognitive inquiry approach to learning is that learners learn about learning. That is, they are able to apply inquiry strategies to novel situations.

Instruction based on cognitive inquiry theory is learner centered and problem based, as opposed to instructor centered and solution based. The reasoning mode is investigatory and inductive. Inquiry instructors say, "Here are some data. What questions arise?" instead of "Here is the rule. Here are some examples of the rule. Work on the examples and reinforce your understanding of the rule."

Instructors who use the cognitive inquiry theory have several goals in mind, including teaching the learner several important skills:

- learning a general rule or theory (content)
- deriving general rules or theories (process)
- knowing what questions to ask in the derivation
- testing and defending a derived theory
- predicting the effects of the derived rules or theories in novel cases

The theory also identifies 10 discrete questioning strategies the inquiry instructor uses in support of the goals. These include selecting positive and negative examples, generating hypothetical cases, forming hypotheses, "entrapping" learners in their mistakes of reasoning, and questioning authority.

Crucial to effective inquiry teaching is the control structure that an instructor uses to manage the learning experience. The control structure consists of four major parts:

1. case selection strategies, including prioritizing and sequencing
2. a set of *a priori* expectations that form a model of the student—that is, what the typical student brings to the learning experience in terms of prior knowledge
3. an agenda sequencing student progress through the learning process—that is, correcting one error in logic at a time
4. a set of priority rules used in determining the order in which the instructor attends to errors and omissions in student thinking

Collins and others have built on their inquiry learning theory to develop related theoretical applications, including situated cognition and cognitive apprenticeship (where the situation in which learning occurs—including the cultural context—and the related authentic activities are important to the learning process).

Origins

Cognitive inquiry theory was developed in the late 1980s by Allan Collins and Albert Stevens, who rigorously analyzed the dialogues between master interactive instructors and their learners. The instructors were all using case, questioning, discovery, or Socratic methods. Collins and Stevens derived the goals, strategies, and control mechanisms used by these instructors that made for effective teaching. The cognitive inquiry theory is descriptive of the expert performances they closely observed. In turn, the theory is prescriptive for nonexperts.

While cognitive inquiry is one of the newer learning theories to emerge, it is based on classical teaching practices that trace their beginnings to Socrates (Greek philosopher, c. 469–399 B.C.). Using dialogue or dialectic, Socrates drew forth existing knowledge from within his learners by pursuing a series of questions and examining the implications of their answers. In this way, he effectively guided his listeners to discover various philosophical insights on the human condition (Plato, 1924).

During the Middle Ages, noted philosopher-theologian Peter Abelard (1079–1142) also used a dialectic-based teaching technique, which he developed in his treatise "*Sic et Non*" (yea and nay). Abelard's method consisted of placing before the learner the reasons for and against a particular thesis on the principle that truth is to be attained only by a dialectical discussion of apparently contradictory arguments.

The theory of cognitive inquiry finds its current roots in educational research based on the premise that learners learn by doing (Dewey, 1990; Vygotsky, 1978). Cognitive inquiry theory doesn't fit neatly into either objectivism or constructivism, the two philosophical categories with which most learning theories are labeled (see Chapter 11). Actually, cognitive inquiry effectively straddles both camps. The theory leans towards learning approaches collectively known as "constructivist" (where learners are provided a resource-rich learning environment from which to construct their own reality), although it has strong underpinnings that relate to an "objectivist" point of view (where learners are expected to learn what are considered objective truths).

Most of the instructors observed by Collins and Stevens were operating in a pre-adult learner environment. Nevertheless, it is clear that the goals, strategies, and structures espoused by the cognitive inquiry theory are applicable across many domains of knowledge and learner populations (Collins & Stevens, 1989).

New Developments in Cognitive Learning Theory

In collaboration with others, Collins has continued to write on other factors that affect learning. (His thoughts on situated cognition and cognitive apprenticeship are discussed in "Situated Cognition and Cognitive Apprenticeship" on page 202.) These newer developments share some common precepts with his cognitive inquiry teaching theory, and as such can also provide guidance to designers and instructors (Brown, Collins, & Duguid, 1989).

Biographical Sketch

Dr. **Allan Collins**, former principal scientist at Bolt Beranek and Newman, Inc., is Research Professor of Education at Boston College, where he coleads the Research on Learning Communities team in the School of Education. He is also Professor of Education and Social Policy at Northwestern University, where he is currently a member of the academic faculty of the Institute for the Learning Sciences. He is also active in the Learning Environment Design

---

Biographical Sketch, cont.

Group. This group engages in research that advances understanding of how people learn and studies the design of learning environments based on what is known about natural human learning. He is a member of the National Academy of Education and a fellow of the American Association for Artificial Intelligence.

One of the original editors of the journal *Cognitive Science*, Collins is also one of the founders of the Cognitive Science Society. He is a specialist in the fields of cognitive science and human semantic processing. His focus has been on the use of computers in the learning process. In addition to several articles, book reviews, and technical reports, Dr. Collins has published *Retrieval Time from Semantic Memory*, with M.R. Quinllian, and *Natural Semantics in Artificial Intelligence* with J.R. Carbonell.

He is best known in psychology for his work on semantic memory and mental models; in artificial intelligence for his work on plausible reasoning and intelligent tutoring systems; and in education for his work on inquiry teaching, cognitive apprenticeship, situated learning, epistemic games, and systemic validity in educational testing.

From 1991 to 1994 he was Codirector of the Center for Technology in Education, centered at Bank Street College of Education, where he led projects to study the most effective ways to use technology in schools and the use of video in assessing student performance. He currently directs a project with the Army Research Institute to study expert approaches to inquiry in scientific and military analysis. He has also codirected a project with the Department of Defense Overseas Schools to develop a plan to infuse technology into its curriculum, pedagogy, and assessment practices.

Dr. Collins received his PhD in Psychology from the University of Michigan in 1970.

According to Collins, "[Inquiry teaching] is time consuming...but if the goal is to teach students to solve problems or invent theories in a creative way, this may be the only method we have" (Collins, 1987).

Description

"INQUIRING MINDS WANT TO KNOW!" screams the marketing slogan of a tabloid newspaper sold mostly in grocery stores. This unlikely source unknowingly utters a truth about learners that is at the core of Collins' theory on cognitive inquiry teaching. All of us, as instructors, earnestly dream about having motivated learners just as eager to learn as we are eager to teach them. We know that interested and curious learners are a joy to teach. How then, do we instill an inquiring state of mind in learners? An even more challenging question is how to teach our learners consciously to assume an inquiry-driven mode to increase the effectiveness of their learning processes. Collins' cognitive inquiry theory helps answer these universal questions by providing the tools we can use not only to stimulate our learners, but also to teach them how to assume an inquiring mindset when confronted with novel problems to solve.

In a nutshell, cognitive inquiry teaching theory relies on the learner to bring a natural curiosity, an incremental knowledge base of past experiences, and strong intuition. In turn, the instructor is expected to rigorously design and manage an environment within which the learner can play out scenarios leading to guided discoveries. Together, an instructor using inquiry methods and a learner with a modicum of curiosity, experience, and intuition can create a dynamic learning synergy. The power of this blend derives from enhancing and sharpening a learner's natural curiosity—an inquiry-driven approach.

Cognitive Inquiry and Guided Discovery

Cognitive inquiry questioning technique can be used effectively in tandem with "discovery" approaches to the learning process. Both methods employ an inductive reasoning paradigm.

Inquiry methods start with a question, and the ensuing instruction—usually structured with a series of additional questions—brings the learner to an understanding of the answer to the initial question. In a *discovery* mode, the learner is not presented with a rule or generality until after the learner has discovered it (Collins & Stevens, 1989). The distinction between these two approaches is the level of instructor involvement in the process. Instructors using a pure inquiry approach are actively shaping the process with complex questioning techniques (discussed in "Inquiry Teaching Strategies" on page 199). Instructors using discovery methods usually employ a less-structured approach, allowing learners the freedom to discover new content in their own way.

While the above distinction is perhaps important in discussing various learning theories, the heuristic techniques of inquiry and discovery are both useful to the interactive instructor who wishes to engage learners in participatory rather than passive learning.

Inquiry Teaching Goals

Inquiry instructors attempt to reach several overarching goals in preparing and conducting their learning sessions. The first goal is to teach their learners about a general rule or theory—a content focus. The second goal is to teach their learners how to derive the general rule or theory—a process focus (Collins & Stevens, 1989).

Teaching the General Rule or Theory. Examples of a general rule or theory are the relationship of distance from the ocean and air temperature or the principles to follow when teambuilding. In teaching the general rule or theory, the inquiry instructor has two subgoals that support this major goal:

1. Detect and correct invalid hypotheses concerning the instant case.
2. Make predictions in novel cases.

In teaching about rules or theories, instructors often elicit invalid hypotheses and then try to get the learner to recognize and then correct them. When learners confront their own errors in logic, they may be less likely to fall into the same traps later on. Presenting learners with a novel scenario or case allows them to use the rule derived earlier in the lesson to deal with new problems. For example, once a basic rule has been derived, mathematics instructors using inquiry methods often present new problems of increasing difficulty and ask learners to predict their answers.

Teaching How to Derive the General Rule or Theory. The teaching subgoals that support this major goal are as follows:

1. Ask appropriate and searching questions.
2. Describe the nature of a theory.
3. Test the rule or theory.
4. Verbalize and defend derived rules or theories.

Teaching learners the proper sort of questions to ask is primarily a function of the particular knowledge domain being taught. For example, when teaching morality, derived rules can be evaluated by asking how fair they are. Questions about the effects of differing inputs or changing circumstances on outcomes may be appropriate.

To teach about deriving a rule or theory, it is also important to educate learners about the various forms that rules may take. Again, the particular form depends somewhat on the knowledge domain.

Testing derived theories is an important subgoal in teaching about how to derive theories. Applying derived theories to the real world is one way this can be done.

Finally, inquiry teachers take pains to have learners challenge derived rules and theories and then defend them. Here, the strategy of questioning authority is brought to bear.

Inquiry Teaching Strategies

Choosing Positive and Negative Exemplars. This strategy is used primarily to highlight relevant factors. A positive exemplar is a pattern where all the factors are consistent with a particular value of the variable being sought. For example, if the variable being sought is for team leaders to stimulate desired behaviors (e.g., team members voluntarily sharing the team's workload amongst themselves), a positive exemplar would be team leaders who consistently encourage and reward such desirable behaviors. Negative supervisory behaviors that demonstrate none of the relevant factors (such as ignoring desired employee actions when they do occur) could also be chosen to allow learners to discern relevant factors from graphically different examples. Later, exemplars with a more complicated pattern of relevant factors can be selected for review.

Varying Cases Systematically. This strategy is excellent for highlighting the relevant factors that learners must isolate and consider in their inquiry. Inquiry instructors present cases where the relevant factors are systematically varied. For example, in teaching about motivation, the instructor can present cases where the motivational behaviors are systematically varied, such as the type and degree of reward.

Selecting Counterexamples. Another strategy that inquiry instructors use in selecting cases is selecting counterexamples. This strategy forces students to pay attention to different factors affecting the variable (desirable employee actions) under consideration. For example, when learners discussing employee motivation propose a rule about supervisors needing to recognize and reward desired actions, the instructor might bring up a counterexample of a supervisor who constantly praises even minor instances of desired actions. The instructor could then ask the learners if this behavior will result in motivated employees. Picking counterexamples can illustrate the insufficiency of a derived factor alone or demonstrate that the derived factor is an unnecessary one.

Generating Hypothetical Cases. This strategy is used by inquiry instructors to exercise their learners' reasoning. Again, the cases force learners to consider one or more factors they are trying to derive. For example, when learners are discussing the role of performance reviews with subordinates as a motivational tool, the instructor can generate case after case to help learners isolate critical factors in the conduct of such reviews. One case might be that of a supervisor conducting the review in a public place; another might be where the supervisor reviews the employee's ratings and then summarily ends the conversation.

Forming Hypotheses. Getting learners to generate rules that relate different factors to the variable under discussion is a very useful strategy in inquiry teaching. This is a critical step along the way to learning in an inquiry environment. Once various cases are reviewed, learners can be encouraged to make generalizations that apply to each case.

Testing Hypotheses. Once hypotheses are formed, inquiry instructors encourage their learners to test them. This testing should be done systematically to evaluate the various factors that went into formulating the hypothesis. If learners decide that performance reviews should contain no surprises to the person being reviewed, the inquiry instructor (or others in the class) could construct various scenarios that test that rule. For example, that hypothesis could be tested with a scenario where the supervisor provided a pleasant surprise during the review (e.g., a bonus).

Considering Alternative Predictions. Inquiry instructors often ask learners to consider different levels of value for the factor under consideration. For example, in a discussion about goal setting as a motivational tool, the factor being considered may be the degree to which an employee supports a particular goal. The instructor may ask learners to consider conditions of high, medium, and low support.

Entrapping Learners. One of the more interesting and effective strategies is allowing an inquiry to proceed along an erroneous path until, with close questioning by the inquiry instructor, the learner discovers the error and retreats to logically safer ground to start again. Another way this is done is for the inquiry instructor to take learner observations, turn them into a rule or hypothesis, then suggest a counterexample that demonstrates the insufficiency of the rule.

Tracing Consequences. When a learner's thinking is based on a misconception or an error, inquiry instructors use pointed questions to allow the learner to trace the consequences of that error to a conclusion. When learners see that the derived consequence is absurd or incorrect, in effect they have "debugged" their theory. They benefit in two ways: They learn to evaluate a theory by testing its consequences, and they may be prevented from making similar mistakes in future inquiries.

Questioning Authority. This is not as revolutionary as it sounds. The inquiry instructor, by teaching learners to question authority, encourages them not to look to the instructor or the book for correct answers, but rather to derive rules or theories on their own and test them to their own satisfaction. The important by-product of this strategy is that learners learn to think rigorously and to question those factors that appear to be givens.

Controlling Inquiry Dialogue

Inquiry processes are time consuming, and unless effectively managed by the instructor, can result in goals not reached. Four strategies are helpful:

1. Select and sequence illustrative cases.
2. Build an *a priori* model of the learner.
3. Have an agenda.
4. Follow a set of priority rules in modifying the agenda.

While this sounds like a great deal to keep track of, let alone to follow the course of the ongoing dialogue, the skilled inquiry instructor who keeps uppermost goals clearly in mind can manage the process effectively, particularly if he or she is able to adapt quickly to learner progress and introduce cases with appropriate factors (Collins & Stevens, 1989).

Strategies for Selecting and Sequencing Cases in Support of the Goals. The skilled inquiry instructor observes three discrete case selection substrategies:

1. Sequence of selected cases from the simple to the complex
2. Sequence cases from the concrete to the abstract
3. Sequence from more important and frequently encountered to less important and less frequently encountered

In all cases, these strategies move learners from familiar experiential ground toward deriving a rule or theory they have not encountered before, which is one of the uppermost goals of inquiry instruction.

Establishing an *A Priori* Learner Model. To be most effective, inquiry instructors should not only have a fairly complete picture of the extent of their learners' prior experiences and knowledge bases, but also the ability to gauge and alter this model of the learner based on his or her responses to questions during the inquiry. A skilled inquiry instructor is able to maneuver learners strategically to the edge of their experience base, where new information can be discovered and added.

Setting and Maintaining a Learning Agenda. During the course of an inquiry, the instructor may discover that the learner is laboring under errors or omissions in thought processes. Because these "bugs" can only be debugged one at a time, the instructor needs an agenda of priority rules to follow in attending to these reasoning problems.

The priority rules that a skilled inquiry instructor follows in "debugging" the inquiry process include the following:

- Fix errors before omissions, as errors are more problematic for the inquiry process than omissions.
- Attend to prior steps before later steps, as this ensures a rational order.
- Provide shorter fixes rather than longer fixes, as they are easier to complete and take less time (a shorter fix may even include telling the learner the answer).
- Fix more important factors before the less important ones.

Attending to these priorities moves the inquiry process in a positive direction and at a good pace, rather than bogging learners down in a tiresome guessing game.

Situated Cognition and Cognitive Apprenticeship

Allan Collins, in collaboration with others, has continued to research the impacts of various external factors on the cognitive learning process. A review of his recent writings suggests that he is mainly focused on learning research that can be used to design effective learning environments in elementary, secondary, and college classrooms (Brown et al., 1989). Even so, his findings can be adapted to adult learning environments, including corporate training courses. His studies on situated cognition and cognitive apprenticeship serve to broaden educators' perspective on learning to include factors well beyond those found in traditional classrooms. In many instances, workplace training has used situated cognition (by training people in the actual job context) and cognitive apprenticeship (by placing a novice with a master to work side by side).

Situated Cognition. Collins challenges traditional educators to move beyond teaching simple knowledge to include where and how the knowledge is used. Along with others (Peters, 1987), he criticizes traditional schooling for separating knowledge from the context in which it will be used, thus shortchanging learners. He suggests that activity and situations are integral to learning and cognition. He bases his premise on cognitive research about the way learners acquire knowledge most effectively. He begins by comparing the methods traditional schools use to teach vocabulary to the way children learn the meanings of words outside school in real situations (Miller & Gildea, 1987; Lave, 1988b). He then equates language to all knowledge. Finally, by considering knowledge as a tool, he makes a telling analogy: Many people acquire tools, yet they do not know how to use them, because they haven't been exposed to the real-world context where they are used authentically.

Collins avers that practitioners of a particular skill set make up a community in the fullest social and cultural sense. Thus the process of acquiring the necessary skills to become a member of that community should also include the enculturation that identifies one as an authentic community member, able to perform authentic tasks just as indigenous members do. In the fullest sense, then, effective learning includes not just acquiring "raw" knowledge, but doing so in the entire environmental surroundings that characterize authentic activities (Lave, 1988a).

Cognitive Apprenticeship. Collins builds on his ideas about situated cognition and authentic tasks to create another cognitive theoretical model. Once again, he has, in collaboration with others, reached into antiquity for ideas on effective teaching methodologies. Just as his cognitive inquiry theory has a basis in classical Socratic dialogues, he has focused on craft apprenticeship, a way to train novices dating from the Middle Ages and earlier, as the basis on which to build a learning model (Collins, Brown, & Newman, 1989). However, Collins' cognitive apprenticeship differs greatly from traditional forms of craft apprenticeship in that it recognizes that most current societally required skills are quite different from classical physically oriented craft skills in that they involve substantial amounts of symbolic and computer-based activities. Collins' model describes the ideal learning environment as consisting of four building blocks: content, methods, sequence, and sociology.

Traditionally, content has been thought to consist of concepts, facts, and procedures. Collins would add several items to this mix: tips and tricks of the trade; cognitive management strategies, such as goal setting, strategic planning, monitoring, evaluating, and revising. In addition, Collins includes learning strategies as required content. These strategies include knowing how to learn, especially in new fields; getting more knowledge on a familiar subject; and reconfiguring knowledge in different ways. This fuller definition of content allows learners to function effectively regardless of the setting.

The Collins model includes a variety of teaching methods, with an emphasis on observing, engaging in, or discovering expert behaviors in context. All his recommended methods encourage learner independence and exploration. Instructors coach and provide learners with "scaffolding" (support while learning tasks), and "fading" (gradually allowing students' control over their own learning).

Sequencing is also a critical part of learning in a cognitive apprenticeship model. The objective is expert performance, and to move the learner to that level requires sequencing of tasks from simple to complex, and situations from singular to diverse. The instructor also manages the learning process to give the learner a feel for the overall domain before attending to details.

The key requirement of Collins' precepts is that the learning environment replicate the real world in terms of technological, social, time, and motivational aspects. It is not only the knowledge, but also the real-world social context in which that knowledge exists that is important (Resnick, 1988). For example, in the real world, tasks are mostly accomplished through problemsolving interactions with other people, so this aspect should be simulated in the learning environment.

The Engineering Practices Introductory Course Sequence (EPICS) at the Colorado School of Mines is a real-world exemplar of cognitive apprenticeship in action. The EPICS program, a four-semester, 11-credit hour sequence, is teaching learners many fundamental engineering skills, but in the context of project work. Learners work in teams of four or five to solve real-world, open-ended problems for clients from industry and government. These authentic projects also provide a context in which students learn and practice skills in oral and written technical communications and teamwork. Based on qualitative and quantitative evidence, EPICS positively influences learners' abilities to learn and work in an authentic, experiential environment in which they must create their own knowledge and meaning, rather than relying on passive, lecture-driven instruction (Pavelich, Olds, & Miller, 1994).

Research Support

Collins and Stevens' theory of cognitive inquiry teaching was inductively derived from extensive detailed scrutiny of the dialogues of many interactive master instructors, including Collins himself, Socrates (in the writings of Plato), Roger Schank, and others. It is more than marginally interesting that the behaviors best taught using this theory (looking at many cases, finding the relevant factors in action, making and testing hypotheses, deriving rules, etc.) were, in effect, used to derive the theory.

The theory of cognitive inquiry is based on the prior writings of Collins and others detailing their investigation into the most effective ways to teach others. The validity of the theory has been proven, not so much in academic research, but in the successful implementation of whole inquiry-based curricula at the primary and secondary school levels.

Best Uses

One of the major strengths of cognitive inquiry is that it is a powerful teaching tool across knowledge domains. The expert performers that Collins and Stevens studied were using inquiry and discovery methods to teach diverse subjects ranging from arithmetic and geography to moral education and problemsolving. Inquiry methods are particularly effective in teaching learners about causality (i.e., principles or theories: "This action caused that effect. Why do you think that is so?"). This characteristic has led to its extensive use in the teaching of scientific subjects. Whole elementary and secondary scientific and social studies curriculums have been built using teaching methodology based on cognitive inquiry theory. It is in the act of inquiry that causality is most effectively taught. Carefully crafted questions, framing an effective instructor-learner dialogue, can be used in the pursuit of learning nonscientific domains, such as leadership, teambuilding, general management skills, marketing and sales, finance, maintenance and safety, product development, and other performance-improvement training interventions.

In fact, using inquiry theory to teach adult learners how to solve problems can be extremely effective in workplace training. After all, it is in the workplace where employees and managers are constantly expected to solve novel problems using their incremental experience and expertise. Since content taught using inquiry theory methods tends to be remembered longer than subjects taught didactically, these methods may be used successfully to teach transferable skills that are critically important. A classic example of this use would be teaching nuclear reactor operators to use their observation of operating variables to choose a control methodology to mediate an emergency situation.

There are at least four important considerations to be aware of in applying these inquiry techniques. In the first place, as efficacious as inquiry methods are, they cannot easily stand alone as a teaching tool. Other methods of instruction should be used in conjunction with inquiry, such as advance organizers, demonstrations, and lectures. The inquiry process requires a context of content and background knowledge within which it can occur. Second, the inquiry process is considerably less efficient in terms of time than other expository methods. It takes time for learners to pursue a line of thinking down false trails, discover and correct logical contradictions in their reasoning, and finally derive the rule or theory being taught. Of course, a carefully thought out scenario of inquiry and an expertly applied sequence of questions can shorten the process somewhat. Third, physical resources to accompany and support the inquiry process can become extensive, particularly where experimentation is required. Finally, a seemingly never-ending sequence of questions can become tiring even for the most curious of learners, particularly in an adult learning setting, where a more pragmatic approach may be valued.

Methods based on cognitive inquiry theory are best used when—

- Improved thinking skills, in addition to content knowledge, are needed.
- Sufficient time and resources, including an instructor skilled in inquiry methods, are available.
- Learners have the necessary background and *a priori* knowledge base in the domain being taught.

The Decision to Use Cognitive Inquiry Theory

In deciding whether to use cognitive inquiry in a learning activity, the instructional designer should answer the list of questions in Table 10.1 during needs analysis. If the answers are positive, cognitive inquiry theory may be an effective method to incorporate into an instructional design.

Designing a lesson based on cognitive inquiry theory is a challenge since the exact sequencing, and indeed, the very timing of the inquiry teaching lesson depends on the facility of the instructor in this method and on the progress of learners toward the objectives of the session. Thus, a strict regimen of learning activities cannot be constructed.

Successful learning experiences based on inquiry methodologies require a close collaboration between the instructional designer and the instructor. This can best be achieved by providing a rich context of lesson materials:

- specific guidance on the rules and theories being taught
- the variables used in formulating the rules
- the factors that affect the value of the variables
- a rich supply of cases—hypothetical and otherwise—and their suggested sequence
- a variety of counterexamples the instructor may draw on in guiding the inquiry process

The challenge to the designer is to think through the inquiry process to discern a particular set of rules from start to finish and to provide the instructor with materials that are appropriate to meet the learning objectives of the session.

Needs Analysis Question	Yes	No
Do you want learners to think for themselves? Are they comfortable in an independent learning mode?		
Do learners have the thinking skills needed for inquiry learning to succeed?		
Have the learners' prior experiences and knowledge bases prepared them for an inquiry regarding the rule or theory being taught?		
Does the course of instruction allow for the time inquiry teaching requires?		
Is there ready access to the resources required to support the inquiry process?		

Table 10.1
Cognitive Inquiry Decision Table

Model in Action

Let's listen in as an inquiry instructor uses strategies of cognitive inquiry theory to teach a group of adults interactively about teambuilding. She has shown a video-tape that first depicts a team in the throes of failure, then shows the same team as a well-organized and optimally functioning, successful unit. Before showing the video, she asked the class to makes lists of specific behaviors based on their observations as they watch both scenarios. She begins the inquiry process:

Inquiry Instructor (II): All of you have made long lists of team behaviors from the video. Can we begin to make any comments about the behaviors that set these two team situations apart?

Class Member (CM): Sure. The successful team was able to communicate well with each other. No one was really talking to each other on the other team.

II: OK. Does anyone have an idea about what caused this?

CM: Maybe the team that could communicate well had been together longer. They knew each other better.

II: Let's look at the factor of the time a team has been together then. How many of you know about or perhaps served on teams that had been together a long time, and were still having trouble communicating?

CM: I certainly have. Time together is just one factor. There are others.

II: Can anyone identify other factors that seem to cause better communications between team members?

CM: OK, how about this? The successful team's members seemed to have a goal they were all committed to. The other team was in disagreement over their goals.

II: All right, let's take a hypothetical case about a team that has been together only a short time, but they are in agreement about their goal. Do you think this team has a chance to be successful?

CM: Yes. It seems as though while time together is important, commitment to a goal might be even more important.

II: What do the rest of you think about this rule?

And so the inquiry process goes on. Soon the learners have derived and prioritized by importance a list of rules that govern effective team behavior. Later, they will use these derived rules to develop a team-building process. During the dialogue, the inquiry instructor has in mind her goals of teaching the learners specific rules about teambuilding, and at the same time she is teaching them skills about how to think systematically in deriving rules based on observations.

Note the inquiry instructor's use of several strategies: First, she used the videotape to present both positive and negative exemplars; then she varied cases systematically to force the class to look at variable factors. She also introduced a hypothetical case to cause them to evaluate the importance of one factor against another. If the class members had brought up observed behaviors in a different order, the inquiry instructor would have used her skills in controlling the inquiry dialogue to adapt her agenda to meet her goals. She would have selected cases with different factors to help her learners evaluate the impact of these factors on the team-building process.

Implementation Guide

Step	Design Instructions
1	List the rules or theories you wish to teach.
2	Identify realistic and stimulating problems for the learners to work on that allow them to derive the rule or theory.
3	Specify some inquiry-based activities the learners could conduct in deriving the rules or theories.
4	List the factors that affect the value of the variable being taught.
5	Develop scenarios and cases in enough variety and with a mix of factors to effectively manage the progress of learners during the inquiry dialogue.
6	Develop counterexamples that will help learners identify the cogent factors that impact the value of the variable being taught.
7	Develop hypothetical cases (what ifs) that encourage learners to consider a range of factors.

References

Brown, J.S., Collins, A., & Duguid, P. (1989). Situated cognition and the culture of learning. *Educational Researcher, 18*, 32–42.

Collins, A. (1987). A sample dialogue based on a theory of inquiry teaching. In C.M. Reigeluth (Ed.), *Instructional design theories in action*. Hillsdale, NJ: Lawrence Erlbaum Associates.

Collins, A., Brown, J.S., & Newman, S.E. (1989). Cognitive apprenticeship: Teaching the craft of reading, writing, and mathematics. In L.B. Resnick (Ed.), *Knowing, learning and instruction: Essays in honor of Robert Glaser* (453–494). Hillsdale, NJ: Lawrence Erlbaum Associates.

Collins, A., & Stevens, A.L. (1989). A cognitive theory of inquiry teaching. In C.M. Reigeluth (Ed.), *Instructional design theories and models: An overview of their current status* (247–278). Hillsdale, NJ: Lawrence Erlbaum Associates.

Dewey, J. (1990). *The school and society* and *The child and the curriculum*. Chicago, IL: University of Chicago Press.

Lave, J. (1988a). *Cognition in practice*. Boston, MA: Cambridge.

Lave, J. (1988b). *Word problems: A microcosm of theories of learning.* Paper presented at AERA annual conference, New Orleans, LA.

Miller, G.A., & Gildea, P.M. (1987). How children learn words. *Scientific American, 257*(3), 94–99.

Pavelich, B.M., Olds, B.M., & Miller, R.L. (1994). Real-world problem solving in freshman/sophomore engineering. In J. Gainen & E.W. Willemsen (Eds.), *New directions in teaching and learning*. San Francisco: Jossey-Bass.

Peters, R. (1987). *Practical intelligence: Working smarter in business and everyday life*. New York: Harper & Row.

Plato. (1924). *Laches, Protagoras, Meno, and Euthydemus.* (W.R.M. Lamb, Trans.). Cambridge, MA: Harvard University Press.

Resnick, L.B. (1988). Treating mathematics as an ill-structured discipline. In R.I. Charles & E.A. Silver (Eds.), *The teaching and assessing of mathematical problem solving* (32–60). Hillsdale, NJ: Lawrence Erlbaum Associates.

Vygotsky, L. (1978). *Mind in society: The development of higher psychological processes*. Cambridge, MA: Harvard University Press.

Bibliography

Collins, A., & Stevens, A.L. (1982). Goals and strategies of effective teachers. In R. Glaser (Ed.), *Advances in instructional psychology* (Vol. 2). Hillsdale, NJ: Lawrence Erlbaum Associates.

About the Author

Peter J. Pallesen, senior information trainer for San Diego, CA-based High Technology Solutions, Inc., has leveraged his extensive and varied business and management background into a career providing just the right kind of performance improvement interventions at just the right time. He develops and delivers various technical and soft skills training in support of a human resources re-engineering project for a large federal agency, including a complete team leader's workshop curriculum for supervisors and managers. His Basic Computer Skills workshop has been distributed agencywide. In addition, he is responsible for developing and delivering a broad variety of proprietary application-specific computer training based on the Lotus Notes and PeopleSoft platforms. He has his graduate certificate in Instructional Design and his MA in Human Performance Systems from Marymount University.

CHAPTER 11

Constructivism

Theresa Falance

Although much has been written about constructivism, it is a concept defying easy description or classification. More accurately described as a philosophical approach than an instructional model, constructivist principles can be effectively incorporated into the very teaching models that its proponents reject. Current debates between practitioners of conventional teaching models and professed constructivists enrich the educational community by questioning accepted ideals and furthering the evolution of inquiry into the nature of learning.

Constructivism asserts that knowledge cannot be transmitted from teacher to student. Rather, knowledge is constructed in the mind of the learner as a consequence of working through real-world situations. Emphasizing the construction of knowledge in the learner's mind, constructivism shares a point of view with cognitive models of teaching. The philosophy reveals social underpinnings by suggesting that learners are more likely to construct new ideas when they are engaged in creating and sharing useful artifacts with others.

As a philosophy, constructivism can be traced to the 18th-century work of the Neapolitan philosopher Giambattista Vico, who held that humans could only clearly understand what they have themselves constructed. Many others worked with these ideas, but the first major contemporaries to develop a clear idea of constructivism as applied to childhood development were Jean Piaget and John Dewey ("Building an Understanding of Constructivism," 1995). Further support for constructivist theories can be found in the works of Lev. S. Vygotsky and Jerome T. Bruner.

With the advent of the information age, constructivism came to the forefront of educational debate. Duffy and Jonassen wrote—

> It is not that constructivism is a new perspective. Rather, we think that the two changes in our society—the volume of information we must manage and the new opportunities provided through technology—have caused us to revisit constructivism. The effect has been indirect. The information age and the technological capabilities have caused us to reconceptualize the learning process and to design new instructional approaches. Both the learning theories and the instructional approaches are consistent with the constructivist epistemology (1992).

Elsewhere, Duffy and Jonassen conclude, "constructivism provides an alternative epistemological base to the objectivist tradition" (Duffy & Jonassen, 1991).

Constructivists distinguish their views from other teaching theories by labeling nonconstructivists as objectivists. While constructivism calls for the development of authentic tasks as fundamental learning activities, objectivists attempt to guide learners through a series of objectives to incorporate knowledge existing in external reality. Objectivists believe that knowledge exists outside the learner's mind and can, indeed, be transmitted from teacher to student.

Constructivist authentic tasks share a commonality with any learning model based on experience. A learner who is totally immersed in an activity is more likely to internalize the experience, building new ideas or thought processes. Today's new media tools—virtual reality environments, "just-in-time" information searches, and multimedia—provide learners with new tools for creating collaborative products of personal meaning. Constructivist theories have great value in the exploration of computer-assisted learning.

Origins

Constructivist concepts can be found in philosophies dating over the past four centuries. In modern times, when educators engage in the quest to understand the nature of learning, components of the constructivist theory emerge.

John Dewey, 1859–1952, the American educator, regarded democracy as the center point of philosophy. By rejecting authoritarian teaching methods, his theories had great impact on progressive education. In his writing, Dewey asserts that knowledge can only emerge in situations from which learners can draw meaningful, personal experiences. According to Dewey, these situations were likely to occur where students joined together in manipulating materials, constructing knowledge together as a "community of learners" (Dewey, 1916).

Jean Piaget, a Swiss psychologist, studied child development over six decades. Piaget's constructivism is based on his view of the psychological development of children. Piaget called for teachers to understand steps in the development of the child's mind. The fundamental basis of learning, he believed, was discovery:

> To understand is to discover, or reconstruct by rediscovery, and such conditions must be complied with if, in the future, individuals are to be formed who are capable of production and creativity and not simply repetition" (Piaget, 1973).

The writings of J. T. Bruner (1961, 1968, 1973) amplify Piaget's theories. He is often quoted on the necessity of "going beyond the information given." Bruner, a cognitive psychologist, contends that the instructor's responsibility is to encourage students to incorporate new principles through discovery. According to Bruner, when learners are given information solely through a verbal presentation, the information tends to "go in one ear and out the other." Even if the student is able to repeat the concept verbatim, if no internal processing takes place, the concept remains unincorporated. A learner cannot use an unincorporated concept in a processes of building new information.

Duffy and Jonassen (1992) extend constructivist theories to the role of instructional designers. In their book *Constructivism and the Technology of Instruction*, they bring together the many voices of contemporary educational theory to explore the relationship of constructivism to other teaching models. Duffy and Jonassen challenge the designer to use technology to develop learning environments that will help students encounter and define reality. Representing constructivist practitioners in the age of technology, the book calls for great innovation in educational practices, as exemplified by a comment by David N. Perkins: "We have the technology for this adventure; can we shift the shape of education at every level?" (1992).

Biographical Sketch

David Jonassen, EdD, is an outstanding contributor to literature on educational technology. A prolific writer, Dr. Jonassen has authored and edited more than 20 books on ISD, hypermedia, cognitive learning tools, and constructivism. Notable contributions include *Constructivism and the Technology of Instruction* (with Thomas M. Duffy) and *Handbook of Research for Educational Communications and Technology*.

Jonassen is a sought-after speaker, having chaired or lectured at educational and psychological conference events worldwide. He has served as an officer or active participant in a number of distinguished groups, including the Association for Educational Communications and Technology, The White House Task Force on Libraries and Information Services, and The American Educational Research Association.

Dr. Jonassen's research interests include mapping knowledge representations in software, computer mindtools for critical thinking, designing constructivist learning environments, constructivist approaches to ISD, and research on needs assessment, task analysis, and front-end analysis.

Currently a professor at Pennsylvania State University, Dr. Jonassen teaches a variety of courses in instructional systems and educational technologies. Before coming to Penn State, he taught at the University of Colorado.

Dr. Jonassen stands out among his constructivist colleagues for his ability to reconcile the philosophy with other models of instructional design. In his own words, "I believe that we need to learn how to use different perspectives as lenses for understanding different aspects of the human condition."

Description

Definition

Constructivist concepts are based on the fundamental belief that knowledge does not exist in the exterior world. All knowledge is constructed in the mind of the learner. To construct new knowledge, learners must experience an activity, either in its actual environment or in a simulated environment "real" enough to allow their total immersion in the situation.

By gaining hands-on interaction with a situation, learners translate experience from external reference to internal reality. Constructivists believe that the acts of creating artifacts with real-world usefulness, in an appropriate setting, and sharing these products with others causes an individual to create a new cognitive structure that makes sense of the encounter. Collaborative work with peers is important in the interpretation of new information. Since humans are social animals, other individual perspectives in the journey of discovery help a learner "negotiate" the meaning of new concepts in a social context.

Designers of constructivist-inspired learning environments are forever in search of the authentic task. The authentic task is an activity that offers an opportunity for learners to enter a real situation, work with the customary tools of that environment, and create a product that has meaning in the learner's world. Instructors set up environments and await the outcome of a learning experience, interacting only as mentors or facilitators to help the learners over stumbling blocks they encounter. Since each person absorbs physical surroundings in a highly personal manner, constructivists believe that it is impossible to set up a series of objectives for achievement through an authentic task.

Constructivists also advocate learning through cognitive apprenticeship. Designers should so arrange the learning environment that learners can interact extensively with experts in the content domain, experiencing how the experts think and solve problems. In this way, learners can "apprentice" themselves and build their own expertise by considering and perhaps trying out the thought process and actions of the expert. This is a different process, however, from behavior modeling, in which the learner attempts to follow exactly the behaviors of the "correct" model of performance. In a constructivist environment, learners are encouraged to construct their own ways of thinking and doing, based only partly on the expert's example. Additionally, the learner is expected to explore other resources and experiences. Ideally, the learner is able to consult multiple experts (and nonhuman resources as well) who hold different views. This important constructivist concept is known as multiple perspectives.

One way to explain constructivism is to contrast it to objectivism. Objectivism is defined by constructivists to be all teaching philosophies and methodologies existing outside the constructivist paradigm. Table 11.1 summarizes how constructivism and objectivism view knowledge and knowledge acquisition differently.

Constructivism	Objectivism
• Knowledge is represented internally as a personal interpretation of an individual's experience. Meaning is imposed on the world by us, rather than existing independently of us. There is no one right way to impose meaning on the world.	• Knowledge exists outside the person in objective reality. The external world is completely and correctly structured in terms of entities, properties, and relations. Meaning exists in the world independently from personal experience.
• There is no correct meaning for which we are striving. All truth is relative.	• Teachers and learners strive for a complete and correct understanding of objective truth.
• A lesson attempts to influence how learners think in a content domain; therefore, designers must attach themselves to a content domain in order to learn how experts solve problems in the domain.	• Instructional design is separated from any particular content. General principles of learning apply across all content domains, with an emphasis on the acquisition of content knowledge.
• Emphasis is on developing thinking and learning skills.	• Emphasis is on gaining content knowledge and skills.

Table 11.1
Constructivism versus Objectivism in Views of Knowledge Acquisition

The constructivist view of learning activities is a solid differentiator between constructivist and objectivist (nonconstructivist) views. According to Cunningham and Duffy, this fundamental distinction is critical to understanding constructivism:

> Traditionally in instruction, we have focused on the information presented or available for learning and have seen the activity of the learner as a vehicle for moving that information into the head. Hence the activity is a matter of processing the information. The constructivists, however, view the learning as the activity in context. The situation as a whole must be examined and understood in order to understand the learning. Rather than the content domain sitting as central, with the activity and the "rest" of the context serving a supporting role, the entire gestalt is integral to what is learned (1996).

The implications for instructional design practice are significant. Table 11.2 summarizes the key contrasts between the constructivist approach and the traditional or objectivist approach. In general, constructivists create a rich environment in which the learner is free to explore, whereas objectivists impose much greater direction and structure on the learning experience.

Constructivists	Objectivists
• Allow learner to set own objectives or allow objectives to emerge.	• Prespecify learning objectives: knowledge, skills, and attitudes to be learned.
• Create a learning environment that encourages construction of understanding from multiple perspectives.	• Use principles from psychology and media to design and sequence the instructional message, both at the macro and micro levels.
• Allow learners to control sequence and perspectives.	• Predefine the perspective that will be taught and the sequence of instruction.
• Do not focus learner attention in ways that depart from the real world.	• Use real-world situations, but not at first. Start with clear-cut, simplified examples and exercises.
• Situate learner in real-world contexts.	• Practice newly learned concepts in real-world contexts but usually only after prerequisites are achieved.
• Teach through cognitive apprenticeship and individual discovery.	• Teach through a variety of methods within a controlled set of learning conditions.
• Evaluate learning based on individual's emerging goals, using real-world criteria if possible.	• Evaluate learner's progress against preset objectives.

Table 11.2
Constructivism versus Objectivism in Instructional Design Practices

Design Principles

David Lebow (1993) proposed Five Principles Toward a New Mindset as constructivist values that might influence instructional design. Lebow describes traditional instructional practices as a "potentially damaging." He sees the ideal teacher's role in the classroom as one of facilitating, managing and guiding students toward an expanded understanding of their world. This point of view is directly opposed to the traditional method of imparting and transferring knowledge. If learners spend their time memorizing data for an upcoming exam, little time is left for dissecting, debating, and reconstructing concepts for incorporation into the learner's thinking process.

The Five Principles Toward a New Mindset are as follows:

1. Maintain a buffer between the learner and the potentially damaging effects of instructional practices.
    - Increase emphasis on the affective domain of learning.
    - Make instruction personally relevant to the learner.
    - Help learners develop skills, attitudes, and beliefs that support self-regulation of the learning process.
    - Balance the tendency to control the learning situation with a desire to promote personal autonomy.
2. Provide a context for learning that supports both autonomy and relatedness.
3. Embed the reasons for learning into the learning activity itself.
4. Support self-regulated learning by promoting skills and attitudes that enable the learner to assume increasing responsibility for the developmental restructuring process.
5. Strengthen the learner's tendency to engage in intentional learning processes, especially by encouraging the strategic exploration of errors.

The usefulness of these principles is clearly demonstrated when applied to the design of computer-based training. In a technology-based system, the computer has to act as an effective teacher by providing a supportive structure. The interface must, therefore, facilitate, manage, and guide students as they actively engage in knowledge construction.

Design Steps

To design activities that are consistent with the constructivist philosophy, an educator must set up a situation where the following features are a natural occurrence (Wilson, 1995):

1. *Observation*—Students make observations of authentic artifacts anchored in authentic situations.
2. *Interpretation Construction*—Students construct interpretations of observations and arguments for the validity of their interpretations.
3. *Contextualization*—Students access background and contextual materials of various sorts to aid interpretation and argumentation.
4. *Cognitive Apprenticeship*—Students serve as apprentices to teachers to master observation, interpretation, and contextualization.
5. *Collaboration*—Students collaborate in observation, interpretation, and contextualization.

6. *Multiple Interpretations*—Students gain cognitive flexibility by being exposed to multiple interpretations.

7. *Multiple Manifestations*—Students gain transferability by seeing multiple manifestations of the same interpretations.

To achieve these features, the designer has several tasks. Typical design tasks for a constructivist learning environment include the following:

- Select an ill-defined, ill-structured problem (e.g., How can we reduce infant mortality in poor countries?).

- Describe the environment in which the problem occurs (e.g., Who works in this environment? Who are the performers and stakeholders? What are the values, beliefs, and power structures involved?).

- Represent the problem in an engaging manner (e.g., a video, story, or virtual reality scenario).

- Provide a problem manipulation space (e.g., physical or symbolic means for learners to manipulate a real or simulated environment).

- Provide related cases (e.g., analogies or similar experiences from which learners can generalize and create mental models).

- Provide information resources and cognitive tools (e.g., databases, websites, and text documents related to infant mortality, as well as computer-based tools that help learners reason, visualize, model, or make decisions).

- Foster and support communities of learners (e.g., encourage collaboration among learners with similar learning goals).

- Make experts and models available (e.g., experts on infant mortality can provide a variety of perspectives on the problem. Other performers can model thinking skills or coach learners).

- Scaffold as needed (e.g., reduce task complexity, help the learner do part of the task, or prescribe the use of cognitive tools when the learner lacks prerequisite skills).

Practical Tips

In an ideal world, all learner experiences would be personal explorations, fully equipped with state-of-the-art tools and mentors of Einstein's stature serving as personal tour guides. In reality, some experiences cannot be authenticated. In a unit discussing the composition of the lunar surface, few will get the opportunity for a "hands-on" exploration of the moon's surface. Radical constructivist thought would reject this unit as useless information since external fact has no basis for incorporation into the learner's cognitive skill set.

Applying the best of constructivist theory to the non-authentic task will deepen an activity's meaningfulness. Perhaps an instructor can't take students to the moon. But a search for the authentic task that would make moon exploration "real" has many possibilities. Students can handle rocks found on earth with similar composition to lunar artifacts. The instructor can move the study environment to a museum facility that surrounds the learner with sensory simulations of lunar environmental conditions or expose students to just-in-time hypermedia that allows them self-paced absorption of relevant content. The instructor can put his or her knowledge of constructivism to good use by taking steps towards personalizing the experience for each learner.

Applications for constructivist techniques occur frequently in the workplace. From experiences as complex as preparing for interstellar flight to those as routine as overcoming client objections, learners will best integrate new learning by running through the paces using authentic situations.

Best Uses

Constructivism and Educational Technology

Current constructivist best practices involve the use of advanced technologies—distance learning, distance collaborative projects, computer simulation environments, and hypermedia searches. In the preface to their book, Duffy and Jonassen make important observations about instruction in the information age. Rapidly increasing and changing information demands a new approach to learning. They point out—

> Traditional models of learning and instruction emphasized forms of mastering the information in a content domain. Storing information and being able to recall it was central to the missions of both schools and business training. However, it simply is no longer possible (there is too much) or even reasonable (it changes too rapidly) to master most content (technical) domains (1992).

When content is a moving target, it is increasingly critical to emphasize development of sophisticated cognitive structures preparing learners to process ever-new information. As Duffy and Jonassen assert, "The goal is not to master the content, but rather to understand and use information to solve a real world problem" (Duffy

& Jonassen, 1992). Fortunately, advanced educational technologies allow users to gather just-in-time information to feed internal processing mechanisms and grind out new answers.

As technology approaches virtual reality capability, the constructivist dream of teaching solely through authentic tasks promises to be fulfilled. Future classrooms may be "holadeck" grids awaiting the learner's simulation program du jour. Since applications of educational technology support constructivist methodologies, its implications are important to designers of future instruction.

In today's instructional design practice, it is possible to merge objectivist and constructivist theory in creating course material. The designer can introduce new skills and concepts using a variety of objectivist techniques such as advance organizers or mnemonics. This groundwork can raise the learner's level of comfort when the learner is confronted with novel experiences offered in an authentic task. Carrying along some useful tools in the journey of discovery would not necessarily disengage a learner's sense of exploration.

Limitations

Until recently, traditional designers found constructivism to be a philosophical approach with little actual instruction published under its banner. That criticism is no longer applicable. Major websites at the University of Colorado and Columbia University are linked to a wealth of sites featuring constructivist lesson plans, most prevalent in middle school mathematics and science. At the time of this writing, a simple Internet search for the combination of "constructivism" + "lesson plan" yielded 33,031 matches, including National Science Foundation and American Mathematical Society recommended links.

In the face of its apparent popularity, constructivism is now challenging instructional designers to reconsider the theories they use in their design work. However, some traditionalists believe that as a model of teaching, constructivism leaves many significant questions unanswered.

Walter Dick evaluated several documents by constructivist authors (1992). Dick questions the scope of constructivist theory, the broad parameters of its instruction over a particular domain, its failure to address entry-level learner behaviors, the difficulty of assessing student learning with a program without stated goals, and the lack of accountability for student learning.

The latter points were recently countered in correspondence between this chapter's author and Dr. Jonassen. When asked to comment on the difficulty of assessing student learning, Jonassen pointed out, "It is presumptuous to believe that we can ever assess (not evaluate) what someone has learned. We can assess some things reliably. But those things are usually the least meaningful, personally or otherwise. That's why so much learning and instruction engages only memorization: because we know how to assess it reliably. But assessing what someone makes of an idea is stochastic, conjectural, nondeterministic, and unpredictable."

Much has been written on how constructivism contrasts with more traditional design approaches. Some experts still contend that important points addressed in "objectivist" styles of teaching have not been thoroughly addressed by constructivists. Although Dick acknowledged the benefits of constructivist interventions, he expressed the hope "...that you [constructivists] will continue to research and evaluate, to identify the real strengths and weaknesses of your approach and to continue to interact with instructional designers about your findings."

And, indeed, constructivists have continued their research in learning and mental models. Scholars like David Jonassen have shared their work with the educational community, successfully exploiting new technologies to reach a large and interested audience.

Traditional instructional designers are usually more willing to employ aspects of constructivist philosophy in more advanced instruction, after basic skill levels have been mastered. But the concept of infusing traditional instruction with constructivist philosophy may be redundant. As Jonassen put it, "They [constructivist principles] will be there anyway. Learners will make whatever sense of instruction they need to. We really only run into trouble when we take the learning out of its natural context and impose it on some very unnatural school context."

Perhaps the strongest proof of constructivist theory applicability is taking place in the corporate world. Products and services that rely on innovation, such as telecommunications and computer networking, need a ready supply of managers, designers, and technicians who already have basic cognitive structures in place to tackle challenges that were not yet imagined when they took their training. Constructivist learning is occurring at the desktop, in the laboratory, and in corporate classrooms, where creative solutions are needed for authentic tasks and multiple perspectives abound.

Research Support

Since there are no stated objectives preceding a constructivist learning experience, performance is difficult to measure by traditional means. However, constructivists can use feedback research to compare actual performance with a set standard of performance. Error analysis can pinpoint any dysfunctional thought processes. The use of student portfolios, including learner-produced artifacts resulting from a set of instruction, can demonstrate a learner's competency.

Constructivism, both as a theory in cognitive psychology and as an educational philosophy, has an extensive research base. Currently, the design of constructivist learning environments is the subject of a great deal of qualitative analysis. Other prominent topics for research include the design of problem-based curricula, computer support for collaborative learning, and instructional models for computer-based learning environments.

A survey of the literature reveals an overwhelming selection of titles on constructivist topics. Additionally, many universities are currently engaged in research in constructivist methodology, particularly as the theory is applied to teaching mathematics, sciences, and educational technology, as well as designing corporate help systems.

The Institute for Learning Technologies (ILT), founded in 1986 at Teachers College, Columbia University, is devoted to research in constructivism and related theories. The Institute works to advance the role of computers and other information technologies in education and society. ILT implements real-world projects, according to constructivist principles, using multimedia and network technologies to create sophisticated learning environments. The Institute maintains a large, well-organized website listing myriad research projects under the constructivist banner.

The National Science Foundation has funded a great many projects involving constructivist methodology. Examples include Purdue University's The Calculus, Concepts, Computers and Cooperative Learning (C4L) and Northwestern University's Materials World Modules (MWM).

Research Support, cont.

The University of California currently has a large research study underway that focuses on the use of computer technology in education. The study, entitled, Computer Technology and Instructional Reform: A National Survey of Teachers and Their School Contexts, will determine the prevalence of constructivist perspectives and constructivist-compatible instructional practices among teachers.

Examples of current constructivist projects that can be found on the World Wide Web include the following:

- Learning Through Collaborative Visualization Project (CoVis)
- Computer-Supported Intentional Learning Environments (CSILE)
- Jasper
- Archetype
- Computer Clubhouse

Model in Action

The constructivist's authentic task is deeply rooted in progressive education. Early examples consistent with the theory include the Foxfire Program, initiated by Elliot Wigginton in 1968. Wigginton, just out of teacher's college, was finding it difficult to maintain order in his ninth and tenth grade English grammar classes in the north Georgia Appalachian community of Rabun Gap. To overcome this problem, he transformed the class into a journalistic exploration of Appalachian culture. Students interviewed elderly community members and converted local knowledge and lore into a series of newspaper and magazine articles, best-selling books, and videos. By taking a collaborative approach to a real-world problem, set in an appropriate environment, under the guidance of an expert mentor, learners created products of genuine value to share with an eager nation. Thirty years later, the program still survives. Foxfire continues to turn out students skilled in journalism, publishing techniques, promotion, project management, and teamwork. Followup with alumni of the Foxfire program suggests that students are able to transfer these skills to employment situations (Puckett, 1989).

The Foxfire experiment demonstrates Lebow's five principles. While engaging learners in real relationships with their subjects, Wigginton maintained a position as mentor and resource, dispensing his knowledge as an expert in journalism as the situation demanded. Students were encouraged to write articles from their unique points of view within an autonomous process. Journalistic and photographic processing skills were incorporated as needed to fulfill the publication goals. Student writers were given increasingly higher levels of responsibility in developing each product. Later studies confirmed the learners' tendencies to engage in intentional learning processes by pursuing careers in areas touched on by their involvement in Foxfire.

A 1995 issue of *Educational Technology* published several examples of more recent constructivist teaching units. The following excerpt demonstrates constructivist guidance in exploring an information domain:

> In the Archaeotype program, students study ancient Greek and Roman history by using observations of simulated archaeological digs to construct interpretations of the history of these sites, while drawing upon a wide variety of background information. The Archaeotype program ... presents the students with a graphic simulation of an archaeological site, then the students study the history of the site through simulated digging up of artifacts, making various measurements of the artifacts in a simulated laboratory (Observation), and relating the objects to what is already known using a wide variety of reference materials (Contextualization). The students work cooperatively in groups (Collaboration), while the teacher models how to deal with such a site then fades her involvement while coaching and supporting the students in their own study efforts (Cognitive Apprenticeship). The students develop ownership of their work by developing their own interpretations of the history of the site and mustering various kinds of evidence for their conclusions (Interpretation Construction). By arguing with the other students and studying related interpretations in the historical literature, they get a sense of other perspectives (Multiple Interpretations). By going through the process a number of times bringing each contextual background to bear on a number of different artifacts, the students learn and understand the many ways that the general principles behind what they are doing become manifest (Multiple Manifestations) (Wilson, 1995).

The example above meets the definition of an authentic task. The learner revisits the dig for more artifacts under different points of view. Students are motivated by their individual interests and set their own pace. Teachers maintain an advisory role. Problemsolving skills are engaged in the collaborative interpretations of data. The challenges built into the project are intentionally multidisciplinary, requiring the use of math, science, history, and philology. Students need to involve different disciplines to solve the problems.

Although constructivism is frequently applied to middle and high school situations, its benefits are not limited to school situations. Adult education specialists generally agree that adults learn what they think is relevant; adults learn through practice; and adults learn at their own pace. Given these principles, it is easy to understand why context is central to adult learning situations:

> Adults learn by constructing meaning from their experiences. Situations that aren't viewed as meaningful are typically rejected as a source of learning. An important aspect of these meaningful learning experiences is that they not only involve one's intellectual faculties, but one's emotional capacities as well. Thus, incorporating elements of social and developmental learning will undoubtedly enhance the impact of standard learning activities (Hermanson, 1996).

Learning in context is, perhaps, more important in the field of medicine than in most other human endeavors. The ability to conduct virtual reality operations on robotic bodies has opened up new worlds of experience for students, previously relegated to practicing on cadavers. The cadavers offered no feedback, while robotic bodies offer a wealth of risk-free information. Constructivist principles are also emerging in the literature about adult literacy. Adults rise up out of illiteracy in their need to read street signs, shopping lists, and bus schedules. Contextual learning is key to maintaining learner interest.

Rapid prototyping is a currently popular methodology for developing new computer software. A programmer using this method will work collaboratively with a prototypical end user, throwing up "straw men" of various functional components. The user/collaborator will either "prove" the component effective or ineffective, working in concert with the programmer. This close association makes use of collaborative work, just-in-time learning, and authentic tasking demonstrating the efficiency of constructivist principles in the workplace.

Implementation Guide

The central component to constructivist design remains the development and implementation of lessons containing authentic tasks and techniques to anchor that new learning to existing cognitive structures.

Although the philosophy behind constructivism demands freedom from setting specific learning objectives in favor of fostering the learner's voyage of discovery in the real-world environment, common objectives for the designer have been documented. A constructivist framework for instruction shapes learning as an individual construction within the learner's environment. Instructional principles derived from constructivism include the following objectives:

1. Anchor all learning activities to a larger task.
2. Support the learner in developing ownership of the task.
3. Design an authentic task.
4. Design the task to reflect the complexity of the environment the learner will face.
5. Support and challenge the learner's thinking.
6. Encourage testing ideas against alternative views and alternative contexts.
7. Provide opportunity for reflection on the content learned and the learning process (Savery & Duffy, 1995).

Considerations in Meeting the Planning Objectives

Considering the objectives listed above, the designer should ask some basic questions in preparation for lesson plan development.

What Are You Trying to Teach? Enacting the authentic task may bring to the forefront some unforeseen advancements in the learner's skill set, critical thinking and/or social skills. Going in, the designer should have a firm concept of the probable outcomes of the experience. For example, in a re-enactment of a paramedic call, practice in making critical decisions could be a likely outcome, but the purpose of the authentic task might be something as simple as learning a series of important steps to a rescue procedure. The design should prepare the facilitator to identify and amplify important developments in the learning process, as they occur.

Why Should the Learner Do This? One big advantage to the "just-in-time" approach to learning favored in the constructivist model is its means of clarifying the reason that a task or procedure is presented. Using this approach, the learner sees the necessity to accomplish a given task as it occurs, within a larger context. When the user is convinced of the need for a particular instruction, ownership is naturally established.

If a human resources manager is practicing counseling techniques and the subject of sexual harassment arises during a routine discussion, the necessity for understanding recognized guidelines for dealing with the situation becomes readily apparent. Instead of designing a presentation as a preamble to set context, the ideal situation occurs when the designer sets up the conditions from which the need for a given skill set will naturally become apparent. The question, "Why should we do this?" should never occur. Instead, the learner should express a need such as, "My photographic enlarger is out of calibration. How can I recalibrate?" while trying to print photographs. In this case, the well-prepared facilitator is ready with materials to support a lesson on recalibration within his or her mentoring role.

What Are the Factors in Designing an Authentic Task? While preparing to launch an authentic task, the designer will need to give ample consideration to the following factors:

1. What are the characteristics of the physical environment where this particular task is usually done in the real world? Will the learners have access to the actual environment or can its characteristics be readily and convincingly simulated?

2. What is the usual set of equipment used by professionals to accomplish this task? Will the learners have access to the equipment or a reasonable facsimile?

3. Is the facilitator a recognized authority in this field, or can he or she present sufficient credentials supporting the role of "expert"?

How Does the Experience Translate to Changes in Thinking? As stated earlier, "The goal is not to master the content, but rather to understand and use information to solve a real-world problem." The more experience individuals have, the larger their pool of resources from which to draw conclusions. While building an authentic task, it is important to design a degree of conflict into the otherwise smooth flow of any procedure. Activities that cause the learners to hypothesize about real-world mysteries such as, "Why does a nurse shark migrate?" are valid even if the learner cannot readily arrive at an answer that would withstand scientific scrutiny. The key is not in making a profound discovery but in acquiring the necessary intellectual tools to formulate a reasonable hypothesis.

How Will You Judge the Learner's Progress? Evaluation poses a challenge to the constructivist lesson planner, because its objectives target higher-order thinking skills. The key to developing evaluation criteria within an authentic task is to use the same criteria that professionals in a real-world situation would use to judge the success of a project. For example, if a project involved implementation of a website that would function smoothly online, a clear evaluation criterion would be met when the site was accessed by a number of different computers without causing the computers to crash or the connection to be broken.

How Will You Help Learners to Reflect on Lessons Learned Through the Experience? In a constructivist lesson, a project "debriefing" session is an important part of the overall experience. A military campaign or a marketing strategy implementation usually concludes with a discussion among participants to document obstacles encountered and overcome them. Similarly, the authentic task is reinforced and cataloged in the learners' minds through a social dialog about the process, conclusions drawn, and by the development of new plans to further the experience.

Steps in Constructivist Lesson Planning

In summary, when attempting to create a constructivist authentic experience for learners, the instructional designer might find the following steps useful in developing a lesson plan:

Step	Action
1	Assess the skills needed by a professional attempting to perform a real-world task.
2	Research the environment and tools required to match the real-world experience.
3	Engage an instructor with sufficient credentials to play the role of mentor.
4	Prepare backup material to teach needed skills "just-in-time" while the task is live.
5	Develop a set of real-world evaluation criteria.
6	Prepare to stage a debriefing session to summarize the learners' experience processing.

References

Bruner, J.S. (1961). *The process of education.* Cambridge, MA: Harvard University Press.

Bruner, J.S. (1968). *Towards a theory of instruction.* New York: W.W. Norton.

Bruner, J.S. (1973). *The relevance of education.* New York: Norton.

Building an understanding of constructivism. (1995). *Classroom Compass, 1*(3), Winter.

Cunningham, D.L., & Duffy, T.M. (1996). Constructivism: Implications for the design and delivery of instruction. In D.H. Jonassen (Ed.), *Handbook of research for educational communications and technology.* New York: Simon & Schuster Macmillan.

Dewey, J. (1916). *Democracy and education.* New York: The Free Press.

Dick, W. (1992). *An instructional designer's view of constructivism: Constructivism and the technology of instruction.* Hillsdale, NJ: Lawrence Erlbaum Associates.

Duffy, T.M., & Jonassen, D.H. (1991). Constructivism: New implications for instructional technology? *Educational Technology, 31*(5), 7–12.

Duffy, T.M., & Jonassen, D.H. (Eds.). (1992). *Constructivism and the technology of instruction.* Hillsdale, NJ: Lawrence Erlbaum Associates.

Hermanson, K. (1996). *Enhancing the effectiveness of adult learning programs: The importance of social and development learning.* New Horizons for Learning, Seattle, WA. [On-line]. Available: http://www.newhorizons.org

Lebow, D. (1993). Constructivist values for instructional systems design: Five principles toward a new mindset. *Educational Technology Research and Development, 41*(3), 4–16.

Perkins, D.N. (1992). Technology meets constructivism. In T. Duffy and D. Jonassen (Eds.), *Constructivism and the technology of instruction.* Hillsdale, NJ: Lawrence Erlbaum Associates.

Piaget, J. (1973). *To understand is to invent.* New York: Grossman.

Puckett, J.L. (1989). *Foxfire reconsidered: A twenty-year experiment in progressive education.* Chicago: University of Illinois Press.

Savery, J.R., & Duffy, T.M. (1995). Problem based learning: An instructional model and its constructivist framework. *Educational Technology, 33*(1), 31–38.

Wilson, B. (Ed.). (1995). *Constructivist learning environments: Case studies in instructional design*. Englewood Cliffs, NJ: Educational Technology Publications.

Bibliography

Vygotsky, L.S. (1978). *Mind in society: The development of higher psychology processes*. Cambridge, MA: Harvard University Press.

Vygotsky, L.S. (1986). *Thought and language*. Cambridge, MA: The MIT Press.

About the Author

Theresa Falance holds an MA in Human Performance Systems and a graduate certificate in Instructional Design from Marymount University. A practicing multimedia producer, Ms. Falance specializes in the design and creation of computer-aided and web-based instructional programs. Ms. Falance is currently a member of the adjunct faculty at George Mason University, where she teaches user interface design tools.

Humanistic, Social, and Affective Models and Strategies *PART III*

This part of the book includes two humanistic models, one social model, and one motivational (affective) model, as well as one "meta" model that seeks to encompass a variety of perspectives, including experiential learning. These models were chosen because they demonstrate diverse yet related theoretical perspectives that consider the learner as a whole person. They are especially useful with adult learners.

Humanistic Models and Strategies

If the theme of behaviorists is "reinforce it," and the two themes of cognitivists are "pour it in" or "discover it," then the theme of humanists is "draw it out." Humanistic models and strategies emphasize respect for the learners' existing knowledge, their judgment about what they need to learn, and their ability to engage in self-directed learning activities and evaluate their own learning. Humanistic educators and trainers believe in developing the whole person, including feelings and values, as well as the intellect. The core purposes of humanistic instruction are self-discovery and self-development, including the enhancement of creativity, self-expression, and self-esteem.

Humanistic approaches to teaching and learning are based, in part, on humanistic models of counseling, such as those of Carl Rogers (1961) and Abraham Maslow (1962). Considering a client's emotional needs first and helping the person satisfy needs for safety, self-esteem, affiliation, and personal growth, humanists believe, create the best path to emotional health. And these approaches also pave the way for academic learning and achievement. Rogers' counseling style was nondirective. Since the client usually knows better than the therapist what needs to be done, the counselor's role is to listen for and reflect feelings. By paraphrasing content, encouraging the expression of feelings, and accepting and reflecting the client's feelings, the therapist leads the client to discover for himself or herself what needs to be done. Transferring this model to instruction (Rogers, 1969, 1982; Rogers & Freiberg, 1993), the teacher becomes a nondirective facilitator and resource person. The learner retains the responsibility to set goals, make learning plans, and carry them out. This model requires tremendous patience and self-discipline on the part of the instructor.

The humanistic model as set forth by Rogers also emphasizes the importance of a genuine, caring, personal relationship between teacher (or therapist) and student (or client). This interpersonal relationship or "way of being" with the learner itself establishes an atmosphere of exploration and encounter. Often called person-centered education, the Rogerian approach emphasizes individual growth and development in the context of a nondirective, supportive mentor. People will learn what they want and need to learn, on their own, when they are emotionally ready and have the proper support.

This notion of the self-directed learner casts a different light on the roles of the instructional designer and instructor, in contrast with both behavioral and cognitive views. It demands, at least, collaboration with the learner, which goes beyond the usual needs assessment, in which learners are often seen as objects to be studied. Adult learning models, two of which are included here (Knowles and Vella), are based in humanism and its notion of the self-directed learner.

Adult Learning

Adults engage in both formal and informal learning. However, adult learning as a separate field of study is relatively new. The field draws extensively, but not exclusively, on humanistic philosophy. Malcolm Knowles (1978) popularized the term *andragogy*, which he defined as the art and science of helping adults learn. Knowles and his followers identified several characteristics that differentiate adult learners from pre-adult learners and require special instructional approaches. For example, adults have a large experience base on which to draw in a learning situation, so this experience should be respected and used in the learning process. According to this model, adults prefer problem-centered, self-directed learning, rather than subject-centered, teacher-directed learning. Adults are ready to learn something when they have a specific life or career need to learn it, so they should be encouraged to learn what they choose, when they choose, and how they choose.

The Knowles school of thought has come under criticism from those who point out that most of the characteristics of adult learners are actually true of pre-adults as well. That is, many children and youth prefer to learn something they can use right away, benefit from building on their previous experiences, enjoy active rather than passive learning activities, and deserve respect from their teachers. Further, some adults in some circumstances prefer and benefit from a more teacher-directed style of learning. Nevertheless, the principles of androgogy are intuitively appealing, widely used with both children and adults, and worthy of consideration for inclusion in any learning design.

Popular (Learner-Centered) Education

Building on the work of Knowles and Brazilian educator Paulo Freire (1974, 1993), Jane Vella (1994) has developed a model for popular or learner-centered education, which she has applied mainly in developing countries. Vella's approach focuses on intense learner involvement at all phases: needs assessment, design of learning activities, delivery of training, and evaluation. Key to this approach are the establishment of a psychologically safe and affirming environment, praxis (a continuous action-reflection cycle), true and equal dialogue between learners and facilitator, treatment of learners as subjects rather than objects, learning of what is immediately useful, and active work in small groups. (Thus, popular education can also be classified as a social model). Vella's model adds to humanistic adult learning principles an extra element of political consciousness raising and empowerment among the learners.

Social Models and Strategies

An idea compatible with humanism is that better learning occurs in groups. Social learning models emphasize the advantages of groups or teams in which learners facilitate each others' learning. Self-directed learners can facilitate other self-directed learners and be facilitated by them. Thus humanistic and social models can go hand-in-hand.

Cooperative Learning

The idea of cooperating to learn academic content and to prepare learners for their roles in social and political life can be found in the writings of Aristotle, Plato, Thomas Aquinas, and Horace Mann. Early in the 20th century, John Dewey (1916) gave expression to the idea of cooperative education and launched a movement in this direction. Contemporary advocates of social approaches have studied ways of structuring learning groups, activities, and rewards to improve results, and impressive learning gains have been achieved (Joyce & Weil, 1996). Nearly every study has shown at least modest effects, compared with control groups, and sometimes very large effects are demonstrated. These results are applicable across different levels of schooling, from elementary through postsecondary education, across different levels of cognitive learning, and across different types of learning outcomes such as attitudes and social skills. Cooperative learning includes various ways of peers teaching peers and ways for groups or teams to be held accountable through various cooperative reward structures.

Affective Models and Strategies

Related to humanism are affective models of instruction, which are concerned primarily with improving learner motivation. Some affective models go so far as to advocate that activities be developed that engage people on an emotional level, and then see what learning objectives emerge from these activities. This, of course, is backward, from the usual systematic instructional design approach, in which objectives are set first, then (sometimes engaging!) activities are developed to promote learning of the objectives. The affective-first approach has been successful, especially in school settings with hard-to-reach learners. Doing something fun and emotionally engaging can make students like school for the first time, so that they grow as people and gradually become willing to participate in academic pursuits.

The affective model chosen for inclusion in this volume, however, is one that draws from various theoretical approaches. Keller's ARCS model is derived from behavioral, cognitive, and affective research findings. The ARCS model has wide applicability, because its principles can be combined with most other instructional design models to add motivational elements to the instruction.

Motivation Through ARCS

Keller's ARCS model (Keller, 1983) integrates a variety of motivational theories and bodies of research evidence on motivation and applies them to the design of learning experiences. Based on this integration, he identifies a collection of motivational factors that affect effort and performance in a learning task. He divides the resulting motivational strategies or prescriptions into four components: attention, relevance, confidence, and satisfaction. The model is included in this part of the book (Chapter 15), because it relates directly to affective concerns in the design of instruction for any type of learning outcome, and it can be used with many other models.

Experiential Learning

Another idea arising from humanism is that of experiential learning. This term may imply the use of general, cumulative life experience as a resource for reflection and learning, and it may also refer to the deliberate provision of active, hands-on experiences as part of the immediate learning experience. In the latter definition, methods such as games, simulations, role plays, case studies, drama, field trips, internships, and team-building exercises are seen as central to the learning process, especially in contrast to more passive or abstract methods of learning, such as reading and listening to lectures. Out of experiences, learners can draw meaning. If experiences are well chosen, and if the followon processing is carefully facilitated, experiential activities can lead to deeply meaningful and lasting learning, because the whole person (intellect and emotions) are involved.

Lancaster: A Meta-Model

The Lancaster model (Chapter 13) encompasses experiential learning but does not limit itself to that modality. Instead, Lancaster presents experiences in the "outer world" as an essential but variable element of a total learning experience, to be balanced by the designer (and the learners) with "inner world" reflection and integration.

This model, developed by a group of scholars at Lancaster University, encompasses aspects of behavioral and cognitive learning approaches, but it especially highlights the importance of direct experience in the overall learning cycle. Recommending both personal action in the outer world and reflection in the inner world (thus involving cognitive and affective aspects of the learner), as well as input from external sources (e.g., readings and lectures), the model seeks to cover learning modes comprehensively. The action-reflection cycle is similar to "praxis" in the popular education model and seems to emphasize the personal and even constructivist nature of learning. Decisions about emphasis and sequence of the different modes (input, action, and reflection) are left to the designer's judgment. Thus the model lays out design alternatives without being prescriptive.

Contributions of Humanistic, Social, and Affective Models and Strategies

Humanistic, social, and affective models of instruction remind designers to consider the whole person, including social and emotional needs as well as intellectual ones. When people are treated with respect, not just as learners but as people, they may be more motivated, and more likely to enter enthusiastically into the learning experience; they may learn more and may transfer more of what they learn to work or life. Models in this family present specific guidance for connecting with learners on a deeper level and ensuring that instruction really meets their needs. Even when using behavioral or cognitive models, humanistic elements can be effectively added to the overall design.

References

Dewey, J. (1916). *Democracy and education*. New York: Macmillan.

Freire, P. (1974). *Education for critical consciousness*. (M.B. Ramos, Trans.). New York: Continuum.

Freire, P. (1993). *Pedagogy of the oppressed*. (M.B. Ramos, Trans.). New York: Continuum.

Joyce, B.R., & Weil, M. (1996). *Models of teaching* (5th ed.). Boston: Allyn & Bacon.

Keller, J.M. (1983). Motivational design of instruction. In C.M. Reigeluth (Ed.), *Instructional design theories and models: An overview of their current status* (383–434). Hillsdale, NJ: Lawrence Erlbaum Associates.

Knowles, M.S. (1978). *The adult learner: A neglected species* (2nd ed.). Houston, TX: Gulf.

Maslow, A. (1962). *Toward a psychology of being*. New York: Van Nostrand.

Rogers, C.R. (1961). *On becoming a person*. Boston: Houghton Mifflin.

Rogers, C.R. (1969). *Freedom to learn*. Columbus, OH: Merrill.

Rogers, C.R. (1982). *Freedom to learn in the eighties*. Columbus, OH: Merrill.

Rogers, C.R., & Freiberg, H.J. (1993). *Freedom to learn* (3rd ed.). New York: Merrill.

Vella, J. (1994). *Learning to listen, learning to teach: The power of dialogue in educating adults*. San Francisco: Jossey-Bass.

CHAPTER 12

Popular Education

Amy A. Greene

Imagine a professor preparing for a traditional university lecture class. Shortly before class, he picks up last semester's notes for the lecture. He intended to review the notes, or maybe even to update them, but he hasn't had the time. As he delivers his lecture, students occasionally ask questions, but he regards these questions as interruptions in the flow of the lecture and dispenses with them as quickly as possible. At the end of class, he doesn't stay to talk with students, but rushes out the door to his research lab, or perhaps to a consulting assignment.

From the popular education perspective, the professor has broken all the rules. He has not designed a class; he has delivered information. The professor's focus is on covering content, not on ensuring that students have mastered the content. His reputation for scholarship is his paramount concern, not the relationship between the subject matter and his students' lives. The professor is the central performer in the classroom, while the students are relatively passive.

Here is an example of a class session that uses Vella's principles of popular education.[1]

---

[1] In her early work, Vella refers to her approach as popular education, reflecting her reliance on many of the principles described by the Brazilian educator Paulo Freire. Vella has begun using the term "learner-centered education" in her recent work. Both terms will be used in this chapter, and both refer to Vella's approach.

Vella was asked to design a program to train college students to teach English to Haitian migrant workers in rural North Carolina. Instead of designing a program for an audience unfamiliar to her, she chose to work for a summer teaching English to the Haitian migrant workers herself. She held her class at the migrants' camp so that the attendees would not need to travel. She began not by teaching but by learning, inviting students to teach her a few words of Creole before they began the English lesson. In the first lesson she asked each participant (all were male) the name of his wife or girlfriend. Each participant then used this name in an English sentence ("I will send Marie a clock"), and then the entire group repeated the sentence.

Vella uses this example to illustrate two of her principles of popular education: the need for careful sequencing of what is to be taught and the need for frequent reinforcement. She begins with names and objects that are part of the learners' experience. She establishes sentence patterns that the whole group repeats. After one participant has recited "I will send Marie a clock," the entire class repeats it: "Jean Pierre will send Marie a clock! He will send Marie a clock!" The next learner supplies his own girlfriend's name and the object to be sent, but the sentence to be learned is otherwise identical: "Antoine will send Annette a pillow!" The sequence is important: Vella begins with sentences that evoke the familiar—the girlfriend's name—and the tangible—objects close at hand. The reinforcement is important: The nearly identical sentences are repeated over and over by the entire group. The personal and the familiar are embedded in the learning of the new skill, speaking English. To some small degree, each student's individuality has been recognized and affirmed.

Vella has designed and facilitated sessions for community development workers in the Maldives, for staff from a substance abuse unit at a veterans hospital, for a voter registration program conducted by a national lobbying organization, and for famine relief workers in Ethiopia. She uses this approach with her own graduate-level classes in public health. The Literacy Volunteers of America has adopted this approach for much of its staff training. Whatever the setting and whatever the skills to be taught, the approach is the same. The instructor and some of the students have worked together on the needs assessment and design, but during the class session, the learners are doing the work. Typically a class of 10 or 12 learners works in pairs or in groups of four on a series of learning tasks. The tasks engage the learner in wrestling with the subject matter; the content is open for critical examination. The instructor is present as a guide, a coach, and a resource, but the learners determine what they will make of the content as they discuss how it relates to their own lives.

Origins

Malcolm Knowles and Paulo Freire are two of the primary influences on Vella's work.

Malcolm Knowles, a leading theorist in the field of adult learning, is best known for developing principles to guide the design of learning events for adults (see Chapter 16). He coined the term "andragogy" to describe the study of how adults learn, as distinguished from pedagogy, the study of how children learn (Knowles and Associates, 1984). Knowles places great importance on a welcoming and nonthreatening climate in the classroom as a prerequisite for adult learning. A podium and rows of desks, implying one-way communication, are replaced by tables for small-group work; the physical environment sends the message that interaction among students will be a significant activity in the classroom. The psychological climate is equally important: Learners must feel respected, comfortable, and welcomed. The classroom event is recognized as a group experience, not an information-delivery session. Knowles uses the term "facilitator" rather than "instructor," reinforcing the idea that the learners—not the instructor—occupy center stage (Knowles, 1984).

Hands-on learning is another hallmark of Knowles' approach. Knowles insists that learning be based on activity on the part of the learners, and based on real and immediate needs. Retention is increased dramatically when learners can actually practice what they are learning, and when as many senses as possible (auditory, visual, kinesthetic) are engaged.

Paulo Freire, the radical Brazilian educator and author of *Pedagogy of the Oppressed* (1972), condemns the traditional educational system for presenting static and generic content to passive students. He labels this approach the "banking approach" to education: The instructor is assumed to be full of knowledge, the students are assumed to be empty, and the process of education consists of the transfer of knowledge intact from instructor to student. In contrast to this banking approach, Freire proposes the problem-posing approach. Students, full partners with the instructor in the learning process, are invited to engage in a discussion of real issues in their lives. Content is presented so as to challenge and invite discussion rather than to provide passive and uncritical consumption. The instructor identifies issues that carry emotional resonance with students—Freire labels these "generative themes"—and presents them to students for discussion. Asking open-ended questions creates an atmosphere of inquiry and reflection, and application to one's own life is encouraged.

Vella has created a very detailed infrastructure for designing adult learning that reflects many of Knowles' ideas. Her focus on group learning tasks as the critical events in the classroom embodies hands-on learning. Her insistence on including learners in the needs assessment and design reflects Knowles' emphasis on process over content delivery and the partnership of instructor and student as collaborators. For both Knowles and Vella, the process orientation does not mean that one is abandoning the content. Instead, it makes the instructor accountable for structuring the content to make it accessible and relevant to learners. It makes both instructor and learner accountable for examining the content critically, challenging it, discussing it, and identifying the parts that can be extracted and used.

Vella has also adopted several fundamental aspects of Freire's approach. She embraces the approach of problem-posing education with its honoring of the learner as the subject of his or her own learning. Following Freire, she bases her approach on the adult as a decisionmaker who learns by making more decisions in the classroom, not by listening to a lecture. She incorporates the use of "generative themes" to make sure that the learning is rooted in the lives of the learners. Vella adopts Freire's distinction between the banking approach to education and the problem-posing approach but refers to the two approaches as "monologue" and "dialogue." The university professor uses monologue (Freire's banking approach), whereas popular education is based on dialogue (Freire's problem-posing approach). For Vella, as for Freire, the dialogue between instructor and student and among students is the process that creates relevant meaning. The dialogue is the mechanism for mediating between the knowledge and experience of the instructor and the knowledge and experience of the participants.

Description

In the popular education (learner-centered) classroom, learners in small groups work through a sequence of tasks. The starting point for the task may be a minilecture, a map or chart included in the student workbook, or a movie clip related to the subject of the course. Participants are provided with open-ended questions to use in discussing the material.

For example, one of the short case studies Vella used frequently with health educators features a nurse teaching in a rural setting. She is trying to teach mothers about proper infant nutrition and how to use growth charts to monitor their babies' growth. The nurse is discouraged because the mothers, who do not read or write, are unresponsive and don't seem to understand the nutrition principles she has presented. For discussing such a case study, Vella prescribes a standard set of four open questions for each small group to use (Vella, 1994, p. 12):

1. What do you see happening here? (description)
2. Why do you think it is happening? (analysis)
3. When it happens in your situation, what problems does it cause? (application)
4. What can we do about it? (implementation)

Biographical Sketch

Dr. **Jane Vella** is the founder and CEO of Global Learning Partners, Inc. (JUBILEE Popular Education Center). Providing both consulting and training services, her organization has trained more than 2500 JUBILEE Fellows in this approach to adult learning. Vella has worked in community education and staff development since 1953, in more than 40 countries around the world. As a Maryknoll Sister, she taught at the University of Dar es Salaam in Tanzania, where she lived from 1955 to 1977. She received her EdD in Adult Education from the University of Massachusetts at Amherst. She lives in Raleigh, North Carolina and is an adjunct professor at the School of Public Health at the University of North Carolina, Chapel Hill, and a member of the Episcopal Church of the Nativity.

Vella's most important books are *Learning to Listen Learning to Teach* (1994), *Training Through Dialogue: Promoting Effective Learning and Change with Adults* (1994), *How Do They Know They Know: Evaluating Adult Learning* (1998), and *Taking Learning to Task: Creative Strategies for Teaching Adults* (2000).

The four questions lead the learner through the phases of description, analysis, application, and implementation or praxis—action combined with reflection. Imagine yourself as a health educator using the four questions. Because the questions are open ended, and because you can draw on your own health education experiences, you and your colleagues would have no difficulty discussing the case study, thinking of alternative approaches for the nurse to use, and learning techniques from each other in the process. This is an example of a problem-posing task; participants are invited to consider and discuss a situation with parallels in their own lives. No instructor or textbook presents health education principles. Instead, students share their reactions to the case study and may generate some principles of their own.

If a well-known health educator has developed a set of principles that students need to know about, these will be presented in the student workbook as resource material for one of the classroom tasks (rather than as a lecture). The task, however, might be worded, "Read the following list of 16 principles for health educators. In your small groups, choose three of these principles that have particular relevance to your own work. Discuss how these principles are applied (or not) in your own work setting and identify their implications. We'll share responses from each group." In this way, students are introduced to the principles but are invited to test them against their own experience.

Work on tasks in small groups, punctuated by debriefing sessions and occasional whole-group activities, is the focus of the learner-centered classroom. These tasks rest on the investigation of learners' current needs and concerns and the creation of a design that incorporates those needs and concerns.

This approach requires a significant amount of preparation time for the needs assessment and design, and a significant degree of care and engagement on the part of the designer/instructor.

Needs Assessment and Design

The popular education approach as practiced by Vella does not lend itself to last-minute design; every training session is a carefully customized event. The approach rests on significant preparation that involves both the instructor and at least a sample of the participants. The focus on preparation is one of the ways in which the design embodies respect for the attendees; the designer knows that attendees will be taking time out of busy schedules and is accountable to the attendees to use the time as carefully as possible.

One person (or a small team) performs the needs assessment, designs the session, and teaches it. The consistency of personnel across phases is essential: It creates the consistency of relationships that sets up the context for the learning. The purpose of the needs assessment phase is two-fold: first, to gather information about the learners' current situation; second, to begin a dialogue with at least some of the learners. This initial contact between instructor and participants serves as a model for their future work together. Even before they arrive at the training site, some of the participants have learned that their preferences and ideas are valued and that their participation is a necessary and integral part of the design. Climate-setting for the classroom has already begun.

To start the needs assessment process, the instructor collects background documentation and visits the learners' work site to experience the environment firsthand and to talk informally with some of the learners. Then the instructor is ready to move into the more focused data-gathering phase.

Vella outlines Seven Steps of Planning, which entail seven critical questions about the proposed event: who, why, when, where, what for, what, and how. The first question to be answered is not just "Who is coming?" as a list of names, but as in "What are their most pressing concerns? What do they already know? What is the session preparing them to do?" The instructor enlists the help of at least a sample of those who will attend the session to work though the steps and answer these questions, outlined in Table 12.1.

Planning Step	Detailed Questions
Who	Who are the attendees?
Why	Why do they need this learning? What are the catalysts for this need?
When	When will the session take place? How can the session be scheduled to be most convenient for the attendees?
Where	Where will the session take place? Can it be held close to the attendees' workplace or home? What arrangements would make the attendees most comfortable?
What	What needs to be learned: skills, knowledge, attitudes?
What For	How will the learning in the session be used on the job or in the community? What are the session's objectives?
How	What will the learning tasks be? What materials will be needed?

Table 12.1
The Seven Steps of Planning

After identifying skills, knowledge, and attitudes that need to be taught, the designer compiles objectives for the session. These are achievement-based objectives, referred to in Vella's later work as ABOs. ABOs are a list of the major activities that learners will engage in during the session. Here is the list of achievement-based objectives that Vella used for a two-hour session on holding more effective meetings (Vella, 1994, pp. 25–26). By the end of the session, everyone will have—

1. Named some problems we have with meetings

2. Examined a list of guidelines for a good meeting

3. Added to that list

4. Named the guidelines that are most useful to us

5. Practiced using at least one guideline
6. Distinguished between a consultative and a deliberative voice

During the session, participants will work through tasks relating to each of these objectives.

During the needs assessment phase, the instructor has identified one or more "generative" themes among the learners. One of the concepts Vella borrowed from Freire, a generative theme is a persistent issue that crops up over and over in conversations with learners. Careful listening and keen observation may lead the instructor to realize that the skill and knowledge gaps identified are not the real issue. Perhaps, instead, lack of resources or inadequate support present significant obstacles to performance. The challenge is to determine how to incorporate these themes into the design.

The instructor then designs a series of tasks to be undertaken in small groups that will address these critical skills. This is the heart of the designer's work: gathering materials that can be included in a workbook together with directions for the task and information about debriefing afterward. Case studies, maps, stories, guidelines from experts in the field—all must be identified and matched with appropriate open-ended questions. Learners will work with and wrestle with the content, validating it or challenging it based on their own experience.

Vella has developed a checklist of competencies toward effective designs in popular education. The competencies are phrased as questions and range from questions about the preparation ("Have you been in dialogue with adult students prior to the course?") through questions about inclusion and engagement ("Have you designed for optimal engagement of all via small group work?" (Vella, 1995, pp. 148–150). The complete checklist of competencies is provided in "Popular Education: Action Indicator" at the end of this chapter.

Relationships and Roles

Relationships between instructor and learners and among learners are considered the primary tools for creating relevant meaning in the classroom.

The approach rooted in dialogue presumes that several elements are in place. The instructor and participants are prepared to engage in dialogue with one another and with other participants, and they accept that the learning resulting from their discussions constitutes the most valuable use of their time together. The participants cannot remain unengaged but are enticed to invest themselves in the occasion. Their participation creates the learning most appropriate to their current needs. This approach places demands both on the instructor and on the learner that differ from those imposed by the traditional classroom lecture model.

Role of Instructor

Before the session begins, at least several students have observed the instructor modeling an open and collaborative approach as part of the needs assessment phase. This frees the instructor to concentrate on the interpersonal aspects of the session: the complex and delicate work of engaging in dialogue with learners as a colearner, open to new ideas and challenges to the subject matter, but firmly in control of getting the group through the planned learning tasks.

The role of the instructor as prescribed by Vella is a challenging one. As he or she designs the session and engages participants early in the workshop, the instructor has an activist role. Once the students are engaged in learning tasks, the instructor must practice attentive restraint. He or she must allow students to perform the learning tasks without interference. He or she monitors the energy level in the group, calling for a change of pace if groups seem to be losing steam or are distracted from the task at hand.

How can the instructor be accountable to attendees to teach the subject of the session while remaining responsive to attendees as adults and decisionmakers? Vella solves this contradiction, in part, by distinguishing between the two types of "voice" present in the classroom. The instructor has the deliberative voice in designing the objectives and the learning tasks. The attendees have the consultative voice; that is, they may make their opinions known, but the instructor has the final say. When attendees are working in small groups on their tasks, the roles are reversed: The students have the deliberative voice on the shape their product will take, and the instructor has the consultative role; he or she may provide advice when asked, and students are free to follow it or not, as they see fit. It is this consultative role that many instructors trained in traditional educational systems find difficult. Vella describes the role this way: "What is the task of the instructor in all this? ... It is to sit still, to pay attention, and to keep quiet. The participants' working through the task independently is their way to learning, and any uninvited 'help' from the instructor can stop that difficult and efficacious process" (Vella, 1995, p. 47).

Vella compares the role of the instructor to that of a back seat driver or a sports coach: The learner is the principal performer of the task, but the instructor is present to provide support, to observe and give feedback, and to answer questions.

Role of Learner

From the beginning of an engagement, the learner-centered instructor demonstrates a commitment to being a partner in dialogue, not a pontificator on a certain body of content. The instructor models respect for the learner, his or her needs, time, and need for relevance and immediacy. The instructor hopes to invite the learner away from his reliance on the instructor as the only authority. He or she hopes to invite learners towards a recognition of their own needs and preferences as the starting point for learning, and toward an appreciation of peers as educational resources.

The learner needs to accept that the real work is done in small groups. The work does not need to be debriefed or reported on to the instructor or discussed by the class as a whole for it to be valid, although all of these things often occur. What constitutes the primary learning is the discussion necessary among members of the small group to understand the task, plan the task, perform the task, report on their outcome to the rest of the group, and reflect on its success.

Popular education alters the traditional balance of power implicit in the teaching relationship. Who is the authority? The instructor has the formal position and the responsibility of planning and conducting an appropriate learning session. The students, however, are the authority on what they need to learn and why. The two come together in a well-prepared learner-centered session.

Principles for Effective Adult Learning

Performing a careful needs assessment and establishing the dialogue between instructor and student are critical starting points. The 12 principles provided in Table 12.2 highlight other important features of the learner-centered approach: an environment of respect, learners working in teams on skills with immediate relevance, the need for clearly defined roles for instructor and student, and the need for affective and psychomotor as well as cognitive engagement.

	Principle	Description
1.	Needs Assessment	At least a sample of attendees must be included in the planning stages of a training session. In this way, dialogue between instructor and student begins even before a face-to-face meeting.
2.	Safety	Tasks are designed for pairs and small groups, providing a safe environment for sharing experiences and practicing new skills.
3.	Sound Relationships	The instructor is a coach, available as a resource to help the learners perform classroom tasks. The instructor needs to engage in dialogue with learners, not to convey information but to work with them toward new understanding.
4.	Sequence and Reinforcement	The tasks that attendees engage in during the class must follow a logical progression, allowing attendees to master simple and less-threatening tasks before moving on to more challenging ones.
5.	Praxis	The design must plan for what attendees will do, not for what the instructor will do. All content must be presented as tasks for attendees to work on in small groups. Group discussion encourages reflecting on the task performed.
6.	Respect for Learners	Learners are encouraged to participate as adults, providing modifications to the objectives based on their needs, sharing their experiences, and making their own decisions about how to carry out the tasks.
7.	Ideas, Feelings, Actions	Tasks are designed to involve as many of these aspects as is practicable.
8.	Immediacy	Learners must be able to find an immediate use for what they're learning.

Table 12.2
Twelve Principles for Effective Adult Learning

Principle	Description
9. Clear Roles	The conduct of a popular education session includes both deliberative (decisionmaking) and consultative (advice-giving) roles. The instructor has a deliberative role in the sequencing of tasks, while learners have a deliberative role in deciding on a topic for their practice teaching sessions.
10. Teamwork	Learners work primarily in small groups of four or six. In these groups, everyone's voice can be heard, questions can be asked in a safe environment, and leaders can readily emerge.
11. Engagement	Tasks must invite learner participation from the start.
12. Accountability	Vella's perennial question is, "How do they know they know?" Learners know they know because they have performed the tasks that the session was designed to teach.

Table 12.2
Twelve Principles for Effective Adult Learning (cont.)

Best Uses

Vella has used this approach extensively with adults for learning related to the workplace and in professional training programs.

The model's success depends on the motivation and behavior of both the instructor and the students. It is dependent on the instructor to do the following:

- Establish a dialogue with students before the session begins through the needs assessment.
- Demonstrate early on that a valuable learning event is possible using the proposed design.
- Model the principles on which the design is based:
    - The primacy of dialogue as a learning tool
    - The responsiveness to immediate concerns

The model is also dependent upon students who—

- Agree to a highly participatory and social experience.
- Agree to abandon the convention of receiving information from a single authority, the instructor.

The success of the model is heavily dependent on the affective qualities of the instructor. It demands an instructor who is genuinely open, curious, engaged, and tolerant of ambiguity and spontaneity. It demands an instructor willing to engage as an equal in the learning process. It demands an instructor who can ensure that the planned learning tasks take place, but who can allow for individuality in the way the tasks are executed.

The key is that the subject matter must be handled in a problem-posing way, allowing participants to relate it to their day-to-day concerns and interests.

While most of Vella's examples are drawn from the nonprofit, education, and government sectors, this approach could also be used in selected ways in the for-profit world. This customized, personal approach might be most useful for a hand-picked group of newly hired employees destined for the executive fast track or for a special high-level task force brought together to solve a critical problem. It could be used to introduce a skill or concept to small groups in cases where implementation is expected to meet with resistance, and when the sponsoring organization is willing to invest the time necessary to hear attendees' points of view.

The approach does not lend itself to widescale implementation for large numbers of employees. It will be more welcome in organizations that encourage diversity and self-expression than in organizations where control and conformity are the goals. This is labor-intensive and relationship-intensive education, highly customized for each small group of learners. The goal is to create a unique event, responsive to and inclusive of all the individuals involved. Such an event takes a significant amount of time for preparation and significant energy for execution.

The popular education approach also lends itself to a partial adoption when a full-scale implementation is not possible. Soliciting participants' reactions to proposed objectives, presenting some if not all subject matter as tasks for small groups rather than in a lecture format, making sure all participants are called by their preferred names—these aspects of a learner-centered approach can often be included as a part of more traditional sessions. Vella currently writes a monthly column for *Convene*, the monthly publication of the Professional Conference Management Association, in which she presents learner-centered ideas that can be adapted to a typical conference format. One of her suggestions is to use a small-group format for a scheduled "panel discussion," but to assign each panel member to a different table to work on tasks along with the participants (Vella, 1999).

Educators use aspects of the learner-centered approach with certain groups of children who have failed in—or have been failed by—more traditional school settings. Programs for gifted children are likely to provide opportunities for students to pursue their own interests. Programs for disruptive teenagers may include small classes and a high instructor-student ratio with the intention of fostering close personal relationships. What do these children have in common? A clear sense of their own drives, needs, and interests; a refusal to be passively and anonymously processed through an educational system; and a need to have their individuality acknowledged and affirmed before they feel respected enough and secure enough to learn. Adults have these needs, too, and a learner-centered approach can successfully meet these needs in a wide variety of settings.

Research Support

Though she possesses academic credentials, Vella considers herself a practitioner—working and reflecting on what she's learned and modifying her approach as needed—rather than an academic researcher. She is continuously refining her approach through both her own experience and reports from students trained in her approach as JUBILEE Fellows through the JUBILEE Popular Education Center.

Model in Action

Vella has successfully practiced her approach in a wide variety of settings. These range from two-hour sessions on how to plan successful meetings to one-week sessions for physicians in Bangladesh on teaching basic hydration principles. Two examples are given here.

The English lesson for Haitian migrant workers, described earlier, illustrates several of the 12 principles. Vella was able to establish a fruitful rapport between herself and the learners by learning some basic phrases in Creole from them at the first class meeting, opening herself up to friendly ridicule and showing herself willing to be a learner before she began to teach. She was able to establish dialogue even in the absence of a common language (sound relationships). She incorporated an affective element by using names of Haitian family members in the English sentences. She drilled the students on the new rhythms of English by having them drum out the sentence patterns on the wall (ideas, feelings, and actions).

A second example, teaching community development workers in rural Nepal, highlights some of the same issues in a different setting. Vella conducted a train-the-trainer session with Save the Children field staff working in rural areas. Participants were lodged in tents, but no classroom space had been provided. Vella charged the group to find a setting that could be used as a classroom. Although she had noticed an abandoned shed nearby and had wondered if it might serve as a classroom, she did not suggest use of the shed herself. When members of the group discovered the shed and suggested it, she concurred. The group worked together to clean up the shed.

Vella uses this example to illustrate the principle of respect for learners. Even before the formal portion of the training session started, Vella involved participants as co-designers of their own learning experience.

Implementation Guide

For those accustomed to traditional instructor-centered instructional models, the learner-centered approach requires a significant adjustment. The demands on the instructor are considerable: The instructor needs to engage in dialogue with students from the beginning of the planning process and must be willing to let spontaneous classroom interactions lead both him or her and the students in unanticipated directions. However, Vella's seven planning steps, the 12 principles for effective adult learning, and the checklist of competencies toward effective designs in popular education provide clear directions as to how to begin.

Step	Action
	Before the Session
1	Gather information about the learners and their learning needs. Involve sample of learners in the seven planning steps. Listen for "generative" themes.
2	Identify skills, knowledge, and attitudes to be taught.
3	Develop achievement-based objectives.
4	Develop and sequence the small group tasks that participants will perform to achieve the objectives. Include both a warm-up (ice-breaker) task and a closing (summary) task. Use the 12 principles for guidance.
5	Use the checklist of competencies to ensure a sound design (see page 259).
6	Prepare workbooks and all additional classroom resources.
7	Prepare for evaluation by identifying predicted effects and outcomes.
	During the Session
1	Discuss the objectives with attendees and modify them as necessary.
2	Make yourself accessible as participants work though their tasks.
3	Monitor the energy level in the classroom. Be prepared to switch gears if motivation seems to be flagging. Intervene as necessary if immediate concerns need to take precedence over the planned agenda.
4	Keenly observe group interactions; be alert to disengaged or disruptive participants. Talk one on one with a disruptive participant if necessary.
5	Establish a plan for followup and support for students after the session.
6	Perform formative evaluation throughout the session (for instance, at the end of each day in a multiday session).
	After the Session
1	Reflect on the session and decide what might need to be modified for the next offering. This is praxis!
2	Evaluate the session based on expected outcomes.
3	Dialogue with other popular educators to share ideas and gain support.

Popular Education: Action Indicator

The checklist presented below is intended for use by for those who have had some formal training in the popular education approach. Vella presents the list as an "action indicator" for designers to determine to what extent they are including the popular or learner-centered approach into their designs. It may also be useful as a guide for those who have not attended formal training (Vella, 1995, pp. 148–150).

Checklist of Competencies

Toward Effective Designs in Popular Education[2]

Have you—

1. Been in dialogue with adult students prior to the course?

    Yes___   Not yet___

2. Prepared the course by using all seven steps of planning?

    Yes___   Not yet___

3. Negotiated the size of the group for optimal learning?

    Yes___   Not yet___

4. Set learning tasks for small groups of learners to teach the content?

    Yes___   Not yet___

5. Examined these learning tasks for sequence: easy to more difficult, simple to complex?

    Yes___   Not yet___

6. Designed a warm-up task that is related to the topic and appropriate for the group?

    Yes___   Not yet___

7. Honored in your design the fact that adult learners are subjects of their own lives?

    Yes___   Not yet___

---

[2] *Training through dialogue: Promoting effective learning and change with adults.* Vella, J.K. © 1995. John Wiley & Sons, Inc. Reprinted by permission of Jossey-Bass, Inc., a subsidiary of John Wiley & Sons, Inc.

8. Named content (skills, knowledge, and attitudes) clearly and cogently?

   Yes___   Not yet___

9. Designed achievement-based objectives that can be readily evaluated?

   Yes___   Not yet___

10. Selected a site that lends itself to small-group work?

    Yes___   Not yet___

11. Kept an eye on the time frame so that learning tasks can be accomplished, avoiding too much "what" for the "when"?

    Yes___   Not yet___

12. Used open questions to stimulate dialogue throughout?

    Yes___   Not yet___

13. Examined each learning task for its cognitive, psychomotor, and affective potential?

    Yes___   Not yet___

14. Designed for safety of teacher and learners?

    Yes___   Not yet___

15. Set up processes and structures (small groups, breaks, gallery walk review of charts) to assure inclusion?

    Yes___   Not yet___

16. Used brainstorming or associative processes without judging or editing?

    Yes___   Not yet___

17. Designed for optimal engagement of all via small-group work, learning tasks, affirming responses, echoing?

    Yes___   Not yet___

18. Avoided monologue by designing for dialogue?

    Yes___   Not yet___

19. Designed a synthesis learning task to summarize all that has been learned?

    Yes___   Not yet___

20. Designed in quiet, reflective time for learners to think about what they are learning?

    Yes___   Not yet___

21. Designed adequate closure tasks?

    Yes___   Not yet___

22. Designed an opportunity for small groups to examine their own group and task maintenance?

Yes___   Not yet___

23. Used a wide variety of techniques?

Brainstorming via snow cards

Critical incident and open questions

Echoing or paraphrasing

Lavish affirmation

Lecture that is not monologue but part of the learning task

Song, dance, mime, artwork

Found objects

Gallery walk for review

Handouts, summary notes

References

Freire, P. (1972). *Pedagogy of the oppressed.* (M.B. Ramos, Trans.). New York: Herder and Herder.

Knowles, M. (1984). *The adult learner: A neglected species* (3rd ed.). Houston, TX: Gulf Publishing Company.

Knowles, M., and Associates. (1984). *Andragogy in action.* San Francisco: Jossey-Bass Publishers.

Vella, J.K. (1994). *Learning to listen, learning to teach: The power of dialogue in educating adults.* San Francisco: Jossey-Bass Publishers.

Vella, J.K. (1995). *Training through dialogue: Promoting effective learning and change with adults.* San Francisco: Jossey-Bass Publishers.

Vella, J.K. (1999). Start . . . Don't stop the learning. *Convene,* pp. 17.

Bibliography

Freire, P. (1973). *Education for critical consciousness.* New York: The Seabury Press.

Freire, P. (1999). *Pedagogy of hope: Reliving pedagogy of the oppressed.* (R.R. Barr, Trans.). New York: Continuum.

hooks, b. (1994). *Teaching to transgress: Education as the practice of freedom.* New York: Routledge.

Shor, I. (1987). *Freire for the classroom: A sourcebook for liberatory teaching.* Portsmouth, NH: Boynton/Cook.

Shor, I. (1992). *Empowering education: Critical teaching for social change.* Chicago: University of Chicago Press.

Shor, I. (1996). *When students have power: Negotiating authority in a critical pedagogy.* Chicago: University of Chicago Press, 1996.

Shor, I., & Freire, P. (1987). *A pedagogy for liberation: Dialogues on transforming education.* South Hadley, MA: Bergin and Garvey Publishers.

Vella, J.K. (1979). *Learning to listen: A guide to methods of adult nonformal education.* Amherst, MA: Center for International Education.

Vella, J.K. (2000). *Taking learning to task: Creative strategies for teaching adults*. San Francisco: Jossey-Bass Publishers.

Vella, J.K., Berardinelli, P., & Burrow, J. (1998). *How do they know they know: Evaluating adult learning*. San Francisco: Jossey-Bass Publishers.

About the Author

Amy A. Greene is a senior instructional designer at RWD Technologies, Inc. based in Columbia, Maryland, where she develops training materials. She holds a BA from Vassar College and an MA in Human Resource Development from Marymount University in Arlington, Virginia. Her experience includes classroom teaching on the high school and college levels and service as a Peace Corps Volunteer in Senegal.

CHAPTER 13

Lancaster Model of Learning

Kristina M. Holdsworth

A structurally simple design model by nature, the Lancaster model of learning is an extremely versatile design tool. It incorporates three broad, inter-related methods of learning, which can be easily adjusted to draw on individual student knowledge and experience and adapted to a variety of content and learning needs. The Lancaster model encompasses learning in both the *inner* and *outer* worlds, addressing learning processed internally as well as learning received from external surroundings. This model directs designers to whole-loop learning cycles, encompassing learning through the modes of receipt of input, reflection, and discovery. The sequence and emphasis of each mode vary, depending on the content, context, and the learner's own knowledge and experience.

The Lancaster model of learning includes elements of both the cognitive and personal/humanistic theoretical perspectives. If it must be classified, it fits most closely into the personal/humanistic family due to its heavy reliance on the learner's personal experience and its lack of emphasis on specified learning outcomes.

The Lancaster model attempts to be a sort of "megamodel." By its flexibility, it incorporates the possibilities of discovery-based or experiential learning, traditional lecture and reading-based instruction, and the kinds of learning that result from inner self-reflection. While advocating a balance among the three modes of receipt of input, reflection, and discovery, the model does not prescribe particular emphases for particular situations, leaving such decisions to the designer's judgment and creativity.

Origins

The Lancaster model of learning was created by a group of professors and students from the Centre for the Study of Management Learning at the University of Lancaster, United Kingdom. Those involved include John Burgoyne, Roger Stuart, and Don Binsted, among others. The model was conceptualized prior to 1980, but no exact development dates have been identified.

The model was designed to reflect a whole-loop learning cycle encompassing three different learning modes within both the inner and outer learning parameters. The creators of the model believed that instruction that addresses combinations of learning modes is more effective than a singular mode approach. This model demonstrates such combinations, accounting for design adjustments to be made in several areas depending on the information to be taught and the prior knowledge and experiences of the learners. The sequencing of the modes of learning can be adjusted to capitalize on the most effective starting point, whether it be information-based, experience-based, or reflective from the learner's perspective.

The model has not been extensively published, thus its utilization has most likely been limited to the original authors and their colleagues in the United Kingdom. No formal research on the model or publications on specific applications of the design principles have been located.

Description

The inner and outer worlds comprise the two dimensions of the Lancaster model of learning. The dimensions of the model are based on where the learning takes place. Learning can come from information and experience received externally (outer world) or from cognitive processing and self-discovery of the student (inner world) (Stuart & Binstead). Three modes of learning are used within the two dimensions. Learning is achieved by receipt of input, reflection, and discovery (Figure 13.1). There are many variations in the application of these elements.

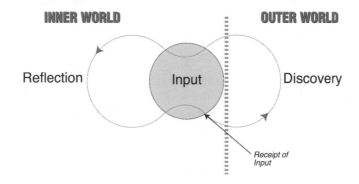

Figure 13.1
Lancaster Model of Learning[1]

The Inner and Outer Worlds

According to the Lancaster model, the learning process occurs in two dimensions: the inner world and the outer world. The inner world consists of each individual's personal knowledge, based on and interpreted through internal constructs of definitions, interpretations, and aptitudes. The outer world is the place where each individual's knowledge and meaning may be discovered, tested, and applied—where an individual acts on his surroundings. Information from which learning is derived can come from original thought and from outside sources but should always be applied to the learner's inner-world framework. All operations in the outer world are based on the schema defined in one's inner world (Stuart & Binstead).

The outer world is where the learner actively provides a stimulus (acts) and observes the response. For example, a student may apply a proactive management concept to his or her outer world (a real situation at work). This stimulus and the subsequent response represent an outer-world experience. The stimulus in this case is an experimental action, but such stimulus can be generated from knowledge from the inner world. However, new learning is being generated in the outer world.

Continuing the learning process based on the experimental action in proactive management, the next step will be to reflect (inner world) on the stimulus and subsequent observations. For example, when the manager contemplates information, considering it within the framework of previously developed constructs, learning

---

[1] *Lancaster Model of Learning* (Stuart & Binstead)

occurs in—and as a result of—the learner's inner world. Any understanding the learner generates is then held in the same framework within the inner world.

Three Modes of Learning

The Lancaster model describes three distinct yet interwoven modes of learning, each occurring within the inner and outer worlds: receipt of input, reflection, and discovery (Stuart & Binstead). They can occur in any order and will vary in their levels of emphasis depending on the desired learning outcome and the philosophy of the designer.

A computer training scenario can illustrate concepts of each mode. The scenario is based on the following:

- **Co., Inc. Example:**

  Company Incorporated (Co. Inc.) has just designed a new intranet system for its employees. Employees can use the new system to access business development information, intellectual capital, HR benefit forms and information, employee contact information, etc. The training task is to educate employees on the capabilities of the system and train them to use it to efficiently access information that will contribute to business development, task completion, and accessing personnel services. In designing the training for this initiative, the instructional systems design staff will use the Lancaster model of learning, concentrating on the whole-loop cycle. Elements of their design are used to illustrate applications of each mode of learning.

In the following sections, each mode is described independently, and illustrated with a short example of the concept. However, the intended use of each mode is in conjunction with the remaining modes. (The integrated illustration utilizing all modes of learning is shown in Figure 13.1).

Discovery. Discovery is a two-step process involving learning by action and observation of the consequences. The first step in the process is an act of experimentation. This action can be either proactive or reactive, but is essentially learning by doing—experiencing something in the outer world. The second step of discovery is the acceptance and understanding of the consequences of the action taken. This acknowledgment can be based on either internal (self-generated) or external (instructor/peer) feedback. Figure 13.2 displays the discovery loop and associated steps (Stuart & Binstead).

- **Co., Inc. Example**

  In the Co. Inc. example, the discovery component of the instruction is centered around a monitored computer training classroom, with each learner at an intranet computer station. Learners are assumed to have a basic understanding of web surfing/searching concepts as well as knowledge of available corporate information. Participants would be asked to identify the types of information accessible through the Co. Inc. intranet. The classroom is monitored by knowledgeable instructors who guide the exploration of individuals on an as-needed basis.

The experience loop can also be accomplished in either past or future tense. Stuart & Binstead propose asking the questions "Did you ever?" and "What happened?" Or you can ask the questions "Could you imagine doing?" and "What would happen?" The "future" option is a sort of "mind experiment" that could substitute for costly, dangerous, or time-consuming hands-on experience.

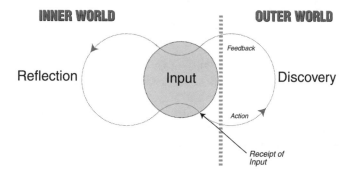

Figure 13.2
Discovery Process

Reflection. Reflection is also a two-step process (see Figure 13.3). Both of the steps in reflection take place in the inner world and are entirely self-generated. The first step in reflection is to conceptualize: integrating knowledge, observations, and experiences into a cohesive basis, literally "forming in the mind." The second step is taking the conceptualization one step further by forming hypotheses on how similar situations may play out in the future. It is the application of knowledge in one's mind, in preparation for application to the outer world.

- **Co., Inc. Example**

  In the intranet training scenario, reflection is stimulated by calling on participants to generate realistic scenarios that require (or would be well suited to) use of the Co. Inc. intranet for task resolution/completion. Learners do not have to be at computer stations during this phase but must have knowledge of the specific system capabilities and the steps required for use. When considering the problem or task, the learner must consider his or her knowledge and system capabilities and formulate an approach. The reflection process requires participants to consider what-if scenarios that may create the incentive to use the system (increased efficiency, opportunity for networking, value-added collaboration, etc.).

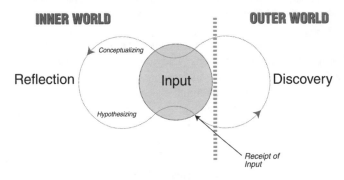

Figure 13.3
Reflection Process

Receipt of Input. The last mode of learning is one most commonly considered in the traditional teaching process. The receipt of input is learning from second-hand information—being given information, aurally through lecture or conversation, or visually through reading materials. Receipt of input is considered an inner-world experience.

- **Co., Inc. Example**

  In the Co. Inc. example, receipt of input is achieved by an instructor demonstration of the capabilities of the intranet. Providing written instructions to the learner on how to use the system in the form of a learner manual or job aid is another means.

Whole-Loop Learning. The Lancaster model (Figure 13.4) points designers in the direction of a comprehensive, multimode approach to learning. Whole-loop learning provides a complete learning experience by including everything prescribed by various learning theories and research (Table 13.1). In addition, whole-loop learning incorporates elements of all of Gagné's nine events of instruction ("The Events of Instruction," page 87).

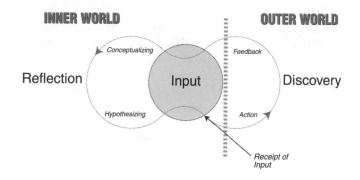

Figure 13.4
Whole-Loop Learning Cycle

Lancaster Element	General Prescription	Theoretical Perspective
Discovery/ Action	Active involvement (experience, hands-on practice)	Cognitive Inquiry, Humanistic
	Reinforcement or natural consequences of action	Behaviorist
Reflection	Cognitive consolidation (restructuring knowledge base)	Cognitive Information Processing
	Personal reflection	Humanistic
	Personal interpretation of new knowledge	Constructivist

Table 13.1
Whole-Loop Learning

Biographical Sketches

Dr. **John Burgoyne** holds a BS from University College London, a master's degree in Philosophy from Birkbeck College London, and a PhD from Manchester. He is currently a professor of Management Learning and head of the Centre for the Study of Management Learning at the University of Lancaster. His past experience includes service to British Airways. Research interests include the learning organization, corporate management development, the nature of management, knowledge and competence, theories of learning, and teaching and training and development methods. He is currently pursuing research in corporate management development as well as theory and practice of learning. Dr. Burgoyne also serves as Associate Editor, *British Journal of Management*; member of the Editorial Board, *Journal of Health Service Management*; and member, British Academy of Management: Research Policy Working Party.

Dr. **Roger Stuart** graduated from Swansea and Leicester Universities and then worked in the private sector. He joined Lancaster University, entered the Department of Behaviour in Organisations and then moved to the Centre for the Development of Management Teachers and Trainers, where he was a teaching fellow. He published a number of articles in the areas of management teacher development. He went on to head The Grove, the British Rail management training centre, and then became an independent consultant and leader of the Centre for Strategic Management Development at the Wadenhoe Centre.

Don Binsted served as the Director of the Center for the Development of Management Teachers and Trainers, University of Lancaster, United Kingdom. He was a senior fellow in the Department of Management Learning at the same university. He published numerous articles in management education and development, as well as in the areas of technology in education.

Implementation

The Lancaster model is primarily based on the combination of learning modes, in various sequences and with various levels of emphasis. This approach allows the designer/instructor to adapt lessons to particular content and objectives. In addition, it takes into account the learner's pre-existing skills and knowledge, as well as the type of information to be processed. It also allows for a variety of activities, making instruction engaging.

Because of the three broad learning modes, the Lancaster model is a versatile design tool that can be used to accomplish specific and precise learning objectives, as well as broadly defined learning goals that allow the learner to affect the learning outcomes. When designing instruction based on this model, you must consider two main variables: sequence of the learning modes and degree of emphasis on each learning mode.

Sequencing. One very important decision is determining what mode of learning comes first. There are six possible combinations:

1. IDR—Receipt of Input, Discovery, Reflection
2. IRD—Receipt of Input, Reflection, Discovery
3. DRI—Discovery, Reflection, Receipt of Input
4. DIR—Discovery, Receipt of Input, Reflection
5. RID—Reflection, Receipt of Input, Discovery
6. RDI—Reflection, Discovery, Receipt of Input

The Lancaster model does not provide a prescription for sequencing the modes. Sequencing depends on many factors. Table 13.2 outlines the sequencing possibilities in relation to samples of instructional content. Key factors to consider when assigning sequence are the type of learning objective(s) and audience characteristics. In addition, environmental factors (time, equipment, etc.) influencing the design should be considered.

Sequence	Topic	Audience Characteristics	Generic Lesson Description
I D R	General Computer File Management Training	Novice/Beginner-level computer skills	**I**-Provide information covering general file management concepts and tools. **D**-Practice using file management system. **R**-Let learners generate structures where they would use their knowledge and skill to organize the files in their job environment.
I R D	Management Skills	Mid-level managers with beginning to intermediate-level experience	**I**-Provide information on corporate policy and best practices (style). **R**-Allow learners to generate a realistic scenario and have them work out their responses using the information provided and their own personal management style. **D**-Set up role-plays in which learners demonstrate their response on actors in a controlled environment. Discuss use of best practices, corporate policy information, and relevant feedback from other participants.
D R I	Diversity Lesson	Experienced managers with knowledge of diversity requirements. Potential problems in supporting diversity initiatives noted by subordinates and peers.	**D**-Have learners observe role-play of an effective team in action using principles of corporate diversity requirements. Discuss best-practice examples that are incorporated into scenario. **R**-Allow learners to reflect on their own situations and how principles from the example observed could be applied to improve performance back in their work environment. **I**-Provide refresher handout on tips and tricks for incorporating identified best practices.

Table 13.2

Whole-Loop Learning Sequence Options

Sequence	Topic	Audience Characteristics	Generic Lesson Description
D I R	Personnel Legal Requirements	Managers with a new legal requirement for a personnel issue	**D**-Observe personnel action and resulting consequences via premade videotape. **I**-Receive information on legal requirements in handling the personnel issue. **R**-Have learners describe a situation based in their own environment where they would need to apply these skills. Provide a forum for them to describe (orally or in writing) how they would incorporate the information into their own management style to legally and effectively handle the situation.
R I D	Sales Strategy Development and Training	New sales team for trial product line	**R**-Using small groups, have teams reflect on possible sales strategies and generate questions about the product line. **I**-Provide information to sales team—answer questions, distribute marketing materials. **D**-Have sales force implement trial runs of sales strategies and report back on successes and failures.
R D I	Computer Application Training	Intermediate to advanced computer users new to the application	**R**-Have learners reflect on their current situation and generate objectives for what they want the application to accomplish for them. **D**-Allow students to experiment with the application in a controlled environment. **I**-Provide additional information on the advanced software capabilities, short cuts, and best practices through demonstration and job aids.

Table 13.2

Whole-Loop Learning Sequence Options (cont.)

Emphasis. Depending on the starting point for the lesson and the information, understanding, and experience the learners bring to the table, the instructional design might concentrate on one mode of learning during a certain part of the instruction. This emphasis can be accomplished in two ways: spending more time on a particular mode of instruction (e.g., Figure 13.5) or increasing the number of times the mode is repeated (e.g., Figure 13.6).

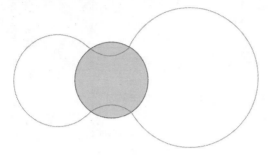

Figure 13.5
Emphasis (Speed)[2]

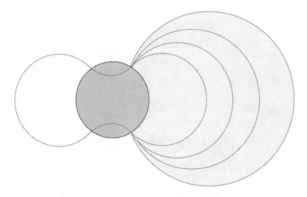

Figure 13.6
Emphasis (Repetition)[3]

The creators of the model acknowledge the use of emphasis on individual modes but do not prescribe specific emphasis for desired learning outcomes. However,

---

[2.] Stuart & Binstead

[3.] Stuart & Binstead

several general guidelines can be inferred for use of emphasis. For example, if students are to perform a skill after the training, it would be wise to concentrate learning efforts in the discovery segment, thus allowing students time to practice or execute the skills they are learning. If the students are to walk away with information only, for use at a later time, instruction should spend more time providing information (receipt of input). If students are to learn something conceptual, like a new theory, design emphasis on reflection, allowing them to incorporate the information into their own schema. Many of the types of learning discussed will use more than one mode of learning, but the concentration of time will be spent on the appropriate mode of learning to accomplish the desired result.

Learner Characteristics

Adjustments to the instructional design can easily be made to accommodate varied learner characteristics, including preferred learning styles and various levels of previously acquired skills. Changing the sequence of the mode implementation, emphasizing specific modes through duration or repetition, can address a wide variety of learner needs.

Learning Styles. Incorporating the three modes of learning into one instructional design ensures the instruction addresses various learning styles. The model allows for, and encourages the use of elements that address both of Kölb's learning activities: perception and processing (Algonquin, 2000).

Kölb used these two learning activities to define four learning dimensions:

1. Concrete experience
2. Reflective observation
3. Abstract conceptualization
4. Active experimentation

Kölb further defined four types of learners, prone to learn in different ways:

1. Type 1—Learns best by concrete experiences and active experimentation
2. Type 2—Learns best by observing concrete examples and reflecting on observations
3. Type 3—Learns best by applying active experimentation to abstract concepts
4. Type 4—Learns best by considering abstract concepts and reflecting internally

Using the guidelines established in the Lancaster model, elements of all preferred learning styles are found in the instructional design. There is something in it for everyone—from real-world examples and active experimentation to reflection and abstract application; most learners will be able to identify with at least one component of the instruction.

Previously Acquired Skills and Applied Skill Requirements. The Lancaster model can also be used to design versatile instruction to accommodate various participant skill sets.

- **Co., Inc. Example**

    In the Co. Inc. intranet training example, the audience is companywide. The participants' entry-level skills range from company executives with minimal computer experience to the technical staff with highly advanced skills. In addition, the required exit skills range from in-depth intranet knowledge for daily use to only a working knowledge of the intranet capabilities.

    Components of the instruction based on the Lancaster model can be quickly and efficiently reorganized to accommodate classes with different entry and exit skill requirements. For example, for learners with little or no intranet experience who need to use the functions of the system in their daily jobs, IDR sequencing may be a good choice: I-Provide information covering computer and intranet use; D-Provide practice time and allow learners to acclimate to the intranet; R-Let learners generate scenarios where they would apply their computer knowledge and skill to corporate tasks they will likely be required to address.

    A second type of audience might be administrative staff who have high-level computer skills and corporate knowledge. DIR sequencing may be appropriate: D-Learners can experiment with operational system while in their job environment; I-During the classroom session, they will receive a comprehensive overview of the types of information accessible from the intranet; R-Have participants consider how the capabilities of the system could be applied to their daily jobs to make more efficient use of their time.

    Further adjustments can be made to the design of the instruction by emphasizing specific sections of the whole-loop cycle. Participants required to use the system should have a relatively large amount of hands-on practice. Participants who only need to be aware of the content areas might be better served with reference materials (job aids).

Consider the previously acquired skills of the audience and the learning objectives of the particular group and alter the sequence and emphasis of the modes to meet these requirements.

Additional Considerations

Linkage. As you design instruction based on the Lancaster model, be sure all modes of instruction support the original objective. The modes must be effectively "linked" together to ensure continuity of instruction. This can be partially the learner's responsibility, but the instruction will usually be considerably more effective if the correlations between the modes are defined for the learners. For example, if the learners are first working on discovery and reflection elements and then provided the job aid, an explanation of what learning the job aid supports and what additional information is provided within would be useful.

Timing. The place and timing of the execution of each mode can also be adjusted. This model can support on-the-job application of the knowledge gained. For example, if discovery is not possible in a classroom setting due to lack of equipment, receipt of information and reflection can be accomplished in the formal training environment. Learners can then be responsible for accomplishing the discovery mode back in their own work environment.

Any of the modes can be designed to occur outside of the primary training environment, but give special consideration to the willingness and ability of the learner to accomplish the learning outside of a structured training environment.

Duration. Sequencing can greatly affect the amount of time required to deliver the instruction. Beginning with the discovery mode usually requires a substantially larger amount of instructional time. Generally, beginning with the receipt of information mode will decrease instructional time.

Focus. Due to the versatility of this model, you must give special attention to the focus of the instruction. A thorough needs assessment must be accomplished to effectively evaluate the entry-level skills and knowledge of the learner population. A comprehensive analysis will help ensure that learners have a foundation of comprehension in the beginning modes of the instruction. In addition, it helps to ensure they are not wasting their time on known information or previously acquired skills.

Best Uses

The variation possibilities in the Lancaster model of learning make it extremely versatile for any type of subject matter, acquiring skills, retaining cognitive information, or developing affective behaviors.

Incorporating the concepts of whole-loop learning into your design helps to ensure that the modes of learning are appropriate to the context of the instruction. Whole-loop design takes into account pre-existing skills and knowledge and can be used efficiently to provide the appropriate instruction from each of the three modes. In addition, more learners are reached by providing multiple modes of instruction that support their need for information, practice, and incorporation.

Use the following questions to ensure your design meets the basic requirements of whole-loop learning:

1. Does it have all parts of the whole-loop?
2. Is the emphasis appropriate?
3. Are the three modes integrated?

While an extremely versatile and effective model, it is difficult for a novice designer to use. The model is not prescriptive: There is no guidance on how to determine appropriate sequencing or necessary emphasis. However, the whole-loop concept provides a comprehensive approach for the experienced designer to incorporate into most any training design.

Model in Action

At company ABC, new managers are rebelling against corporate management policy. ABC has just bought out CDF and instituted new management over a group of individuals who are used to being in charge of themselves. After repeated attempts to disseminate information and provide an overview of the policy at management meetings, mid- and lower-level managers are still having an extremely difficult time dealing with insubordination.

At a management training seminar, participants see a video segment on insubordination. Because of the diverse backgrounds of the participants (some are first-time managers, others have been in the role for years), a multifaceted approach is used to acclimate each participant into the learning environment. The goals of the seminar are to educate participants on corporate policy, provide them with simulated experiences dealing with typical problematic situations, and ensure that each participant incorporates the corporate philosophy and best practices into his or her own management style.

In order to equalize the experience base of all the participants, the module begins with a vignette on a situation with an insubordinate employee. The employee has just demonstrated to the manager his insubordinate behavior. The students are put into small groups and then asked to *reflect* on the situation. Have they had similar experiences? What are some possible responses to the scene?

The next segment of instruction is based on conveying the company policy. Lecture, corporate representative guest speakers, the manager's handbook, employee reference manual, and various job aids are used to deliver the information to the participants (*receipt of input*).

Once the information has been conveyed and distributed, students participate in an experiment (*discovery*). A situation taking place in a scene similar to the individual participant's work environment is acted out by the instructor team, and the learners respond using the guidelines established in company policy and their own frame of reference. After the response is completed, students and instructor staff debrief the participants on their behaviors and provide feedback on the outcome (consequences) of the action taken. The students will also take part in analyzing other students' responses, thus furthering the experiential nature of the exercise (discovery loop repetition).

Implementation Guide

Step	Action	Factors to Consider
1	Define objectives.	• Specific • General
2	Determine existing skill sets.	• Knowledge • Experience
3	Design whole-loop learning.	• Emphasis • Sequence • Learner Characteristics
4	Consider other factors.	• Linkage • Timing • Duration • Focus

References

Algonquin. (2000). *Learning styles.* [On-line]. Available: http://algonquinc.on.ca/
edtech/gened/styles.html

Stuart, R., & Binstead [sic.], D. *Some notes on the Lancaster model of learning.*
Lancaster, England: University of Lancaster, Centre for the Study of Management Learning.

Bibliography

Binstead [sic.], D. (1978). A framework for the design of management learning
events. *Journal of European Industrial Training, 2*(5), 25–48.

Binsted, D. (1980). The training of teachers of management subjects. *Journal of the
Operational Research Society, 31*(1), 29–41.

Burgoyne, J., & Stuart, R. (Eds.). (1978). *Management development: Context and
strategies.* Farnborough, England: Gower Press.

Snell, R., & Binsted, D. (1981a). The tutor-learner interaction in management
development, part 1: The effect of relationship and tutor facilitating strategy on
feelings, learning and interest. *Personnel Review, 10*(3), 1–13.

Snell, R., & Binsted, D. (1981b). The tutor-learner interaction in management
development, part 2: Games tutors play: How covert tutor manoeuvres affect
management learning. *Personnel Review, 10*(4), 2–13.

Snell, R., & Binsted, D. (1982a). The tutor-learner interaction in management
development, part 3: The facilitation of learning via input/lecture. *Personnel
Review, 11*(1), 2–14.

Snell, R., & Binsted, D. (1982b). The tutor-learner interaction in management
development, part 4: The facilitation of learning by discussion. *Personnel
Review, 11*(2), 3–14.

Snell, R., & Binsted, D. (1982c). The tutor-learner interaction in management
development, part 5: Facilitating learning from the de-briefing of exercises.
Personnel Review, 11(4), 3–14.

About the Author

Kristina M. Holdsworth is a training consultant with Booz·Allen & Hamilton, serving various government clients in the areas of ISD and program evaluation. Kristina has considerable experience designing and teaching technology systems as well as various technical and regulatory training programs. Kristina holds an undergraduate degree from the University of Kansas in Environmental Science. She received a certificate in Instructional Systems Design and an MA in Human Performance Systems from Marymount University in Arlington, VA. Kristina is a member of the adjunct faculty at Strayer University in the greater Washington, DC area.

CHAPTER 14

Cooperative Learning

Bill Combs

While most models of learning concern themselves with how individuals acquire knowledge that leads to some behavior change, cooperative learning also takes into account the social environment in which learning occurs. Assuming that a learner will eventually demonstrate his or her learning among other people, cooperative learning demands that other people be involved in the learning process. Proponents of this model take the position that in the context of small groups, individuals become responsible for not only their own learning but also that of others. In so doing, they not only acquire the knowledge at hand but also an improved self-concept, motivation, and drive for achievement.

There is much to suggest that the small-group approach endorsed in cooperative learning resembles a philosophy rather than a model; indeed, there are few concrete steps put forth that describe how cooperative learning experiences should be structured. Yet repeated studies suggest that significant learning advantages can be realized by having individuals share responsibility for learning.

Johnson and Johnson, along with Robert Slavin and Shlomo Sharan, emerged as key developers of the model in the late 1990s. Their work suggests ways that cooperative effort, teamwork, and overall performance can be enhanced, especially in environments that actively encourage collaboration.

Origins

As a "social" model, cooperative learning focuses on the interpersonal context in which learning takes place. Until the early 20th century, and indeed for much of its duration, the acquisition of skills or knowledge and the resultant behavioral change was understood in terms of the individual: Some instructional methodologies typically focused on how individuals responded to stimuli, while others focused on understanding internal information-processing schema. Cooperative learning, on the other hand, stands in contrast to behavioral approaches. Though cooperative learning supports the methodologies of the cognitive models, it has a stronger kinship to approaches that emphasize relationships with others: cognitive inquiry, for example, in which a puzzling situation is presented and responses are developed in a group, or behavior modeling, which incorporates feedback from a peer group. Further, because cooperative learning has a motivational aspect, it bears a resemblance to the "motivational" models, in which relevance of the content to a "real" application is explored.

As with much contemporary educational theory, a considerable portion of the basis for cooperative learning is attributed to John Dewey, who proposed that schools be structured as small democracies, with an emphasis on individual self-worth and motivation. Paradoxically, the development of healthy individual esteem occurs in a social context: One contributes to the progress of a group, which in turn contributes to the nurturing of the individual's ability to contribute. When the same is true of all members of the group, interdependence develops, as does the ability and motivation to continue learning (Sharan, 1994).

These motivational aspects of cooperative learning and its application in social contexts have been explored by Johnson and Johnson at the University of Minnesota, Shlomo Sharan of the University of Tel Aviv, and Robert Slavin of Johns Hopkins University. Their work supports cooperative learning as a means of providing an opportunity for learners to work collaboratively, to learn faster and more efficiently, and to increase retention while feeling positive about the learning situation.

Description

Cooperative learning depends on small groups of learners. Although instructor-provided content and guidance characterize part of the instruction, cooperative learning deliberately incorporates small groups so that the members work together to maximize their own and each others' learning. Each member is responsible for learning what is presented and for helping his or her teammates learn. When this cooperation takes place, the team creates an atmosphere of achievement, and thus learning is enhanced.

General Approach

As an instructional model, cooperative learning endorses this general approach: After receiving instruction from the facilitator, classes are organized into small groups and given clear direction regarding expectations about outcomes and suggestions about group processes. The small groups then work through the assignment until all group members successfully understand and complete it (Johnson & Johnson, 1989).

Cooperative learning can be applied to almost any assignment in any curriculum for any age learner. In addition to providing a means for learners to master instructional content, cooperative learning seeks to make each group member a stronger individual by teaching team skills in a social context. Much of the appeal of cooperative learning is that it provides a way for learners to learn essential interpersonal life skills and to develop the ability to work collaboratively—behaviors that are especially desired in an era when most organizations endorse the concept of teamwork.

Required Elements

Cooperative learning requires considerable talent and preparation on the part of the instructor; passive involvement rarely leads to learning that, by definition, is cooperative. The instruction must be designed carefully so that, for example, every participant is involved in an instructional project by taking turns with different roles such as facilitator, recorder, and timekeeper. Instead of putting high-achieving learners in the role of leader, for example, the instructor must structure the small groups so that all the participants take leadership roles and strive for mutual benefit (Johnson, 1993).

Cooperative learning is often described in terms of what it is not. Cooperative learning is not designing instructional delivery in such a way that competitive or individualistic efforts are promoted. When learning takes place in a competitive learning environment, participants tend to work against each other to achieve a goal that they feel only a small number can attain. The learners may further perceive that they can obtain their goals only if other learners fail, a perception that often results in some learners taking it easy because they believe they don't have a chance to win

(Deutsch, 1962). Evaluation of learning in such an environment is unsatisfactory because participant performance is assessed through norm-referenced means.

Further, in an atmosphere that emphasizes individual accomplishments, participants are seen as working alone to accomplish goals unrelated to those of classmates. Although this environment is conducive to evaluating performance on a criterion-referenced basis, the fact that learner goals are independent contributes to learners' perceptions that the achievement of their goals is unrelated to what other participants do. In this case, the opportunity to grow through collaborative means is lost.

Cooperative learning can thus be seen as a reaction against competitiveness and individualistic outcomes in instruction. But simply incorporating groups in instruction does not constitute cooperative learning. What is required of the instructor is to structure the training so that members of the small groups believe they share a common outcome. Moreover, guidance should be given to the groups that the members are to gain from each other's efforts—that group members need to assist and encourage others to achieve. To do that, every group member, individually, shares accountability for doing his or her part of the group's work. That accountability rests on each team member's mastery of the required interpersonal and small-group skills to be an effective group member. Key among those skills is the ability to discuss how well the group is working and what could be done to improve the group work (Johnson, 1991).

Unless these elements are included, the small groups are not cooperative. But precisely how to structure cooperative learning and its small groups is something the model does not address clearly. There are particularly few details about how to construct a cooperative approach, especially for training adult learners. In this regard, cooperative learning seems to be largely a philosophical approach; what cooperative learning does suggest more strongly is that instructors understand the components that make cooperation work. According to Johnson & Johnson, and Sharan, the essential components of cooperative learning are as follows:

1. Positive interdependence
2. Face-to-face promotive interaction
3. Individual and group accountability
4. Interpersonal and small-group skills
5. Group processing

Positive Interdependence. Positive interdependence takes place when group members perceive that they are linked with each other in such a way that one cannot succeed unless everyone succeeds. It can be understood as a kind of nautical analogy: The members of the small groups are all in the same boat. Once underway, the crew needs to realize that they will sink or swim together. The instructor must design and communicate group goals and tasks in ways that help group members reach that understanding. Although the model is unclear how best to generate this belief among adult learners, it is clear that each group member must recognize that his or her efforts are required and indispensable for group success and, further, that each member has a unique contribution to make to the joint effort. The instructor should clearly define the group's role and task responsibilities and refer to the members' individual strengths.

Face-to-Face Promotive Interaction. This concept refers to face-to-face interaction, which, in small group work, is preferred over other media such as telephone or email. Learners need to do real work together in real time, either in the training room or in outside meetings. In addition to processing information in working toward achieving a goal, members must promote each other's success by sharing resources and helping, supporting, encouraging, and applauding each other's efforts. The instructor should provide examples of how the groups should function, such as orally explaining how to solve problems, teaching one's knowledge to others, checking for understanding, discussing concepts being learned, and connecting present with past learning. Doing so enhances interpersonal dynamics that facilitate learning: Through promoting each others' learning face-to-face, members become personally committed to each other as well as to their mutual goals. In this sense, cooperative learning groups become an academic support system in which everyone has someone who is committed to him or her as a person.

Individual and Group Accountability. Proponents of cooperative learning suggest that two levels of accountability be structured into cooperative lessons: The group must be accountable for achieving its goals, and each member must be accountable for contributing his or her share of the work. The facilitator promotes individual accountability by assessing the performance of each individual in order to ascertain who needs more assistance, support, and encouragement in learning. The instructor must recognize that one purpose of cooperative learning groups is to make each member a stronger individual in his or her own right—students learn together so that they can subsequently gain greater individual competency.

Interpersonal and Small Group Skills. Cooperative learning is more complex than unstructured group interaction, which usually leads to competitive or individualistic learning because students have to engage simultaneously in taskwork (learning the subject matter) and teamwork (functioning effectively as a group). In addition to the taskwork dimension, facilitators of cooperative learning need to focus on social skills that must taught just as purposefully and just as precisely.

Leadership, decisionmaking, trust-building, communication, and conflict-management skills enable learners to manage both teamwork and taskwork successfully, and they need to be addressed during instruction. Since cooperation and conflict are inherently related, the procedures and skills for managing conflicts constructively are especially important for the long-term success of learning groups (Johnson & Johnson, 1989; Johnson, 1991).

Group Processing. Most instructional processes emphasize the importance of transmitting instructional content efficiently: Clearly specified objectives, logical sequencing of content, and awareness of the conditions of learning all determine how well material will be learned. Cooperative learning endorses all these approaches in addressing taskwork, while it gives equal importance to teamwork by addressing the concept of group processing. In one sense, leadership, trust-building, and communication abilities can be taught directly (taskwork); in another sense, they can be experienced in a small group (teamwork). It's just as important for group members to discuss how well they are achieving their goals and maintaining effective working relationships as it is to assist each other's acquisition of knowledge. Groups need to describe what member actions are helpful and unhelpful and make decisions about what behaviors to continue or change. The process of learning is continually enhanced when the group members analyze how well they are working together, and for small groups to reach an instructional goal successfully, they must consciously address their process.

Best Uses

Owing to cooperative learning's origins as a means of developing children's abilities to learn in a group context, practitioners of cooperative learning for adults are often in the position of developing their own best application of the model. There persists a relative lack of research on the model's applicability with groups of adult learners. If one is looking for a way to incorporate tenets of cooperative learning with adult learners, one either has to adapt approaches that have been successful in K–12 education, or one has to develop new instruction or redesign existing processes to incorporate aspects of cooperative learning.

Limitations in research with adult learners notwithstanding, there are a number of situations in which cooperative learning has been applied with success to workplace training. "Executive" programs are one example. Through small-group interaction and joint work toward resolving a case problem, team members can learn in an environment that maintains or enhances their self-esteem, strengthening both technical and interpersonal skills that industry leaders need. Each can learn from the various strengths of the others in a mode that is engaging and motivating.

Case studies that consciously incorporate the tenets of cooperative learning are effective in a number of settings. One software-engineering firm uses a week-long case study to prepare its new hires to join a development team and become productive—hence billable—more quickly. This particular firm's core values rest on teamwork and collaboration; it accomplishes its design work in the context of small development teams that work on separate aspects of a programming problem concurrently. Its new-hire training program, though, does not focus on retraining the object-oriented programming languages the new hires already know. Instead, the firm presents small groups of new hires with a case problem that closely resembles a typical work situation. In the context of a team, the new hires identify resources, divide their labor, and develop a solution—all while communicating their progress and problems with each other. Participants who complete this cooperative case problem consistently report that they are subsequently able to join a "real" project with little disruption and are able to begin productive work quickly and with a great deal of satisfaction.

Other areas in which cooperative learning can be applied are work situations in which a structured, group approach is employed: for example, military task forces, management teams, research and development groups, ad agency teams, political campaign staffs, and quality improvement teams.

Research Support

Most of the research on cooperative learning assesses its applicability in traditional school settings, its effects on academic achievement, and its effects on motivation and self-confidence. The literature is clear, of course, that cooperative learning's best documented application is among elementary and secondary students; more than 500 studies of its use among that target group and in traditional schools is persuasive evidence of its effectiveness.

While the preponderance of research suggests cooperative learning's effectiveness among school-age learners in a traditional setting, the research also suggests that some approaches can be modified for adult learners. For example, structuring group investigations that require analysis and evaluation in the context of guided group work seems to characterize much of management training.

> ## Research Support, cont.
>
> The research is particularly strong in terms of demonstrating a relationship between cooperative learning and achievement. When group goals and individual accountability are emphasized together, there is a consistent, positive effect on measures of achievement. Studies have also suggested that cooperative learning is related to significant gains in increased motivation, enhanced critical-thinking skills, and positive relations among different ethnic groups (Joyce & Weil, 1996).

Model in Action

Total quality management gained large numbers of adherents in the 1980s. It endorsed objective approaches to improving business processes, such as statistical process control and quality circles. Team Leader Training is a five-day course that was developed in that tradition, and its goals of addressing business problems in the context of a small group (a "team") are still valued. Many problems are often best addressed by the employees who are in the best position to understand their causes, and the employees can therefore implement ways to correct the problem. The goal of effective quality-improvement teams is to achieve a "breakthrough" increase in performance. To do that, teams need to adopt a structured approach to decisionmaking, and they need to stay focused in their efforts to do so. Central to this effort is the role of the team leader, who trains members in that approach and facilitates their efforts to arrive at a response. Team leader training, then, seeks to develop those capacities in employees designated as team leaders.

When the trainees arrive for the first day, they notice right away that the training room tables are arranged in a large "U" shape that can accommodate up to 25 learners. There are also five "roundtable" arrangements in the corners of the training room or in separate breakout rooms. During the first hour of instruction, which occurs as a lecture, the trainees discover that quality-improvement projects have seven phases:

1. Reason for Improvement
2. Current Situation
3. Analysis
4. Countermeasures
5. Results

6. Standardization
7. Future Plans

The course is structured so that the first five steps will be covered in detail, one step per day.

The participants then follow a sequence of activities that will remain the same for each subsequent day: a lecture and discussion of some two hours, a one-hour demonstration of quality-improvement "tools" appropriate for the particular step, and a one-hour overview of "group dynamics," which describes the stages of team formation and effective ways of facilitating group behavior.

The participants are then introduced to a real-world problem that can be addressed through a quality-improvement team. Documentation is provided, relevant data presented, and the roles that team members typically assume are described. The class is then divided into quality-improvement teams of five learners each. The teams examine the problem to be addressed in the context of a quality improvement team; select members to take a different role, whether facilitator, recorder, or team member; and begin work to address the problem. They have four hours to complete the work normally associated with each stage of the decisionmaking process.

The team members assume a different role each day and thus become familiar, first-hand, with the duties that each team member is expected to perform. The team also requires participation from every member as it attempts to reach consensus: The team leader doesn't decide, and no individual dominates. To reach that end, the team members have to draw on each other's experience. The facilitator stays in touch with the teams throughout the week to ensure that everyone is participating and that the teams' success rests on the contributions of everyone. The team leader is reminded to do the same.

Implementation Guide

While the model is not as prescriptive as others regarding how to specifically structure instructional content, a trainer can take steps to make learning more cooperative in nature. The steps, based on the components of cooperative learning, constitute a set of guidelines.

Step	Description
1. Select Appropriate Tasks	The course designer should ascertain that the application, practice, or hands-on portion of instruction is appropriate for group activity. The social aspects of the content should be addressed. For example, foreign language instruction should include the opportunity to speak the language with others in a group. Writing a term paper in the new language, on the other hand, is largely an individual activity and might be better addressed through other means.
2. Establish Positive Interdependence	If group activity is important to learning the new skill or content, the instructor must clearly state that group members "sink or swim" together. The result of their work is a reflection of all the team members' contributions, and not just those of the high producers.
3. Facilitate Cooperative Teamwork	The instructor must encourage the group to find the unique strengths of each member. For the group to succeed, its work must reflect the strengths that are present among all its members.
4. Provide Face-to-Face Promotive Interaction	Adequate time must be given in the instructional period for face-to-face interaction. The instructor should demonstrate or describe acceptable group norms for either the current groups or provide descriptions from experience. The instructor may otherwise state expectations of what may be included in face-to-face meetings, such as sharing knowledge, experience, and rewards.
5. Establish Group and Individual Accountability	The facilitator should develop a means of evaluating individual performance as well as group work, and communicate how group work will be evaluated. The group evaluation may be a composite of individual scores, for example.
6. Assess Both Taskwork and Teamwork	Time must be provided for small group members to discuss their process, perhaps at the end of each group meeting. A Plan-Do-Check-Act format can be used: The team members describe their objectives for the meeting, the extent to which they accomplished the goal, what worked well and what could be done differently, and they make plans to include the feedback for the subsequent meeting.

References

Deutsch, M. (1962). Cooperation and trust: Some theoretical notes. In M.R. Jones (Ed.), *Nebraska symposium on motivation*. Lincoln: University of Nebraska Press.

Johnson, D.W. (1991). *Human relations and your career* (3rd ed.). Englewood Cliffs, NJ: Prentice-Hall.

Johnson, D.W. (1993). *Reaching out: Interpersonal effectiveness and self-actualization* (6th ed.) . Needham Heights, MA: Allyn & Bacon.

Johnson, D.W., & Johnson, R.T. (1989). *Cooperation, competition: Theory and research*. Edina, MN: Interaction Book Company.

Joyce, B.R., & Weil, M. (1996). *Models of teaching* (5th ed.). Boston: Allyn and Bacon.

Sharan, S. (Ed.). (1994). *Handbook of cooperative learning methods*. Westport, CT: Greenwood Press.

Bibliography

Aaronson, E. (1978). *The jigsaw classroom*. Beverly Hills, CA: Sage Publications.

Dishon, D., & O'Leary, P.W. (1984). *A guidebook for cooperative learning*. Portage, MI: Cooperation Unlimited.

Kagan, S. (1985). *Cooperative learning: Resources for teachers*. Riverside, CA: University of California.

Sharan, S., & Sharan, Y. (1976). *Small-group teaching*. Englewood Cliffs, NJ: Educational Technology Publications.

Slavin, R.E. (1986). "Learning together: Cooperative groups and peer tutoring produce significant academic gains." *American Educator, Summer*, 6–13.

About the Author

Bill Combs has more than 25 years' experience as a trainer in technical, manage-
ment, and leadership processes at Burroughs Corporation, Litton, TRW, and Sprint
International, and as a consultant to Fortune 500 organizations. He is currently
Director of Corporate Learning at Cysive, Inc., a builder of e-commerce systems.
Bill is also an adjunct professor at Marymount University's Graduate School of
Business and is full professor in the Graduate School of Management and Technology at the University of Maryland University College. His undergraduate degree is
from the University of Tennessee and his graduate degrees are from Virginia Poly-
technic Institute and State University (Virginia Tech).

CHAPTER 15

ARCS Motivational Design

Fran Peters

John M. Keller (1979, 1983) developed the ARCS model of motivation design. The model provides a comprehensive and systematic approach to increasing the motivational appeal of instruction. The ARCS model prescribes four conditions that must be present to motivate learners—attention, relevance, confidence, and satisfaction—with suggested motivational strategies for each condition. ARCS is not a stand-alone model, but rather a model designed to supplement models of instructional design.

The model is based on the premise that an individual's motivation (effort) can be influenced by changes in the learning environment and the instructional events that define the individual's perceptions concerning value and/or "expectancy" for success.

Origins

The ARCS model of motivational design is the result of several years of research and application in the field of motivation. Until the late 1970s, much of the research on motivation concentrated on theories attributing learner differences in achievement to learner abilities. Many of the instructional design models were focused on instruction that would be effective if the students wanted to learn; little had been written to prescribe methods to make the instruction more appealing.

While the ARCS model is a synthesis of a variety of theories, its foundation lies in the fundamentals of the expectancy-value theory (Porter & Lawler, 1968). The expectancy-value theory contends that individuals are motivated (will expend effort) to do or learn an activity if it is perceived to be of value to the individual and if there is a positive expectancy for success. Using value and positive expectancy for success as the first two categories of the ARCS model, Keller synthesized other theories with similar attributes into the model.

The value category is based on research in areas such as curiosity and arousal (Berlyne, 1965), personal needs (Maslow, 1954), fear of failure and anxiety (Atkinson & Raynor, 1974), and beliefs or attitudes (Feather, 1975; Rokeach, 1973). All of these phenomena except curiosity are concerned with understanding how an individual's internal needs and beliefs are related to how much or little effort will be exerted.

The expectancy category integrates research in areas such as locus of control (Rotter, 1972), attribution theory (Weiner, 1974), self-efficacy (Bandura, 1977), and learned helplessness (Seligman, 1975). A common element in all of these theories is the attempt to explain the formation and effect of personal expectancies for success or failure in relation to behavior and its consequences.

The value category was subsequently divided into two categories called interest and relevance to make a distinction between factors concerned with attention and arousal versus those concerned with need for achievement and perceived utility. A fourth category, outcomes, was added to describe theories associated with individual satisfaction.

Using the four categories—interest, relevance, expectancy for success, and outcomes—motivational strategies relating to each category were developed and divided into useful subcategories. Two of the four original categories were later renamed: Interest was renamed attention; and expectancy was renamed confidence, providing what is known today as the ARCS model.

The ARCS model provides designers with an easy-to-use prescriptive model for obtaining and maintaining motivation. Today, it is one of the most well-known and widely applied models of motivation.

Description

Four categories of motivating factors constitute the ARCS model, all with accompanying motivational strategies. Attention and relevance comprise ways to make the instruction stimulating, to meet the learner needs, and to build on the learner's experiences. Confidence and satisfaction include ways of creating positive expectancies of success and rewards with the amount and the quality of effort expended. Within each category, there are three motivational strategies (see Table 15.1).

	Condition	Strategy
A	Attention	Perceptual arousal
		Inquiry arousal
		Variability
R	Relevance	Goal orientation
		Motive matching
		Familiarity
C	Confidence	Learning Requirements
		Opportunities for Success
		Personal Responsibility
S	Satisfaction	Intrinsic Reinforcement
		Extrinsic Rewards
		Equity

Table 15.1
ARCS Motivational Strategies

Attention

Gaining attention involves capturing and maintaining the learner's interest. Gaining attention is often fairly easy; the challenge is how to sustain the attention or interest level throughout instruction. Keller recommends three types of strategies for gaining and maintaining the learner's attention: perceptual arousal, inquiry arousal, and variability.

Perceptual Arousal. What can I do to capture learner's interest?

Use new, surprising, or unexpected events to capture the learner's interest. A cartoon, a staged event such as an engaging physical demonstration, a story told with animated gestures and movements, and animation used on computer applications are some examples of strategies that can be used to capture learner's attention and interest.

Inquiry Arousal. How can I stimulate curiosity?

Inquiry arousal occurs when curiosity is aroused and the learner feels compelled to get more information to solve a problem. Stimulate curiosity by posing or having the learner generate questions or a problem to solve. Using riddles or puzzles is also an example of a strategy for inquiry arousal. Create an atmosphere in which learners feel comfortable about raising questions and can test their theories through discussions, brainstorming, or experimenting.

Variability. How can I maintain interest?

Use a varied range of methods and media to match student interest. By varying the delivery occasionally and unpredictably, attention can be regained or maintained over longer periods. Vary the tone of your voice and use body movements and props. When feasible, walk around the room rather than standing in one place. Use a mixture of lectures, demonstrations, media presentations, group or individual exercises, debates, and learning games. For printed media, vary the text through the use of paper color, paper size, different type sizes or fonts, and diagrams or pictures. Use special effects, graphics, or animation on computer-based applications.

Biographical Sketch

John M. Keller is a Professor at Florida State University. Dr. Keller's work has centered on aspects of ISD, with a special emphasis on problems of motivation and human performance in instructional settings.

Dr. Keller received his undergraduate degree in Philosophy from the University of California at Riverside. After teaching in the secondary schools in San Diego County for a number of years, he began doctoral study at Indiana University. He was awarded a PhD in Instructional Systems Technology with a minor in Organizational Behavior in 1974.

Relevance

Relevance refers to the personal significance and value the learner attaches to achieving the learning objectives (i.e., "What's in it for me?"). In training programs where the instruction is relevant to the learner's current or future job, a thorough needs analysis will help ensure relevance. In general, training should occur just before the learner needs the skills so that he or she can apply the skills immediately. Relevance can also come from the way something is taught. For example, learners high in need for affiliation tend to enjoy classes in which they can work in groups. Similarly, people high in need for achievement enjoy the opportunity to both set moderately challenging goals and take personal responsibility for achieving them. Even if design follows these strategies, some learners may question the relevance of the training content. In these cases, strategies to establish relevance are necessary. Keller recommends goal orientation, motive matching, and familiarity.

Goal Orientation. How can I meet my learners' needs?

Provide written objectives and goals and/or have the learners define them. To be relevant to the learner, instruction must be focused on goals that the learner wants to achieve. Ensure the instruction meets an immediate or near-future need. If the instruction is related to job performance, ensure the goals are clear and demonstrate how they are related to job performance. Allow the learners to define their own goals as related to the instruction. If your predefined objectives and goals do not match the learners' defined goals, make on-the-spot adjustments as necessary.

Motive Matching. How can I match learning styles?

Use teaching strategies that match the learning styles and personal interests of the learner. If learners perceive that instruction meets their needs (achievement, affiliation, and influence), then motivation will be increased. Motivate learners with high achievement needs by providing opportunities to reach challenging goals with moderate risks. Provide opportunities for group projects to meet those with high affiliation needs.

Familiarity. How can I tie the instruction to the learner's experiences?

Present content using language, examples, and concepts that are related to the learner's experience. Most learners enjoy learning more about what they already know; therefore, relating the content to previous knowledge will enhance relevancy. Ask learners to share their previous experiences and tie the instruction to their experiences, modifying the instruction as necessary. Use analogies to enhance familiarity when teaching similar concepts in different disciplines.

Confidence

Confidence relates to the learner's expectation of success. Keller's theory is that past successes or failures in an activity will have an influence on how the learner will expect to succeed in a similar activity. Adults learning a new skill need an opportunity to acquire and practice the skill in a safe environment. In training, learner motivation depends in part on a positive learner expectancy for success. Providing successes through increasingly difficult activities will increase the learner's confidence. Confidence can be improved through the following strategies:

Learning Requirements. How can I ensure the learners will know what is expected for success?

Provide learners with clear goals, learning and requirements criteria, and assessment criteria. Break unreachable goals into manageable subgoals to increase the learner's expectation for success. Arrange conditions to maximize chances for success on early learning tasks to provide for a series of meaningful successes. These tasks must not be too easy, because easy successes do not contribute to expectancy of success on harder learning tasks.

Success Opportunities. How can I provide opportunities for meaningful successes?

Provide multiple achievement levels that allow learners to set personal standards of accomplishment and performance opportunities that allow them to experience success. Structure learning tasks in such a way that the learners must perform something that they are not quite capable of performing but can perform with practice or assistance. Achievement occurs when the assistance is gradually withdrawn. Organize the content with increasing levels of difficulty, with the learner understanding that the material can be learned progressively even though the content may seem complex.

Personal Responsibility. How can I ensure the learners know their successes are based on their efforts and abilities?

Provide feedback that reinforces the idea that successful learning depends on the learners' efforts and ability rather than on external forces. Enhance self-attribution by having the learners assume more personal control over their learning processes, such as goal-setting. Provide detailed, unambiguous feedback so the learners understand that both immediate success and performance improvements are under their control. Provide moderately difficult self-evaluation tools so the learners can access their own competence as they move through the program.

Satisfaction

Learner satisfaction is derived from achieving the performance goals. Learners can become unmotivated rather quickly if the outcomes of their efforts are inconsistent with their expectations. For example, if learners lack opportunities to apply their new skills to their jobs, they may lack motivation for further training. Even worse, coworkers or supervisors may ignore or punish new behaviors on the job, rather than reinforcing them; or trainees may try out newly learned behaviors only to find that they do not work in their job setting. Satisfaction comes through control of consequences: natural consequences, positive consequences, and equity.

Intrinsic Reinforcement. How can I provide meaningful opportunities to practice learned skills?

Provide opportunities to use the skill in a real or simulated setting. With just-in-time training, learners will have nearly immediate opportunities to apply the new learning to the job. If learning is not just-in-time training, simulate job application within the training so the learners can experience the natural consequences of the behaviors.

Extrinsic Rewards. How will I provide reinforcement?

Provide constructive feedback as well as verbal reinforcement to increase the learner's pride in accomplishment. Provide opportunities to practice new skills or behaviors in a safe environment.

Equity. How can I aid the learner to have a positive feeling about accomplishments?

Maintain consistent standards and consequences for task accomplishment. Perceptions of inequities can be extremely demotivating. Take care to set clear and consistent expectations at the beginning of a training program and to consistently follow through on expectations.

Four Phases of Implementation

The four categories form the basis of the model by providing prescriptive motivational strategies. The question then becomes, "How do I use it?" There are four phases that easily correlate to most instructional design models:

1. Perform an audience analysis.
2. Develop motivation objectives.
3. Select appropriate strategies.
4. Design evaluation mechanism.

To illustrate the use of these phases, consider the job of a telephone worker who must climb poles to install new or repair broken telephone transformers.

Perform an Audience Analysis. Analyze the audience to determine which of the four motivational categories (attention, relevance, confidence, and satisfaction) are weak and which are strong. For example, the group may be very confident of their ability to learn the content, but they may not see its relevance to their job. If time is available, use surveys to gather motivational data relevant to the course objectives. Analyze the data to determine which motivational strategies should be used when designing the training.

The audience analysis of the telephone worker group found that the workers were definitely interested and recognized the relevance of climbing poles to their job but lacked confidence in their ability to climb the pole. Therefore, confidence-building strategies were needed.

Develop Motivational Objectives. In this phase, develop motivational objectives based on the results of the audience analysis. The objectives should specify behaviors relative to motivational factors and should address any motivational problem areas identified by the audience analysis. For example, the following motivational objective would be used with the telephone worker group that did not feel confident in climbing the pole safely:

- On a questionnaire, learners will express confidence in their ability to climb the pole safely.

Select Appropriate Strategies. Develop strategies that accomplish the motivational objectives. The strategies should follow these guidelines:

1. Do not take up too much time.
2. Complement—do not overshadow—the learning objectives.
3. Be compatible with the time, money, and implementation constraints of the overall instruction.
4. Be acceptable to the audience.
5. Be compatible with the delivery system, including the instructor's personal style.

For example, a strategy to build confidence for the telephone worker group would be to simulate actual pole climbing by providing poles of varying heights for practice. Chunking by degree of difficulty, in this case poles of increasingly difficult heights, would allow the workers to build confidence in their climbing ability.

It is important to note that *more is not always better*. An excessive number of motivational strategies or strategies focusing on the wrong need could slow the class and detract from the task. For example, for the telephone worker group, strategies that emphasize the relevance of pole climbing would slow the class because the analysis indicated the workers already recognize the importance of climbing the pole. Additionally, in chunking the segmented portion of the pole-climbing exercise, care would have to be taken to determine the correct heights to increment the poles. Otherwise, a false sense of confidence or goals that are seemingly unattainable could occur.

Design Evaluation Mechanism. Include motivational factors in your overall course evaluation. Use direct and indirect measures of persistence, intensity of effort, emotions, and attitude. The assessment tool should measure the level of attention, satisfaction, relevance, and confidence. Subsequent training should be modified, if needed, based on the evaluation results.

Best Uses

The ARCS model can be used to supplement any instruction; however, it is most useful when motivation is lacking or low. Key elements of implementation follow:

1. Maintain a balance between motivational strategies and instructional strategies.
2. Maintain a balance among the motivational strategies.
3. Match strategies to learner needs.

Too few strategies results in boredom, while too many strategies may result in anxiety for the learners. To identify the optimal number and type of motivational strategies to apply, first complete an audience analysis. Consider factors such as age of learners; needs; incoming skills, knowledge, and abilities; initial motives; and the inherent motivational appeal of the topic. All of these factor into selecting the appropriate number and type of motivating strategies for instruction and for establishing a balanced approach.

Model in Action

Background

The Leased Housing Negotiations Course is a required course for all leased housing negotiators, who are responsible for locating and negotiating residential rental apartments for the U.S. Coast Guard. They are responsible for locating apartments according to a strict cost guideline and for ensuring that the lessors understand the responsibilities of both the government and lessor. They are also responsible for discussing every term of the lease with the lessor to eliminate potential misunderstandings.

To negotiate the lease properly, the negotiator must understand the terms and constraints of the lease contract. The negotiator sometimes performs this negotiation function as a collateral task and may view it as not being very important; conversely, others perform this function as a full-time job and view it as very important. The lease contract is complicated, very restrictive in nature, and quite often requires some sales skills to get the lessor to agree to rent apartments to the agency. Therefore, the negotiator must know the complexities of the contract (negotiator constraints) as well as have the ability to sell the good points of the lease agreement. Furthermore, the negotiator does not have the authority to sign the contract, only negotiate the agreement between the agency and the lessor.

The negotiators come to this job with a variety of experiences and backgrounds; some may be experts in administrative fields, while others may be pilots or ship drivers. They typically remain in the job three to four years, after which they are transferred to perform another function. Although the course is required, for various reasons, a course participant may have been on the job for some time before attending the course. The learners' negotiating and leased housing experience ranges from none to 1½ years of experience.

Those new to the job can be categorized in two ways: those who do not know the terms of the contract and have no experience in negotiating, and those who do not know the contract but feel confident in their negotiation skills.

Research Support

Keller advocates applying all four ARCS components to any instructional design because of their relationships to expectancy-value theory. He suggests that the *attention* and *relevance* components help illustrate the value of learning, while the *confidence* and *satisfaction* components help build expectations for successful learning.

Some evidence supporting this assertion was found in a research study by Myke Gluck and Ruth Small (1994), which was conducted to determine the relationship of 35 instructional attribute terms to Keller's four motivation conditions. They found that some relationships exist between certain attributes (strategies) and each of the ARCS conditions, and that adult learners perceive both the instructor and the learner to be closely related to each condition. They also found *attention* and *relevance* (value factors) to be significantly different than *confidence* and *satisfaction* (expectancy for success factors).

Newby (1991) used the ARCS model as a framework for categorizing motivational strategies used by elementary school teachers. He found a strong positive correlation between the number of relevance strategies and on-task student behaviors but a negative relationship for satisfaction strategies. He discovered that more than 58% of the strategies used were satisfaction strategies while relevance strategies only accounted for 7% of those used. This would suggest the importance of maintaining a balance of strategies and following the guideline of *more is not always better.*

Small, Dodge, and Jiang (1996) used the ARCS model to classify instructional episodes that college students described as either interesting or boring. They found that *attention* and *relevance* were the most effective strategies for stimulating interest and reducing boredom.

Those who are midway in the experience level usually understand the terms of the contract but may lack confidence in their ability to verbally sell the contract to the public. Those with the most experience feel very confident in their selling ability, feel they understand most of the contract, and are seeking to understand those parts they don't know. The audience analysis also indicated that while most of the learners recognized the importance of knowing the terms of the contract, some don't really understand the significance of discussing each of the terms to the pro-spective lessors.

Motivational Design

Perform Audience Analysis. The first phase of the effort involves an audience analysis, which includes identifying goals of the lesson and surveying a sample of the audience to determine existing motivations within the four ARCS categories.

For example, the following subgoal has been established for the lesson:

- Personnel will demonstrate technical knowledge of the lease contract while transacting lease negotiations with the lessors by pointing to and explaining the intent of each paragraph of the lease.

A traditional paper-based survey was used to capture the current motivation levels of the target population sample. Furthermore, the target population sample was divided into three groups based on the experience levels of the participants. This division enables the designer to identify motivational strategies for each subgroup within the entire target population. A portion of the survey instrument is shown in Table 15.2.

	Little				Very
How *relevant* is this goal to you?	1	2	3	4	5
What parts of this goal *interest* you the most?					
All	1	2	3	4	5
Technical knowledge	1	2	3	4	5
Public speaking	1	2	3	4	5
How *confident* are you that you can successfully learn to perform the goal?	1	2	3	4	5
How *satisfying* would it be to you to be able to perform the goal?	1	2	3	4	5

Table 15.2
Leased Housing Sample Survey

The data were then categorized and analyzed. Table 15.3 outlines a sample of the survey responses.

	Little			Very
Relevance		7	5	13
Attention (Interest)				
All		7	4	14
Technical knowledge		6	12	7
Public speaking	5	10	8	
Confidence	13	7	5	
Satisfaction			7	18

Table 15.3
Leased Housing Sample Survey Responses

The data received from the survey results indicate that the *relevance* ranges from average to high but that *confidence* is low. Consequently, strategies to increase and maintain *relevance* and to increase the learner's expectancy for success should be incorporated in this instruction. *Satisfaction* and *attention* (*interest*) are medium to high; strategies will be applied to maintain both the *satisfaction* and *attention* (*interest*) level.

A summary of the comprehensive audience analysis provided the following descriptions for each experience level category:

- **New Person.** Likely to have a high attention level because he or she is new to the job and will hang on to every word and tip to get the tools to do job. Because these learners are new, they may not understand the relevance of either knowing the contract or negotiating. They lack the knowledge of the contract and are unsure of their ability to negotiate with the lessors, although some may come into the job having had previous personal experiences with negotiating.

- **Person With Seven to Eight Months' Experience.** Likely to have a high attention level because he or she is relatively new to the job and will be seeking answers to questions. These learners may be overly confident about their knowledge of leases, particularly if they have not attended previous leased housing training. They generally have a medium to high confidence level for negotiating with lessors, depending on past experiences.

- **Person With 1½ Years' Experience.** Likely to have a low to medium attention level because they are experienced and are only seeking answers to specific questions. Their attention will be easily lost if answers are not provided. They are confident about their knowledge of leases, particularly if they have attended previous leased housing training. They generally have a medium to high confidence level negotiating with lessors, depending on past experiences.

Develop Motivational Objectives. Phase 2 requires the development of motivational objectives to support the content-based objectives. The following motivational objectives were included to address the most important motivational issues identified in the analysis phase.

- Learners will stay focused and attentive throughout the lesson. (A)

- Learners will identify, based on previous experiences, reasons why knowing the meaning of the lease is relevant to the job. (R)

- Learners will express confidence in their ability to articulate the meaning of the lease contract. (C)

- Learners will rate themselves as satisfied or very satisfied regarding newly acquired lease negotiation skills. (S)

Select Appropriate Strategies. Based on the analysis in Table 15.3, the strategies will focus on gaining and maintaining the attention level (it will be easy to lose the experienced persons); ensuring that the course meets the needs of all attending; and increasing the confidence level by providing simulated negotiations sessions. Table 15.4 summarizes the motivation strategies selected in Phase 3 of the process. Greater detail on how the motivational strategies were implemented in the flow of an actual lesson is shown in Table 15.5.

	Beginning	During	End
A	• Use overhead with a shocking leased housing statistic. • Display/discuss the course objectives.	• Use clear, concise overheads. • Use variations in tone, humor, and interactive communications to keep students alert and attentive.	• Go back to the initial objectives and ensure they have been covered.
R	• State that the course is designed to assist the learners to perform their job better. • Ask the class their experience level to determine skills and knowledge.	• Encourage students to provide real-life experiences. • Use familiar language with the audience. • Design role plays to simulate actual lease negotiations.	• Refer back to posted real-life experiences and question how this class experience would have changed the outcome.
C	• Clearly outline the course objectives and procedures. • Have copies of training materials available for class.	• Use role-playing to provide opportunities to practice, test, and challenge learners. • Ask what-if questions and encourage students to respond. • Let the teams stage the role-playing in any way they want.	• Provide time for one-on-one feedback.
S	• Ask learners what they would like to accomplish and their expectations.	• Learners' objectives remain posted. • Provide feedback to questions during the lesson. • Provide praise when learners give answers and feedback.	• Provide feedback to questions presented after class. • Review the objectives to ensure all have been accomplished.

Table 15.4
Selected Motivational Strategies

Motivating Factor(s)	Activity
A, R	The instructor opens the class with an overhead that depicts a shocking leased housing statistic. The objectives have been posted, and the class discusses details of the objectives.
R	Additionally, the instructor solicits input from the class on what their expectations and objectives are.
S	These learner expectations and objectives are written on a chart and remain posted throughout the course.
A, R	During the course of instructional events dealing with understanding the intent of the contents of the lease form, the instructor asks the students to describe or relate real-life experiences demonstrating the importance of knowing and understanding the lease, including both negative and positive impacts.
R, C, A	Encourage frequent question-and-answer sessions.
C, A	When the students seem reluctant to ask questions, the instructor asks "what if" questions and encourages the students to respond and participate.
C, A	At the end of this portion of the lesson, the instructor introduces role-playing.
A, C, S	The students are grouped in teams of four; two students assume the role of *negotiator* and two students assume the role of *lessor*. The negotiators have the task of explaining the lease to a prospective lessor. The lessors have the task of asking questions that demonstrate they may not understand what the negotiator explained. The teams are given the opportunity to stage the role-playing in any way they want; the rest of the class must be able to observe.
A, C	As the role-playing occurs, the observers are taking notes to recommend alternative positive behaviors to the role-players.
A, C, S	At the conclusion of each role-play, the team has an opportunity to express feelings regarding the role-play activity and the observers have an opportunity to provide alternative positive behaviors to the team members.
A, S	At the end of the role-plays, the instructor solicits any additional questions and answers from the group to ensure clarity and understanding.
A, S	The instructor concludes and the class reviews the objectives to check off what it has accomplished.

Table 15.5

Motivational Strategy Activities

Evaluation. The final phase of the ARCS model is an evaluation of the strategies used. Table 15.6 shows a sample evaluation instrument. The results of the evaluation serve as the basis for adjusting the motivational strategies used in the course.

To what degree did the following activities hold your interest?

	Attention Levels				
	Little				Very
Observing other class members explain the lease	1	2	3	4	5

To what degree do you believe the following activities are relevant to help you explain leases in the lessor-employee meetings?

	Relevance Levels				
	Little				Very
The role-playing exercises with other class members	1	2	3	4	5

What level of confidence do you have that you can use the following skills in negotiating a lease?

	Confidence Levels				
	Little				Very
Articulating the meaning of the lease	1	2	3	4	5

Overall, how satisfied were you with the following factors?

	Satisfaction Levels				
	Little				Very
Yourself, relative to your new skills and knowledge	1	2	3	4	5
The pace of the instruction	1	2	3	4	5

Table 15.6
Sample Evaluation Tool

Implementation Guide

Phase	Activity
1	**Perform an Audience Analysis.** Conduct an audience analysis to collect information from the target population. Include questions relating to *attention*, *relevance*, *confidence*, and *satisfaction* as related to the goals of the instruction. This requires the completion of the following activities:
	1. Identify the goals and/or subgoals of the lesson.
	2. Design and develop a survey instrument to administer to target population collecting data regarding the attention, relevance, confidence, and satisfaction as related to the goals.
	3. Collect data and categorize using the conditions of motivation.
	4. Analyze the results.
2	**Develop Motivational Objectives.** Specify behaviors relative to motivational factors and address problem areas as defined in the audience analysis.
3	**Select Appropriate Strategies.** Develop appropriate motivation strategies that accomplish the motivational objectives.
	• Do not take up too much time.
	• Complement, do not overshadow, the learning objectives.
	• Be compatible with the time, money, and implementation constraints of the overall instruction.
	• Be acceptable to the audience.
	• Be compatible with the delivery system, including the instructor's personal style.
	More is not better. Focus strategies on weaker motivational conditions.
4	**Design the Evaluation Mechanism.** Develop motivational factor assessment questions to include in your overall course evaluation. Use direct measures of persistence, intensity of effort, emotions, and attitude to evaluate motivational consequences. The evaluation tool should measure the level of *attention, satisfaction, relevance,* and *confidence*.
	1. Gather your list of motivational strategies.
	2. Write a statement describing what the learner experienced.
	3. Incorporate the statement into an evaluation tool under the categories of *attention*, *relevance*, *confidence*, and *satisfaction*
	4. Based on the analysis of the evaluation, increase, decrease, or change the motivational strategies for this course.

References

Atkinson, J.W., & Raynor, J.O. (Eds.). (1974). *Motivation and achievement.* Washington, DC: Winston.

Bandura, A. (1977). Self efficacy: Toward a unifying theory of behavioral change. *Psychological Review, (84)*, 191–215.

Berlyne, D.E. (1965). Motivational problems raised by exploratory and epistemic behavior. In S. Koch (Ed.), *Psychology: A study of a science* (Vol. 5). New York: McGraw-Hill.

Feather, N.T. (1975). *Values in education and society.* New York: The Free Press.

Gluck, M., & Small, R.V. (1994, October). The relationship of motivational conditions to effective instructional attributes: A magnitude scaling approach. *Educational Technology,* 33–39.

Keller, J.M. (1979). Motivation and instructional design: A theoretical perspective. *Journal of Instructional Development, 2*(4), 26–34.

Keller, J.M. (1983). Motivational design of instruction. In C.M. Reigeluth (Ed.), *Instructional design theories and models: An overview of their current status* (383–434). Hillsdale, NJ: Lawrence Erlbaum Associates.

Maslow, A.H. (1954). *Motivation and personality.* New York: Harper & Row.

Newby, T. (1991). Classroom motivation: Strategies of first-year teachers. *Journal of Educational Psychology, (83)*2, 195–200.

Porter, L.W., & Lawler, E.E. (1968). *Managerial attitudes and performance.* Homewood, IL: Richard D. Irwin.

Rokeach, M. (1973). *The nature of human values.* New York: The Free Press.

Rotter, J.B. (1972). *An introduction to a social learning theory of personality.* New York: Hold, Rinehart & Winston.

Seligman, M.E. (1975). *Helplessness.* San Francisco: Freeman.

Small, R.V., Dodge, B.M., & Jiang, X. (1996). Dimensions of interest and boredom in instructional situations. In *Proceedings of Annual Conference of Association for Educational Communications and Technology*, Indianapolis, IN.

Weiner, B. (1974). Self-efficacy: Toward a unifying theory of behavioral change. *Psychological Review, 84,* 191–215.

Bibliography

Arnone, M.P., & Small, R.V. (1995). Arousing and sustaining curiosity: Lessons from the ARCS model. In *Proceedings of the 1995 Annual National Convention of the Association for Educational Communications and Technology,* Anaheim, CA (see IR 017 139).

Bohlin, R.M., & Milheim, W.D. (1994). Applications of an adult motivational instructional design model. In *Proceedings of Selected Research and Development Presentations at the 1994 National Convention of the Association for Educational Communications and Technology,* Nashville, TN.

Carson, C.H., & Curtis, R.V. (1991). The application of motivational design to bibliographic instruction. *Research Strategies*, *9* (3), 130–138.

Gagné, R.M., & Medsker, K.L. (1996). *The conditions of learning*: *Training applications*. Fort Worth, TX: Harcourt Brace.

Keller, J.M. (1983a). Development and use of the ARCS model of motivational design. Paper based on lectures presented at Vakgroep Instruktietechnologie Toegepaste Onderwijskunde Technieche Hogeschool Twente, January-June 1993.

Keller, J.M. (1983b). Use of the ARCS model of motivation in teacher training. IDD&E Working Paper No. 10, March.

Keller, J.M., & Kopp, T.W. (1987). An application of the ARCS model of motivational design. In C.M. Reigeluth (Ed.), *Instructional theories in action* (289–320). Hillsdale, NJ: Lawrence Erlbaum Associates.

Main, R. (1993). Integrating motivation into the instructional design process. *Educational Technology*, *33*, 37–41.

Reigeluth, C.M. (1987). *Instructional theories in action.* Hillsdale, NJ: Lawrence Erlbaum Associates.

Small, R. (1997). Motivation in instructional design. (Report No. EDo-IR-97-06). East Lansing, MI: National Center for Research on Teacher Learning (ERIC Document Reproduction Service No. EDO-IR-97-06).

Small, R. (1998). *Designing motivation into library and information skills instruction.* [On-line]. Available: http://ala.org/aasl/SLMQ/Small.htm#instruct

About the Author

Fran Peters is employed by U.S. Coast Guard and works in the Housing Programs Division at Coast Guard Headquarters, Washington, DC. She has developed Leased Housing Contracting Training and Leased Housing Negotiations Training and is responsible for developing and delivering the annual Area Housing Officer Training for field-level housing managers throughout the Coast Guard. She has an MA in Human Performance Systems from Marymount University and a BS in Education from Appalachian State University.

CHAPTER 16   *Adult Learning*

Cynthia J. Demnitz

Many think of Malcolm Knowles (1913–1997) as the father of adult education. Knowles is widely credited for introducing American adult educators to the theory of andragogy, the art and science of helping adults learn. Andragogy comes from the Greek *aner*—man or adult—and *agogus*—leader of. In contrast, pedagogy is the art and science of teaching children (from Greek *paid*—child—and *agogus*). Knowles didn't originate the term, and he incorporated the thinking of many others in developing his ideas. Yet his is the name most strongly associated with andragogy in the United States. Central to his theory is the belief that adults are active participants in their own learning. The role of the instructor is that of facilitator and resource, a "pointer-outer" of ideas. Knowles' book *The Modern Practice of Adult Education: Andragogy Versus Pedagogy* (1970) presents the andragogy model. According to the original model, four basic assumptions distinguish adult learners from children:

1. **Self-Concept**—Children are naturally dependent; adults have a deep need to be self-directing.
2. **Experience**—Children's experience is limited; adults' broad experience is a valuable learning resource.
3. **Readiness to Learn**—Children's readiness is more subject centered; adult's readiness is more related to skills and knowledge needed to fulfill their roles in society.

4. **Orientation to Learning**—Children's orientation is subject centered (they master content to pass a course); adults are problem-centered (they seek skills or knowledge to apply to real-life situations).

Knowles originally viewed andragogy and pedagogy as two opposing models, and he stirred much debate among adult educators. He continually modified his assumptions, conceding that many children learned well using andragogical principles, and adults often learned well in a pedagogical setting. Knowles later maintained that the most effective instruction depends on the individual and the situation.

Origins

Knowles' own career path is a key to the formation of his assumptions about adult learners. He had substantial real-life experience with adult learners before completing his formal graduate education. In the introduction to *Andragogy in Action* (Knowles & Associates, 1984), he describes his entry into the field of adult learning. After college he had hoped to join the U.S. Foreign Service, but there were no positions open. He took a "holding" job as director of training for the National Youth Administration (NYA) in Massachusetts, a work-study program for unemployed young adults. He began to follow emerging theories of adult education, particularly those of Eduard C. Lindeman. He continued to apply these ideas in his next position, director of adult education at the Huntington YMCA in Boston. In 1946, Knowles became director of adult education at the Central YMCA in Chicago. He enrolled in the graduate program in adult education at the University of Chicago, where he was greatly influenced by his major professor Cyril O. Houle. There he also met Arthur Shedlin, an associate of Carl Rogers, who introduced Knowles to self-directed learning principles.

Knowles' master's thesis drew on literature in the field and his own real-life experience to formulate an integrated, albeit "informal" theory of adult education. This became the basis for his first book, *Informal Adult Education*, published in 1950. In 1951, Knowles became executive director of the Adult Education Association of the U.S.A., and he shifted his focus from individual learners to the broader adult education movement.

Knowles describes the roots of andragogy. In 1967, Dusan Savicevic, a Yugoslavian adult educator, introduced the term andragogy to Knowles, who popularized it in the United States. However, the term had been used in Europe for some time. It is believed that the term was coined in 1833 by Alexander Kapp, a German teacher,

Biographical Sketch

Malcolm Shepherd Knowles (1913–1997) was born in Livingston, Montana, the son of a veterinarian. As a young Boy Scout, he demonstrated strong motivation and individualism, once applying himself to win 50 merit badges to a major national Boy Scout prize. From 1930 to 1934, he attended Harvard University on scholarship, graduated, and enrolled in the Fletcher School of Diplomacy. Unable to fulfill his intention to enter the U.S. Foreign Service, he entered the adult education world with several early positions in adult education and training with the National Youth Administration (NYA) and the YMCA. He received his MA in Education from the University of Chicago in 1949 and became executive director of the Adult Education Association of the U.S.A. in 1951. In 1960, he received his PhD in Education from the University of Chicago. He was a professor of adult education at Boston University from 1966 to 1974, followed by a professorship in adult and community education at North Carolina State University from 1974 to 1979.

Knowles was a prolific author, publishing more than 19 books and 200 articles, some with his wife, Hulda. He was widely sought after as an organizational consultant, conducting workshops for corporations and organizations worldwide. Known for his authentic personal style, he was himself a lifelong learner and remained active professionally until very late in life. Some of his major publications include the following:

- *The Modern Practice of Adult Education: Andragogy Versus Pedagogy* (1970)

- *The Adult Learner: A Neglected Species* (1973)

- *Andragogy in Action: Applying Modern Principles of Adult Learning* (1984)

- *The Making of an Adult Educator: An Autobiographical Journey* (1989)

Knowles received numerous awards and honors, including membership in the HRD Hall of Fame. He considered that his greatest legacy was preparing many adult educators from around the country. When he died on Thanksgiving Day 1997, there was an outpouring of appreciation from his many followers and admirers. *The New York Times* called him "an adult education pioneer." Many education and training professionals consider that principles of learning that we take for granted have a foundation in Knowles' theories.

who used the term andragogy to describe the educational theory of Plato (although Plato himself never used the term). The term appeared again in Europe in 1921 as used by the German social scientist Eugen Rosenstock, who believed that adult education required special teachers, methods, and philosophy. There are many recorded uses of the term in the 1960s in France, Holland, and Yugoslavia. Since 1966, the University of Amsterdam has offered a doctorate for "andragogues," referring to andragogy as any professionally guided activity that aims to effect a change in adults (Knowles, 1990).

The term andragogy had been used in the United States before Knowles popularized it. Davenport found references to the term in the United States by Martha Anderson and Eduard Lindeman in 1926–1927. Lindeman's ideas about the unique characteristics of adults as learners, and the need for methods and techniques for helping adults learn, were early strong influences on Knowles' thinking (Knowles & Associates, 1984). Both Lindeman and Knowles are viewed as having played important roles in the development of andragogy in the United States (Davenport, 1987).

Description

Assumptions About Learners: Pedagogy Versus Andragogy

When Knowles first presented the andragogy model in 1970 (in *The Modern Practice of Adult Education: Andragogy Versus Pedagogy*), it had four basic assumptions (see numbers 2 to 5 below). He added the motivation assumption (number 6) in 1984. Knowles practiced his own philosophy of learning and continued to refine the model over time based on input from his peers; the "need-to-know" assumption (number 1) was last to be added.

1. **Need to Know.** Pedagogy assumes that the teacher is responsible for all learning decisions; children depend entirely on the teacher's direction. Thus, children need to know only that they must learn material to move to the next level; they don't need to know how learning will apply to their lives. In contrast, adults need to know why they need to learn something. The facilitator helps the learner become aware of this "need to know." One way to develop such awareness is to use assessment tools to help learners discover the gaps between where they are and where they would like to be.

2. **Self-Concept.** While children are dependent, adults have a strong need to be self-directing. Knowles says dependency gradually decreases as children mature. Pedagogical practices are appropriate in the early years of education,

but they are increasingly inappropriate in later years. Knowles claims that adults resent training situations that put them into the dependent role of children. Such learners can revert back to their early school conditioning, becoming passive or resistant. Adults prefer situations that are aligned with their self-concept of being responsible for their own decisions and lives. Learning facilitators must create learning experiences that help adults make the transition from dependent to self-directing learners.

3. **Experience.** Children have limited life experience to draw on as a learning resource. But adults have accumulated a reservoir of experience that can be a resource for learning, as well as a broad base to which new learning can be related. On this last point, andragogy is consistent with the cognitivist philosophy. Experiential techniques such as group discussion, problemsolving, or peer-helping activities can tap into learners' experience. Knowles notes that a given group of adults will have a wider range of individual differences than a comparable group of children. This calls for individualized learning strategies. But in addition to gaining valuable experience as we age, we also collect biases and resistance to new ways of thinking. Learning facilitators should help learners examine these biases and open their minds to new ideas.

4. **Readiness to Learn.** Children depend on the teacher, who tells them that they must learn if they want to be promoted. Adults become ready to learn new skills and abilities to help them deal with real-life situations. This may mean attaining the skills or knowledge needed to fulfill a role in society such as worker, spouse, parent, or retiree. When a person moves to a new role, such as from worker to supervisor, he or she becomes ready to learn new skills.

5. **Orientation to Learning**. Children have a subject-centered orientation to learning, focusing on the content of what they are learning. Thus, learning experiences are organized according to the logic of the subject matter. Adults tend to have a life-centered or problem-centered orientation to learning. Knowles says that adults will spend time and energy on learning something if they believe it will help them deal with real-life problems. An example is designing literacy materials around real-life situations, like reading instructions at work or going to the doctor. Knowles presents an example from the early 1980s of learning to use a computer. He soon tired of the command memorization approach outlined in the instruction manual, preferring instead to learn the commands he needed to know in order to write a letter—a task he wanted and needed to learn (Knowles, 1990).

6. **Motivation.** Children's motivators are external—grades, teacher's approval, parental pressures. Adults, too, have some external motivators, such as pay raises or promotions. But they respond more to internal motivators such as a desire for increased job satisfaction or better quality of life.

Knowles originally saw the two models in opposition—andragogy versus pedagogy. He later rethought his position, conceding that children sometimes learn better in an andragogical setting and adults sometimes prefer and perform better in pedagogical situations. He maintained that most effective instruction depends on the situation, the learner, and the task.

Principles of Andragogical Instruction

1. **Prepare the Learners.** This initial step, added after Knowles presented his original principles, recognizes the importance of laying the groundwork for successful learning. Examples of activities that prepare learners include the following:
   - Providing advance information about what a learning situation will involve
   - Working with learners to formulate realistic expectations
   - Preparing learners to participate in the learning situation

2. **Set the Climate.** Knowles considered this to be one of the most important elements of the process, and he describes it in detail. Climate-setting is widely practiced, as seen in the opening phases of countless training sessions, workshops, and conferences. Climate setting elements include the following:
   - A pleasing and comfortable physical environment. Knowles relates how he and his students fixed up a dreary classroom with inexpensive paper collages and mobiles to lighten the mood.
   - Classroom arrangements that facilitate small-group interaction and promote a cheerful learning environment—not the traditional, auditorium-style setup.
   - A psychological climate of mutual respect and trust. Knowles states that people are more open to learning if they feel respected (Knowles & Associates, 1984).
   - An atmosphere of supportiveness and collaboration. Opening exercises create collaboration among participants right away.
   - A pleasurable learning experience. Learning should be fun, not a chore.

3. **Involve Learners in Mutual Planning.** People are more committed to decisions they help to make. Options for involving participants include the following:
   - Have learners serve on committees to design courses.
   - Present several options for learning activities and let the group decide.

4. **Involve Learners in Diagnosing Their Own Learning Needs.** Knowles presents several strategies for doing this. He states that one of the challenges is

meshing learners' felt needs with the needs of the organization. Options include—
- •Simple interest-finding checklists
- •Assessment tools
- •Use of a competency model that reflects both individual and organizational needs and allows learners to see the gap between where they are and where they need to be.

5. **Involve Learners in Formulating Their Learning Objectives.** Here Knowles introduces his "learning contract" process, which translates learning needs into learning objectives. Such contracts are appropriate in both long-term settings (such as university courses) as well as in short-term workshops, where learners leave with a contract saying how they will continue their learning on their own. Contracts may be reviewed by peers as well as the instructor. The learning contract also does the following:
- •Identifies resources to help meet the objectives
- •Specifies what evidence will be used to judge how well the objectives have been met
- •Determines how the evidence will be used for evaluation

6. **Involve Learners in Designing Learning Plans.** As part of the learning contract, learners identify resources and define strategies to meet the objectives. Examples of resources include the instructor, other knowledgeable experts, group activities with peers, and independent study.

7. **Help Learners Carry Out Their Learning Plans.** As a partner in learning, the instructor/facilitator works with learners to help them carry out the obligations in the contract. This includes being available as a consultant and resource.

8. **Involve Learners in Evaluating Learning.** Knowles describes having learners present the instructor/facilitator with their "portfolios of evidence," including papers, tapes, and observer rating scales. Learners are involved in evaluating whether the learning objectives are achieved, as well as the training program itself.

Characteristics and Implications of Adult Learning Theory

Table 16.1 summarizes key characteristics and implications of Knowles' theory, related implications for adult learning, and implications for presenters.

Adult Learner Characteristics	Implications for Adult Learning	Implications for Presenters
Self-Concept: The adult learner sees himself as capable of self-direction and desires others to see him in the same way. In fact, one definition of maturity is the capacity to be self-directing.	• Climate of openness and respect is helpful to identify what the learners want and need to learn. • Adults enjoy planning and carrying out their own learning exercises. • Adults need to be involved in evaluating progress toward self-chosen goals.	• Recognize participants as self-directing…and treat them accordingly. • The presenter is a learning reference rather than a traditional instructor; presenters are, therefore, encouraged to "tell it like it is" and stress "how I do it" rather than tell participants what they should do. Avoid "talking down" to participants who are experienced decisionmakers and self-starters. Instead try to meet the participants' needs.
Experience: Adults bring a lifetime of experience to the learning situation. Youths tend to regard experience as something that has happened to them, while to an adult, that experience is the individual. The adult defines who he or she is in terms of his or her experience.	• Less use is made of transmittal techniques, more of experiential techniques. • Discovery of how to learn from experience is key to self-actualization. • Mistakes are opportunities for learning. • To reject adult experience is to reject the adult.	• As the adult is his or her experience, failure to utilize the experience of the adult learner is equivalent to rejecting him or her as a person.
Readiness to Learn: Adult developmental tasks increasingly move toward social and occupational role competence and away from the more physical developmental tasks of childhood.	• Adults need opportunities to identify the competency requirements of their occupational and social roles. • Adult readiness to learn and teachable moments peak at those points where a learning opportunity is coordinated with a recognition of the need to know. • Adults can best identify their own readiness to learn and teachable moments.	• Learning occurs through helping participants with the identification of gaps in the learner's knowledge. • No questions are "stupid"; all questions are "opportunities" for learning.
A Problem-Centered Time Perspective: Youths think of education as the accumulation of knowledge for use in the future. Adults tend to think of learning as a way to be more effective in problemsolving today.	• Adult education needs to be problem-centered rather than theoretically oriented. • Formal curriculum development is less valuable than finding out what the learners need to learn. • Adults need the opportunity to apply and try out learning quickly.	• The primary emphasis in the course is on students' learning rather than on teacher's teaching. • Involvement in such things as problems to be solved, case histories, and critical incidents generally offer greater learning opportunity for adults than "talking to" them.

Table 16.1

Implications of Knowles' Theory

Humanistic Psychology Foundation

Knowles is considered to be a major influence in the shift in educational theory from behaviorism toward a theory more grounded in humanistic psychology. Two humanistic psychologists, Carl Rogers and Abraham Maslow, strongly influenced his work. In *The Modern Practice of Adult Education: Andragogy Versus Pedagogy*, Knowles (1980) presents Maslow's well-known theory of human motivation—his hierarchy of human needs. At the lowest level of the hierarchy are physiological needs such as hunger and thirst. These must be satisfied before one can deal with the next higher level, safety needs. After safety needs are fulfilled, we address the next levels: love and belonging, self-esteem, and self-actualization. Self-actualization may be described as a person's desire to become all he is capable of becoming. For Knowles, Maslow's concept—

> implies that the adult educator's mission is to help individuals learn what is required for gratification of their needs at whatever level they are struggling. If they are hungry, we must help them learn what will get them food; if they are well-fed, safe, loved and esteemed, we must help them explore undeveloped capacities and become their full selves (1980, p. 29).

The goal of most learning, according to the humanists, is self-actualization—realization of one's full potential as a person.

Carl Rogers' influence on Knowles was very strong, and Rogers was the foundation for many concepts of the andragogy model. Knowles pointed out that Rogers was concerned with learning that leads to personal growth and development. Knowles (1990) wrote that, according to Rogers, such learning has the following characteristics:

1. **Personal Involvement**—The whole person is involved in the learning event.
2. **Self-Initiation**—The sense of discovery comes from within.
3. **Pervasive**—Learning makes a difference in behavior, attitudes, even the personality of the learner.
4. **Evaluation by the Learner**—The learner determines whether the experience meets a need.
5. **Essence is Meaning**—When learning takes place, the element of meaning to the learner is built into the experience.

Rogers' student-centered approach also strongly influenced Knowles. Rogers considered that we cannot teach a person directly, but can only facilitate learning; the student has a strong responsibility for his own learning. Rogers also stressed the importance of an accepting and supportive environment for learning.

Knowles incorporated Rogers' concept of authenticity into his own teaching practice. In the autobiographical *The Making of an Adult Educator*, Knowles describes his experience as a new professor of education at Boston University in 1960. A senior colleague advised him to play a dignified and professorial role—one that was at odds with his self-concept. His first year, he became so uncomfortable, he considered resigning. Instead, in his second year, Knowles decided to try being himself, applying student-centered and participative approaches. He discovered that he could be a good professor and still be himself—with few compromises (Knowles, 1989, quoted in Bell et al., 1989).

Comparison of Knowles and Rogers

Because much of Knowles' work is based on Rogerian thinking, there are strong similarities between Knowles' approach and that of Rogers, with a few significant differences. Both are humanists, emphasizing the learner's potential for growth and development. Both stress the self-directedness of adults, the freedom of the individual, and the value of experience in learning. For both, the instructor role is that of a facilitator of learning, with strong emphasis on the relationship between the learner and the facilitator. Knowles focuses more on a prescribed step-by-step approach (diagnosing learning needs, spelling out goals, following a plan to achieve them), while Rogers' approach is less structured. For Rogers, the psychotherapist, the facilitator acts more as a nonjudgmental reflector of the student's ideas, and much of the goal of the learning experience is personal insight. Rogers also strongly emphasized the facilitator's role as a reflector of feelings. For Knowles, the facilitator is more of a guide, resource, and advisor. Unlike Rogers, Knowles was more focused on educational program development and administration, a result of his strong background in adult and continuing education programs.

Research Support

Some experts have criticized andragogy for a perceived lack of research support. Davenport (1987) notes several studies that contradict some of the andragogy assumptions. He suggests that educators should concentrate on discovering which approach, pedagogy or andragogy, is appropriate for a given learning situation, rather than which is best overall, a focus consistent with the Knowles' later thinking.

Still, many proponents of andragogy are apt to prefer andragogical approaches for a majority of adult learning situations. Perhaps the most convincing evidence of support for the model is the widespread acceptance of its principles by countless practitioners who find the concepts intuitively appealing and effective in real-life learning situations.

The fifth edition of *The Adult Learner* (Knowles et al., 1998) was published after Knowles' death. ("A Neglected Species" was intentionally left off the title—the authors no longer considered the adult neglected). In this latest edition, the authors discuss perspectives on andragogy that have emerged from research and comparison with other theories. These perspectives continue to suggest a more situational approach to learning—or for choosing pedagogical or andragogical approaches. The authors' discussion from *The Adult Learner*, summarized in the following six paragraphs, revolves around the assumptions of andragogy.

Learner's Need to Know. Because the use of collaborative techniques for planning learning is so widespread and generally accepted, few researchers have felt the need to study this. Several studies of learners in organizational settings support the notion that learners who know how learning will be conducted, what learning will occur, and why learning is important will demonstrate higher levels of satisfaction. For example, Baldwin, Magjuka, and Loher (1991, cited in Knowles et al., 1998) tested the idea that involving trainees in planning their learning would positively affect learning. In the study, trainees who had a choice about attending training and attended their choice were more motivated to attend training and learned more.

Research Support, cont.

Self-Directed Learning. Most experts agree that not all adults are fully capable of teaching themselves and having autonomy in every learning situation. Grow (1991, cited in Knowles et al., 1998) suggests that self-directed learning depends on the situation, and that teachers should help to match styles with the student. Grow (1991, cited in Knowles et al., 1998) proposes four stages in learning autonomy: dependent, interested, involved, and self-directed. The role of the teacher varies with each stage, with the greatest involvement at the dependent stage, the least involvement at the self-directed stage.

Prior Experience of the Learner. Here modern theories of mental models help explain how experience influences learning, often creating biases. Argyris is cited as stressing the difficulties in overcoming resistance to new learning if such learning challenges the existing mental schema created from experience. Senge's concept of mental models describes how such models can limit our ways of thinking. Research by cognitive psychologists suggests that the prior experience of adults can both help and hinder learning (Knowles et al., 1998).

Readiness to Learn. Pratt (1988, cited in Knowles et al., 1998) suggests a useful model within which adults vary in learning situations. He proposes a four-quadrant model with combinations of direction (a learner's need for assistance) and support (learner's need for encouragement). A learner's need for direction versus support varies according to the learning situation.

Orientation to Learning: Problemsolving. Adults are oriented to learning within the context of real-life situations. Experiential approaches have thus been used extensively. Kölb (1984, cited in Knowles et al., 1998) provides a four-stage model for experiential learning that includes: concrete experience, observation and reflection, abstract conceptualization, and active experimentation.

Motivation to Learn. Adults are motivated to learn by internal needs. Several models are consistent with this notion. For example, Wlodowski (1985, cited in Knowles et al., 1998) suggests that adults seek the following learning characteristics: success in learning, volition (choice) in learning, value (learning something that is valued), and enjoyment. His model helps to explain why adults are more motivated by internal than external needs.

Best Uses

The best uses of andragogy can be seen most clearly in the light of a consideration of the model's limitations and strengths. Such an analysis reveals that the model's applicability depends both on the content and the learner's characteristics.

Limitations

Many of the principles and practices of andragogy are widely accepted among trainers and educators. Frequently, conference presentations, university classes, and training sessions begin with some climate-setting exercises, followed by discussion of participant expectations and participatory goal-setting. Commonly, training session leaders and classroom instructors apply facilitated approaches, drawing on the collective experiences of the learners. However, while andragogical practices are certainly widespread, the underlying theories have taken some critical hits.

In 1988, several years after andragogy was established among many adult educators, an article questioning the principles and practice of andragogy was published. In it, Sharon Merriam, professor of adult education at the University of Georgia, summarizes the controversy: "Andragogy has caused more controversy, philosophical debate, and critical analysis than any other concept/theory/model proposed thus far" (Feuer & Geber, 1988). Detractors faulted Knowles for everything from a perceived lack of research support to faulty use of the Greek root words in introducing his definition of the term andragogy (Davenport, 1987). Much of the criticism of andragogy has focused on Knowles' assumptions about adult learners, as compared with pre-adult learners:

Self-Concept. The assumption that adult learners have a deep need to be self-directing is central to the andragogy model, but not everyone agrees. Detractors say that rather than being self-directing in their learning, many adults react with confusion and anxiety when presented with a self-directed curriculum. At the same time, many children are not the dependent learners depicted by Knowles—they can be very independent learners. Experts ask: Is self-directedness characteristic of the typical adult learner, or is it a desired goal for adult educators?

Experience. Many adult educators agree that this is the one area in which there is an enduring distinction between adults and children—it makes intuitive sense and is the most empirically valid of the assumptions. However, one criticism is that experience and prior learning in adults may work to prevent new learning from occurring.

Readiness to Learn. Cyril Houle (Knowles' graduate professor) and others took issue with the assertion that children are more subject centered, while adults are more life centered. Many adults learn for the innate joy of learning, and children often question the utility of subject-centered curricula.

Orientation to Learning. Again, many disagreed with the andragogy camp. Not all adults have a problem-centered orientation to learning. Certain adults are learning oriented—continually inquiring into new knowledge or skill domains. And many adults learn with no specific problemsolving goal. Conversely, children often demonstrate a problemsolving approach to learning.

Motivation. Andragogy asserts that adults are more motivated to learn by internal factors. However, there are many instances of adults being motivated to learn by external rewards, such as pay raises or awards. And children frequently display natural curiosity and engage in learning without external rewards.

Knowles responded to the criticisms by refining his concepts over the years and agreed that adults and children were similar in self-directedness, motivation, orientation and readiness to learn. The only universal characteristic of adult learners is their experience. However, he and his followers continued to assert that andragogical methods are most often superior to pedagogical ones. Knowles asserted that the best mode of instruction depends on the situation. If, for example, the subject matter is highly technical, and there is one best way to perform a certain task, a pedagogical approach is more effective.

Strengths

Examples of the use of andragogy include such diverse subjects as carburetor rebuilding, dental hygiene, cake decorating, and accounting (Zemke, 1998). Yet the principles are more appropriate in some settings than in others. Andragogical approaches are especially effective when learners are highly motivated by personal development or self-improvement, as in health and wellness or stress management workshops. These uses are consistent with the andragogical life—or problem-centered orientation to learning. Career-planning workshops, in which participants may take a variety of assessment instruments, determine their skills and aptitudes, and focus on career planning, can make effective use of andragogical principles. Learners can draw on each other's experience and offer mutual support. The learning goals include increased self-knowledge, and the process is as important as the final outcome.

Management development is another good use of andragogy. Learners tend to be highly motivated, have a variety of individual learning needs, and are most likely in a setting where learning can be immediately applied to day-to-day concerns. Such learners may be improving their management skills in order to move to a new position or to better carry out their current responsibilities. The learning may be applied in the relationship between the learner and a supervisor or mentor, who helps facilitate learning and acts as a learning resource.

Knowles and Associates (1984) provide examples of the application of andragogy in many different settings. These include business, industry, government, colleges and universities, and professional and continuing education. The knowledge and skills taught in these programs include both technical and "soft" skills. One example is an adult English as a Second Language (ESL) program, an excellent application of the model. A typical ESL class is a diverse group of individuals with a wealth of experience that a creative instructor can draw on for material for an English language curriculum. Adult ESL classes also provide excellent opportunities for addressing adult learners' life- or problem-centered orientation to learning—they must learn English in order to live, work, and study in a new country. Many ESL materials reflect this focus on teaching adults the language skills within the context of life situations they encounter.

Feuer and Geber (1988) note that choosing a pedagogical or andragogical approach depends on the situation. If there are many ways to perform a given task, or there are various options in solving a problem (as in management situations), andragogy may be a good approach. But if options are few and there is only one "best way" to perform a task—for example, performing CPR—a pedagogical approach makes more sense. In the case of computer-based training (CBT), the learning program is often set, which limits learner control. However, the learner does have some control over the sequence and pacing of instruction, and the learning is in this sense self-directed. CBT is compatible with andragogy if it is viewed as a part of a larger program of learning in which the learner is involved in setting objectives and determining the learning plan. In this case, a CBT program is one of several resources at the learner's disposal.

Model in Action

The following information describes the implementation of a training session designed using the adult learning model. Table 16.2 illustrates the implementation of andragogy phases.

Learners. The learners participating are adults who have enrolled in a 10-week seminar in stress management offered at a community center.

Instructor/Facilitator. The course is conducted by an expert in stress management, who is also well schooled in the use of self-directed learning concepts. The instructor's role will be that of learning facilitator and resource.

Overall Course Goal. Participants will develop and apply strategies to manage stress in their daily lives.

Model Phase	Activities
1. Prepare the learners.	Distribute course description materials to participants in advance. Materials include an overall course description and a short self-assessment diagnostic instrument on coping with stress. Request that participants take the test and score themselves. Ask them to review their results and think about their individual learning expectations.
2. Set the climate.	Set up the initial session with a U-shaped layout, with snacks and coffee. Arrive early, and be available for informal discussion as participants arrive. Begin the session with ice-breaker exercises.
3. Involve learners in mutual planning.	Discuss the concept that participants will be planning the course together. Introduce idea of the instructor/facilitator as a resource and partner in learning. Review individual participant expectations. Brainstorm an initial list of course activities.
4. Involve learners in diagnosing their own learning needs.	Ask participants individually to review their scores on the self-assessment instrument they took before the start of the course. Discuss findings in small groups. In the large group, develop a consolidated list of stressors in their lives. Based on the results of the assessment and awareness of stress in their lives, participants (with the facilitator's guidance, as needed) individually identify learning needs (where they are now, where they would like to be, and the gap between the two).
5. Involve learners in formulating their own learning objectives.	In small groups, participants formulate learning objectives based on their individual learning needs. Groups consolidate their objectives into three to four objectives per group. Objectives are merged into a common list for the whole group.
6. Involve learners in designing learning plans.	The facilitator works with the participants to brainstorm a list of available resources. In addition to those provided by the facilitator, the participants draw on their personal knowledge and experience. The list includes action items for areas to investigate further (e.g., guest speakers). In the next session, participants develop individual learning plans.
7. Help learners carry out their learning plans.	Over the course of the 10 weeks, the facilitator is available as an active resource in helping participants carry out their learning plans.
8. Involve learners in evaluating learning.	At the time that participants develop their individual learning plans, they determine how to evaluate their learning. Periodically during the 10-week session, participants evaluate their progress against the agreed-upon criteria. The facilitator acts as a consultant in evaluating learning.

Table 16.2

Andragogy Implementation Sample

Implementation Guide

Step	Action
1	Prepare learners.
2	Set the climate.
3	Involve learners in mutual planning.
4	Involve learners in diagnosing their own learning needs.
5	Involve learners in formulating their own learning objectives. Learning contracts are one way to do this.
6	Involve learners in designing learning plans. Describe in the learning contracts how the plans will be carried out.
7	Help learners carry out their learning plans.
8	Involve learners in evaluating learning based on learning contracts.

Guidelines for Working With Learning Contracts

Knowles considered the learning contract to be a powerful tool in putting the principles of andragogy into practice in different settings. In formal education, a contract between a student and an instructor may help the student develop a strong sense of ownership and commitment to the learning plan. On the job, an employee may contract with management to achieve competency in certain areas as part of an individual development plan. Or a contract may be planned and carried out completely by an individual, as, for example, when a person develops a learning plan to achieve the knowledge and skills necessary for a career change.

Steps to Developing an Individual Learning Contract

Knowles (1990) outlines eight steps to developing a learning contract. Table 16.3 shows a setup for a sample contract.

1. Diagnose your learning needs—the gap between where you are now and where you want to be in regard to a particular set of competencies.
2. Specify your learning objectives, translating each need in Step 1 into an objective.
3. Specify learning resources (human and material) and strategies (tools and techniques).
4. Specify evidence of accomplishment for each objective.

5. Specify how the evidence will be validated (criteria you propose to judge the evidence).

6. Review your contract with consultants—friends, supervisors, other expert resource people.

7. Carry out the contract, revising it as appropriate.

8. Evaluate your learning (your consultants can assist in evaluating the evidence in Step 5).

Learning Objectives (What I want to learn)	Learning Resources and Strategies (People, materials, tools, and techniques)	Evidence of Accomplishment of Objectives (Written reports, taped performance, feedback from observers)	Criteria and Means of Validating Evidence (How evidence will be judged)

Learning Contract for

Name: _____ Activity: _____

Table 16.3
Learning Contract

Adapted from *The Adult Learner*, 5th edition (Knowles et al., 1998, p. 211–216).

References

Bell, C.R., and Friends. (1989). Malcolm. *Training and Development Journal, 36*(4), 38–43.

Davenport, J. (1987). Is there a way out of the andragogy morass? *Lifelong Learning: An Omnibus of Practice and Research, 11*(3), 17–20.

Feuer, D., & Geber, B. (1988). Uh-oh...second thoughts about adult learning theory. *Training, 25*(12), 31–39.

Knowles, M.S. (1950). *Informal adult education.* New York: Association Press.

Knowles, M.S. (1970). *The modern practice of adult education: Andragogy versus pedagogy.* Chicago: Follet Publishing Company.

Knowles, M.S. (1973). *The adult learner: A neglected species.* Houston: Gulf Publishing Company.

Knowles, M.S. (1980). *The modern practice of adult education: From pedagogy to andragogy.* Chicago: Follet Publishing Company.

Knowles, M.S. (1989). *The making of an adult educator: An autobiographical journey.* San Francisco: Jossey-Bass.

Knowles, M.S. (1990). *The adult learner: A neglected species* (4th ed.). Houston: Gulf Publishing Company.

Knowles, M.S., & Associates. (1984). *Andragogy in action: Applying modern principles of adult learning.* San Francisco: Jossey-Bass.

Knowles, M., Holton, E., Swanson, R.A., & Holton, E. (1998). *The adult learner* (5th ed.). Houston: Gulf Publishing Company.

Zemke, R. (1998). In search of self-directed learners. *Training, 35*(5), 60–68.

Bibliography

Hatcher, T.G. (1997). The ins and outs of self-directed learning. *Training and Development, 51* (2), 34–39.

Henschke, J. (1997). In memoriam: Malcolm S. Knowles. *Adult Learning, 9*(2), 2–5.

Knowles, M.S. (1989). Everything you wanted to know from Malcolm Knowles. *Training, 26*(8), 45–49.

Lee, C. (1998). The adult learner: Neglected no more. *Training, 35*(3), 47–52.

Long, H. (1975). Self-directed learning: A guide for learners and teachers. In G. Confessore & S. Confessore (Eds.), *Guideposts to self-directed learning* (36–47). King of Prussia, PA: Organization Design and Development, Inc.

Merriam, S., & Caffarella, R.S. (Eds.). (1991). *Learning in adulthood*. San Francisco: Jossey-Bass.

Merriam, S., & Cunningham, P.M. (Eds.). (1989). *Handbook of adult and continuing education*. San Francisco: Jossey-Bass.

Pratt, D. (1993). Andragogy after twenty-five years. In S. Merriam (Ed.), *An update on adult learning theory* (15–23). San Francisco: Jossey-Bass.

About the Author

Cynthia J. Demnitz is a senior consultant with Canal Bridge Consulting in Bethesda, Maryland. She specializes in facilitating strategic planning, business analysis, and organizational change management projects with a range of commercial and government organizations. An experienced presenter and trainer, she has presented at the American Society for Training and Development international and DC Metro Chapter conferences.

Prior to beginning her consulting career in 1988, she coordinated and taught English as a Second Language (ESL) courses for university and adult education programs in the United States and overseas. She developed and published ESL materials, including an ESL reading textbook.

Ms. Demnitz has master's degrees in Linguistics from Georgetown University and Organizational Development from Marymount University, and an Information Systems Specialist certificate from the George Washington University. Her bachelor's degree from Syracuse University is in English Literature.

Applying the Models and Strategies

PART IV

Tools and Guidance

While the authors and editors of this volume have tried to communicate each instructional model and strategy in ways that render it usable to the practitioner, these two final chapters provide additional assistance in selecting and applying the models and strategies to actual projects.

Selection Tool

Chapter 17 presents and explains a decision table for selecting models and strategies. Several people, in addition to the chapter authors, worked on this job aid, as it turned out to be a major project! The difficulties were in identifying the critical attributes that distinguish the action choices and in narrowing the choices in each category to a list that was short enough to provide useful guidance. Depending on the openness of the designer's attitudes, some cases (instructional situations) we tried seemed to admit a wide variety of viable choices, making it difficult to identify rules for narrowing and final selection. In the final analysis, we decided to incorporate the following variables to guide selection:

- Measurability of learning—The need to measure specific learning outcomes
- Learning time—Whether the time available for participant learning is limited
- Learner control—The extent to which learner control (of objectives, content, activities) is desirable
- Designer control—The extent to which designer control is desirable.

Finally, some "add-on" models and strategies were identified that could be used in conjunction with the stand-alone models. As expressed by the authors, this job aid is intended as general guidance, not as a prescriptive algorithm. We do expect, however, that users of the job aid will find that it increases their design options and thus enhances their creativity in design projects.

Guidance for Technology-Based Design

Much discussion preceded the development of Chapter 18. The authors and editors are often asked, "How do you design for technology-based instruction? How do these design projects differ from those for classroom-based instruction? Which models work better for technology-based instruction?" This chapter is a brief answer to that set of questions. Of course, entire books are devoted to these issues, but we believe the key points to consider are these:

- Instructional design is at least as important for technology-based projects as it is for classroom-based projects—perhaps more so.

- Most of the instructional design models and strategies in this book can be adapted to either classroom or technology-based delivery systems. Some models drastically influence the way instruction is designed and controlled, while other models affect the way instruction is utilized.

- Technology-based instruction demands additional front-end analysis and requirements development. These are in addition to the typical needs assessment used for traditional classroom instruction.

- Technology-based instruction requires additional considerations during the design, development, and testing phases of a project, such as selection, allocation, and management of assets (e.g., animation); identifying appropriate granularity of content; creating frequent and meaningful interaction; and user interface and navigation design.

Chapter 18 provides an overview of these issues and should be helpful to the instructional designer faced with a technology-based learning project.

CHAPTER 17

Selecting Models and Strategies

Brandy Christin
and Peter J. Pallesen

Tool Description

This book discusses 16 different models and strategies for training design. How in the real world is an instructional designer to make an instructionally sound selection from this group when facing an actual design project? Each of these models and strategies has a set of features, strengths, and limitations, but these attributes often overlap in confusing ways, making a choice difficult. The job aid in this chapter is a way of bringing reason to the selection process.

We assume that different types of learning outcomes require somewhat different teaching/learning conditions and strategies and, therefore, that distinguishing among intended learning outcomes is a good starting point for model selection. A relatively high-level "taxonomy" of learning outcomes seems adequate for this purpose. Therefore, the job aid is divided into four parts, one for each broad category of intended learning outcomes.

Cognitive Skills

These are the "ordinary" cognitive skills that are the bread and butter of most instruction, including recognition and recall of information, application of concepts, and demonstration of rules. This category includes Gagné's verbal information, intellectual skills (discriminations, concepts, rules, and higher-order rules), and simpler cognitive strategies; Bloom's cognitive domain levels of comprehension, application, and simpler analysis and synthesis; and Merrill's performance categories of remember and use for facts, concepts, procedures, and principles. (The taxonomies referred to here can be found in Bloom, 1956; Krathwohl, Bloom, & Masia, 1964; Gagné & Medsker, 1996; Merrill, 1983.)

Affective and Social Skills

This category includes Gagné's attitudes and Bloom's affective domain. Interpersonal skills are also included here. While interpersonal skills do involve cognitive skills (e.g., concepts and principles), their large component of feelings, values, and personal behavior choices gives them learning requirements that are somewhat different from more purely cognitive skills.

Motor Skills

These learning outcomes are physical skills that often require strength, agility, and coordination to perform with accuracy, smoothness, and good timing. Bloom calls this category psychomotor, while Gagné uses the term motor skills. Because of the need for physical practice, this category has special learning requirements.

Creative and Problemsolving Skills

This category encompasses what we might call thinking skills, including Gagné's higher-order cognitive strategies, also known as metacognition (managing one's own thinking processes). Bloom's highest cognitive level, evaluation, is included here, and perhaps also more complex analysis and synthesis tasks. Merrill's "find" level of performance also fits this category. This category of learning outcomes requires learners to "go beyond the information given."

Application

The job aid can be used to select a model or strategy for a single objective, a module, or an entire course, depending on the homogeneity or diversity of learning outcomes included in the total amount of instruction. Of course, multiple models and strategies can be combined within a course, module, or even for a single objective.

Once you have chosen the unit of instruction you are dealing with and have identified the major category of learning outcomes represented, go to the corresponding decision table.

Within each table, you are asked to decide first whether you need to measure specific learning outcomes. Generally, the answer will be affirmative if all learners must demonstrate mastery of specific skills or competencies (for example, those related to job task performance or those measured on a standardized test). The answer will be negative if learners are expected to learn different things or nothing in particular, or if the learning outcomes are very personal and/or difficult to assess, as they might be in an executive development seminar or career exploration workshop. Several of the models support measurement better than others, but the more measurement-oriented models can still be used where measurement is not a strong requirement.

The next decision is whether learning time is limited or abundant. This decision does not refer to the designer's time, because all the models require significant design time if executed properly. This decision refers to learning time, and of course "limited" and "abundant" are relative terms. The decision is here because some of the models make less "efficient" use of learning time than others. The trade-off, of course, is often increased learning and retention of what is learned.

Next you are asked to select a model either from the "learner control" column or from the "designer control" column. Designer control means that the models lend themselves to the designer making more of the decisions about what will be learned, how, and in what sequence. Learner control means that the learner makes more of these decisions.   The column in which models appear is somewhat arbitrary and should not be taken as a rigid classification. Adult learning is listed as a learner control model, because it allows relatively more learner control than other models. Yet the proportions of learner and designer control are flexible. Similarly, designer control models can be adapted to include more learner control. Note that behavior modification is listed in both columns, because it can literally be used in either fashion. Both columns contain models that are stand-alone models—models that are complete in themselves and can be used without assistance from others. Designers may use either their own preferences or the needs and preferences of the designated learners, to determine which locus of control to emphasize, and which model within that locus best meets their needs.

Within each cell, the applicable models are listed in descending order of "goodness of fit." This ranking is somewhat subjective, but substantiation should be evident from explanations in previous chapters in the book. Some of the reasons for ranking a model higher include the following:

- The model is more comprehensive in its coverage of learning outcomes in this category.
- The model is more detailed in its prescriptions for this learning category.
- The model is applicable to a wider range of learners.

Readers are encouraged to take these rankings as general guidance and to consider carefully the specific requirements of their content, learners, and situation in making a final decision.

In the last column of the table, "add-on" models and strategies that cannot be used by themselves are suggested. These can comfortably be used in combination with the stand-alone models. For example, structural learning theory can be used to identify and sequence elements in a procedure, component display theory can be used to structure the lesson activities, and mnemonic devices can be added to help learners remember elements of the procedure in order. The models and strategies in the last column are not listed in rank order.

One final note: The intent of this job aid is to be suggestive, not prescriptive, and to point the instructional designer in an appropriate general direction. No manageable job aid could include all the important, but sometimes subtle, variables involved with the model-selection process. These include such things as the culture of the learners and their organization; the strengths, weaknesses, and preferences of the designers and the instructors; time available to learn new models; and even physical facilities available for the instruction. The best selection device of all is the incremental experience of the designer, over time, with different models for various learning tasks and learner groups. In fact, the hallmark of a truly effective instructional designer is the ability to match a learning challenge with an appropriate mix of models and strategies.

Job Aid: Cognitive Skills

IF YOU AND	Learning TIME is	SELECT one of these models that allows more LEARNER CONTROL	OR	SELECT one of these models that allows more DESIGNER CONTROL	AND	CONSIDER using one of these models or strategies:
DO need to MEASURE specific learning outcomes	Limited	Adult Learning Popular Education Component Display		Behavioral Approach Component Display Advance Organizer Conditions of Learning Lancaster		Cooperative Learning ARCS Mnemonics Structural Learning
	Abundant	Adult Learning Popular Education Component Display		Behavioral Approach Component Display Advance Organizer Conditions of Learning Behavior Modeling Lancaster		Cooperative Learning ARCS Mnemonics Structural Learning
DO NOT need to MEASURE specific learning outcomes	Limited	Adult Learning Popular Education Component Display		Behavioral Approach Component Display Advance Organizer Conditions of Learning Lancaster		Cooperative Learning ARCS Mnemonics Structural Learning
	Abundant	Cognitive Inquiry Constructivism Adult Learning Popular Education Component Display		Behavioral Approach Component Display Advance Organizer Conditions of Learning Lancaster Behavior Modeling		Cooperative Learning ARCS Mnemonics Structural Learning Synectics

Job Aid: Affective and Social Skills

IF YOU	AND Learning TIME is	SELECT one of these models that allows more LEARNER CONTROL	OR	SELECT one of these models that allows more DESIGNER CONTROL	AND	CONSIDER using one of these models or strategies
DO need to MEASURE specific learning outcomes	Limited	Adult Learning Popular Education Behavior Modification		Conditions of Learning Behavior Modification Lancaster		Cooperative Learning ARCS Mnemonics
DO need to MEASURE specific learning outcomes	Abundant	Adult Learning Popular Education Behavior Modification		Behavior Modeling Conditions of Learning Behavior Modification Lancaster		Cooperative Learning ARCS Mnemonics Synectics
DO NOT need to MEASURE specific learning outcomes	Limited	Adult Learning Popular Education Behavior Modification		Conditions of Learning Behavior Modification Lancaster		Cooperative Learning ARCS Mnemonics
DO NOT need to MEASURE specific learning outcomes	Abundant	Adult Learning Popular Education Behavior Modification Cognitive Inquiry Constructivism		Behavior Modeling Conditions of Learning Behavior Modification Lancaster Cognitive Inquiry		Cooperative Learning ARCS Mnemonics Synectics

Job Aid: Motor Skills

IF YOU *AND*	Learning TIME is	**SELECT** one of these models that allows more **LEARNER CONTROL**	*OR*	**SELECT** one of these models that allows more **DESIGNER CONTROL**	*AND*	**CONSIDER** using one of these models or strategies:
DO need to MEASURE specific learning outcomes	Limited	Adult Learning Popular Education		Conditions of Learning Behavior Modification Lancaster		Cooperative Learning ARCS Mnemonics Structural Learning
	Abundant	Adult Learning Popular Education		Conditions of Learning Behavioral Approach Behavior Modeling Lancaster		Cooperative Learning ARCS Mnemonics Structural Learning
DO NOT need to MEASURE specific learning outcomes	Limited	Adult Learning Popular Education		Conditions of Learning Behavioral Approach Lancaster		Cooperative Learning ARCS Mnemonics Structural Learning
	Abundant	Adult Learning Popular Education Constructivism		Conditions of Learning Behavioral Approach Behavior Modeling Lancaster		Cooperative Learning ARCS Mnemonics Structural Learning

Job Aid: Creative and Problemsolving Skills

IF YOU	AND Learning TIME is	SELECT one of these models that allows more LEARNER CONTROL	OR	SELECT one of these models that allows more DESIGNER CONTROL	AND	CONSIDER using one of these models or strategies
DO need to MEASURE specific learning outcomes	Limited	Adult Learning Popular Education Component Display		Conditions of Learning Behavior Modification Lancaster		Cooperative Learning ARCS Mnemonics Structural Learning
DO need to MEASURE specific learning outcomes	Abundant	Adult Learning Popular Education Component Display		Conditions of Learning Behavioral Approach Behavior Modeling Lancaster		Cooperative Learning ARCS Mnemonics Structural Learning
DO NOT need to MEASURE specific learning outcomes	Limited	Adult Learning Popular Education Component Display		Conditions of Learning Behavioral Approach Lancaster		Cooperative Learning ARCS Mnemonics Structural Learning
DO NOT need to MEASURE specific learning outcomes	Abundant	Constructivism Cognitive Inquiry Adult Learning Popular Education Component Display		Component Display Conditions of Learning Lancaster Behavioral Approach		Cooperative Learning ARCS Mnemonics Structural Learning

References

Bloom, B.S. (1956). *Taxonomy of educational objectives, handbook I: Cognitive domain*. New York: McKay.

Gagné, R.M., & Medsker, K.L. (1996). *The conditions of learning: Training applications*. Ft. Worth, TX: Harcourt Brace.

Krathwohl, D.R., Bloom, B.S., & Masia, B.B. (1964). *Taxonomy of educational objectives, handbook II: Affective domain*. New York: McKay.

Merrill, M.D. (1983). Component display theory. In C.M. Reigeluth (Ed.), *Instructional design theories and models: An overview of their current status* (279–333). Hillsdale, NJ: Lawrence Erlbaum Associates.

About the Authors

Brandy Christin

Brandy Christin, an associate with Booz·Allen & Hamilton, has more than 20 years of consulting experience in training analysis, design, and evaluation. She currently designs and develops distance learning courses for a large federal agency. Ms. Christin holds a Graduate Certificate in Instructional Systems Design from Marymount University and is nearing completion of an MA in Human Performance Systems from Marymount University.

Peter J. Pallesen

Peter J. Pallesen, senior information trainer for San Diego, CA-based High Technology Solutions, Inc., has leveraged his extensive and varied business and management background into a career of providing just the right kind of performance improvement interventions at just the right time. He develops and delivers various technical and soft skills training in support of a human resources re-engineering project for a large federal agency, including a complete team leader's workshop curriculum for supervisors and managers. His Basic Computer Skills workshop has been distributed agencywide. In addition, he is responsible for developing and delivering a broad variety of proprietary application-specific computer training based on the Lotus Notes and PeopleSoft platforms. He has his Graduate Certificate in Instructional Design and his MA in Human Performance Systems from Marymount University.

CHAPTER 18

Design Considerations for Multimedia Programs

Craig Locatis

Technology-based training delivery systems, such as CD-ROM-based and web-based multimedia, offer unique environments for developing training and performance support programs, and each has distinct design requirements. While these requirements are in addition to the design requirements for typical classroom instruction, they do not obviate the need for traditional instructional design models and strategies. Human beings do not evolve as quickly as technology, and their fundamental learning processes remain essentially unchanged. Indeed, technology-based delivery systems make instructional design knowledge more important than ever, because without such guidance, developers may employ the technology superficially, exercising its bells and whistles to create programs loaded with pyrotechnics but little educational value. Multimedia effects can be used in ways that make little, if any, contribution to learning or—worse—in ways that actually intrude on the learning process. Distance learning experiences, without the benefit of a live instructor (or even other trainees), usually suffer more from poor instructional design than do traditional classroom courses. Instructional design principles provide strategies for ensuring that technology-based delivery systems will achieve desired learning outcomes. Developers need to know how these strategies can be applied in multimedia and distance learning environments. They also need to be aware of some additional design and development issues that arise when the technology-based systems are used.

This chapter begins with a definition of multimedia and a brief description of multimedia trends, to establish a context for understanding its remaining sections. This background information is followed by a discussion of how the use of multimedia affects the entire instructional development process and a discussion about how instructional design theories relate to the application of multimedia technology. Additional multimedia design and development issues are then delineated—issues relating specifically to the unique features of the technology.

Multimedia Technology and Technology Trends

Technically, the term "multimedia" refers to a program that uses two or more of the following types of information: text, graphics, pictures, animation, audio, and video. Today, the term refers to programs that are computer-based and interactive. Interactive programs are nonlinear and alter the content presented and/or the order in which it is displayed, based on user input. The foremost interactive multimedia device currently is the computer, and when people talk about interactive multimedia programs today, they usually are referring to programs that are computer-based (Ambron, 1988). Consequently, this chapter uses the term multimedia to describe any instructional delivery system that is computer-based and interactive, including delivery by CD-ROM or by the Internet. Typically, multimedia programs are also self-paced. In addition, when distance learning or performance support is involved, there usually is some presumption that the programs are provided via networks. Hypermedia is a closely related term referring to multimedia content that is composed of interlinked units of information that users can browse and explore (Shneiderman & Kearsley, 1989). The pre-eminent example of networked multimedia and hypermedia is the World Wide Web. Early multimedia programs were not as integrated as they are today, in part because computers lacked sufficient power. Multimedia content was recorded as analog television and presented via special peripheral devices that the computers controlled. Students would interact with text on computers that would direct the devices to display still images or motion episodes on separate television monitors.

Four major trends have contributed to making the computer a multimedia appliance: conversion, convergence, capacity and costs, and commonness.

Conversion. Conversion means being able to convert analog content to digital, but it also means that devices that were previously analog are becoming digital. Compact audio discs, digital still and video cameras, and digital telephones are, perhaps, the most prevalent examples, but digital radio and television broadcasts also are possible.

Convergence. The conversion to digital has helped fuel a second trend, convergence, or the coming together of heretofore separate technologies. It is now possible to view digital movies or place phone calls with computers because computing, telephony, and television are coming together. Convergence not only applies to hardware but software. At one time, desktop publishing and word processing software were very different. Eventually, the layout, graphic, and WYSIWYG (what you see is what you get) features of the former became integrated with the font, spell check, and grammatical features of the latter, so that functionally the two types of software tools are almost indistinguishable. Many of the applications built with software tools are converging also. Authoring tools that formerly created computer-based instruction for delivery on standalone computers or CD-ROM can now generate instruction for delivery on the Internet. While some of the programs generated provide electronic performance support systems (EPSS) and others provide more formal instruction, many programs incorporate both. In these cases, it is sometimes difficult to determine just where the online support ends and training begins, since users can move seamlessly from the support system to more directed instruction.

Capacity and Costs. The third trend driving multimedia computing concerns capacity and costs. The former keeps going up, while the latter keeps declining. New capabilities engender new demand and economies of scale lower production costs.

Commonness. Cost and capacity factors have contributed to the forth trend—commonness. It used to be that computers were the exclusive domain of a privileged, knowledgeable few. Now, computers are ubiquitous, in the workplace and at home. And, as computers have become more common, they have become easier to use and readily available as a means of providing multimedia instruction.

Multimedia in Instructional Development

Early in every training development project, the developer-client team faces the task of choosing an appropriate delivery system. Since many factors, such as content, learner attributes, cultural context, and costs, must be considered and balanced, models have been developed to facilitate this complex decision (e.g., Pallesen et al., 1999). Once a decision has been made to use multimedia in some form, additional decisions still have to be made about hardware and software and the various features that will be required. Computers may need a certain amount of memory and storage to accommodate the large multimedia files, and they may need to accommodate external storage media such as CD-ROM or digital videodisc.

Machines may also may need to be networked, and the network may require certain transmission speeds and other quality factors. Multimedia developers face a unique challenge. Since technology changes rapidly, there is always an excuse not to use it; something better and cheaper is always on the horizon. But such reasoning can lead to postponing adoption decisions forever. If the potential benefits of technology are to be used to advantage, adoption decisions will have to be made, and the timing of these decisions becomes paramount. Adopt too early and the technology may be too expensive, unstable, nonstandardized, or non-interoperable with other technologies. Adopt too late and the older technology may prove to be more expensive and cumbersome than newer technology or, worse, no longer supported (Locatis & Al-Nuaim, 1999).

Technology's role in instructional development extends beyond the choice of delivery platforms and affects the development process itself. Most development models have an initial analysis phase, where performance problems are appraised to determine whether they would be most appropriately resolved through training, performance support, or some other intervention. Often, the learner population and the context in which training and/or performance support may be provided is assessed. In the design phase, the goals and objectives of the intervention are established, and strategies are planned for achieving them. Detailed media choices are made, and storyboards, scripts, and screen layouts are devised. These strategies are often refined and realized in the form of a training and/or performance improvement product in a development phase. Finally, most models have an evaluation phase, during which the interventions developed are tried out and their effectiveness determined. Multimedia affects this development process in at least three ways.

1. **Technology Assessment.** Multimedia adds a requirement to do some technology assessment in the early analysis stage. If multimedia are likely to be part of the solution to a training or performance problem, then some of the up-front analyses of these problems should include an appraisal of technology options as well. What technologies are being used currently in the workplace and how comfortable are people with them? How receptive are the organization and the various groups within it to new technology? Sometimes, no additional technology investment may be required when existing infrastructure is leveraged. Other times, modest technology upgrades, such as sound cards or higher resolution displays for existing desktop computers, may be needed. On the other hand, major upgrades to faster computers or higher speed networks might be necessary, or older technology must be replaced completely. Even when appropriate technology is in place or management is willing to invest in new technology, the attitudes and readiness of employees may argue against it—at least not without some additional traditional classroom instruction or personal mentoring. Much

depends on previous experiences with technology and the confidence with which people use it.

2. **Development Stages.** Multimedia affects the development process by making it possible to overlap and shorten the development stages. Much of the up-front analysis, planning, and design in instructional development is done on the computer and, when multimedia programs are to be created, it may unnecessary to create screen layouts, tests, and other instructional assets on paper that later will be programmed. Instead, easy-to-use authoring tools and markup languages can be employed to generate immediate approximations of the final product. Such rapid prototyping allows early review of the content and design alternatives and speeds development. The prototypes are concrete objects, not theoretical plans, having specific features that developers and their clients can experience and discuss. Moreover, these mockups can be tested with small numbers of users and the feedback used to develop more refined, working prototypes.

3. **Pilot Testing.** The use of multimedia usually accentuates the importance of pilot testing in development projects, especially when the development projects are large and the investments in deploying technology widely are substantial. Pilot testing one or a few completed, working prototypes can help determine whether these program components are effective enough to justify further development and whether the technologies employed will prove cost effective if deployed on a wider scale. Unlike some traditional pilot tests in instructional development, multimedia testing uses program components, not the entire program. For example, if an instructional program is to consist of 10 multimedia modules, the pilot test may involve one or two of the first prototypes. If an EPSS is to support a dozen different task areas, one or two areas might be rapidly prototyped, further developed until they are functionally complete, and pilot tested. After pilot testing, additional instructional modules may be developed or further functionality might be added to the EPSS.

Instructional Theory and Multimedia Development

One of the greatest threats to the integrity of multimedia projects is for developers to become so enamored with the capabilities of the technology that they attempt to use them all, even if they add expense and have marginal utility. Instructional design theories and models provide guidance for designing multimedia programs that will achieve a range of learning outcomes. The key is to determine what outcomes one wants to achieve and then to identify the appropriate instructional theories for attaining them. Is the objective to obtain a certain knowledge or skill, to solve problems, to apply procedures, or learn about oneself? Is it to motivate, to foster reflection, or to encourage individuals to learn together? Since most multimedia programs have multiple goals and objectives, several approaches may be relevant. While the theories sometimes seem contradictory, they usually are not. Instead, each theory tends to emphasize particular aspects of the learning process. The theories that figure more prominently for one given set of learning outcomes may be totally irrelevant or only tangentially applicable to a different set of objectives.

At least three reasons support the use of instructional design models and strategies in the design of multimedia programs for learning and performance support. First, these models and strategies have stood the test of time. Indeed, some are based on teaching traditions dating back to ancient Greece. Second, they have empirical support. While in some cases this support is based on field experience, most of the models are supported by substantial scientific research. Finally, the models offer concrete, practical guidelines for bringing about different educational outcomes. When a model is relevant to given instructional goals, it usually offers a blueprint for constructing learning experiences that will facilitate their attainment.

In sum, the theories are authoritative sources for making informed design decisions. They provide rational frameworks for thinking about and discussing design options that can be more productive and have greater payoff than exchanges between developers and clients about their personal preferences and predilections. Although it is not possible in a single chapter to describe how each model and strategy in this book can be applied in designing multimedia programs, the models can be discussed categorically, depending on whether they have a behavioral, cognitive, or humanistic/social/affective orientation.

Behavioral Models and Multimedia Design

Behavioral models emphasize the responses learners make during instruction. The responses are made to some stimulus, but other than acknowledging that some cuing or prompting may be necessary to evoke responses, behaviorists have little to say about how knowledge or information should be presented and portrayed externally, not to mention the thinking that transpires internally inside the learner's head. The models do, however, have something to say about sequencing instruction and how learners should progress.

The primary tenet of behavioral theories is that responses that are appropriate to attaining learning and performance outcomes should be reinforced and those that are inappropriate should not. One implication for interactive multimedia design is that learners should be actively responding to the program content, not passively viewing it. This principle avoids the unappealing and ineffective "page turning" approach to multimedia, apparent now in much web-based material. Moreover, opportunities for interaction should contribute directly to attaining a program's goals. That is, practice should be on the criterion behavior or some approximation of it. A multimedia program that teaches about workplace diversity, for example, may quiz learners on demographic facts. A more appropriate form of interaction might be to react to workplace scenarios, identifying the most appropriate action a manager should take. Another implication is that learners need immediate knowledge of results after they respond and, possibly, remediation. Feedback might be provided in games, for example, by having a counter score each response. The games might have text or sounds encouraging students to try again when their responses are incorrect and that route students to remedial learning events when they fail to attain a certain performance threshold. In one multimedia simulation, the victim of a gunshot wound dies if the student/doctor does not order the right tests and make the correct diagnosis within the proper time frame.

Behavioral theories also hold that certain skills are prerequisite to others and that learning should progress in small steps. Adding and subtracting single digits, for example, is preparatory to adding and subtracting multiple digits where carrying and borrowing may be involved. Consequently, behaviorists also prescribe mastery of earlier skills before allowing students to progress to later ones. The approach has intuitive appeal and works well in cases where prerequisites can be identified. The problem is that it is not always clear that prerequisites for certain skills exist, or what constitutes mastery. Swimmers, for example, do not have to master dog paddling before progressing to the crawl stroke, and when physicians learn medical diagnosis they need not have mastered history-taking skills before learning what laboratory tests to order. Even when the identity of prerequisite learning tasks is clear, there may be a range of sequencing options. In addition or subtraction, for example, it is possible to teach the steps from first to last or to teach the last step first, then the next to the last step, and so on.

Prerequisites and mastery learning, advocated by most behavioral models, raise questions about learner control of instruction and generally argue against it. Most multimedia developers, however, are loath to handcuff their users electronically and usually provide a range of tools for exploring their programs. Research on aptitudes, however, indicates that students with well-developed self-learning skills can thrive in open environments (Snow & Lohman, 1984). Older students or students who already have substantial knowledge of the subject matter are more likely to have these skills than novice learners. Two design options are popular when learners are novices. One is to provide advice about how to proceed through a program, based on students' previous performance. Another is to provide programs having mechanisms for activating or deactivating learner control (cf., Shin et. al., 1994). Some may allow instructors to set the learner control function, while others may allow students freedom at first, but impose more direction when performance is low.

Behavioral models dictate that instruction should proceed in small steps, but the need for very small steps has largely been discredited. Small steps are not only boring; they lead to instruction that is inefficient. Most multimedia developers break instruction down into logical steps that reflect the subject matter and the tasks that are performed in the real world, rather than divide content into arbitrary subskills. If there is any question about step size, they are prone to opt for large steps initially, dividing instruction into smaller steps only if tryouts indicate learners are having difficulty. While this approach ensures development of lean programs, concerns arise that the programs provide insufficient instruction when used in conjunction with learner control (Schnackenberg & Sullivan, 2000). Some developers also opt for creating adaptive programs that dynamically adjust the size of step and difficulty of the information presented based on previous performance. These programs are more sophisticated than those imposing more direction when performance is low, because the programs have algorithms that constantly compute estimates of each learner's knowledge level during the course of interaction (Tennyson et al., 1984).

In summary, behavioral models may be best applied to multimedia design when specific, concrete behaviors are to be learned (when there is a right way to perform a task). If program control is desirable, and prerequisite sequences are well defined, behavioral approaches will work well. In any multimedia program, frequent, active responding and immediate feedback are recommended. Indeed, these are distinctive features of multimedia delivery systems; not to use them is to waste the system capabilities.

Cognitive Models and Multimedia Design

Cognitive models fall into two camps: those that endorse expository teaching and those that favor letting students discover and construct knowledge on their own. Most cognitive models focus on the stimulus (how knowledge is presented to the learner) as well as the thinking that goes on inside a learner's head. Where the two cognitive camps diverge is on how much guidance should be provided. Those advocating expository approaches are similar to behaviorists in favoring program control. Unlike the behaviorists, however, cognitivists are more tolerant of allowing learners to progress without mastering prerequisites. Students may only partially comprehend component concepts and skills initially, and it is only when they have been exposed to all components that the pieces "fall into place" and understanding occurs. Constructivists argue that since all learning is constructed in the head of the individual learner, the learners should be free to explore rich environments and make sense for themselves from a variety of data sources and experiences. Thus, they favor extremes of learner control.

The most pervasive influence of cognitive models on multimedia development is, perhaps, in the area of knowledge representation. Both camps want to ensure that knowledge is appropriately portrayed and that conceptual relationships and problemsolving strategies become internalized appropriately by students. Expository models particularly stress content organization though tables of contents, concept maps, graphical displays, and other mechanisms that make explicit subject relationships. Information visualization strategies from screen layout to the use of color in multimedia programs are of special concern (cf., Lynch & Horton, 1999; Shneiderman, 1998; Tufte, 1990).

One popular multimedia design strategy is to employ metaphors to depict content. A program teaching accounting may use a spreadsheet metaphor, while one teaching research skills might situate the instruction in a virtual library setting. Another strategy is to use analogies. While metaphors establish more global context for representing knowledge, analogies provide more specific ones. A heart, for example, may be likened to a pump, a brain to a computer. Metaphors and analogies are often employed in noninstructional multimedia applications. An airline's website, for example, may use a ticket counter metaphor that users can interact with to obtain information about fares, destinations, and schedules. When metaphors and analogies work, they are spectacular, but when they fail, results can be abysmal. Thus, they should be chosen carefully.

Cognitive theories have also influenced multimedia design in the development of intelligent tutoring programs and expert systems. While adaptive instructional programs dynamically adjust instruction, the adjustments are based on statistical probabilities calculated from previous performance in the program. Intelligent tutoring programs can be much more sophisticated, presenting problems intentionally designed to detect reasoning errors and repair them. Some compare student performance to an underlying expert model and intervene when a student's performance begins to diverge. Others have underlying knowledge bases of rules experts employ to solve problems that they explicitly teach, and they may have the capability to solve the problems they present to students themselves because they are integrated with expert systems (Wenger, 1987). There are also experts systems that exist independently of tutoring programs; these are not used so much to detect reasoning errors as to prevent them. The systems can be viewed as a special type of EPSS that renders advice based on information users provide. The systems are intended to reduce the amount of information people need to keep in their heads and to suggest solutions that might be overlooked (Shortliffe, 1990). In medicine, for example, it is impossible to keep track of all drug interactions, and some interactions produce side effects mimicking diseases and syndromes. Expert systems can inform physicians of interactions in the medications they may consider prescribing or, if a patient presents with certain symptoms that can be ascribed to drug interactions or a disease, they may suggest drug interaction as a possible cause to help guard against possible misdiagnosis.

Cognitive theory's influence on interface design has been to encourage development of simpler interfaces and to reduce the amount of cognitive overhead students need to interact with programs (Norman, 1993). Anyone who has stared at a computer screen understands that the notion of metaphor extends beyond multimedia applications to the computer's operating system. Users no longer need to know commands but can interact with a "desktop," and they use programs with graphical user interfaces that enable them to place "files" into "folders" or to "bookmark" their favorite websites.

Constructivist cognitive theories have added a dimension of openness to multimedia development (Hannafin et al., 1997). Of special importance is the development of case studies and simulations to allow learners to discover underlying concepts and problemsolving strategies. Sometimes the cases and simulations have fidelity with the real world, and sometimes they do not. A multimedia chemistry program may offer a virtual laboratory with devices and substances that the users can manipulate to conduct experiments much as they would in a real lab. A program teaching map reading and computational skills, on the other hand, might place learners in a completely hypothetical situation, such as being in a mythical land, and require them to use maps, compasses, and other devices to locate treasure. Constructivist theories support the use of databases and online information sources to solve problems. The Internet and World Wide Web constitute a vast information space for addressing research questions or for browsing and exploration that can be employed to teach the metacognitive skills of learning how to learn on one's own.

A designer of multimedia programs can use a variety of tools and strategies derived from cognitive instructional models. If using expository teaching methods, one can structure procedural or rule-based content using algorithms (Scandura); present information and concepts using an advance organizer (Ausubel); insert mnemonics to aid recall of facts, lists, and associations; or structure lessons around the nine events of instruction (Gagné and Briggs). Merrill's component display theory, with its detailed prescriptions for each type of content and performance outcome, is particularly well suited for multimedia instructional design. If inquiry, discovery, or constructivist methods are more appropriate, multimedia environments allow extensive access to different resources (databases, simulations, expert opinions, picture files, etc.) and learner control to access those resources as desired.

Humanistic/Social/Affective Models and Multimedia Design

Humanistic, social, and affective theories address emotional and cultural factors in learning, educational outcomes related to learning how to work in groups, and the development of attitudes toward both subject matter and learning. They also are concerned with motivation. Although they are diverse, they have impacted multimedia design. Cultural factors are an important factor in multimedia development. For example, care is taken to avoid stereotypes. If programs require characters, they usually are representative of the target population for which programs are intended. A number of motivational strategies—such as employing cues to gain and direct attention, offering encouragement, and providing problems that are challenging but still doable to instill confidence and feelings of accomplishment are used routinely in multimedia programs. Keller's ARCS model, for example, is just as applicable to multimedia training as it is to traditional classroom training.

Of all the theoretical perspectives, those in the humanistic, social, and affective realm probably have more to say about how multimedia programs are used than about how they are designed. The ways multimedia programs are used can dramatically affect learning outcomes in ways developers might not have anticipated. For example, skilled teachers can use the most culturally pugnacious and biased websites of extremists groups as springboards for learning about fear and hate and for encouraging critical thinking.

The adult learning model (Knowles) and the popular education model (Vella) can certainly incorporate multimedia instruction. Since the adult learning focus is on the independent, self-directed learner, the availability of multimedia resources on the World Wide Web can greatly facilitate the learner's ability to locate relevant information and instruction. However, adult educators advocate personal attention by an instructor/facilitator, so that multimedia approaches alone would not be entirely consistent with the model. Popular education, which focuses on face-to-face group activity, could employ multimedia instruction as an adjunct to classroom work, rather than as the main teaching mode. However, technology advances, such as desk-to-desk computer videoconferencing, may soon make humanistic models more possible to implement via technology-based delivery systems.

Most multimedia programs are intended for individual use, but research shows additional benefits accrue by having students use them in groups (Hooper, 1992). Peer discussion fosters further elaboration of the content and allows more advanced learners to help their cohorts. Cooperative learning approaches identify specific strategies for fostering such outcomes while discouraging competition and ensuring that all students contribute. While most group learning with computers has occurred in classroom settings, online communication tools are enabling students to learn collaboratively at a distance (Hiltz, 1994). While some tools, such as email and discussion groups, allow for asynchronous communication, others, such as chat, videoconferencing, and streaming video applications allow for one-to-one, one-to-many, and many-to-many communication (Locatis & Weisberg, 1997). Both synchronous and asynchronous modes of distance learning have recently been used in higher education and in business, and cooperative learning is possible even in these virtual classrooms. A challenge for multimedia developers will be to create environments where multimedia resources and online collaboration tools are integrated to allow knowledge sharing and advancement (Scardamalia et al., 1992).

Multimedia Design and Development Issues

All the design and development decisions in traditional instruction development and performance improvement projects should also be addressed in multimedia development projects. The performance and training needs must be identified, the characteristics of the performers must be assessed, and the organizational contexts and cultural environments need to be appraised. Decisions about objectives, content sequencing, instructional methods and strategies, and media choices must be made. Resolving these issues correctly becomes even more critical in multimedia projects, because greater startup and development costs are often involved. But the prospect of using multimedia often raises additional concerns, beyond those evident in traditional instructional design or performance improvement projects.

Asset Use and Allocation

It is one thing to have the capability to present content using a range of media and another actually to use those capabilities. First, every modality employed adds to development costs, and some modalities are more expensive than others. A program having video, animation, and graphics will generally be more expensive to create than one having just graphics and text. Moreover, use of some media boost delivery system requirements. Audio and video may require more powerful computers with CD-ROM or DVD drives and sound cards or, if delivered via the Internet, a certain level of network performance and capacity. Second, use of some modalities or too many modalities may be counterproductive. For example, while it may seem clever to have continuously running animations on a text page, they distract from reading. A better option may be to allow users to activate and control them on their own. If the animations are gratuitous and do not add substantive content, they will have little benefit, even when interaction is added. Novice developers often use varied backgrounds and colors, moving text, and other gimmicks that usually only contribute to eye strain. Ironically, abuses such as these are more likely because authoring tools have made it easier to create so many varied multi-media assets. Having a clear purpose and strategies based on an instructional design model helps developers select and use assets wisely.

Content Granularity

Many multimedia programs are excessively long and linear. Most users work with computers interactively and exercise a high degree of control over the work that they perform with them. Long audio and video sequences or reams of text can turn an active technology into a passive one. Selecting appropriate granularity of multimedia content is a difficult problem. Old adages such as "Limit information to what can be displayed on a single screen" are not very useful. Not everyone has the same size screen, and most users can adjust its resolution anyway. As computer use has increased, more users know that they can scroll down displays and that there may be more information than what fills a single screen. Moreover, when text is involved, many users may print it for use offline. They may prefer to print the entire resource, or sections of it, rather than individual pages. Finally, convergence has made it possible to broadcast audio and video as streams over the Internet. These programs may be archived and offered on demand or live, but are usually just as passive as regular radio and television programs. The granularity problem depends on how the multimedia information is to be used and what users may expect. Users may tune into a live video broadcast of a symposium on the Internet expecting to see it in its entirety. Users accessing an archive of the conference, however, may prefer to choose among different presentations that were made during the symposium instead of the whole program. Again, thorough analysis and design using a coherent model helps determine appropriate granularity.

Meaningful Interaction

Learning and performance improve when users can interact with content meaningfully. Of the many levels and types of interaction, the simplest is paging forward and backward through successive displays. For an EPSS, such page turning may suffice, since most users are simply looking up information for immediate application. When learning is required, higher levels of interaction are warranted. Some of the types of interaction are the following:

- Problems and selectable options for solving them. Simple links that provide feedback may be used, or learners may be routed to different parts of a program.

- Constructed response items. Users must compose their answers in writing, and they are given feedback and routed through the program based on their responses.

- Monitoring the time participants take to respond and scoring their performance.

- Complex computer simulations. These may involve problemsolving and time-sensitive performance, such as solving trauma cases in emergency rooms. In this example, the computer may alter the condition of the simulated patient automatically, introducing new complications, if certain interventions fail to be made, and each option students choose may be used to calculate problemsolving performance.

Developers and clients must trade off the level of interactivity and the corresponding development cost. To evaluate any input students compose themselves is much more difficult than to assess their selections from a list of options. Adding time as a variable and/or scoring algorithms often requires formidable programming. Using a well-chosen instructional design model based on research and experience often helps in determining when sophisticated interactions are worth the additional time and expense—when and to what extent they add learning and performance value.

Human Interaction. One type of interaction that often is overlooked in multimedia program development and use is interaction among students or between students and teachers. The presumption that students should individually use multimedia programs has a long history. As more tools evolve that allow collaboration online, multimedia developers need to define ways to incorporate them into their programs, since student-to-student and student-to-teacher interactions are by nature much more open and freewheeling than any that can be realized between a computer and a single user. While the asynchronous communication tools such as email predominate today, synchronous tools such as videoconferencing are becoming more feasible at the desktop. Human interaction also can be designed into applications involving live streaming audio and video broadcast of lectures, seminars, and other events over the World Wide Web. In addition to providing a link on a web page to the broadcast, links also can be provided that allow users to send email or chat messages to the program presenters. If planned appropriately, audience participation can be encouraged, and the broadcasts may assume some of the character of radio and television talk shows. These capabilities will allow technology-based delivery systems to provide closer adherence to humanistic and social instructional models.

User Interfaces

Human factors and human-computer interaction are important considerations in multimedia program development. Computer displays should not have the density of print media, and care must be taken to ensure fonts and images are legible and displays are clear and uncluttered. An overarching goal is to make the interface transparent, so that users can concentrate on learning the content from an instructional program or obtaining support of an EPSS without being preoccupied with the computer as an intervening tool. One way to accomplish this is by devising "affordances" or creating interactive multimedia objects with functionalities that are intuitive and obvious. Forward and backward arrows for paging and printer icons for printing are popular examples. Another way to accomplish this is by making parts of the interface similar to the computer operating system or other application tools users are likely to understand already. For example, if the computer operating system and most other applications for the computer use drop-down menus, then this method of making menu selections should be considered. One benefit of offering resources on the web is that browsers provide a standard interface for accessing content. Finally, the overall design should be consistent. Screen layouts should follow a standard format and navigation tools should be uniformly placed so users know exactly what to expect as they interact with the program.

User Navigation

While navigation is part of the interface, it deserves special consideration. With linear media like video, users are guided through the program. While books are non-linear, their size and organization are usually apparent at a glance. Not so with computer programs, and disorientation is common. While care should be exercised to provide navigation features that are consistent with program- or learner-control strategies developers choose to adopt, it is often advisable to provide tools allowing users to exit the program, go to the start of the program, or access "landing pads" in the program (such as indexes and tables of contents) that let them jump to other parts. In addition, users should not have to traverse more than three menu layers to access content. Search features also may be important, especially if users are expected to look up information, as in an EPSS. When multimedia is designed for the web, links outside the program to other resources and websites need careful consideration. Linking to existing databases and other related online resources is a unique advantage, enabling developers to leverage resources and not have to develop them themselves. However, placement is crucial. The overall goal is to encourage users to stick with the program and the website, so users should not be encouraged to leave. Users may become perplexed if they select a link to an outside resource that they expect to be internal. External links should be grouped in one section of the program and appropriately labeled, rather than riddled throughout. Since external resources are beyond developer control and may be moved or deleted by those in charge of these sites so as to make the links inoperative, this strategy also has the advantage of making the links easier to maintain.

Asset Management

One of the most labor-intensive efforts in multimedia development is the identification, creation, and/or capturing of resources. When existing photographs, artwork, or other resources are identified for inclusion in programs, permissions, clearances, or copyrights may have to be obtained. Many graphics, sound, and video resources also may have to be developed from scratch. While these resources may already be in digital format, they often are not. Photos may have to be scanned and audio and digital recordings digitized. The higher the resolution of a digitized image or the fidelity of a digitized audio source, the larger its file size. More storage space will be consumed when it is stored on a CD-ROM and more bandwidth will be consumed if the file is delivered over the Internet. Consequently, many developers may create or capture them in lowest resolution acceptable. A better strategy, however, is "capture large; deliver small." Since so much effort is involved, digitize resources at the highest resolution, archive them, and then export them at a lower, acceptable quality. The reason is that technology improves rapidly. As the resolution of computer displays improves and bandwidth increases, standards of acceptable quality will rise also. When programs are updated, it will be easier to re-export the high-resolution resources at the new standard of acceptability than to have to recapture them. Even if a program is not updated, many of the multimedia resources in it might be re-used in future projects, and it may be worthwhile to catalog individual assets and place them in a database so they can be retrieved and re-purposed.

References

Ambron, S. (1988). New visions of reality: Multimedia and education. In S. Ambron & C. Hooper (Eds.), *Interactive multimedia*. Redmond, WA: Microsoft Press.

Hannafin, M., Hill, J., & Land, S. (1997). Student centered learning and interactive multimedia: Status, issues, and implications. *Contemporary Education, 68*(2), 94–99.

Hiltz, S. (1994). *The virtual classroom: Learning without limits via computer networks*. Norwood, NJ: Ablex Publishing.

Hooper, S. (1992). Cooperative learning and computer-based instruction. *Educational Technology Research and Development, 40*(3), 21–38.

Locatis, C., & Al-Nuaim, H. (1999). Interactive technology and authoring tools: An historical review and analysis. *Educational Technology Research and Development, 47*(3), 63–75.

Locatis, C., & Weisberg, M. (1997). Distributed learning and the Internet. *Contemporary Education, 68*(2), 100–103.

Lynch, P., & Horton, S. (1999). *Web style guide: Basic design principles for creating web sites*. New Haven, CT: Yale University Press.

Norman, D. (1993). *Things that make us smart*. Reading, MA: Addison-Wesley.

Pallesen, P.J., Haley, P., Jones, E.S., Moore, B., Widlake, D.E., & Medsker, K.L. (1999). Electronic delivery systems: A selection model. *Performance Improvement Quarterly 12*(4), 7–27.

Scardamalia, M., Berieter, C., Brett, C., Burtis, P., Calhoun, C., & Smith L.N. (1992). Educational applications of a networked database. *Interactive Learning Environments, 2*(1), 45–71.

Schnackenberg, H., & Sullivan, H. (2000). Learner control over full and lean computer-based instruction under differing ability levels. *Educational Technology Research and Development, 48*(2), 19–35.

Shin, E., Schallert, D., & Savenye, W. (1994). The effects of learner control, advisement, and prior knowledge on young students' learning in a hypertext environment. *Educational Technology Research and Development, 42*(1), 33–46.

Shneiderman, B. (1998). *Designing the user interface*. Reading, MA: Addison-Wesley.

Shneiderman, B., & Kearsley, G. (1989). *Hypertext hands-on!* Reading, MA: Addison-Wesley.

Shortliffe, E. (1990). Clinical decision support systems. In E. Shortliffe & L. Perreault (Eds.), *Medical informatics: Computer applications in health care.* Reading, MA: Addison-Wesley.

Snow, R., & Lohman, D. (1984). Toward a theory of cognitive aptitude for learning from instruction. *Journal of Educational Psychology, 72*(3), 347–376.

Tennyson, R., Christensen, D., & Park, O. (1984). The Minnesota Adaptive Instructional System: An intelligent CBI system. *Journal of Computer-Based Instruction, 11*(1), 2–13.

Tufte, E. (1990). *Envisioning information.* Cheshire, CT: Graphics Press.

Wenger, E. (1987). *Artificial intelligence and tutoring systems: Computational and cognitive approaches to the communication of knowledge.* Los Altos, CA: Morgan Kaufman Publishers.

About the Author

Craig Locatis is an educational research specialist and project officer at the National Library of Medicine (NLM), where he has worked on research and development projects involving new technology for 20 years. Projects have ranged from developing an interface for one of the first online library catalogs to creating prototype multimedia applications. Dr. Locatis was one of the founders of the Library's Learning Center for Interactive Technology, a national center for demonstrating interactive health care programs. He also was responsible for a project connecting the national medical libraries of eight republics in the former Soviet Union to the Internet. His current assignment is with NLM's Office of High Performance Computing and Communication, where he manages Next Generation Internet contracts and experiments with applications involving broadband networks. Dr. Locatis reviews for several professional journals and has published widely. While at the NLM, he has taught or guest lectured at universities in the metropolitan Washington, DC area and at Vilnius University in Lithuania.

Index

Eliciting Stimulus 11
Encoding 79
Encoding Mnemonics 123, 126
English, H.B. 176
Entrapping Learners 200
Equity 303
Equivalence Class 156, 158, 162, 163
Evaluation 305
Events of Instruction 77, 87–91
Expectancy
   in motivation 298
Expectancy-Value Theory 298
Experiential Learning 239
Expert Systems 363
Expository
   method 105, 106
   models 67, 67–69
Expository Advance Organizer 181
Expository Models
   multimedia 363
Extinction 15
Extrinsic Rewards 303

F

Facilitation 219, 327
Facilitator ix, 245, 319, 328
Fact 103, 104, 106
Fading 111, 112, 115, 116
Familiarity 301
Fantasy Analogy 143, 144
Feedback 46, 58–59, 108
   rules 58
Find 104, 105
First-Letters 125, 132
Foreign Language 121
Forming Hypotheses 200
Freire, P. 237, 243, 245, 246

G

Gagné, R.M. x, 100, 101, 104, 176, 185, 270
Gagné-Briggs Model 69, 99, 101
Generality 103, 105, 106, 112, 114
Generalization 28, 31
Gilbert, T.F. ii
Goal Orientation 301
Goldstein, A.P. 47, 48
Gordon, W.J.J. 70, 137, 138, 140
Green Book xi
Greeno, J.G. 76

Gropper, G. 4, 25–42
Group Processing 288, 290

H

Hands-On Learning 245, 246
Harlow, H.F. 76
Help 107, 108
Hierarchical
   categories 79
   relationships 75, 82, 85
Higher Order Rules 80, 82, 85, 158, 160
Hilgard, Ernest 176
Hirumi and Bowers 184
Human Performance Technology (HPT) i
   philosophy ii
   systematic methods ii
Human Resource Management x
Humanism 71
Humanistic Models 235–237
Humanistic Psychology 327–328
Humanistic, Social, and Affective Models and
      Strategies ix
   multimedia design 365–366
Hypermedia
   See Multimedia
Hypothetical Cases 200

I

Individualized Instruction 53
Individually Prescribed Instruction (IPI) 5
Inductive Reasoning 193
Information-Processing Model ix, 77–79
Inquiry Arousal 300
Inquiry Methods 197
Inquiry Models ix, 67, 69–72
   See also Discovery Models
Inquiry Teaching Strategies 199–201
Inquisitory Method 105, 106
Instance 105, 112
Instructional Curriculum Map 85, 92, 93
Instructional Design Certificate x
Instructional Systems Design (ISD) vii, viii,
      77
   five phases vii
   model selection strategies 346–353
Instructional Transaction Theory 112
Instructor as Facilitator
   See Facilitator
Instructor Authenticity 328

Medsker, K.L. x
Memorization 69, 224
Merrill, M.D. 68
Metaphor 141, 142–144
  use in multimedia 363
Mnemonics 69, 112, 121, 175
  acronym 125
  acrostic sentence 121, 125, 131, 132
  alliteration 126
  digit-consonant method 121, 127–128
  digit-letter system 122
  encoding 123, 126
  first-letters 125, 132
  in Component Display Theory 108
  keyword method 121, 122, 126, 128, 131
  loci, method of 122, 124, 128
  methods 121
  multimedia 364
  organizing 124
  peg system 122
  pegword system 124, 128
  rehearsal 129
  rhyme 121, 122, 124, 126, 132
Modeling 12, 15
Modes of Learning 268
  discovery 268–269
  receipt of input 268, 270
  reflection 268, 269–270
Moore, D.W. 184
Motivational Design 308
Motivational Models 286
Motivational Objectives 304, 310
Motivational Strategies 238, 299, 304
Motive Matching 301
Motor Skills 75, 81, 84, 86, 88, 89
  model selection strategy 346, 351
Multimedia 362
  adult learning model 365
  advance organizer 364
  analogy 363
  ARCS motivational design model 365
  asset management 370
  asset use and allocation 366
  behavioral models 360–362
  cognitive models 362–364
  component display theory 364
  constructivism 362, 364
  content granularity 367
  cooperative learning 365

  definition 356
  effect on development process 359
  effect on ISD 358
  expert systems 363
  expository models 363
  human interaction 368
  humanistic, social, and affective
     models 365–366
  mastery learning 361
  meaningful interaction 367
  metaphor 363
  mnemonics 364
  nine events of instruction 364
  pilot testing 359
  popular education 365
  role in ISD 358
  self-directed learner 365
  structural learning theory 364
  technology assessment 358
  trends 356–357
  use of ISD models 360
  user interfaces 368
  user navigation 369
Multimedia Trends
  capacity and costs 357
  commonness 357
  convergence 357
  conversion 356

N

Negative Exemplar 199
Negative Reinforcer 11
Nine Events of Instruction 270

O

Objectives
  achievement-based 249
  behavioral 25
  Gropper's 28
  motivational 304
  sequencing 4
Objectivism 195
  in contrast to constructivism 217
Objectivist ix, 71, 195, 224
On-the-Job Reinforcement 50, 59
Open-Ended Questions 247, 250
Operant Conditioning 1, 2, 8, 26
  See also Reinforcement Theory
Operant Responses 11

Operation 158, 159
Operational Creativity 139, 140
Organization Development x
Outcomes 298

P

Path 156, 162
   selection strategy 163
   subordinate 162
   superordinate 162
Pedagogy 245, 319
   comparison with andragogy 322–324
Peg System 122
Pegword System 124, 128
Perceptual Arousal 300
Performance Gap vi, 13
Performance Improvement
   See Human Performance Technology
      (HPT)
Performance-Content Matrix 100, 114
Perkins, D. 215
Personal Analogy 143
Personal Responsibility 302
Phonetic 127, 128
Piaget, J. 213, 215
Popular Education 237, 243–263
   checklist of competencies 250
   multimedia 365
   needs assessment and design 248
   role of instructor 251
   role of learner 252
   seven steps of planning 249
   twelve principles 252–254
   See also Learner-Centered Education
Porter, L.W. 298
Positive Exemplar 199
Positive Expectancy for Success 298
Positive Interdependence 288
Positive Reinforcement 46
Positive Reinforcer 11
   See also Reward
Practice 46, 245
   exaggerated 35
   graduated 34
   units of 33
   varying difficulty 34
Praxis 237, 239, 247
Prerequisite 108, 114
Pressley, M. 121, 123, 126

Primary Presentation Form 105–107, 112
Primary Reinforcer 8
Principle 103, 106
Procedure 103, 104, 106, 107
Prochaska, J.O. 17
Programmed Instruction 3, 8, 9
Promotive Interaction 289
Prompting and Fading 15, 111, 112, 115, 116
Punishment 11, 15

Q

Questioning Authority 201

R

Random Order 111
Range 158, 159
Range of Examples 111, 116
Readence, J.E. 184
Receipt of Input
   See Lancaster Model of Learning
   See Modes of Learning
Reception Learning 177
Reflection
   See Lancaster Model of Learning
   See Modes of Learning
Rehearsal 129
Reigeluth, C.M. xi, 157
Reil, J.C. 8
Reinforcement 2, 244
   positive 15
   social 19
   See also Reward
Reinforcement Theory 1
   See also Operant Conditioning
Reinforcer 12
   continuous 12
   effectiveness 12
   intermittent 12, 13
   positive 7
   saturation 13
Relevance 301
   in motivation 298
Remember 104, 105
Response 11
Response Generator 79
Reward 2, 7
   systematic use of 12
   See also Positive Reinforcer
   See also Reinforcement

Rhyme 121, 122, 124, 126, 132
Robinson, J.C. 5
Rogers, C. 235, 236, 320, 327, 328
    comparison with Knowles, M. 328
Rotter, J.B. 298
Routine Treatment 32–33
Rules 79, 82, 85, 156, 158

S

Satiation 15
Satisfaction
    in motivation 303
Scandura, J.M. 68, 155–172
Scientific Method 69
Secondary Presentation Form 107, 108, 112
Secondary Reinforcer 9
Selection Job Aid 349–352
Self-Directed Learner 236, 237
    multimedia 365
Self-Directed Learning 320
Self-Paced 3
Self-Paced Instruction 356
Self-Study 9
Seligman, M.E. 298
Sensory Register 78
Sequence 244
    objectives 36
    reverse 35
    See also Backward Chaining
Shaping 2, 15
    progression 33
    treatment 35
    See also Behavioral Approach
Sharan, S. 285, 288
Short-Term Memory 76
Simile 142
Situated Cognition 195, 202
Skill Practice Exercise 50
    design 54–55
    rehearsal, coaching, and practice 55–58
Skinner, B.F. 1–2, 8, 17, 26, 76
Slavin, R. 285
Small Group 286
    learning 246, 252
    skills 288, 289
Social Learning Theory 5, 45, 47
Social Models 237–238, 286
Social Reinforcement 5, 47, 50, 58
Socrates 194

Soft Skills 45, 52, 54, 60
    See also Interpersonal Skills
Solution Rule 162
Sorcher, M. 47, 48
Specialized Treatments 35–36
Specific Example 103, 105, 106
Specific Feedback
    See Feedback
Speculation 138, 142
Standard Verbs
    learning objectives 81
Standards of Performance
    varying 34
Stevens, A. 194
Stevens, G.H. 160, 162, 163, 164
Structural Analysis 157–158, 160, 164, 165
Structural Learning Theory 68, 155–172, 175
    atomic rule 158, 160
    atomic solution rule 161, 166, 167
    atomic solution rule path 168
    automated solution rule 163, 169
    automated solution rule path 169
    automaticity 163
    domain 158, 159
    equivalence class 163
    higher order rules 158, 160
    multimedia 364
    operation 158, 159
    path selection strategy 163
    range 158, 159
    rules 156, 158
    simplest path 155, 156
    superordinate path 162
    testing 156, 163, 164
Student Individuality 244
Success Opportunities
    in motivation 302
Symbolic Analogy 144
Synectics 70–71, 137–152
    analogy 137, 138, 141, 142, 143–144
    assumptions of 139
    compressed conflict 144
    creative problemsolving 139, 142, 145
    creativity 138, 139, 140, 141
    deferment 138, 142
    detachment 138, 142
    direct analogy 143, 144
    fantasy analogy 143, 144
    involvement 138, 142

making the familiar strange 137, 142, 147, 148
making the strange familiar 137, 142, 149
personal analogy 143
sample exercise 146
speculation 138, 142
symbolic analogy 143, 144
Systematic Variation 199

T

Target Behavior 11, 13
Taskwork 289, 290
Technology-Based Training
    See Multimedia
Tennyson, R.D. vii
Testing Hypotheses 200
Thinking Skills 69
Tosti, D. 45
Total Quality Management 292
Tracing Consequences 200
Transfer Strategies 50, 59
Tulving, E. 76

U

Unconditioned Stimulus (UCS) 8
Use 104, 105, 106, 107

V

Value
    in motivation 298
Vella, J. 237, 243, 247
Verbal Information 75, 80, 83–84, 86
Verbal Learning
    meaningful 175
    See also Advance Organizer
Vicarious Reinforcement 47
    See also Reinforcement
Vico, G. 213
Videotape 53
Vygotsky, L.S. 214

W

Watson, J.B. 8
Weil, M. xi, 184
Weiner, B. 298
Whole-Loop Learning Cycle 265, 266, 270
Wigginton, E. 226
Working Memory 78

Z

Zemke, R. 90